Voices of the Nakba

'Through the pages of this book the reader can hear, feel, experience and understand more about the Nakba than by reading any other book on the subject.'
—Raja Shehadeh, author of *Going Home: A Walk Through Fifty Years of Occupation*

'Moving and thoughtful [...] With their silences, ellipses and jags of storytelling, the refugee voices invite us to imagine the lives torn asunder by the violence of the Nakba.'
—Laleh Khalili, Queen Mary University of London and author of *Heroes and Martyrs of Palestine: The Politics of National Commemoration*

'Brings to life the experiences of ordinary Palestinians in pre-1948 Palestine and the traumatic experience of war and exile, written by leading scholars in the field. Of special value in this volume is the section on control and resistance during the Mandate dealing with policing, and narratives of rebellion.'
—Salim Tamari, Professor of Sociology (Emeritus), Birzeit University

'A truly impressive collection [...] An opportunity to reconsider whether what the Palestinians faced was victimhood rather than an act of colonialism.'
—Dawn Chatty, Emeritus Professor of Anthropology and Forced Migration, University of Oxford

'Imaginatively curated and framed [...] A brilliant contribution to the current moment as the world finally understands the true nature of the Palestinian struggle.'
—Ahdaf Soueif, author of *The Map of Love*

'The stories gathered here are the fruit of perseverant gathering. Their careful, deliberate, loving translation bear the sense and sensualities of Palestinian existence. *Voices of the Nakba* shows how and why those who will not forget will never be forgotten.'
—Fred Moten, cultural theorist and author of *The Feel Trio*

'The oral history of colonised people is a lifeline against the coloniser's official history with its violent erasure. This excellent book centres the marginalised voices of Palestinians, reflecting the rich and complex tapestry of their experiences.'
—Ibtisam Azem, author of *The Book of Disappearance*

'A comprehensive, illuminating and moving work of scholarship, which is also, quite simply, a work of art.'
—Liron Mor, Assistant Professor, Department of Comparative Literature, University of California, Irvine

'A monumental achievement [...] Enhancing the use of oral history as a research methodology, this book is a major addition to Nakba Studies and the living history of modern Palestine. A must read for those interested in the roots of the Palestinian refugee question and a just future for Palestine.'
—Professor Nur Masalha, Palestinian historian and formerly Director of the Centre for Religion and History at St Mary's University, Twickenham

Voices of the Nakba
A Living History of Palestine

Edited by Diana Allan

Translations by
Hoda Adra, Rayya Badran and Lindsay Munford
with the assistance of Farah Atoui, Jessica Hollows
and Cynthia Kreichati

Foreword by Mahmoud Zeidan

Afterword by Rosemary Sayigh

PLUTO  PRESS

First published 2021 by Pluto Press
New Wing, Somerset House, Strand, London WC2R 1LA

www.plutobooks.com

This book has been selected to receive financial assistance from English PEN's 'PEN Translates!' program, supported by Arts Council England. English PEN exists to promote literature and our understanding of it, to uphold writers' freedoms around the world, to campaign against the persecution and imprisonment of writers for stating their views, and to promote the friendly co-operation of writers and the free exchange of ideas. www.englishpen.org

Supported using public funding by

**ARTS COUNCIL
ENGLAND**

British Library Cataloguing in Publication Data
A catalogue record for this book is available from the British Library

ISBN   978 0 7453 4292 4   Hardback
ISBN   978 0 7453 4291 7   Paperback
ISBN   978 0 7453 4272 6   PDF
ISBN   978 0 7453 4293 1   EPUB

The cover shows Nakba Archive co-founder Mahmoud Zeidan's mother, grandparents and older siblings in Ayn al-Hilweh refugee camp (1966).

This book is printed on paper suitable for recycling and made from fully managed and sustained forest sources. Logging, pulping and manufacturing processes are expected to conform to the environmental standards of the country of origin.

Typeset by Stanford DTP Services, Northampton, England

Simultaneously printed in the United Kingdom and United States of America

For Rosemary Sayigh

Contents

PART I Life in Pre-1948 Palestine

PART II The British Mandate and Palestinian and Arab Resistance

List of Figures

Figure 1   Combined 1940s survey maps of Palestine showing the villages and towns of origin of interviewees. Courtesy of Palestine Open Maps.

Acknowledgements

Forced displacement defines the modern Middle East and shapes its demographic and political realities today. Since the start of the Syrian civil war in 2011, more than 12 million Syrians have been displaced from homes and communities; half of these are now exiled refugees. Within the current global imaginary of displacement, the figure of the refugee is Syrian. However, this latest 'crisis' forms part of a long, layered history of forced migration in the region. The twentieth century opened with the Armenian genocide, scattering survivors throughout Greater Syria. Like the Circassians, who had fled wars in the Northern Caucasus 50 years earlier, Armenian refugees were able to establish new identities as ethnic minorities and assimilate into host communities. Other displaced populations in the Middle East have been less fortunate. Many of the Kurds, Iraqis and Palestinians who have sought refuge in the wake of colonial and imperial wars, ethnic cleansing and expulsion over the past century are still stateless. Palestinians, now in their eighth decade of exile, are one of the world's oldest and largest extant refugee populations. Their swift and brutal uprooting during the founding of the State of Israel in 1948 – and the long displacement that has followed – is referred to as 'the catastrophe', *al-Nakba*. As remembered by refugee elders in Lebanon, it is the subject of this book.

Voices of the Nakba has evolved from years of work by many people. Our greatest debt is to the elders who allowed us to record their experiences: their voices are the source and inspiration for this collection. Almost two decades have passed since Mahmoud Zeidan and I established the Nakba Archive and began recording narratives in the camps in Lebanon. The Nakba Archive was created by a remarkable collective of Palestinian researchers in camps across Lebanon: Ibrahim al-Ali, Amira Elwan, Ahmad Faour, Ahmad Ghneim, Suhair Haddad, Sylvia Haddad, Rami Abu Hamdeh, Jaber Abu Hawash, Inass Abu Samra, Rania al-Haj, Jihad Idriss, Ghada Kaddoura, Amina al-Khatib, Muhammad al-Masri, Jalal Marzuk, Khaled Maw'ad, Bushra Mughrabi, Ramez Muhammad, Nader Muhammad, Mayssun Mustafa, Nawal Mustafa, Rasha Najdi, Abir Omar, Nuha Qurdieh, Riham Shriedeh, Shafik Shammas, Ashraf Shouli and Sonia Rifai. The project was enabled by generous support from the Welfare Association, the Ford Foundation and contributions from private sponsors.

I would like to thank Mahmoud Zeidan's family for all that they have given to the Nakba Archive over the years, and for allowing us to use the beautiful photograph from their own family archive for the book's cover.

The Nakba Archive and this book have also benefited in direct and indirect ways from the support of many colleagues and friends. Kaoukab Chebaro, Hana Suleiman and Rami Khouri have long been advocates of the Nakba Archive and helped establish the Palestinian Oral History Archive (POHA) at the American University of Beirut (AUB), which now houses the collection. Mona Assi, Sara Sweidan, Hana Haidar and Nourhan Shehab, at POHA, have provided invaluable support in sourcing material for this book. I would also like to thank Rayan El-Amine, Salman Abu Sitta, Dawn Chatty, Moataz Dajani, Beshara Doumani, Munir Fasheh, Sherna Berger Gluck, Elaine Hagopian, Nadia and Nuhad Hamad, Sumaya al-Haj, Sari Hanafi, the late Barbara Harell-Bond, Bayan Nuwayhed al-Hout, Kholoud Hussein, Anne Lesch, Sarine Karajerian, Hicham Kayed, Rebecca Murray, Karma Nabulsi, the late Roger Owen, Ilan Pappe, Laila Parsons, Emma Playfair, Mezna Qato, Hilary Rantisi, Eugene Rogan, Sara Roy, Areej Sabbagh, Ahmad Sa'di, Yasmine Eid-Sabbagh, Sandra El-Saleh, Musaed el-Saleh, Ruba Salih, Yezid Sayigh, Hala Sayegh, Nadia Sbaiti, Bassem Serhan, Avi Shlaim, Jaber Suleiman, Mayssun Soukarieh, Samia Tabari, Salim Tamari, the late Adel Yahya, Leila Zacharia and Souhad Zendah for their support.

Realizing this book – with its many moving parts – has been possible thanks to the hard work of an exceptional group of scholars and editorial assistants. I thank the contributors for their thoughtful engagement with the interviews, and for writing such carefully researched, illuminating chapters. Farah Atoui has been a wonderful research assistant, who helped review translations and, in myriad ways, kept things on track. While Jessica Hollows would not want special mention, her contribution to this book has been critical: it has benefitted immeasurably both from her insights and commentary on individual essays and her exceptional editorial skills. Hoda Adra, who translated many of the interviews in this collection, has also made a pivotal contribution to its realisation. Her considerable gifts as a translator have helped to render the Palestinian vernacular – and its unique rhythms of speech, thought and emotion – vividly and vitally in English. Rayya Badran, Suhaila Nassar, Tahani Nassar, Salma Miqdadi and Lindsay Munford have also provided invaluable assistance with translation and transcription. Cynthia Kreichati's final review of the translations alongside the recordings, and her careful listening, caught nuances and distinctions that otherwise would have been missed. I would also like to thank David Shulman from Pluto Books for first inviting me to work on a book about the

Nakba Archive, and for his patience and encouragement at every stage of its slow development, and Thérèse Wassily Saba for her meticulous editorial assistance. The research and translation were made possible thanks to grants from the Fonds de Recherche du Québec Société et Culture and the Social Sciences and Humanities Research Council, Canada, whose contributions are gratefully acknowledged.

My family is also owed special thanks. My husband, Curtis Brown, has supported the Nakba Archive and all that has grown from it for almost two decades. He has patiently read many drafts of many texts and has been unstinting in his intellectual and material support. While my daughters, Layla and Freya, have expressed weariness with my work on the Nakba, which appears neverending, they have been mostly enthusiastic enablers and a source of joy and inspiration.

It remains for me to thank Rosemary Sayigh, a valued mentor and friend, who is also a contributor to this volume. She was among the first scholars to recognise the importance of recording the histories of 'ordinary' Palestinians in Lebanon – refugees, the urban and rural poor and, most importantly, women – whose experiences had not been accounted for in official histories. Sayigh is the North Star of Palestinian oral history; her scholarship has illuminated and constellated this field of study for more than half a century, and is distinguished by its tireless, unwavering commitment to the people whose lives it describes. As a feminist scholar, attuned to the experiences of women and the vital role they have played in sustaining Palestinian life, Sayigh's work has troubled gendered ideologies and transformed our understanding of Palestinian history – who makes it, who narrates it, the form it takes. Her feminist methods model an exemplary 'politics of listening' that first inspired the work of the Nakba Archive and now inform this book, which we dedicate to her.

Note on Translation and Transliteration

Translating the interviews for this collection from Palestinian vernacular into English raised critical questions about how to convey the broader communicative range of speech in writing. Our aim has been to make the voices of Palestinian elders audible and accessible to English-language readers, while retaining the singular syntactical marks of their origin in spoken Arabic. The translators have sought to preserve the fluid qualities of oral expression by maintaining conversational rhythms and minimising editorial intervention. Ellipses indicate time-code breaks and silence. In an effort to uphold the interviewees' language and the world it describes, we often retain Arabic transliterations, which are explained in the Notes and a Glossary. These terms are spelled so as to clearly convey their vocalisation in Palestinian dialect to English-language readers. *Ta' marbuta* is thus often transliterated as 'eh'; and the long vowels *waw* and *ya'* are rendered as 'ou' and 'ee' respectively.

Transliterations of proper nouns follow the *International Journal of Middle East Studies* (*IJMES*) simplified system, with some exceptions. Diacritics are used only to denote the letters *ayn* (') and *hamza* ('), with double consonants indicating the Arabic *shadda*. Spellings at variance with the *IJMES* rubric appear for ease of reading (e.g. Beirut, rather than Bayrut), and where a person's preference is known (e.g. Mahmoud, in lieu of Mahmud). Names of organisations and institutions are translated in parentheses, to facilitate comprehension. While interviewees often use the adjective *ingleez* for their foreign occupiers during the Mandate, in the interest of clarity and consistency we use 'British' throughout. For the names of Palestinian villages and locales, we adhere to spellings adopted by the Institute for Palestine Studies (IPS) and Walid Khalidi's *All That Remains* (1992), which continues to be an authoritative reference on the Palestinian villages destroyed or depopulated in 1948. With respect to Palestinian and Arab cities and regions, we privilege Arabic toponyms over English exonyms throughout the interviews ('Akka not Acre, al-Quds not Jerusalem, al-Nasira not Nazareth, al-Jalil not the Galilee, Sur not Tyre), in keeping with speakers' usage. English exonyms appear in the essays, according to the preferences of individual contributors to this multivocal work.

These concerns represent some of the challenges of rendering voice and oral performance in text. Media context is critical in these editorial decisions: the subtitling of these same interviews on the Nakba Archive website, for example, generally incorporates more hesitation, repetition, and circling back than we've chosen to include here. Such questions should be borne in mind by readers as core to the subject of this book.

Foreword

Refugee Archives and the Nakba Archive

Mahmoud Zeidan

My relationship with history began with what I learned in primary school about peoples of the region, from the Canaanites to the Ottomans. Its recent past, particularly in Palestine, we saw not as history but rather as lived events and stories vitally animating the present. These stories were either inherited from our parents and grandparents or directly experienced and narrated by us.

I was born in ʿAyn al-Hilweh camp in South Lebanon, into a family of refugees. They were forcibly expelled from Safsaf when my eldest brother was two, following a massacre perpetrated by Zionist gangs that left approximately 80 dead, most of whom were unarmed peasants. The remaining inhabitants of the village fled, along with those of neighbouring villages who heard of the atrocities in Safsaf and, before that, in Dayr Yasin.

I never read about these events – or even our village itself – in history books. I don't know how I came to know what I know about it. I know the stories of Safsaf as I know the houses of ʿAyn al-Hilweh, its alleys and its people. Like many others in the camp, I know these stories as if by instinct. They blend with our present everyday lives to the extent that we don't regard them as belonging to past time or history. They present themselves naturally, without effort and in any occasion. They don't result from a question or seek permission.

These stories thrummed the tents of the camp and flew like the driving rain. They hung in the air in later years, among tin houses, spreading like the scent of food and attracting neighbours, relatives and passers-by. They echoed through time from tin houses to serried concrete flats, passing through winding alleyways from home to home during the very many occasions that gathered together parents, neighbours, relatives and loved ones.

I knew how our neighbour Hasan Zaghmut had become an orphan at six, how he was taken from his father's shoulders as they fled Safsaf, then watched his father shot to death. I learned why our disabled neighbour Abu Kamil Yunis' right arm was always stretched away from his chest. He was returning from the village mill when he encountered Zionist soldiers, who stood him against a wall, along with 40 others (relatives and neighbours, including some who'd fled to Safsaf from nearby villages that had already fallen to the Zionists), and shot them all. Abu Kamel was hit in the arm, and when he heard the soldiers muttering in Hebrew, which he understood, that they intended to kill anyone who remained alive, he played dead and survived the second round of killing. He waited until the soldiers left and the villagers came to bury their victims. I knew why our neighbour Jamil was raising his nephews: his older brother had been killed in the same massacre.

The stories of refugees took various forms, including narratives of heroism or defeat, elegies for home and lamentations of exile, and sardonic tales contrasting past and present, the beautiful and the bitter. Genres ranged from lyric to epic to anecdote. Even ghost stories were part of the repertoire, redolent as they are of loss and shame, of the unquiet dead. When I walked the dark alleys of the camp after dinner, I trembled in fear of a ghoul that had accosted my father long before I was born, while he slept in our home in Safsaf. It seized and shook him violently, demanding he return a stake my father had taken from the grave of a pious man who'd been buried in the garden of our home.

We laughed out loud on winter nights, huddled over a fireplace and listening to our elders. They told these stories in the presence of the people who lived them and everyone would laugh. Our neighbours, Mustafa, Khalil and Hasan, used to steal a small goat from fellow villagers when multiple herds mingled at the wellspring. They would swiftly slaughter the goat and roast it under cover of night before its owners noticed the loss and reported it to the Mandate authorities. Their reputation was such that they were immediately accused whenever a sheep went missing. Before one of their furtive feasts, Khalil repeatedly said to the sheep while slaughtering it: 'You die, damn your owner'. When he woke the next morning, he realised from the sheepskin that the animal was his; his two comrades had plotted against him.

Stories are a medium of intimacy. One of my favourites was a sort of joke of my father's, which he told to tease his friend from Dalata village, poking fun at the naivety of its villagers. The people of Dalata saw the moonlight reflected on the water's surface in the village fountain, thought it was a slice of cheese and threw a cat in the fountain to retrieve it. My father would relate this story in their dialect: 'Float you tigress cat! Float! Get a slice for us and a slice for you!' The cat drowned.

Our history was refracted through these tales and through the camp relics that jewelled them. Another neighbour, Abu Khalid, would show us his passport, indicating the number of times he had travelled to Beirut and Damascus before the Nakba. A photograph of my uncle Saleh, taken while he served in the British police during the Mandate, was framed and placed prominently in the living room; it was cited midstream of a story as a sort of oral footnote. Many other neighbours displayed photographs of themselves in Haifa or 'Akka, and took great pains to prevent them from being damaged.

As a teenager, I started becoming aware of my own experiences and developed my own repertoire. Stories would come to me without effort or even conscious choice. I survived the Israeli invasion and bombardment in 1982. I saw with my own eyes the enemy who had driven my parents out of Safsaf and dispersed them across the world, now putting an end to my childhood. In the aftermath, we were displaced from 'Ayn al-Hilweh to Sayda city. I was 13 years old when I began recording in personal diaries what I had seen and experienced in the camp. As a high school student in 1985, I witnessed the battles in East Sayda between the Lebanese Forces and the Lebanese National Movement. By then, we were displaced to Beirut. Two years later, I survived the War of the Camps between Palestinians and the Amal Movement, which prevented me from pursuing my studies at university.

My friends and I shared the same bitter fate, and came to consciousness as part of a generation whose stories seemed different from those of our parents: stories of migration and multiple displacement, of bombings and booby traps, of kidnappings and killings at checkpoints. We began seeing pictures of martyrs – some of them friends – filling the walls, streets and alleys; political slogans blackened the walls of the camp, for example, 'No agreement, no negotiations, and no surrender'. Our interest in the past waned; we were burdened by the weight of our own reality and experience. We were not yet alive to the deep continuity between what our parents had lived and what we were living.

Our parents' ingenious strategy for connecting our present to their past was to make the latter more beautiful and romantic. During my university years, I became interested in narrative technique, which most elders of the Nakba generation had mastered. When my father listened to daily news bulletins he unleashed, without fail, the anger he felt towards the Arab regimes and the international community that failed to protect the Palestinian people and remained silent on their decades of exile, but he would weave into the harangue a lyrical evocation of the past. I soon realised that for his generation storytelling was not only transmissive but also expressive and cathartic. They were not only passing stories on to their children but also freeing themselves of their grip and burden. It was then that my brother and I started to record my father's stories as a way to remember him. Death soon caught up with him and we only managed to record his voice on a few cassette tapes.

I began to research. I read manuscripts – finished or fragmentary – by the many refugees who raced against time to write books about their own villages. My brother and I attempted one of our own, about Safsaf. We tracked down village elders and began to catalogue oral and material traces spanning 50 years: one kept property documents of land and buildings, another had an ID or birth certificate, another an old photograph; so-and-so kept his school grade books, another held on to a map or the plan for the village, and there were those who kept kitchen utensils. These materials were enmeshed in a trove of stories, tales, proverbs, anecdotes and laments.

My uncle Muhammad had had his picture taken with two of his fellows from Safsaf, Sheikh Husayn and Muhammad Merhi, during their service with the British police in Haifa. The photograph never left Sheikh Husayn's pocket. It was wrinkled and covered with a transparent adhesive to protect it from water, but sweat had leaked in and gave it a yellowish hue. Sheikh Husayn always refuses to lend it but will proudly display it when the occasion calls for it.

When my uncle left to work in Kuwait in 1951, he kept a diary. He described being injured while defending the village and being transported to a hospital in Tyre in South Lebanon. In Kuwait, he met other survivors of the massacre and wrote up their accounts as well. The diary was brief and its pages were worn away, but it represents a unique record, of a kind researchers are only beginning to look into.

The remaining mosaic of experiences, stories, photographs, news clippings, artefacts and heirlooms shaped historic Palestine for refugees and proved they belonged to it. This history came to life on big occasions and later died down. It is dispersed and fragmented, in this respect mirroring the realities of refugee life in exile. Early attempts to collect, preserve and exhibit this history were not carried out according to appropriate professional and technical specifications.

I met Diana Allan in 2002, when she was beginning her doctoral research on the Beirut camps. We agreed on the need for an archive of first-generation oral testimonies, both to preserve our heritage and to provide a resource to researchers, educators and human rights defenders. We agreed the archive should be built using a unified methodology. The first challenge we encountered was the formulation of questions, which I hadn't previously considered. Earlier and in informal contexts, refugees would talk without much prompting. Now they were warier: 'Why do you ask?' 'Why now?' 'Where will these accounts be used?' Chains of such challenges and misgivings unfurled. One person was hesitant to speak, fearing for his family in Europe; another worried about his children in exile. Others wondered about the nature of the questions themselves, or the criteria determining who was to speak.

Over five arduous years, we gathered accounts from those who were expelled, whose villages were cleansed or destroyed. This material became the Nakba Archive that we have in our hands today. I cannot pretend we collected all we had intended to. The Nakba Archive is a modest brick in the rebuilding of the modern history of Palestine. It has motivated other initiatives and will continue to do so, more than 70 years on from the Nakba.

There is still an urgent need for an official organisation to collect the dispersed and endangered remnants of Palestine's oral history, and to preserve what has been already collected. It is imperative that this archive be accessible not only to current and subsequent generations of refugees but also to scholars, research centres and history departments in universities. Material like this represents not merely a past history but also a rumbling present. To understand Palestine's history and the Palestinian cause, serious researchers must come to grips with this, for the Nakba continues.

Figure 2   Madi Issa, al-Bassa, Palestine.
Courtesy of Rania Adib el-Hajj Issa.

Introduction: Past Continuous

Diana Allan

It was the Syrian intellectual, Constantin Zurayk, who first coined the term *al-Nakba* to describe the disaster that befell Palestinians and Arabs during the creation of the Israeli state in 1948.[1] In his short, incisive book, *Ma 'na al-Nakba*, '*The Meaning of the Disaster*', Zurayk sought its causes and cure, and excoriated Arab states for failing to recognise the Zionist threat, or to mount a united front against it. Like other modernising Arab intellectuals, Zurayk saw the loss of Palestine as revealing not only the absence of unity among Arab states but also the cultural backwardness of Arab society, which he felt lacked the political awareness to perceive or respond to the dangers it faced.[2] Zurayk wrote his book during the summer of that year, with hostilities barely over and the scope, significance and duration of their aftermath unknown, but his choice of title proved prescient. If '*al-Nakba*' captured the despair, confusion and intense recrimination of Arab nationalist intellectuals at that time, it also had the inadvert effect of deflecting from, if not absolving, Zionist aggression.[3] It is usually translated as 'catastrophe', 'disaster' or 'calamity', suggesting *force majeure* or an act of God rather than a carefully planned expulsion. Periodisation is also obscured: if in 1948 'a country and its people disappeared from both maps and dictionaries', as Elias Sanbar puts it, the dismantling of Palestinian life in fact had begun decades earlier, in the late nineteenth century, with the sale of lands by absentee landlords and the first waves of Jewish colonial settlers to Palestine.[4] Incremental dispossession intensified under British colonial rule, between 1920 and 1948, and gathered force after it, both through Israeli settler-colonialism in the Palestinian territories and through the disenfranchisement, marginalisation and confinement of Palestinian refugees living outside of them. Support for a national homeland for the Jewish people was core to British Imperial policy. The promise of the Balfour Declaration of 1917 (which helped secure the establishment of a Jewish state in Palestine) not to 'prejudice' the rights of 'non-Jewish communities' in Palestine and Transjordan was swiftly betrayed following the collapse of the Ottoman Empire.[5] The international community under the leadership of the United States picked up where the British left off, perennially making and breaking promises of impartiality and Palestinian rights.

This book returns to the question Zurayk first posed about the meaning of disaster and formulates a response through the recollections of those who lived it. Drawing on narratives recorded by the Nakba Archive with Palestinians expelled to Lebanon, it marks a shift of focus from the colonial machinations that produced these events towards an experiential understanding of their unfolding. In the wake of the destruction of 531 Arab villages by Zionist forces between 1947–48, an estimated 750,000 Palestinians were uprooted. Some 110,000 fled to Lebanon, where they were placed in camps administered by the United Nations Relief and Works Agency (UNRWA).[6] These camps have become home to at least five generations of refugees, who live without citizenship or rights. Their accounts attest to oppression and injustice in the longue durée and invite a reconsideration of the Nakba's temporality and scope. Determining where catastrophe begins and ends is both epistemologically necessary and politically significant. 'To identify the Nakba as a past and finished event is to insist that there is no longer a struggle to define it,' writes the Palestinian historian Joseph Massad. 'It is to grant it historical and political legitimacy as a fact of life, but also to endow all its subsequent effects as its natural outcome.'[7] Displacement and dispossession remain vital to Zionism, as a racist, settler colonial ideology, while erasure and confinement are experienced with increasing intensity by Palestinians living under occupation as well as in exile. It is now commonplace to speak of the Nakba as *mustamirra*, 'ongoing' – a process still happening rather than a discrete historical event. For refugees struggling in camps in Lebanon, the Nakba is a way of life, inclusive both of the defining event in modern Palestinian history and the lived condition of its present.

Those expelled in 1948 have responded to protracted exile by insisting on these histories of forced displacement and their right of return to their lands and homes and to self-determination. Passed down through families and communities, these accounts of mass expulsion and exile challenge the silencing and 'juridical erasure' of Palestinian experience.[8] They affirm existence, demand redress and imagine what justice might look like. They are vivid reminders of the uprooting of almost 80 per cent of Palestinian society by 1949.[9] As Salman Abu Sitta writes in Chapter 8, these accounts forcefully counter Zionist claims that the systematic destruction of Palestinian society was the unintended consequence rather than a central aim of the campaign by Zionist forces. Narrators detail the swift and brutal attack on Palestinian communities through methodically executed policies of ethnic cleansing, population transfer, de-Arabisation and cultural genocide, hastened by the terrors of psychological warfare and massacre. More than half a century ago, Edward Said observed that Zionist assertions of *terra nullius* sought to 'cancel and transcend an actual reality – a group of resident Arabs – by means of a future wish – that the land be empty for the development of a more deserving power'.[10] Zionist racial and moral hierarchies were a seamless continuation of British colonial policies towards Palestinian Arabs (the unnamed 'non-Jewish majority'), whose sovereignty both colonising forces refused to recognise. The termination of the Mandate in 1948 set in place a settler-colonial regime that has continued to dehumanise and dismantle Palestinian life ever since.[11]

This book revisits the violent events of the creation of the State of Israel and details the Palestinian life-worlds destroyed. Elders recall the rhythms of peasant life, the forms of education and intellectual institutions that existed, the cosmopolitanism of Jaffa, relations between Arab and Jewish communities in Palestine, the ambivalent pride of working for the British as policemen and colonial administrators, nationalist fervour, revolution and flight. Colonial subjugation – first, at the hands of the British, who crushed a viable Palestinian resistance movement, and subsequently by Zionist settlers – is a pervasive theme. British officials haunt refugee memory – foot-whipping civilians, wantonly destroying crops and property, ruining precious food stores, confiscating weapons, imprisoning and hanging resistors, and engaging in plunder and brutal collective punishment. ʿAbd al-Rahman Saʿad al-Din's account of the scorched-earth attack on the village of al-Zib in May 1948, ordered by Moshe Carmel (then commander of the Zionist Carmeli Brigade), discussed by Jacob Norris in Chapter 6, includes familiar examples of colonial counterinsurgency. The tactics and forms of torture developed and refined across the British Empire to subdue and control colonial subjects were redeployed by Zionist leaders in their newly created state. Elders describe singular experiences of plunder, loss and intimidation, while tracing the collective contours of forced expulsion and societal obliteration. Recorded mostly in camps and informal gatherings, these accounts also chronicle exilic life and the costs exacted by survival. The craft of storytelling has been pivotal in sustaining the collective memory of the Nakba in exile. Elders recount these events with acuity and deliberation, communicating not only facts but also truths lived and felt, and with an ear and eye to the present scene of narration. They and their interviewers revisit the destruction and make sense of what remains, mapping a topography of relation to Palestine not simply as place of origin, but also as a site of belonging and way of life.

Most of the interviews in this book were recorded in the early 2000s, in the wake of the 1993 Oslo Accords, when the Palestinian leadership appeared to have abandoned refugees, implicitly signalling its willingness to exchange their right of return for statehood.[12] These betrayals and the failures of the 2000 Camp David Summit were still fresh in people's minds. The fiftieth anniversary of the Nakba, the need to affirm the right of return, and the drive to symbolically reclaim the 1948 expulsion as central to refugee identity were all integral to the context of recollection. The liberation of South Lebanon in 2000, after 18 years of occupation, also raised hopes of Israeli vulnerability. Both the Nakba Archive itself and the testimonies it collected were inflected by the political urgencies and aspirations of that time. Returning to these accounts two decades on, when many of their narrators are no longer alive, is to be reminded of a sense of fervour and possibility now gone. With every passing decade, the unresolved plight of Palestinian refugees resurfaces briefly in global consciousness, only to be eclipsed by a fresh regional crisis. But to return to them is also to be reminded of the enduring capacity of refugees to sustain life-worlds, both autochthonous and exilic.

In 2010, the Nakba Archive's collection was donated to the Palestinian Oral History Archive (POHA) at the American University of Beirut Libraries.[13] Over the past decade, these interviews have been redigitised, cross-indexed and made searchable by key terms. In an effort to privilege the orality and integrity of the time-based audio-visual medium, POHA's indexers and archivists eschewed transcription and instead produced detailed, bilingual descriptions and tagging systems for each interview. This vast undertaking was masterminded by a group of researchers who listened to hundreds of hours of recordings many times over. The metadata they gathered was then used to develop an expansive catalogue and search engine, allowing users to enter textual search terms and identify correlating time-coded moments in the video interviews.[14] This repository, containing over a thousand hours of audio-visual recordings, was launched as an online, open-access archive in June 2019. The interviews in this book can be viewed through both the POHA and Nakba Archive websites (in the latter case, with English subtitles); the time-code citations provided for each interview will allow readers to locate the specific passages in the original recordings.[15] The experience of listening and watching elders speak deepens and enriches historical understanding. As viewers, and now readers, our visceral and affective response flows from recognition of the 'immeasurable weight in actual existence' of another human being and 'the cruel radiance of what is', as James Agee once said of another ethnographic project striving, as this one does, to transverse the printed page.[16]

LIVING HISTORIES

In the historiography of the modern Middle East, Palestinian oral history and refugee narratives have occupied a marginal place. In both Zionist histories and the revisionist works of New Historians, Israel's founding continues to take narrative precedence over Palestine's destruction. A definitive history of the Palestinian Nakba, as told by Palestinians, has yet to be written. Said himself noted that in spite of all that has been written about Palestine, 'Palestinians remain virtually unknown'.[17] With notable exceptions, few studies of the Nakba have been driven by the accounts of ordinary Palestinians.[18] Despite growing recognition of how oral sources compensate for incomplete written records (systematically destroyed or dispersed as they often are, or beyond reach in state archives),[19] mainstream histories of this period continue to rely on texts. First-person accounts consulted with interest tend to be memoirs and letters of prominent political actors. The accounts of illiterate refugees are meanwhile seen by many scholars as unreliable, biased and digressive (one Palestinian historian who listened to recordings in the Nakba Archive described them as 'rambling', temporally unmoored and non-linear). While advocates argue that oral history can fill gaps and shed light on the collective significance of events through recurring motifs, what is rarely considered is how the spoken might transform our understanding of history itself – its form, substance and purpose, and the matter of who tells it. Neither supporters nor detractors have reckoned with the forensic and expressive power of embodied voice, with what the philosopher Mladen Dolar calls the 'vocal fingerprint'.[20]

This distrust of oral sources has been costly for our understanding of the Nakba, since the majority who fled in 1948 were peasants who could neither read nor write, and left no memoirs or written record.[21] Rosemary Sayigh, whose afterword closes this book, was among the first scholars to recognise the importance of recording the experiences of ordinary Palestinians driven into exile. Sayigh's interest in documenting refugee histories, not broadly shared, began in the 1970s, and she recalls the scepticism with which some of the Palestinian elite viewed the 'people of the camps'. They were seen as backward, conservative peasants, objects of compassion and charity rather than authoritative subjects, mired as they were in ignorance and superstition.[22] This earlier generation of Palestinian intellectuals, ideologically rooted in secular pan-Arab modernism, regarded the 'fallibility' of oral sources as a liability threatening the legitimacy of Palestinian revisionist scholarship when it was most needed. For progressive Arab intellectuals like Zurayk (but also Musa Alama, Hisham Sharabi and others) cultivating rational, scientific methods of knowledge production was seen as the means by which to reform and revolutionise Arab society and political organisation, within a broader framework of anti-colonial struggle. Oral traditions were less a resource to be tapped than an index of societal stagnation separating Palestinians from Western modernity and the 'march of progress'. Many feared that uneducated refugees might unwittingly echo Israeli propaganda that Arab leaders had told them to leave so that their armies might enter and slaughter Zionists.[23] While early avoidance and neglect of refugee testimonies is understandable in hindsight, it had the inadvertent effect of placing the experiences of camp communities outside the historical frame.

The marginalisation of refugee narratives lingers as a legacy. Since the Oslo Accords, camp communities have hovered awkwardly at the edge of diplomatic discussions that deliberate their fate. Overwhelmed by the exigencies of daily life, refugees are often presumed to lack the presence of mind to analyse their past or imagine a political future.[24] Enduring life in camps across the region they are muted reminders of a 'problem' that will not resolve, of international negligence and Western guilt, whose suffering – in sharp contrast to that of other survivors and witnesses to history – has made them unreliable. This silencing is institutionally underwritten: UNRWA schools are not permitted to teach the history of the Nakba to refugee youth; the events that produced their exilic condition are not part of the curriculum. What is lost in the double deference to Western textual dogmatism on one side and political risk-hedging on the other is not only vital information about what actually took place in the hundreds of villages that were razed, but also the dense, experiential reality of pre-1948 Palestine, the Nakba, and its afterlives. Paradoxically, those who lost most in 1948 – whose lives were fundamentally and irrevocably transformed – have not yet been meaningfully accounted for. Though the Nakba symbolises the existential zero point of Palestinian collective consciousness, its granular details are still undocumented. They have instead taken tenuous hold in the fissures of family lore, passed down in fragmentary form. In the last two decades, a number of archival initiatives like Al-Jana, Palestine Remembered and the Palestinian Revolution have sought to reclaim these histories for the historical record.[25] While precious time was wasted, and this work comes decades late, some gaps have been closed through oral history research with elders. The Nakba Archive is similarly founded on the premise that such understanding, as much if not more than any other, shores historical memory against oblivion.

Voices of the Nakba is concerned with not only the content but the form of Nakba narratives. The authors attend to the energies and expressivity of

6

voice, and the distinctive properties and possibilities of the spoken word for rethinking the history of 1948. For elders whose stories exist only in spoken form, remembrance takes up residence in the voice, and is preserved through the reciprocity of transmission. The stories carry the collective weight of remembrance, while communicating the preoccupations of exilic life. Elders who do not know the year of their birth describe in meticulous detail the routines and spatial layout of their villages – the arrangement of houses, wells, shrines and mosques, where each family lived, the surrounding orchards, forms of land tenure, the songs sung at different social occasions, what was grown and gleaned, the model and make of their Ottoman-era firearms. The elegiac density of memory – the lists of things named and accounted for – is often staggering. Remembrance is by turns commemorative, compensatory, a form of relation, a mode of critique, an inheritance, a work of love. The inventories that structure and ballast recollection in many narratives carry the imprint of felt relation, and enable refugees to hold their losses close: description is itself a refuge. If narrators do not always follow linear chronology, their stories evoke an inner experience of time, and forms of knowledge situated in place and in the body. Worlds rematerialise in description. This is not to sentimentalise oral histories as more authentic or true, but to acknowledge their distinct epistemological and ontological value for understanding the lived experience of displacement and loss. In conjuring Palestine in all its phenomenological richness, these narratives give meaning to its disappearance. To dismiss them would be to echo and consecrate the original dispossession.

Intimacy takes many forms in these accounts, including depictions of friendship between Arabs and Jews before 1948. Fifi Khouri remembers the beautiful hats made by a family of European Jewish milliners in Jaffa, with whom her family socialised; Hamda Jum'a recalls her sisterly bond with 'Fifati', her Jewish neighbour who promised (and failed) to protect her; Muhammad Jamil 'Arabi wistfully recounts the wedding feasts where everyone 'blended together in a very lovely way'. For Amirah Silmi, the sharp limits of friendship in 'Arabi's account of his Jewish neighbour's vision of coexistence – 'we are the mind, you are the arm, mind and arm work well together' – evidence the colonial mentality undergirding social relations. On the other hand, these affective relations, in certain moments, seem to destabilise clear distinctions of self and other, colonised and coloniser, and perhaps for this reason have been largely effaced in nationalist histories both Israeli and Palestinian, lest they unsettle state-centric imaginaries of national-ethnic partition. For refugee narrators, descriptions of erstwhile solidarity and connectedness underscore the bewilderment, betrayal and helplessness Palestinians experienced in 1948. Asked what he felt after he was forced to flee his village, Husayn Mustafa Taha is unequivocal: 'A feeling of desperation, and a feeling of subjugation, and a feeling that the British and the Jews defeated us. And a feeling of lack of power to resist against them! That was the feeling. We left. We left.'

ARCHIVING EXILE

I met Mahmoud Zeidan in 2002, and we soon began recording interviews with elders in the Palestinian camps and informal gatherings in Lebanon. That modest if urgent enterprise gradually evolved into a more ambitious one. Over the next five years, we recorded close to 500 interviews with refugees hailing from 135 villages and towns, mainly in the northern Galilee and coastal areas of Palestine.[26] From the outset, the initiative was conceived as a grass-roots collaboration and, by 2005, it involved a network of 28 fieldworkers and researchers from all 12 official UNRWA camps in Lebanon. Our overarching aims were to give elders and community members an opportunity to represent their histories in their own terms, and to document as many eyewitness accounts of a passing generation as we could.[27] Both the research practices and the interviews are the result of the long-standing commitment of community members who worked with us.[28] Interviews were conducted with men and women from diverse social, geographic and religious backgrounds, and included Christians, Muslims, landless agricultural labourers (fellahin), fishermen, Bedouin and poor city dwellers. The range of experiences and perspectives expands our understanding of what constitutes history, unsettling gender logics that have reflexively privileged political deeds over domestic work, or the sacrifices of nation over those of family. While the majority of interviews were recorded by refugee researchers in camps, in the later stages of the project, we also conducted interviews with the elite outside the camps – businessmen, intellectuals and wealthy Palestinians. At the time of interview, most subjects were in their late seventies and eighties, having left Palestine as teenagers and young adults.

Like the archive, this book sets out to highlight legacies of ongoing colonialism and challenge the proscriptive power of Zionist narratives. It reclaims and celebrates refugee narrators as authoritative chroniclers of their past, and attends to the experiential aftermath of 1948. For decades, public awareness of the 'Palestinian refugee problem' has been shaped by the so-called 'peace process', and more recently by its failure and the attendant collapse of the two-state solution. Israeli authorities have steadfastly denied the Palestinian narrative, refusing to acknowledge its history of ethnic cleansing (now broadly accepted by most informed observers) or to recognise the right of return for refugees (on grounds that such recognition would mean the end of the state). Meanwhile, the Palestinian Authority leverages refugees as pawns in a political game in which they have little say. They figure by turns as living symbols of a historic injustice, speechless victims in need of humanitarian aid, and immiserated impediments to 'peace', but only very rarely as political subjects endowed with voice. Such agency as they are accorded is abstract, monolithic and vaguely menacing, its material and affective dimensions subsumed into the political demand of the right of return, for its part no sooner invoked than dismissed as quixotic and destructive. Both the archive and this book are an attempt to move discussion of refugees beyond the statistical, anecdotal and mythical, to bring their histories, rights and desires into focus in a way not dictated by – or reducible to – political symbolism or diplomatic pragmatism, and to reconstitute them as historical subjects.

When Mahmoud and I began, relatively little oral history work had been undertaken with Palestinians in Lebanon and none of it had been filmed.[29] In turning to video, our intention was to take seriously the embodied, performative power of these narratives. Oral testimonies convey forms of affective experience and knowledge that are non-verbal, and to see and hear elders speak is quite different from reading transcripts. 'My biggest ambition was to learn to write my name. Really … What can I say? I swear, I would cry – I would cry my heart out wanting to be able to write my name,' says Hasna Mana', recalling how girls were denied an education. 'What was I to do? I would clean and sweep … make bread on the *taboun*, I would go to 'Akka, run errands for my family with my father. But my wish was to be able to write my name.' Frustration suffuses her words but only in the potent pauses that punctuate them do we sense the submerged magnitude of thwarted desire. Each voice is driven by a different set of preoccupations, and each has rhythms and urgencies that mediate perception and foster imaginative engagement. Intonation, the sound of words caught in the throat, the repetitions – *we left, we left* – are all vital to meaning, as is silence, a structuring presence in all of these narratives, stealing across these pages like a tide.

Moments when speech fails or when something is conspicuously withheld are reminders of all that resists or eludes inscription. In the interview with Mahmud Abu al-Hayja, discussed by Laila Parsons, al-Hayja describes the loss of the village of al-Birwa after a valiant battle. 'You are a young educated man and I assume you have done your research,' he says to the interviewer, his voice trembling. '*This* is history, and history is merciless!' He speaks of a betrayal still keenly felt, but it is the sound of his voice, elliptical and perforated, and the intensity of his gaze that register grief. Hovering between aural impression and discursive expression, al-Hayja's voice conveys a lingering pain. Absences and gaps interrupt the complacencies of meaning-making, modulating the terms of engagement between interviewer, subject and audience, exposure and privacy, insufficiency and surplus. The speaker pushes back – reality holds representation in check.

While interviews focused on the experience of expulsion, the recordings document its legacy for five generations of refugees. Video registers the stark contrast between the recollected past and lived present, transposing one upon the other. Camp homes – cramped and crowded, insufficiently lit, abuzz with the interjections of relatives and neighbours and the hum of generators – give meaning and context to remembrance. Initially regarding these technical constraints as lamentable but unavoidable, we came to recognise their significance and value. The recordings not only make visible the concrete material circumstances that precipitate and give form to recollection, but also the social and relational dynamics that have sustained it, shaping how refugees narrate and listen. These stories are told not only to communicate experiences to younger generations who did not live them, but also as a form of sociality and entertainment, a way of passing time and whiling away the tedium of camp life. Refugee elders are often gifted storytellers with a keen sense of revealing detail and narrative arc. The social and material environments captured on film situate the Nakba as a condition and inheritance that continues to evolve across generations, in conditions of deepening deprivation. As Lena Jayyusi, one of the authors in this collection, observes elsewhere, every act of Palestinian remembrance has to be understood in cumulative relation to 'the continuing figure of erasure and denial that marks the contemporary Palestinian condition'.[30]

Interpenetration of past and present suffering is a defining characteristic of refugee narratives. In Kamila al-'Abd Tahir's testimony, discussed in Chapter 9 by Saleh Abdel Jawad, she describes her brother's death in the massacre in Saliha in 1948 and her own narrow escape. 'Whenever I tell these stories, blood boils over from my heart', she tells the interviewer, recounting how Zionist soldiers had rounded up and gunned down villagers in the village mosque, and how she lay surrounded by the bodies of dead relatives for days stroking her dying brother's hair. 'We wept, all we could do was weep', she tells the interviewer, before shifting mid-sentence to the present tense: 'Saliha is full of worries. It is, my dear'. Her story also reminds us how in the aftermath of violence, the labour of burying and remembering the dead often falls to women. But what happens when loss goes unrecognised or when there is no body? In her analysis of Amina Hasan Banat's narrative, Ruba Salih begins with a bucolic description of life in Shaykh Danun, before charting its brutal destruction by Zionist paramilitaries. Dwarfed by a wall of photographs commemorating children lost during Lebanon's civil war, Banat recalls her journey to Lebanon in 1948, carrying her two infant daughters in a tray balanced on her head. Her account segues into recollections of the Israeli invasion of Beirut in 1982, when her husband was killed and four sons disappeared. She describes nightly conversations with her missing sons and their spectral appearances in the alleys of the camp. These digressions tacitly insist that her losses as a wife and mother in Lebanon form part of her Nakba story. Banat's account challenges the nationalist rhetoric of lost children as martyred heroes for the national cause: 'My country, I could never forget it, it remains in my thoughts, but not as much as my children,' she says. 'My children were born from my heart.'[31] These exchanges reveal explicitly and painfully the extent to which recollection – even of a past as canonically epic as the Nakba is for Palestinians – is experienced as part of a lived present.

In the complex rewiring of space and time that occurs in speech, chronology is as much a function of emotion as time. A question may elicit a flood of images, all rushing in at once, sparking further associations or derailing thought altogether. The voice that breaks off from a painful episode in one setting may fuse several such episodes in another. Banat's braiding together of her expulsion from Palestine in 1948 with the losses she sustained in Lebanon in 1982 makes explicit a fluent continuity of political forces ranged against her. Fatimah 'Abdallah's testimony, discussed in Chapter 7 by Ted Swedenburg, similarly merges revolutionary moments: when asked about songs sung for the revolutionaries of 1936, she responds with a verse extolling PLO Chairman Yasser Arafat, 'Abu Ammar' (suggesting she heard people singing it in her village in Palestine, when she must be speaking of the *thawra* in Lebanon).[32] Such spatio-temporal jumps reveal persistent structural dynamics shaping and transforming individual lives. For the reader without rhythmic cues they can be hard to follow, but to listen to recordings of Banat and 'Abdallah is to hear continuities – of war, revolution, dispossession, disenfranchisement, statelessness, family upheaval, births and deaths – carried over decades and across borders on the current of voice. Seamless conflations in their narratives are as illuminating as gaps and silences in those of others.

Elders were sometimes reluctant to be interviewed and expressed doubt about our intention to record their testimonies. Many saw it as too little, too late ('*Why did you not come when our memories were still fresh?*'). One elder made the point that only when something disappears do we researchers come study it (echoing as he did a familiar critique of salvage ethnography – that it captures worlds on the wane in a spirit of complicity and complacency, while simultaneously midwifing their departure). Almost all questioned the capacity of language to convey what they had lived ('*What can I tell you? What can I say?*'), pointing to the abundance of evidence already gathered of violence against Palestinians, none of which had brought justice or reparations; indeed, it only reaffirmed their powerlessness and suggested that fruitless rhetorical insistence on their *human* rights had ultimately annulled their political rights, while leaving that very humanity in question. Mahmud Abu al-Hayja's challenge to the interviewer – *you* study what happened – is one example of this resistance to the moral presumptions of bearing witness, which lays the burden of claims-making on victims. It stands as an admonishment to researchers and activists who ask refugees to narrate their suffering while doing little to address the structural conditions that perpetuate it. Parsons also notes Abu al-Hayja's palpable weariness with his role as witness and supplicant. Such moments of reluctance and refusal are significant. Refugees evince a hard-won, salutary scepticism about archives as a necessary good, about the value of eyewitness testimony in producing justice or resolution for victims, and about the liberal pieties of forms of advocacy that only reproduce unequal power relations. Who archives, who gets archived and who, ultimately, benefits from such projects?

If archives are traditionally the preserve of the state, exile dismantles and disperses them. 'Slowly our lives – like Palestine itself – dissolve into something else,' Edward Said wrote. 'We can't hold to the center for long.'[33] Centrifugal drift has only quickened in the 35 years since he wrote that. What is an archive without a centre? What relation does a form so statist and institutionally grounded have to a stateless, deterritorialised people? What archive might capture the dissolution and transformation of Palestinian society? The archive built from refugee accounts is one that, in a sense, already existed in the storied world of camps, the living, changing repositories of the Nakba experience. Refugees' accounts offer a decentred vision of Palestine and what it means to be Palestinian, set at an oblique angle to statist projects. Forever cast outside the modern state system, they are its staunchest critics. As Shaira Vadasaria observes, 'Palestinian refugees are both the outcasted subject of settler colonial nation building and its greatest threat.'[34]

Over more than seven decades, exile has forged its own language of rights and justice, one that derives as much from a felt relation to lands and homes lost in 1948 as from the colonial and international legal codes that have excluded them. Through it, refugees challenge erasure and exclusion. While they continue in political discourse to invoke UN Resolution 194 (the article legally enshrining their right of return), their claims sustained in narrative draw variously on family lineages, on their lived experience as *ahl al-ard* (stewards of the land), or the intimacies of communal belonging encompassed by *ahaali*, attachments that precede and prefigure citizenship but also in some ways obviate it. With the failure of the two-state solution and the so-called peace negotiations, the Palestinian struggle is increasingly seen in terms not of state building but of decolonisation, reviving deeply rooted frameworks of anti-colonial struggle. This is something refugees have long understood. Their narratives, instinctively ranged against the exclusionary colonial logics of states and borders, articulate a vision that speaks forcefully back to this political moment.

THIS BOOK

Voices of the Nakba introduces readers to the depth and breadth of the Nakba Archive and exemplifies its potential use in interventions both academic and political. The chapters are organised chronologically around 30 interviews recorded with men and women from diverse socio-economic and geographic backgrounds. The interviews were selected both for their historical and thematic range and their aesthetic form; narrators speak to different aspects of life under the British Mandate, the events of 1947–48 and their aftermath. The short accompanying essays provide context and analysis, inviting readers to think critically about the experience and representation of displacement and exile, and about what is at stake for speakers in these acts of remembrance. Writing from a range of disciplinary perspectives, the authors consider how refugees make sense of their experiences, attending to what narrative forms tell us about temporal perception, intergenerational and class relations, and the other dynamics shaping refugee memory. The decision to include extended interview excerpts (selected by contributors) rather than interspersed passages is motivated by the desire to preserve integrity of voice, idiom, and rhythm of recollection.

Structured as a series of conversations, this book consciously extends the dialogic setting of the interview: interviewers pose questions, subjects respond, authors listen and comment. It represents a sustained enquiry into the reciprocal act of remembrance and reflects on what it means to engage accounts of profound societal rupture and loss. While refugees speak to and from a particular social and political context, they also appeal to a world beyond it, one understood to have betrayed them and grown deliberately deaf to their entreaties. Allusions to this imagined audience that must listen and respond abound – 'they will laugh', 'let them hear this' – or in the exhortations to 'hear my words!' At other points, the audience is the self: 'God what a dupe I was!' Hamda Jum'a exclaims, struck anew by the trajectory of her life. 'Arabs are dupes. *Astaghfirullah*, record this so that Arabs can hear me say they're donkeys!' In these moments of address – to an international community indifferent to injustice, to Arab brethren who have abandoned them, to a naïve younger self – readers are brought into the circle of exchange, implicated not only as auditors but participants. The book's form invites acts of listening in which complacency is flushed and exposed; self-recognition is the precondition to candour, empathy and critical engagement. Cynthia Kreichati, reflecting on the ethical demands narratives make of the reader, exhorts us to imagine the people and places in Fatima Sha'ban's account of her life in al-Zib through a process of 'attunement', so that they might impress upon us and take root.

In this way, the book explores the affective ecology of memory, approaching elders not simply as historical 'sources' but also as living archives of verbal and non-verbal knowledge. Poetic formulae convey loss and longing, revolt and resilience, underscoring the vitality and plasticity of oral culture. The songs Husayn Lubani sings about the Great Revolt (1936–39) against the British bristle with angry satire – 'Our flag floats above the clouds, Delegate, go tell your country, London is our horse stall.' As Swedenburg observes, these songs that chronicle popular histories of anti-colonial struggle are also a medium of subversion and critique. Lyricism serves both as shield and weapon. Spoken Palestinian – linguistically and syntactically distinct from standardised literary Arabic – lends itself to nimble improvisation, irony and banter. The sayings, curses and hypnotic ritual laments of 'ataba constitute a vivid aural palette that imbues ordinary speech, enabling the leaps of consciousness characteristic of spoken discourse. When asked about her work for the British Mandate at Qadas airport, Hamda Jum'a's response was gnomic: 'My dear, I tell you a he-goat and you tell me, "Let's milk it!" And I'm a *taltamees* (a discombobulated person) who can't even distinguish Friday from Thursday!' As with words heard through a wall, meanings are lost but the energy of the exchange is clear, as are the intergenerational tensions, the pointed scepticism of the young interviewer's question and the tactical deflection of Jum'a's self-deprecating reply. Such instances of incommensurability are not so much gaps as openings, making visible the simmering resentments and moral grammars that shape refugee life.

The words and phrases elders intuitively reach for are also repositories of knowledge. Rochelle Davis, reflecting on Hasna Mana''s account of village life in al-Manshiyya, considers the significance of particular words that have fallen out of use and return like spectres. Colloquial terms – sometimes specific to particular villages or districts – evoke the physical and social world of work in pre-1948 Palestine, its aesthetic and sensual dimensions. Mana' speaks of *bayadir*, a communal outdoor threshing floor where villagers congregated; *bayyarat*, the orchards that surrounded the village; and *shawahat*, the blades used for harvesting. These words, heavy with memory, are linguistic remnants of a communal, agrarian life that no longer exists. Like pins in a map, they anchor experience in space and time and register its displacements. Recalling the large-wheeled carriages driven by villagers from al-Sumayriyya during Eid festivities, Mana' pauses to ask the interviewer if he understands her – 'You don't know what a *karra* is, do you?' Such terms – many of them unknown to Palestinians raised in Lebanon – are seeds of a unique experiential and cultural heritage held in dialect. Language also registers the impress of colonial relations, discernible in the odd word or phrase spoken in English. Caught jaggedly but with eerie fidelity, they register linguistic encroachments. Skips in the phonograph from another time, the clipped imperatives of British bureaucracy – '*It's not regular!*', '*Who made this?*', '*Get out!*' – are startling reminders of an audible politics of voice.

VOICE

The translators of these interviews were tasked not only with reproducing their vernacular complexity in another language but also conveying their intimacy in another medium. The aim has been to make these voices accessible to English-language speakers, while retaining the rhythm and cadence of the spoken. Hoda Adra, who translated many of the narratives in this book, responded to the need of narrators to deliver 'both as messenger and affective release', and tuned in to the 'intimate veracity' of refugee remembrance that resurfaces in these accounts, erased by a Zionist narrative that negates the personal and familiar.[35] Adra's translations are alive to the interconnectedness of remembering and speaking, to the twinning of rhythm and emotion in a leaderless tension, 'galloping side by side'.[36] The listening she models is absorptive rather than detached. It is concerned not only with semantic content and facts but with intimate truths as lived and felt.

These meanings, conveyed as an affective charge – as sound, rhythm and the 'grain' of voice, which for Roland Barthes 'reactualizes, in the subject's speech, the totality of his history' – are not the after-effect of thought so much as a sonic manifestation of presence.[37]

Dolar laments that, in the Western metaphysical tradition, voice 'makes the utterance possible, but disappears in it, it goes up in smoke in the meaning being produced.'[38] His figure of the 'vocal fingerprint' elegantly rematerialises speech as sound, voice as person, which helps distinguish between speaking as interpellation (the discursive production of identity and claims-making) and speaking as an act of refusal, challenging statist exclusion through assertion of a sovereign self. Lisa Stevenson, hinting at the power of voice as presence in Arctic Inuit sound recordings, writes that speech must also be understood as 'a call to the self ... constitutive of being humanly alive', its primary function 'not intelligibility but sound as it communicates, as it moves between and ties people together'.[39] This conception of voice is both empirically instructive and politically imperative. It performs an epistemological break of sorts, revising what counts as 'content', plausibility and truth. It also reminds us that when refugees recall the past they are not only reclaiming their experiences for the historical record but also asserting their presence, humanity and grounding as political subjects. Refugees challenge political exclusion in terms both semantic and embodied: by attending to voice *as* content – as manifesting a particular social and political ontology of exile – we may begin better to understand the lived condition of the ongoing Nakba.

Just as storytelling and the inscription of memory entail forgetting and loss, transcription and translation risk compromise and betrayal. Oral performance 'lives by its fluidity', a fluidity jeopardised by the conversion to text.[40] Both the work that went into making the Nakba Archive and the POHA project to index it prompt reflection about experiential knowledge that print and digital media cannot catch in their nets, about the costs incurred by the move from life as lived, through life as narrated and recorded story, to life as searchable text. When I consider how I have catalogued these interviews in my own memory over the years, it is not by village, profession, gender, age, political activity and so on, but rather by the particular effect they elicit. In our enthusiasm for digital archives, a note of wariness is warranted. There are traces of experience in these pages not easily sifted by Boolean operators: the soundscape of church bells Hasan al-Husayni remembers enveloping the Jerusalem of his youth, or the feel of the pressed dress Fifi Khouri laid upon her bed in Jaffa in anticipation of imminent return, to which Sherene Seikaly directs our attention. Following

Adra's injunction, this collection aims to receive and reflect these luminous details, shining forth as they do from the dimmed stars of a fading world.

* * *

The first of the many voices that make up Jabra Ibrahim Jabra's 1978 novel *In Search of Walid Masoud*, describes how memories 'obsess us, sweetening the bitterness, deluding us', likening them to 'clouds over the expanses of the mind' and 'precious diamonds compressed within the folds of the soul'. 'Dr Jawad Husni Inherits a Heavy Legacy', that first section is called. The solace, burden and bitterness of that mnemonic legacy feature centrally in Palestinian storytelling on and off the page, as does a kind of vigilant ambivalence. Diamonds compressed from the cinders of experience are held close for safe keeping, sharp synecdoches of loss, in turn yielding the nacreous seeds of futurity. Heirlooms can be a burden. Palestinian historiography and remembrance are burdened by the political imperative to document and transcend destruction, to uphold claims against inimical forces of obfuscation and indifference. The urgency informing them arises from the need at once to order and transmit a traumatic past, and to take hold of an imminently uncertain present and future.

Mahmoud Zeidan's preface to this book extends that tradition, oral and literary, in which memory is in the air you breathe, the soundscapes you take in, the spaces you inhabit. Zeidan describes 'Ayn al-Hilweh camp, south of Sayda, as *storied*: its history – and that of the cleansed villages in Palestine, like Safsaf, that fed into it – is environmental, absorbed through the senses rather than consciously acquired. It is a world mediated by voices:

I never read about these events – or even our village itself – in history books. I don't know how I came to know what I know about it. I know the stories of Safsaf as I know the houses of 'Ayn al-Hilweh, its alleys and its people. Like many others in the camp, I know these stories as if by instinct ... These stories thrummed the tents of the camp and flew like the driving rain. They hung in the air in later years, among tin houses, spreading like the scent of food and attracting neighbours, relatives and passers-by.

Storytelling, wrote Walter Benjamin, a few years before the Safsaf massacre and cleansing, 'does not aim to convey the pure essence of the thing, like information or a report', but rather 'sinks the thing into the life of the storyteller, in order to bring it out of him again'.[41] Benjamin traced in that essay

17

how modernity had 'gradually removed narrative from the realm of living speech, and at the same time is making it possible to see a new beauty in what is vanishing'.[42] He wrote out of love and longing for the art of the storyteller and the work of Nikolai Leskov, but there was also a warning in those words: we fetishise what we are complicit in eradicating. He sets the morally ambiguous detachment of the solitary reader, who turns to his novel with 'the hope of warming his shivering life with a death he reads about', against the tremulously vital deathbed tableau that is, for Benjamin, the ur-scene of storytelling:

> Not only a man's knowledge or wisdom, but above all his real life – and this is the stuff that stories are made of – first assumes transmissible form at the moment of his death. Just as a sequence of images is set in motion inside a man as his life comes to an end – unfolding the views of himself under which he has encountered himself without being aware of it – suddenly in his expressions and looks the unforgettable emerges and imparts to everything that concerned him that authority which even the poorest wretch in dying possesses for the living around him. This authority is at the very source of the story.[43]

This is death set in the midst of life, drawing on it and in turn replenishing it. It is a scene of sociality, solidarity and radiant transmission. It is not a vanishing.

In 2012, during one of the last interviews I filmed for the Nakba Archive, a man in his nineties from the village of Taytaba, then living in Burj al-Barajneh camp in Beirut, concluded by telling Mahmoud and I that he had little expectation of seeing his village again. 'I don't have hope to return,' he said, matter of factly. 'Palestinians from 1948 will die here. We dream in Palestine – we remember our villages and return to them in our dreams – but one day this too may not be permitted.' His comment suggests defeatism and defiance in equal measure. It registers faith in the oppositional, emancipatory force of the unauthorised refugee narrative: what disappeared in 1948 continues to pulse and circulate. In a fundamental sense, resistance to the ongoing erasure of Palestine and to the Israeli settler-colonial project – which ethnically cleanses Palestinian neighbourhoods, seizes land, destroys Palestinian homes, infrastructure and archives, removes Arab street names, plants pine forests over the ruins of Palestinian villages, immobilises, incarcerates and dislocates communities, and denies the rights, attachments and humanity of Palestinians – is still a struggle of remembering against forgetting.

To speak of archives creates an illusion of distance and permanence that are lacking in the camps where these interviews were conducted. As deprivation deepens for Palestinian refugees across the Middle East, cycles of rupture and crisis revive and revise the erasures of 1948. The exigencies of the present are experienced both as the continuation of a traumatic past and the past of some diminishing future. Anne Stoler put it well when she observed that Palestinian pasts demand a 'recursive analytics'.[44] A friend born and raised in Shatila camp in Beirut made the same observation more simply: 'I know the Nakba because I live in Shatila.'[45] The Palestinian refugees displaced from Yarmouk, Deraa, Neirab and other camps in Syria since 2011, like those resisting eviction in East Jerusalem and the Naqab in Israel, surviving brutal carceral siege in Gaza, embarking on perilous 'irregular' journeys to Europe in search of resettlement, or now contemplating Israel's re-annexation of the West Bank, are simply living the latest chapters in this long, unfolding history of dispossession, displacement and statelessness. The disaster continues. But so does a way of knowing and being formed in opposition to erasure, an orientation to the future as well as the past.

Figure 3   Fifi Khouri and her sister in Yafa,
Palestine, circa 1920. Courtesy of
Nakba Archive.

PART I

Life in Pre-1948 Palestine

1
Village Life in Palestine
Rochelle Davis

In Palestine, in the first half of the twentieth century, land was the cornerstone of villagers' economy as well as identity. Villages were closely linked to others in the same region, as well as to nearby urban centres. The British Mandate government regulated village life through taxation, various registration requirements, security patrols and, to a much lesser extent, public service provision.[1] At the same time, village life was undergoing significant changes due to urbanisation and the development of urban areas. When Mandate authorities conducted their first census of Palestine in 1921, two-thirds of the population was categorised as rural. By 1944, the estimated total population of 1.7 million (1.14 million of whom were Palestinian Muslims and Christians) comprised rural and urban residents in equal measure.[2] The urban population had increased by almost 100 per cent, while rural growth stood at just over 50 per cent. Much of that urban growth was a result of migration from villages to cities for work.

Despite this rapid urbanisation, village life remained anchored to the land both for economic livelihood and as a source of local and national identity. Across Palestine, village life centred on agricultural production. Growing grains, tobacco, vegetables and fruits, and raising sheep and goats for meat and milk were essential parts of villagers' livelihoods and economic activities. Hasna Mana' was born in the village of al-Manshiyya, home to over 900 residents in 1948 and located 3 kilometres east of the coastal city of 'Akka (Acre). When asked about her father's occupation, she states that he kept herds of sheep and goats, and opened a *diwan*. Ibrahim Blaybil is from Taytaba, a village of over 600 people that lay approximately 10 very hilly kilometres north of Safad. His father was a farmer. Ibrahim excelled academically and became a teacher after graduating from secondary school. Villages usually had local blacksmiths and truck drivers, and larger village populations included small shop owners and mechanics, among other skilled workers.

Village economies were deeply enmeshed with one another and with nearby urban economies.[3] Villagers traded the crops and animals they raised with other villages or urban merchants, in exchange for cloth and other commodities. Both women and men travelled to nearby urban areas to sell produce – in particular, fruits, vegetables and home-made cheeses. Ibrahim describes the villagers growing watermelons and 'yellow melons', but these were not money-makers – nor was tobacco, a crop highly regulated by the government. He tells of Taytaba's success with tomatoes, which he describes taking to market in Tel Aviv in the full interview. Ibrahim also details the villagers' relationship with a Jewish man from Safad, who would come to Taytaba to buy milk products, meat, wool, and sheep and goat hides. With the cash they earned, villagers could purchase goods from the city markets. Villagers also provided labour for urban enterprises and infrastructures, working in ports as stevedores, and as policemen. Hasna mentions that a variety of people came to live in al-Manshiyya due to its location close to 'Akka. Indeed, villages near urban areas were often bedroom communities for migrant workers from more remote villages, who travelled to the city for jobs.

As Hasna's stories from al-Manshiyya show, the villages of the coastal plains adopted mechanised agriculture practices because grain harvesters could work on flat terrain (unlike the hills around Taytaba). The motorised irrigation pump she describes would have been rare in the highlands, which relied on rain-fed agriculture and lower temperatures.

Urban centres were also hubs for education and entertainment. Imams and teachers often came to live in villages from larger towns and urban areas with better access to education; and children travelled to larger villages and towns to pursue their studies, once they had finished school in their own villages. After completing primary school in Taytaba, Ibrahim and some other boys rented weekday accommodation in the city of Safad, in order to continue their studies until age 14. He then had to travel to the village of al-Bassa for upper secondary school. Hasna's childhood memories include going to celebrate the Big and Small Eid holidays in 'Akka, where children congregated in their new clothes, played on swings and ate special treats. She also recalls trips by girls and women to the communal bathhouse in the city.

Across Palestine, village life centred on certain physical spaces. If villagers had sufficient resources, they built schools, mosques and churches. Ibrahim explains that in Taytaba, in the late 1920s, he and the other boys went to school in the mosque, where they learned maths, Arabic, religion, drawing and sports. The mosque building became a full-time place of worship after the villagers built a school in 1935. When he became a teacher himself in the 1940s, Ibrahim taught Arabic, English and maths to boys and girls in the village of 'Alma, about 15 kilometres north of Taytaba.

Every village had a *baydar* (*bayadir* in the plural), a hard-packed outdoor threshing floor for the harvest of grains (wheat and barley) and pulses (lentils, beans and chickpeas). Weddings were often held on this flat, smooth, communal space as well. Grains and pulses were harvested and threshed in late summer and early autumn. Throughout the seasons, everyone worked in the fields, planting, harvesting or tending animals. Ibrahim says he hated working with sheep and goats, a chore he escaped once he went to Safad and al-Bassa for secondary school. Women worked both in the fields and at home preparing the harvest for winter storage. Tomatoes, okra, peppers and mallow were dried. Milk was turned into yoghurt, then *labneh*, which was made into balls and packed in olive oil or dried with cracked wheat in large, hard balls of *kishk* to be reconstituted and cooked with grains and lentils. Such subsistence living characterised Palestinian village life.

The British colonial authority targeted this subsistence livelihood as part of their crackdown on Palestinian resistance. Historical documentation of the British crackdown on Palestinians during the 1936–39 revolt tell of British soldiers dumping villagers' winter stores on the floor, breaking olive oil storage jars, and pouring kerosene on supplies. These actions by the governing authorities resulted in hardship and food insecurity for whole families, who would have to rely on other villagers for their livelihoods for the year. Hasna describes seeing British forces burn down suspected revolutionaries' houses and destroying food supplies in al-Manshiyya.

Such accounts of collective punishment are told in every village. Palestinian anticolonial and nationalist activists – who organised, mobilised and fought against the British Mandate and Jewish Zionist settlers – relied on villagers to hide and supply them while they participated in clandestine resistance efforts. Hasna explains that political activity and armed resistance was happening all around her, but she was instructed not to talk about it as a child, for fear of leaking secrets to the British. Ibrahim tells the story of leaving his village for Safad at the beginning of the school week, when British soldiers stopped him and his cousin, who were both on horseback. The soldiers first demanded the two teenagers inform on whomever had built trenches and walls – which the army presumed to be the work of Palestinians resistance fighters – in the steep valleys outside Taytaba. When the boys could not provide an answer, the soldiers forced them into an army vehicle and took them back to the village. Along the way, they passed by another cousin, who was ploughing the fields with two bulls. When the British troops beckoned to him, he tried to unleash his bulls before approaching, but a soldier shot him dead. Hasna shares similar memories of British actions in her village. These stories testify to the ways that Palestinian anti-colonial activism was violently suppressed that took the form of collective punishment that colonial forces meted out to villagers.[4]

The British Mandate government administration penetrated into the villagers lives in other ways, evidenced in the records that villagers still possess, both at the individual level (identity cards and passports; birth, death and marriage certificates; driving licenses) and the economic level (receipts for taxes paid, licenses to grow tobacco, animal immunisation records, tithe receipts, land documents).[5] British Mandate governmental departments appointed teachers, who were either locals trained in established institutes and hired to work in their home villages, or professionals sent to villages from other parts of the country. Ibrahim's life story traces a trajectory from Taytaba's village school to schools in Safad and al-Bassa, and on to 'Alma, where he eventually worked as a teacher. At the same time, Hasna describes how villagers kept the British Mandate governmental apparatus distant from internal community conflicts, which were resolved through a committee of elders who determined fault and punishment.

For many, village life in Palestine before the Nakba conjures up a romantic, agrarian existence. Those who lived it often contribute to its romanticisation, usually because they faced impossibly difficult circumstances after the Nakba, when they were made refugees. They lost homeland, herds and livelihoods, and were reduced to the indignity of life in refugee camps; whereas, when living in the village, despite the difficulties, it was life on their own land, in their own country and on their own terms. Others describe village life without glossing over the hardships – no indoor plumbing or electricity; limited education for children and even less for girls; and the dominance of patriarchal norms of proper behaviour. Hasna describes how disputes were resolved between husband and wife or family members; how women were coerced into dressing in certain ways; and the social acceptability of what today we would label domestic abuse. She repeatedly says, 'This is how we did things', suggesting she knows how much times have changed, and that actions and beliefs that were acceptable then may not be so now. Hasna's one dream as a child was to learn to write her name, but her village did not send girls to school, a fact she laments.

Remembering village life is also a generational documentation of change and rupture. Hasna, in particular, defines items and practices that she thinks would be unfamiliar to younger generations. As she tells her stories, she asks her interlocutor regularly if he knows to what she is referring to, even though he is from a refugee camp in Lebanon, and originally from a village in Palestine. She knows that the terms she uses to describe bygone ways of life have not always been passed down to younger Palestinians – not only because of the passage of time but also because of the ruptures of forced displacement and dispossession, which uprooted villagers from their traditional life. Why would one need to know about a *bayyara* (small irrigated orchard) or *shawahat* (harvester blades) when these things ceased to be part of Palestinians' lives after their villages were taken from them? While this type of knowledge may be fading, village life has taken on symbolic importance to Palestinians wherever they are. Village traditions such as *thawb* dresses embroidered with *tatreez* cross-stitch, *kaffiyeh* scarves and olive cultivation have been embraced by all Palestinians – even those who hail from urban areas or coastal plains, where these customs and practices were less widespread. Their adoption reveals how Palestinian village life has become, in the post-Nakba period, symbols of greater Palestinian cultural heritage and national struggle.

Ibrahim Blaybil
born 1920 in Taytaba, Palestine
Interview with Mahmoud Zeidan
'Ayn al-Hilweh camp, Sayda, 2004

4'07"–7'03"

Mahmoud Zeidan: *What was your father's job in Palestine?*
Ibrahim Blaybil: In Palestine, my father used to work in farming, in agriculture. He used to plant wheat, lentils, beans, corn, chickpeas. They would clean and thresh them on the *bayadir* in Taytaba.

Before we get into the subject of agriculture, I would like you to tell me about your childhood in Taytaba.
My childhood … I was born after 1920. We entered school in around 1927 or 1928. We were children and, at that time, children would not go to school when they turned six or seven, they would take longer. The British Mandate was an emerging government and it had not created a school yet. There was a mosque and that is where children would learn. And the government would send an imam, who would be the teacher, and would pay him a salary to teach the children. Later, in 1935 or 1945, they built a school for students.

Was this school founded by the people of Taytaba or by the Mandate?
The mosque had a big square, a big garden, in which they built a school later. It was a government initiative, and the people of the town helped as well.

How many classrooms were there?
There were four or five classrooms. I remember four or five that they made out of cement. And they kept the mosque for praying. But before the school was built, each Friday, when we wanted to pray, we would take the benches out and all the other things, and mop the floor, put down the carpets and pray in the mosque. The village imam would open it for prayer time.

And on normal days, how were you…
On normal days, they would bring the benches back to the mosque and we would go study.

So they didn't pray in this mosque on normal days?
No, only on Fridays and on Eids – during the religious holidays. Otherwise, people would pray in their own homes, or if someone had a spacious house, they would pray there.

Was this mosque very big?
No, it was just a single room, about five by five metres, surrounded by a garden.

10'04"–11'13"

What were the subjects they used to teach?
Mathematics, Arabic, religion, drawing, physical education ... When government schools would close for holidays, we would as well. When government schools were on vacation, our school was as well. The children who went there would help their parents with farming, harvesting ... For about three months. And they would collect the crops on the large *bayadir* and clean and prepare them on the *nawraj*. Children would help their parents. And during springtime as well, we would help our parents plant the tomatoes, the zucchini, the wild cucumbers, the okra...

13'10"–16'25"

People used to own sheep, goats, and they had to take care of them, cows as well. I used to hate it. When I got to fourth or fifth grade, we went to Safad. There were a large number of students from my town, as well as yours. From the Nayif and al-Zaghmut families, as well as the Hamad brothers, Qasim Hamad, Ibrahim Hamad and ʿAli Hamad. No, they were cousins. Two of them were brothers and one of them was a cousin. They were from Syria. We had rented a place in Safad and that is where we studied for the fifth, sixth and seventh grade. When we got to secondary school, anyone who was 14 years old and one month was discharged from the school by the British High Commissioner. In 1939, when they discharged us, we were in secondary one. There was secondary one and secondary two. I then went to al-Bassa for secondary school. I went to al-Bassa with Yusif Kaʿwash, who is still alive, as well as Nayif Muhammad Ibrahim from al-Sammuʿi, and ... God bless the Prophet Muhammad ... Ah, it's ʿAli Saʿid from al-Hula, and we rented a space in al-Bassa and entered secondary school. Later, it became a university and we studied there.

31

Why did you get discharged from the school system?
Because we were over 14. If you were older than 14, they would dismiss you from your school. In order to keep people ignorant! And, at that time, the British Mandate would pressure the *fellahin*. For example, during our growing season, they would bring in wheat, corn and lentil crops from abroad to compete against local Palestinian markets inside Palestine. Until people started hating the actions of the British. This led to the uprisings during the revolution of 1929.[6] I remember it, there were planes flying over our town. And there was another revolution in 1936, I think 'Izz al-Din al-Qassam was martyred in it.[7]

17'53"–18'21"

Why didn't you finish school, and what did you do after?
We were unable to continue, because we would have had to move to al-Quds. Or go where there was an agricultural school: Madrasat Kadoorie al-Zira'iyya (Kadoorie Agricultural School) in Tulkarm. In Haifa, there was a secondary school that went up to secondary four, like the one in al-Bassa.

30'05"–33'12"

I became a teacher and I taught between 1943 and 1945 … Or was it 1946? Something like that, 1946. In 1947, the disruptions started.

What did you teach?
I taught religion, Arabic, English, mathematics … Around 1944 or 1945, the director, whose name I can't recall, was from Safad … They were play-ing with a gun and a bullet hit someone's foot. School was cancelled and I was the only one left teaching there. The school went from grade one to four, and there were maybe two or three rooms. I was the one teaching them. While I was teaching handwriting over here, the best students were making others recite their lessons over there. I was dispatching the best students and sending them to the classes to teach other students, and I was overseeing them. I would write a maths problem on the blackboard in one room, and a maths problem on another blackboard in another room, and see who was able to solve it. And that is how I was simultaneously teaching all these subjects to three or four classes.

So when the director was absent, only you remained in the school?
Only I remained.

Not even other teachers?
Nobody. They caused an accident, one of them was shot while they played with a gun. And I had to pick up the mess. The investigator came, Jamil al-Zaraziri, and he asked me to write a report. I didn't write a thing!

Were you strict with the students?
Yes, of course! Very strict. Nobody dared ... There were about 10 or 15 girls, but most of them were boys. We were very strict with them, oh yes! We would tell a boy: 'You are the *'arif*. Tell us who is playing with marbles in the alleys.' Why were we strict? So that they would study! If a student hadn't memorised, we would hit him. Even the parents would encourage us and say, 'The meat of the child is yours, the bones are ours.' Yes, we taught well. We trained some good teachers. Professor 'Ajawi, if you've heard of him. I was the one who taught him, at that school. 'Abd al-Karim Ta'an, from our village, was also a school director in Rashidiyya [camp] ... I taught him.

34'50"–35'43"

The villagers had weddings and they would invite us because we were the teachers. Also, we would visit the *mukhtar*, who would organise an invitation for the education department inspectors. It was the kind of responsibility he had ... And he would invite the teachers to lunch with them. There was Muhammad Faris, I don't know if he's still alive, who went to 'Alma. There were many others. The Sulayman family came from 'Alma, the *mukhtar* was also from the Sulayman family.

During that period, were you sleeping in 'Alma, or coming and going there?
I was renting, from the family of Faris al-Hajj.

38'27"–39'21"

What did the people of Taytaba do for work?
They cultivated wheat, barley, produce, vegetables. At one point, they grew watermelons, which did not produce enough and did not bring in much profit. Then, they planted yellow melons and its harvest, even though it was only *ba'l*, was as delicious as honey, but they realised they wouldn't profit much from it. Then, they planted tobacco, which did not bring much profit either. In the end, they planted tomatoes, which were highly productive and from which they made a huge amount of profit.

59'03"–1h 00'30"

Do you remember the British ever coming to Taytaba?
One time, when I was a teenager, I was on my way up to school in Safad with Abu ʿAtif Blaybil, who is also here with us. We arrived at ʿAyn al-Zaytun and saw the incoming cars of the British Army. We were riding our horses. I was riding and Abu ʿAtif was on foot, on his way to get things. As soon as we recognised the British troops, we took a path down to ʿAyn al-Zaytun, so they brought their guns out on us. I released the horses, and they left and went back to our town on their own. The soldiers asked us, 'Where are you going?' We told them, 'We are students at Safad School.' I told him in English, and said that we were going there to study. 'Who made this?' The soldiers were asking about the trenches and the terraces, which were this high (raises arm above head). We said: 'We have no idea, we come here every week from Safad' – I spoke to him in English – 'to visit our families'. They made us ride in the last car of the British convoy. The soldier took out his rifle and yelled again at us, 'Tell me who made this!'

1h 01'19"–1h 02'11"

They took us back to our village. Our whole village was not working because they wanted to force the villagers to work and have each village build a military road for the British Army and we refused! Starting from your village until west of Saʿsaʿ. They made us work! But before we arrived at the village in the convoy, my cousin Yusif Abu Muhammad, God rest his soul, was farming. They ran after him: 'Come here! Come here!' He was farming with his two bulls. They wanted him to come to them, but he had to release the bulls because they were attached to the plough. They started shooting at him, and one of them hit him with his rifle and the blood started pouring. Abu ʿAtif started cursing him, I told him, 'Why do you curse? They hit him, it's done.'

1h 09'00"–1h 11'22"

Before the skirmishes started, how was the relationship between the Jews and the Arabs?
The relationship was good, before 1939 … Relationships, yes, they were good. The Jews were not many and not very active. For example, one-quarter of Safad's population was Jewish. Yes, around one-quarter … and the rest was Muslim, and there was a Christian minority.

34

Did any of these Jews ever go to Taytaba to buy things?
Yes, they would come to buy *tarsh*, meat, wool and skins ... normal interactions. There was a tall man called Salim Nisan, who used to wear a *ghabaneh*, a *tarbush* with a *ghabaneh* on it, with a *qumbaz* and a long jacket. He dressed just like an Arab. The *fellahin* used to borrow money from him and pay him back from the harvest. Yes, we treated each other well, and we would eat from their meat and they would from ours, because we were allowed to eat their meat.

Did you know any of these Jews personally?
No, I just remember Salim Nisan. He had a storeroom that was about two or three metres high and it contained all kinds of goods, from mattresses to sheets to blankets, and dresses. People would borrow money from him and go to town to buy their *labneh*, their cheese, the wool, the skins ... There was nothing wrong between us and them. But the situation evolved when they started migrating and coming from abroad. And with the Jews who came, things became different. The interactions changed. Arabs and Jews stopped coming and going to each other.

Hasna Mana' (Dib Munayzil)
born circa 1931 in al-Manshiyya, Palestine
Interview with Mahmoud Zeidan
'Ayn al-Hilweh camp, Sayda, 2003

1'37"–2'35"

Mahmoud Zeidan: *What year did your father move to al-Manshiyya?*
Hasna Mana': To be honest son, I have no idea. I was born in al-Manshiyya, I lived in al-Manshiyya, and my siblings also lived in al-Manshiyya. We
knew nothing other than al-Manshiyya. The land was fallow but we didn't
own it. We owned houses but the land was not ours. We owned *mawashi*.
Do you know what *mawashi* are? Sheep, goats. These are *mawashi*.

What did your father work in?
Nothing at all. My father had a space bigger than this one, full of sheep and
full of goats. He sold it all: their manure, their wool, their milk and their
offspring. That was my father's occupation. He had opened a big *diwan* and
served bitter coffee to the elders. That too was my father's occupation. That
was it.

How many brothers and sisters were you, Hajjeh?
We were two brothers and four girls.

2'49"–6'55"

What do you remember of your traditions? What did your parents teach you?
Well my son, as a little girl, I used to lay low … I remember hanging
around the *diwan* and listening to the men talk. I would eavesdrop on their
conversations! The year was 1936. I would lay low and notice who were
the revolutionaries among them. My mother told me: 'Don't you dare tell
anyone.' One time, they brought in a mine! They hid it in a pile of wood
logs. I began to understand. I told my father, 'Better get rid of it.' The British
were slaughtering us. If they had an ounce of doubt about anyone, they
would shoot him right away, whoever he may have been. Whenever I saw
any of the revolutionaries, I kept my mouth shut, just like my mother told
me. And we would help them. If one of the revolutionaries asked us to hide
his rifle, we would. Don't say anything to anyone. We wouldn't speak of
anything. This is how we were raised.

Once, a man shot a Jew ... they chased him, and he ran away ... from al-Manshiyya, jumping from wall to wall until he reached the fields. The British had police dogs, dogs who could sniff, and it did not cross our minds to sprinkle black pepper behind the man, who would kill and run. We were not aware enough at the time. When the dogs scratched on the rooftop of a house, they let the people out, and burnt the house down and everything inside it. The flames reached the ceilings.

Are there any other scenes you recall vividly? For example, them burning down someone's house?
Oh yes! But of course ... They burnt the house of Khalil Mana'. They burnt the Zahmad house, Abu Hasan's family. They burnt the house of the *mukhtar*, 'Ali Khraybi, from the al-Khraybi family. They burnt many of them. It was random, they chose the houses ... They burnt Hajj Jamil's house. And those they didn't burn, they broke into. Nobody would lock their doors; everybody would leave their house without locking it. If a door was locked, the British would break into the house. They would go in and take the sugar ... We would buy sugar in bulk – rice, too. They would pile the sugar, the rice and the flour, and pour kerosene all over it. They wouldn't even burn the house. Some houses, they wouldn't burn. They would round up the *mouneh*, including large cans of jam and *halawa*. These tin cans cut in half would contain around 10 litres of *halawa*. They would pour kerosene on all the *mouneh*, just so that they could not be eaten. That's what they did to destroy our supplies when they didn't burn the whole house...

6'48"–8'18"

What other things do you still remember from your childhood, like some of the things that you did with your friends?
When Eid came, we used to fast when we were young. My father would say, 'I will give a piastre to those who fast,' to lure us into it. So we would fast. Before Eid, he would buy us new clothes, even if we already had a huge wardrobe. Or we would get new clothes sewn for the occasion. He also bought us new shoes. For Eid, everything has to be new! It's part of our customs. On the day of Eid, our uncles would come to offer us their blessings, and then we would ask to go out for the day with the girls. We were young teenagers this tall, and we would gather food to cook: meat, onions, pepper ... Each one would bring a few ingredients, and we would go to a house to make the *kubbeh*, where there were no men. The head of the house, an older woman, would help us. After eating the *kubbeh*, we

would get up, one girl would play the *dirbakkeh*, and we would dance taking turns. We would sing and dance. We were young teenagers then.

9'07"–10'06"

The next day, we would pack a change of clothes, a *boqja*, a sponge and soap, and a copper bowl. We would call it the hammam bowl; it was made of a hand-hammered, yellow copper. We would go to 'Akka, to Hammam al-Basha, and we would scrub ourselves clean, and then go out to the swings. The swings were set up between 'Akka and al-Manshiyya. The train station was over here, the 'Akka gate was there, the swings over there, and al-Manshiyya was that way. People from 'Akka would come to the swings, bringing all kinds of food with them, from *turmus*, to *ka'b-l-ghazal* which was amber coloured, we used to call it gazelle's heel, it looked like a lump … And we would ride the swings. We would spend the four days of Eid al-Kabir, and three days for Eid al-Saghir there at the swings. We would walk from 'Akka all the way to al-Manshiyya.

13'38"–19'13"

What was the difference between Eid in 'Akka and Eid in al-Manshiyya?
In 'Akka, there were swings for children. People would bring soaked *turmus*, falafel, *ambar*, *awwameh* and trays of *baklaweh* and *harisseh* to the main square. There were many trees and the older women would sit underneath them, while the young teenage girls played on the swings, and the more mature girls would sit and watch them swing, turn and flip. It was a yearly event for the people of 'Akka. The people of al-Sumayriyya would also come, riding on *karrat*. Do you know what a *karra* is? You don't know what a *karra* is, do you? The *karra*, *yamma* … Maybe you've seen one on television, dear. They have wheels, like the ones in the movies, and they're this long … With two big wheels at the back and two small ones at the front, poles in the middle, and a horse on each side wearing a leather harness and pulling the *karra*. They would go from al-Manshiyya to 'Akka and transport vegetable crates, *mulukhiyya*, radishes and eggplants to the market. The people of al-Sumayriyya would come and trade with us. They had fields and orchards.

How did the people from al-Manshiyya, who did not go to 'Akka, spend Eid?
The elderly women would receive visits from their brothers, who would bring them meat. If one of these women did not slaughter [a sheep], her

brother, her father or a relative would bring meat to her. When Eid is upon us – and you too – we slaughter a sheep! And my brother or father would also bring me a share of their meat. Elderly relatives would visit each other to celebrate and drink coffee, younger ones would go to the swings and watch, which is what we did, even when we became young women.

Who would you go to the 'Akka swings with?
It would be me, my sister, my neighbour, my girlfriend; I wouldn't go alone. Many, many young women would go.

Did your father prevent you from going there alone as young women?
No! He didn't. We would get up in the morning, move the rugs and sweep the floor, milk the herd and deliver milk to the milkmen, then we would leave my mother in the house to cook. We would go to the swings dressed in our Eid clothes. We would stay until the Maghrib call to prayer, and leave.

What were your dreams when you were a child? What did you want to be when you grew up?
Oh dear ... My biggest ambition was to learn to write my name. Really ... What can I say? I swear, I would cry – I would cry my heart out wanting to be able to write my name. Here, girls in our communities were not given an education, *yamma*. But boys were, and they brought them to 'Akka for school. There were two grades for them to study in al-Manshiyya, after which they took them to 'Akka. They said it was dishonourable for our girls to get an education. See how narrow-minded they were? ... So I couldn't have much ambition in me. What was I to do? I would clean and sweep ... make bread on the *taboun*, I would go to 'Akka, run errands for my family with my father. But my wish was to be able to write my name. When I married and joined my father-in-law's family, they didn't teach me. In-laws don't teach women, neither do husbands, they want the wife to toughen up. Ah, yes ...

Did any of the women from your village get an education, in al-Manshiyya?
None of them did. Not our generation of women, nor the one before nor after. 'Abid Zalam was a policeman in Haifa. His daughter had finished year two or three, and the day they moved to al-Manshiyya, he interrupted her education. It was over. The girls in 'Akka, Haifa and al-Nasira got an education. Not us. Not the villages. And it wasn't just our village. Many of our villages did not educate, but the Christian ones did, like Kafr Yasin and the villages east and west of it. We did not.

23'29"–24'22"

What types of jobs did the village people work?
What do you mean, jobs? People lived off the land, those who had a *bayyara*. In al-Manshiyya we had many ... Do you know what a *bayyara* is?

An orange grove, right?
No, it is not an orange grove! An orange grove is its own thing. A *bayyara* includes an orange grove, but it also grows apples and other trees ... but not olive trees. It also had figs, cucumbers, tomatoes, *mulukhiyya*, wild cucumber, okra ... All water-irrigated.

How would al-Manshiyya get water?
It had about 20 or 30 *mator*! What's a *mator*? It's the same as that thing that brings water over to the camp, here. The ʿAli ʿUtir family had a *mator*. The Rustum family had a *mator*.

You mean they had a well?
Yes, a well with water coming out of it! A well, which we call *mator*.

28'12"–30'44"

At two in the afternoon, people would take their lunch break, rest for a bit, and go back to farming their lands. They planted cucumbers, planted corn, planted *mulukhiyya* ... After resting, they would receive their pay and continue working the land. We used to have a lot, a lot of money! So much! We were so happy. From ʿArraba people would come to al-Manshiyya, from Sakhnin they'd come to al-Manshiyya, from Majd al-Krum they'd come to al-Manshiyya, from Umm al-Fahm they'd come to al-Manshiyya, from the *Matawleh* – these parts – Qana and the villages around it, to al-Manshiyya.[8] I could enumerate many more. So many Lebanese would come and get their provisions from al-Manshiyya and stay a while because of its abundance. It was not a mountainous region. We never needed to sow seeds, or till the forest soil. No! When we planted the wheat ... The women had nothing to do with this, they only needed to take care of cooking lunch, for the workers. We used to have a machine for harvesting. Do you know what they called it? *Makana*. It had four *shawahat* on the reel and one blade which would move like this and cut the wheat, and the *shawahat* would toss the cut wheat to the side.

Who did this makana *belong to?*
It belonged to my father-in-law's family. It was also used for harvesting in the countryside, and was hired out for one Palestinian lira per hour. Say you had a wheat field that you had just harvested, you would be the one to load the cut wheat. Your wife wouldn't touch a thing. Her only duty was to cook lunch. We would never go down to the fields. They would pile up the wheat using a pitchfork, and fill a truck that would bring it all the way down to the valley, to the *bayadir* for threshing. There was a board wider than this mattress ... Do you know what a threshing board is? Have you ever seen one? Some men used two cows, and others one or two horses, to pull the board over the wheat, which would separate the wheat from the stalks.

37'41"–40'20"

I want to ask you about the different religious sects that were present in al-Manshiyya...
Although people not from the families of the village lived there, al-Manshiyya was united. If your wife and your neighbour were in a fight, your other neighbour could still count on both. We never complained to the government, since the British were there. We never complained, in our own country. There used to be a committee made up of elders. Say your wife had a problem with her neighbour, they would bring you all in, both wives, you and her husband. Whoever's fault it was would pay their share. If it were your fault, you'd put down ten Palestinian lira and go beat your wife to teach her a lesson. The other one would do the same, except if he was innocent, he wouldn't put down any money. If it was his fault, he would pay in order to teach his wife a lesson ... So that she would not repeat the same mistake. Say your wife was walking down the street and that her arm was exposed, or say she was wearing tight clothes in public ... It used to be disgraceful to wear revealing clothes ... All our clothes used to be long. We didn't wear anything short ... If a woman was dressed that way, they would yell at her: 'So and so, go cover yourself!' She would run away, she wouldn't dare say a word. If her husband beat her, she would not retaliate. If she complained about her husband, she would be told: 'Aren't you still alive? If he were a real man, he would have kept hitting you.' No other way. This is how we did things ... Our way. Justice was served our way. We never involved the government. Once, a woman got into a fight with her sister-in-law. She beat her up so badly that she caused her to miscarry. Our justice system says that a child in its mother's womb cannot fend for itself. Injuring an adult is easier than injuring a child. As a young man, you are capable of

41

defending yourself, but a child cannot. For us, a child is equal to an adult, if not superior. I swear to God, they did not escalate the situation to the government. The guy taught his wife a lesson, and when the other husband came, he said, 'We're clear.' They reconciled, it was worked out, and the government was not involved.

2

Of Forests and Trees:
City Life in 1930s Palestine

Sherene Seikaly

It was the first day of May. Fifi was eight months pregnant and craving hearty food. The last two months had been difficult. Persistent shelling had instilled fear in the people of her picturesque city, Jaffa, known to most as the 'Bride of the Sea'. The British had announced that their colonial Mandate would terminate on 15 May, ending a colonial rule that facilitated the establishment of a Jewish state in Palestine from its outset. This equation attempted to strip Palestinians of their political rights and hold their futures in abeyance.

That March, people were fleeing. Some took boats; others walked. Fifi convinced herself, 'I am not afraid'. Her husband was determined to stay, and she was certainly not leaving without him. But staying was getting harder every day. Basic goods had become scarce. Shops and bakeries were mostly shut; when they did open, it was briefly and sporadically. On that auspicious first day of May 1948, Fifi looked out her window to spot a passer-by carrying a bag of meat. She rushed out to ask where the man had found such a scarce and coveted item. He kindly obliged and before long Fifi had secured some ground beef. Back at home, she revelled in the prospect of a normal day, and opened a fresh bottle of olive oil. It splattered on her dress, which she quickly removed to sprinkle talcum powder on the stain. She laid the dress on her bed before returning to the kitchen. With help from her servant, Fifi prepared the meat, rice and lemon juice to stuff courgette and vine leaves. How nice it would be to have a proper meal. The whole family would enjoy it.

These hopes came crashing down as the shelling intensified. A very pregnant Fifi and her husband took the fateful decision to flee. Fear triumphed: they did not want to die; they wanted to protect their children. As they travelled the Jaffa–Jerusalem road, they spotted a Jewish settlement. 'Lower your eyes,' Fifi's husband instructed, 'Don't let the children look, maybe they won't shoot.' The family expected to return home in two weeks;

after all, King 'Abdullah of Jordan had sworn not to abandon Jaffa. Fifi had packed an overnight bag for her family of four, soon to be five. She left the dress on the bed and her prized fur coat in the closet. As for the stuffed vine leaves and courgette, they were Fifi's parting gift to her servant.

Fifi Khouri narrates this story of life and loss from a comfortable living room in Beirut. Her East Asian domestic worker comes in and out of the frame, serving coffee and making herself scarce. Like Fifi's servant in pre-1948 Palestine, she remains unnamed, almost invisible. When asked, Fifi cannot recall how Palestinian elites interacted with 'the poor'. But both before and after the Nakba, she enjoyed class and sect privilege. Like most Christians in the Eastern Mediterranean, her family benefitted from European patronage, capital and expertise throughout the nineteenth and twentieth centuries. Heightened access to social mobility began with education. In Palestine, the literacy rate among Christian men and women was 98 per cent in 1948, compared to just 60 and 30 per cent among Muslim men and women. This differential was a reflection not of culture or capacity, but rather privilege and access to institutions. Proximity to European power had its own consequences. Fifi recalls, with a tinge of resentment, how her French and English were stronger than her Arabic, and how her familiarity with French and British history surpassed her knowledge of the Arab past. She ascribes this alienation from language and history to a specific condition: 'We were colonised'.

Fifi's privilege did not cushion her from patriarchal restrictions. With support from a liberal uncle, she travelled as far as Berlin for her studies, but the First World War cut this adventure short. Back in Palestine, Fifi found herself more constrained than ever by her grandfather, the family's patriarch. Like the rest of the women in her family, she was forbidden from taking a job or attending university. Fifi does not linger over these realities, returning promptly to colourful matters of daily life. She tells of Jaffa's clubs, where Palestinian upper- and middle-class people gathered to play ping-pong, football and tennis. She describes family outings to the cinemas, cafés and restaurants of neighbouring Tel Aviv. She remembers recently arrived Jewish immigrants from Europe selling exquisite pieces of furniture. She recalls, and then curses, one Lola Bear – the Jewish seamstress who sewed her wedding dress. And the handbags! The most expensive handbag store was in Tel Aviv. By the mid-twentieth century, the Palestinian middle classes, like their global counterparts, had embraced consumerism as a way of shaping identity. Fifi's reverie comes to an abrupt halt as she reflects, critically, 'As usual and from now until forever, that is what us Arabs rush towards – the brand.'

When the interviewer enquires about what Fifi would do differently could she turn back time, she balks at this counterfactual. She is wary. She has grown accustomed to younger Palestinians blaming older refugees for fleeing. She pauses to reflect. Knowing what she knows now, she might have stayed – but had she stayed, she would have been consigned to the status of second-class citizen. Ultimately, Fifi's fate is one of dispossession and exile. Still, she reminds us, it is 'heaven' compared to the hell of many of her compatriots' circumstances. Lebanon's sectarian imperatives granted many Palestinian Christians immediate citizenship, while the majority of Muslim refugees were confined to refugee camps, where their descendants remain today.

Fifi's reflections contrast starkly with Hasan al-Husayni's narrative. The latter interviewee traces a national canon of events and figures, among them his relatives. We hear of the formidable and deeply flawed leader Hajj Amin al-Husayni. We hear of the revolutionary leader ʿIzz al-Din al-Qassam, whose social initiatives and political programmes provided refuge for thousands of farmers, mostly from the Upper Galilee, who dwelled in shantytowns in the industrial city of Haifa after they were displaced by the Jewish National Fund's purchase of large swathes of land. We hear of the six-month national strike that evolved into a three-year uprising – the Great Revolt of 1936–39 – that shook British colonial power to its core. Al-Husayni's testimony also offers a window on the contingencies that shape history. He emphasises that Jewish–Palestinian animosity was a product of British colonial policies, Zionist ideology and the repression of collective rights. He cites Israeli diplomat and politician Abba Eban's assertion that 'the height of Jewish civilization was [during its coexistence] with the Arabs in al-Andalus'. Al-Husayni condemns Nazism, asserting that Hajj Amin was aware of the Holocaust in Europe, and he denounces the leader's ill-advised meeting with Hitler in the midst of the Second World War as detrimental to the Palestinian cause. From al-Husayni's testimony, we can glean the metanarratives and themes of Palestinian national history. Yet, his forest of history reveals few trees of everyday life. We hear of outings with his mother to see films featuring the master musician Muhammad ʿAbd al-Wahhab. But perhaps the richest detail al-Husayni brings to life is a soundscape of mid-twentieth-century Jerusalem. One of his most poignant memories is of living in a place 'immersed in [the sound of] church bells' while attending al-Rawda boarding school, located in the al-Aqsa compound and surrounded by churches.

What are we to make of these two divergent accounts of pre-1948 Palestine and what can they tell us? Fifi's unassuming posture, informality, reflexive impulse, and the fact she forgets the name of 'so-and-so' leader or whether or not a revolution took place in 1936, might render her account less properly historical for some. Yet, this same informal quality brings into view a lively, complicated and three-dimensional Palestine. Narratives such as al-Husayni's impose their authority, indicating stories and names we ought to remember. These narrators assume and reinforce a gendered power; al-Husayni narrates the historical, whereas Fifi recollects stories. Referring to Fifi by her first name and al-Husayni by his last, as I have here, reflects this power differential. But this differential also limits al-Husayni, whose impulse to narrate official history leaves little space for his personal memories. Reading Fifi and al-Husayni together is telling of the struggle to balance personal, informal history with the intense need, especially in the Palestinian case, to relay a singular story of events and figures. Here, Fifi and al-Husayni teach us the value of embracing a multiplicity of historical forms, both formal and informal. They teach us that the Nakba was not an inevitability but rather a product of specific historical conditions. Like all the sources in the Nakba Archive, these oral histories give us powerful windows onto Palestinian history, as well as the rich and shifting relationships people forge with memory and the past. Accounts like Fifi's and al-Husayni's, especially when read together and in conversation, help us overcome binaries often drawn between official and unofficial history. They help us piece together the beauty and the loss of Palestine before the Nakba. They give us both the forests and the trees of our past. Most of all, they make possible that brave act of imagining a Palestinian future in the context of an unabating and ongoing Nakba.

Fifi Khouri
born 1922 in Yafa, Palestine
Interview with Bushra Mughrabi
Hamra, Beirut, 2004

8'00"–17'23"

Bushra Mughrabi: *How old were you when you started school?*
Fifi Khouri: Five or six years old. The neighbours' daughter used to hold my hand and take me to school with her, and then bring me back.

Do you remember your first day of school?
No, I don't remember ... Later, at the age of twelve, my parents sent me to a boarding school in al-Quds. That was the trend at the time, girls from good families would go to al-Quds to study and live with the nuns of Sahyun. I was 12 years old.

What was the name of your elementary school?
The Sisters of Saint Joseph's Annunciation. They were all nuns.

It was a private school, of course.
Yes.

Were you paying tuition?
Yes, we were. There were very few government schools in Yafa, too few. I didn't know anybody from our entourage, or our friends, who attended government school. There probably were some who did, but I did not know...

So would people not go because they were scarce or because they themselves were from a specific social class that wanted a private school education?
Do you mean people who went to al-Quds?

No, the ones from Yafa itself.
From Yafa? No, they would go to government schools. Opportunities for education were widely available. People wanted to get an education. There were government schools, but I don't remember exactly where they were. There was a school called Hasan 'Arafa, a private school he himself opened. It was a very good school. And the Missionaries, the Protestants, the Catholics and the Greek Orthodox all had their own schools.

Was your school a missionary school?
A French missionary school.

Do you remember what you used to study in elementary school?
Our education was very good and we received very strong foundations in English, French and Arabic. I used to love mathematics and I felt it was my strongest subject.

Were you studying mathematics in French?
Mostly in French, yes. And our Arabic was not bad. But after that school ...
What do you call what comes after elementary school? Secondary school. When I went to al-Quds, my Arabic was the worst. I was studying it for an hour only each week.

Did you use to have female or male teachers in elementary school?
No, they were all female teachers. There was a priest who used to teach us Arabic. And they did not have sections for each grade. I remember how so-and-so was in my class ... Why was that, if she was a lot older than me? They were not precise about students' ages. They would mix us together and teach us.

And those who were in the same class were at the same level?
That happened in Arabic class, not in other subjects. Only with Arabic. I guess we must have all had the same level ... I don't know, I can't remember much.

Do you remember the names of some of your teachers?
Yes, there was Sœur Elie. I have pictures from that period. Nuns. One of them was from Halab, another one from France and again another one from France. And our principal was French as well. There were very few Arabs. Most of them were French.

Would they teach you anything other than educational subjects? For example, manual activities or sports?
Manual activities, a bit of sewing, which we would try to escape. There weren't any specific physical education classes. We would just play during our free time. We would play a bit. There was not much enthusiasm for sports.

After elementary school...
Usually, secondary education continued in the same school. But, at the time, my parents decided to send me to al-Quds, to the nuns of Sahyun, as they called them. They used to be in the old town. All my girlfriends from my generation, and those slightly older and younger, as well as my aunts, studied in that school. It was famous. The quality of its education was excellent, but Arabic class – one hour a week. I stayed in that school for two years and I took the secondary school test – what they call Brevet. And my father moved me out of it right after. He said: 'Are we foreigners? No, we are Arabs, we should learn Arabic.' He enrolled me in an English school in al-Quds as well.

What was its name?
Jerusalem Girls' College.

What was it affiliated to?
English Protestants as well. The education there was good as well. Because I had received a good foundation in French with the nuns, things went smoothly in English. Arabic was a bit complicated because I had missed out on a lot. I remember an incident with the teacher, Mr ʿAsaf Wahba from al-Quds. He used to teach us Arabic. We each had to read a line from *Diwan al-Mutanabbi* and explain it. I was not understanding anything and I would say to my teacher, 'Why should I care about al-Mutanabbi's thoughts?' As you know, in Arabic, each line can be interpreted in a thousand different ways. I told him, 'Let me read everybody's lines and let them explain them.' He said, 'No, it's not possible'. But it was all right afterwards.

Did you use to learn history?
Yes, of course. But Palestinian history? No.

Which histories would you learn about?
We learned French history with the nuns and English history with the British. We learned France's history from beginning to end, and its geography from beginning to end as well. And it was the same with the British.

Didn't you learn Arab history?
Very little ... Very little. We were colonised...

Did you take part in any activities during patriotic events, for example?
Not at all ... There weren't any. I don't remember anything of the sort at all. During a vacation, I went to study at Birzeit. It was not a university yet. My

parents were travelling to Romania and they placed us there, for about two months, with my sister and brothers and my cousins. There, you could feel the patriotic vibe, the enthusiasm and all of that.

Whose school was that, in Birzeit?
It belonged to Priest Hana Nasir at the time, and his daughter, Sit Nabiha Nasir, was running the school. She was the principal and her two other sisters were teachers. There were also teachers from the al-Tarazi family. It was a very good school.

So it was a national school.
Yes it was.

Were there national schools in Yafa?
No, there was the Orthodox school in Yafa. They would not call it the national school. It was the school I knew, as well as the Hasan 'Arafa school. Those are the only schools I know.

Were there girls from other religions with you?
Yes, of course. In Yafa, we were a mix of Christian and Muslim girls. There weren't any Jewish girls with us in Yafa. But in al-Quds, there were Jewish girls. We were friends.

So there were Jewish girls at the nuns of Sahyun?
Yes, there were Jewish girls there, as well as at the Girls' College. And they would speak Arabic well, like you and I do, and our parents used to know each other and everything.

Where were the Jewish girls from?
From Palestine. It's not like…

So not from Yafa.
They were living in Tel Aviv. But their father, for example … I knew somebody who had a very nice store in Yafa, and we would go buy clothes and shoes from him. What a wonderful man he was! And then when the revolution happened, he closed up shop. The mayor of Tel Aviv was a very good friend of my father's, and when the bombings started, he called him and said, 'Wadi', trust me, tell your people to raise the white flag, so that our people stop bombing.'

43'00"–48'40"

You were telling me about a club, did it have a religious affiliation?
Yes, it was the Roman Catholic Church's club, but anybody could go to it. It was not strictly religious. Although at the time, there was a bit of religious extremism around the question of marriage. For example, an Eastern Catholic girl was not allowed to marry an Orthodox Christian man. And if she did, they would ban her from the Catholic Church. A similar incident happened to one of my friends. It was the talk of the town. They excommunicated her from the church, as well as her mother, because the mother allowed her daughter to marry an Orthodox Christian.

Were they also denied their civil rights?
No, not their civil rights, only their ecclesiastical rights. So, if she died, they would deny her a Catholic burial. Ecclesiastical rights, only.

What activities did the club offer?
There weren't many activities. People would play ping-pong, go on trips, that's it. The Orthodox club had more activities because it was open to young men only. Football, tennis, things like that. Those were the clubs I knew. When we wanted to get some fresh air or go on a family outing, we often went to Tel Aviv. We would go to the cinema, or to a coffee shop, or...

Did you have issues going to Jewish areas?
No, not at all. Had we sensed any problems, it would have surely been better for us. But we didn't ... Whenever we wanted a nice custom-made dress, we would go to the Jews. They would come from Europe ... Talented seamstresses, hat makers. There were shops owned by Jewish immigrants, who were allowed to bring over their furniture and things with them, but not any money. So they began selling furniture and people would purchase beautiful expensive pieces from them. I had my *jihaz* sewn by a Jewish seamstress. You had to book your appointment in the summer to see her in the winter, and in the winter to see her in the summer.

Do you remember the name of this seamstress?
Yes, Lola Bear. To hell with her ... Take handbag stores, for example ... Everybody knew that Harnak in Tel Aviv was the most expensive handbag store. As usual and from now until forever, that is what us Arabs rush towards – the brand. And there were many coffee shops and restaurants and cinemas...

Would you go to the Jewish restaurants?
Yes, we would, of course. Most unfortunately. But there was Musa Nasir, whom I mentioned to you previously, he was a *kaymakam* in al-Quds and al-Nasira, and a very nationalistic man. He was Hana Nasir's father, of Birzeit University. He would come over, and we would offer him chocolates that had the name Bafga written on them, which was the Jewish chocolate brand. He would refuse to take it. He would say, 'This single piece of chocolate will cost you a lot.' I will never forget what he said. There was a third club in Yafa, how could I forget it? The club ... al-Nadi al-Riyadi (the Sports Club), is what they used to call it. It was a family club, it did not pertain to any specific religion. It was on my in-laws' land. There was tennis, ping-pong, card games and, every two weeks, they had dance parties, with a small orchestra and people would dance. It was a very nice club.

Would young women and men go to these parties?
Young women, young men, yes.

Did the Jews go to these parties?
No, at that time, most Jews were living in Tel Aviv; they would not come. They wouldn't come to our areas unless it was for work. After they moved away from Yafa, none of them would come anymore. There used to be nice Jewish-owned shops in Yafa.

What about the British, would they come to Yafa?
No. The British would not mix, except for a few [Palestinian] families, for example, so-and-so who was a high-ranking government officer mixed with the British. But, God forbid, if the British would mix with the [Palestinian] people. The British as colonialists were different than the British in their own country, who were extremely kind. The colonialists were arrogant, to say the least.

You told me the Jews had moved out of Yafa. Were there any Jews in Yafa who then moved out?
Yes, of course, there were some before the revolution. There was a big store called Rabinovitch where we would buy the most beautiful outfits, the most beautiful shoes, everything there was beautiful. And we would speak to the owners in Arabic, and they were friends of the family and all. When the first revolution happened, I think it was in 1936 or 1938, I don't know, they closed up shop and left. They knew they could no longer make a living in Yafa. Can I drink coffee now, or is it not allowed? (she smiles).

59'54"–1h 03'10"

Let us go back to the period before you left Yafa, before you became sur-rounded, before you decided to leave. Which incidents seemed to be occurring in preparation?
On our side, as Arabs, we were lost; we did not know what would happen. We knew that the British would leave on 15 May, they had informed us of it. And we knew that King 'Abdullah would announce every now and then that Yafa would not be...[1] Because Yafa had its own situation, al-Quds had its own situation, Haifa had its own situation, each city had its own situa-tion. He would say, 'The city of Yafa is my port, I will not abandon it.' So we were somewhat reassured that even if bombings happened, we would be protected by Jordan. And I remember, it was a Sunday; it was Palm Sunday and many people had already left. Some would flee and would be afraid to say they were leaving; they did it undercover. Some people sold a few of their properties to the Jews and ran away. And I remember the time someone passed me on the street and I was seven months pregnant, and he said, 'Is your husband crazy, keeping you here?' I answered, 'I am not afraid and I am not leaving without him.' During that week, there was a lot of confusion in Yafa. Some people wanted to leave by boat, other people this and that ... When the last airplane left, the Gargour offices – they were ship dealers – brought a boat to Yafa. The families who had stayed – includ-ing some of my relatives, my mother and father – departed on that boat. As they were taking the small boat to get on the bigger ship, some people's belongings capsized and fell into the sea, other people fell in the water ... It was an ordeal. They finally got on the boat and arrived in Beirut.

During that period, were there any Jaysh al-Inqadh [Arab Liberation Army], or any Arab army arriving to the city?
Not at all. The last day before we left, on 29 April, an officer named Michel al-'Isa, who was originally with the Jordanian Army, arrived with a group of young men. They passed through Yafa claiming, 'Do not be afraid, we opened up the road for you.' See to what extent it got ... These guys came and opened the road, and those who had cars ran away, and even those who did not want to flee fled.

What did he mean when he said he opened the road?
We were under the impression that he had come to rescue us. We were not politically minded then. These days, we know to analyse every word they say. At the time, we did not analyse. We did not use our heads. And so you

had people leaving ... As we were leaving on the Yafa–al-Quds road, we saw a Jewish settlement. We got scared, my husband told me to lower the children's heads so that the Jews would not shoot them. Later, we realised they had not been shooting anybody who was leaving. On the contrary, they wanted people to leave.

During that time, where were the British?
The British were still in Yafa ... I mean in Palestine, in general. They had two weeks left.

1h 4'22"–1h 7'30"

During the period when the situation was no longer normal...
Really not normal, there was confusion.

Yes, how much did it affect your life socially and economically, and what was the time-frame?
During the last four, five months, the economy collapsed. The orange season was ruined. Socially, there was a lot of fear and everybody kept talking about the situation, about why it was happening, and how ... And this guy insulted that guy, these ones blamed those ones ... There was confusion in the city. People were afraid and had no idea what would happen. Nobody planned the next step. Nobody.

Weren't there elders who tried to meet to decide what would happen to Yafa?
(She shakes her head) Let me give you our own example. My brother-in-law and my sister-in-law's husband were members of the municipality of Yafa. Dr Haykal was the mayor. There was no money left and the British had imposed an embargo. They all had a meeting on the very last day, at the Cliff Hotel in Yafa and were wondering what to do, and whether they should raise ... As I told you earlier, my dad had been advised to raise the white flag and he had relayed this message, 'Let's raise the white flag.' But we had no real leader. There was a shaykh among the members, whose name I do not recall, who put his gun on the table and said, 'There is no way we are raising the flag.' You have to know that each person called the other a traitor. So, who is the real traitor, it remains a mystery. Bottom line, they sold us and they bought us, and we had no idea.

Did anybody announce to the people in any official way, 'Let us leave, let us depart from Yafa'?
Nobody told the people, no. People ... Fear. People were puzzled over how they would leave.

What were you afraid of?
Of the bombing! We were afraid it would intensify. If ... Take the recent bombings in Lebanon ... Had we known that, when these things happen, people have the option to remain in their country – and not die – we would not have left. And now, our children are putting huge blame on us, they tell us, 'Why did you leave?' There was no more meat left, the shops and bakeries would close, this store would open briefly ... This is how it was, I remember how on our last day, we saw a passer-by carrying a piece of meat. I asked him where he had got it from and he told us. We went to buy the meat and made stuffed courgettes and stuffed grape leaves, and when the bombing intensified and we decided to leave, I gave them to the woman who used to work for us and told her, 'Take them and God be with you.' We left with very few belongings, a suitcase this small; we were four people and I was awaiting a child. We were supposedly coming back home two weeks later, that was King 'Abdullah's promise, that after 15 May, he would be taking responsibility.

1h 10'29"–1h 11'07"

What did you take with you when you left? What did you bring along, during that time?
Nothing, I only took two weeks' worth of clothes! A suitcase no bigger than that, the one you pack for a weekend trip. I did not take a coat, nor a single sweater or anything. For example, I had a fur coat; it remained in the closet. The children's clothes were left behind. There was even a dress ... I had opened a bottle of oil and it had stained the dress ... I remember taking the dress off, laying it out on the bed and sprinkling it with powder, and it stayed as was.

1h 15'31"–1h 17'24"

September came, and we had no more money left. We moved to a cheaper hotel that only gave us one meal a day. It was the Hotel Belvedere. I had a diamond ring, my engagement ring. One day, my husband said, 'Would you be sad if I went and sold it?' I said, 'No, go sell it, what's it for anyway?'

He went down to the jewellery market and the first shop was too crowded. He went into a second shop and bumped into people he knew, and felt ashamed, so he left. As he walked down the street, someone tapped him on the shoulder. He was one of his customers in Yafa, from the wood business, whom my husband would help by letting him pay in instalments. He said to my husband, 'Where have you been, I heard you left and you were not able to cash out...' His name was Badr Dajani, God bless his soul, wherever he may be. He pulled out ... 400 dinars from his pocket. He told my husband, 'I am going back to Amman and, when I come back, I'll bring you more money'. My husband came back happy and said, 'Here, take your ring back, I don't need it'. A while later, he opened a wood business here, construction wood, with a Palestinian partner. He invested the money and my husband and his brother worked. Later, someone came in from Amman, who was related to this person who had given it to him. He said to my husband, 'I need to ask you ... Badr passed away and there is an entry in his journal that says: 400 dinars, Antoine 'Abd al-Nur. Does he owe you or do you owe him this amount?' My husband said, 'I owe it to him'. But the banks had not been paying us yet, they were paying us in instalments, from the money in our own bank accounts. I will never forget this incident.

1h 19'31"–1h 20'50"

If you could turn back time and go back to 1948, how would you have handled it? Would you have acted the same way, for example, would you have left or what would you have done?
I can't really answer you ... With my current life experience, I would not have left. Or maybe I would have anyway because those who remained there until now are not dignified. They are still living ... How do you say? Like second class. The work opportunities are not what they used to be. Had my husband stayed there, what would he have worked in? Do you think he would have stayed a wood trader? They would have run him down.

Do you get nostalgic about your home in Yafa?
Of course, I get nostalgic about the quality of life we had. Our minds were at peace, my husband dreamt of having five children, three boys and two girls, and that we would buy them a house in London and offer them an education in Britain, you know, those were the dreams ... But also, thank God. I always thank God, because we did not have to endure misery like ... Some people went through a lot of misery here ... Among those who left. When I look at those who are living in the camps, I feel we are in heaven in comparison to them. God help them.

Hasan al-Husayni
born 1925 in al-Quds, Palestine
Interview with Mahmoud Zeidan
Verdun, Beirut, 2003

00'56"–03'58"

Hasan al-Husayni: I was sent to the al-Rawda boarding school. My sisters – even Nada's mother, who was only four years old then – were sent to boarding school because my parents travelled a lot. My father was in charge of foreign affairs with Hajj Amin and they spent a lot of time travelling, so they preferred to send us to boarding school.[2] Al-Rawda was an Arab national school, which still exists today but under a different name, though I have forgotten it. It overlooked the Haram al-Sharif and you could see both al-Sakhra and al-Aqsa.

During Ramadan especially, and every single day before *iftar*, we prayed the 'Asr, either at al-Sakhra or al-Aqsa. It wasn't an Islamic school properly speaking, no. There were Christian teachers and students, but it was a national school. I stayed in that school until 1936 when the revolution started, the al-Qassam revolution of 1936. I remember sitting one day in the living room with my mother and my maternal uncle Musa al-'Alami, who had a long career in politics and philanthropy in Palestine, in al-Quds – and Ariha, where they had a construction project, I don't know if you've heard of it. We were sitting together and suddenly al-Barnawi, who worked with Hajj Amin, entered. He was African but he was Hajj Amin's assistant and confidant. He came in, whispered something in my father's ear and left. In an instant, my uncle, mother and father disappeared and a few moments later, my father came out carrying a small bag. He put a ladder against our neighbours' house, who were our relatives on my mother's side and he disappeared. We didn't see him at all. The next morning, the British Army came and searched the entire house. We were still in bed sleeping; we were small children. They barged in and searched under the bed, they searched every room but they didn't find him of course because he was gone, and they left. We felt like we were treated as suspects and that we were under constant surveillance. So my father and uncle decided that it was time to leave. So we left for Beirut by car.

19'40"–21'32"

How were the social relations between the people of al-Quds and the Jews?

57

At school, for example, at the Saint George's School, which was a British school, the Jews and the Arabs studied together. The others came from their area – because the school was very good – while the Arabs were among those who already lived there. Until today, al-Mutran's School [Saint George's] still exists, until today, in al-Quds. There was a time – after we returned a second time, when I lived in Ramallah and we would go back and play football against al-Mutran. To this day, I still have friends I met back then because we played football together.

What religious landmarks did your neighbourhood or its region have? Did it have churches, mosques or temples?
The most beautiful memories I have from al-Quds was the ringing of the church bells. I told you earlier that the Salesian School was run by nuns. Farther up was the French Hospital and a church. Above it was al-Maskubi-yya, the huge Russian Orthodox Church. I lived in an atmosphere immersed in church bells. In the area of Musrara, I don't recall the call for prayer because there weren't any amplifiers like there are today obviously, so the closest one to us was quite far. The church bells resounded further than a voice without a microphone. This is why all I can remember was the church bells, whether they came from Italian churches – the Salesians were Italian – from the French above us, or the Russians further up the road.

21'58"–26'12"

What kind of entertainment was available for adults?
I remember my mother taking me to the cinema. Cinemas were in the Jewish neighbourhoods at the time. The Arab neighbourhoods got cinemas later on, but back then ... The first time I saw something at the cinema was with my mother and it was an 'Abd al-Wahhab or something like that. It was in the Jewish neighbourhood, at the Edison Cinema, I believe. So, the hatred grew gradually but there wasn't any hatred before. There's a book by Abba Eban, *My Country* or something like that ... It says that the height of Jewish civilisation was with the Arabs in al-Andalus, with its religious phi-losophers to its non-religious ones. Al-Ma'mun and ... That other famous one, a very well-known philosopher, they all stemmed from al-Andalus.[3] They lived with the Arabs. When the Arabs emigrated from al-Andalus, the Jews left with them. There are many Jews in the Arab Maghrib and some people even went to Istanbul. The Sultan took them; he adopted the Jews who left al-Andalus to go to Istanbul. The enmity between Arabs and Jews dates back to Herzl, at the end of the last [nineteenth] century. He created

Zionist thought – although the British proposed land in Kenya, in Africa, but he said, 'Not at all, we want al-Quds. We want Palestine.' There wasn't even a Hebrew language properly speaking. They suddenly arrived and the first families began forbidding their children from speaking to anyone, even to the Jews, so they could learn to speak Hebrew the way it once was. That is how the Hebrew language became the way we know it today.

You told me that this conflict did not use to exist – this hatred.
Yes, incidentally I now recall something. When I was a child, I used to go to the YMCA in the Arab area to play there. On one occasion, the teacher in charge took us on a trip that included Jewish settlements, among other places. We went to the settlements, we entered them, we ate there, we talked to the children and they talked to us. At the time, we didn't feel that we had to hate someone if they were Jewish. I don't know if they saw it differently, but I don't think so, I think they felt the same. We only talked to them for a short while, visited one place after another and returned to al-Quds. The YMCA was one of the recreational spaces for children. We played football, raced, swam and music … We listened to Arnita and I developed a penchant for European music. We listened to Arnita – not to the Palestine Symphony Orchestra but to an orchestra affiliated with the British radio, it had an orchestra with mostly Jews of course; we Arabs didn't have any – at the time – of that calibre. I used to go to the YMCA's auditorium and listen to concerts performed by the Jews. Later on, I went to see the Palestine Symphony Orchestra. The first great symphony orchestra was the Jewish Symphony Orchestra. It's now called the Israeli Philharmonic Orchestra but it is the same one. It started in 1936 and its first conductor was Toscanini, one of the greatest conductors of his time.

27'50"–31'05"

You told me earlier that your father worked with Hajj Amin. Were all of the Arabs in al-Quds loyal to him?
The overwhelming majority. There was the opposition, of course, which I regret to tell you mostly included al-Nashashibiyyin, Raghib Baik Nashashibi. There were foolish sensitivities. If someone wanted to become mayor, then Husayn al-Khalidi was appointed instead, for example. So the one who was loyal to the mufti was not loyal to … So there were these sensitivities but not enough for us to fight each other. There were disputes but there were also marriages among us and the Khalidi family. Al-Quds

was small, there weren't too many people there. Everyone in al-Quds was related.

Let us go back and talk about the Jews. You told me earlier that there wasn't any hatred between you. When did the people of al-Quds start to feel sensitive towards the small minority of Jews? Can you give us a date?
There were barely 6 or 7 per cent of Jews at first. Then the immigrants started coming in large numbers – with the approval of the British, of course – especially after the war between the Allies and Hitler. And let me tell you, no one has harmed our cause as much as Hitler did. The emotive response towards the Jews was caused by his monstrous acts. I know that from Hajj Amin himself. I used to visit him and I always kept in touch with him. He said, 'Yes, Hitler killed millions of Jews.' There were doubts about this at the time, but he said, 'No, no, I know that the Jews ...' And Hitler took care of him in order to use him with the Yugoslavian Muslims, to make them rise up against Tito. He tried to take advantage of him for that. But I think he failed because I don't believe Hajj Amin did anything to exploit the Yugoslavian Muslims. They wanted their independence, not because of Hajj Amin or anyone else. They wanted to stay after the war despite Tito having taken power. They wanted independence; they never felt a total integration with their Slav counterparts.

Hajj Amin's visit to Germany was perhaps seen as detrimental...
It was very detrimental, that is why my father ... The French expelled us when they became allied with the British, so we went to Baghdad.

Tell me about what happened in the beginning, when [Hajj Amin] left Palestine.
We all came to Lebanon.

3

The Margin and the Centre in Narrating Pre-1948 Palestine

Amirah Silmi

This essay attempts a close reading of two narratives by two Palestinians with different modes of being, doing and knowing. Their distinct economic, social and political locations entail different positions, frames of reference and value systems. In the first story, gender, class and nationality intersect to form the marginal position of Hamda, a refugee Palestinian peasant woman originally from ʿArab al-Zubayd, a village destroyed in April 1948. The other involves Muhammad, an urban refugee man from Haifa. This essay will examine how these two narrators' different positionalities are reflected in the way they remember and tell their stories of life in Palestine and Arab–Jewish relations before the Nakba. I neither seek to draw a generalisable picture of these relations, nor to construct a gendered duality of narrative modes; my aim is rather to liberate the different and the particular that these two narratives enfold.

MEMORY FRAGMENTS: HAMDA'S STORIES

Hamda's memories of pre-Nakba Palestine emerge as a network of entangled and overlapping fragments. One fragment leads to another in a non-linear fashion, following the logic of the different instances, happenings and experiences that comprise a life, with all their similarities, differences, inconsistencies and contradictions. Hamda's process of recollecting reminds us that she is narrating something she is digging out of herself. Once exhumed, her memories never take the form of complete images but rather appear as fragments of a whole that can never be revealed as such. Though most of the story remains untold, each fragment has the potential to turn into a living story, one without beginning or end. The fragmented story, while still attached to the life from which it arises, is also able to have a life of its own and even generate another.

Hamda remembers the small things – the closet, the box; she conjures images in song. Then she tells a story, weaving details of marriages, of ceremonies and of what women wore. In Hamda's stories, we cannot locate a discursive practice. She neither gives an analytical interpretation of the relationship between traditions and women's position in society, nor describes her condition as a working-class, Bedouin/peasant woman in a socialist idiom. She does not even invoke nationalist discourse about Palestinian refugees. Still, she tells stories about relations to the people and things of Palestine, to certain pieces of land, to plants and trees, all of which appear in their individual particular form.

Hamda's memories restore specific details of dress and costume, of kitchen utensils and home furniture, of machines, of the wheat and barley harvest, of the beauty of the eggplants and the tomatoes. She retraces the paths and byways she took to work, those where battles took place, and the roads and forests that witnessed her expulsion. She tells us how she could distinguish each and every piece of land and the people to whom it belonged. Describing these details, she underlines the value once ascribed to them – a value that now lies in their being lost and longed for, and which makes them the things that rise to the surface when life in Palestine is evoked.

ON THE MARGINS OF A MODERNISED FOREIGN WAY OF LIFE

Living off the land and livestock, Hamda's early mode of life was one of autonomy, a form of self-reliance that ran counter – not in an ideological or political sense – to a modernised way of life based on institutions, notions of rights and duties, and the accompanying, constructed dualities of self and other. Her self-sufficiency manifests itself in a certain kind of indifference, in the positive sense of the word, to all possible others or selves who would easily, in their mode of being, transform Hamda into an Other: the English, the Zionists, and urban bourgeois Palestinians.

Hamda describes the harvesting of wheat meticulously, how it was done by her people. What seems most important to her, what she remembers, is that her father had goats and sheep, and that the wheat they harvested would fill a space four times as big as a house. Hamda points to Zionist settlers' use of machinery to cultivate the land and the resultant increased produce, which filled boxes instead of cloth bags. She tells us that they, too, had livestock, but she did not really care to know the details of this material wealth, for her father had his own.

Hamda, the daughter of Bedouin/peasant tribe, did not enjoy this condition of self-sufficiency throughout her years in Palestine. In another fragment of her story, she tells us how, when her father became sick and unable to work, she had to take a job at the airport the British were constructing in Qadas. Hamda does not present this labour as 'hers', and it did not produce anything she can describe with the same pride with which she recalls the wheat harvest, the eggplants or the tomatoes. Instead, she interrupts the story about her runway construction work to declare her realisation that, 'We worked so much for the Jews, God what a dupe I was!'

Hamda does not describe poverty or exploitation as such; she remembers her salary inconsistently, and notes her good health and strength. She also mentions how her English employer would ensure that there was always another girl working with her; and how he treated her like a child, calling her nicknames, which Hamda took to indicate that he liked her. One could think that Hamda, a 15-year-old peasant girl with a different mode of doing and knowing, was unfamiliar with the colonial practice of treating colonised people as children in need of protection – that is to say, exploitation and dispossession.[1] Nevertheless, if we try to adopt a position/perspective closer to Hamda's, we are again confronted with the relative insignificance of paid work in her life as she remembers it.[2] This irrelevancy is evident in the details Hamda emphasises when speaking of the Blida women who came to work with her and her colleagues.[3] Hamda does not talk about competition between the two groups of women; instead, she goes into an elaborate description of the Nabi Yusha' festival in which both groups participated.[4] Detailed fragments of a past life lost seem of more value to remember and narrate than poverty and colonial exploitation. One might even think that it is the poverty of the present – a present to which Hamda is not oblivious – that leads Hamda to remember that which is no longer.

MEMORIES OF WAR: DISPLACEMENT AND DISPOSSESSION

Expulsion in Hamda's memory does not happen at a precise moment or take the form of events that can be narrated in chronological order. Indeed, she becomes upset when asked to remember the exact dates of discrete events. Stating clearly that she is saying what she can remember, Hamda can tell stories of the Nakba, but she cannot be its witness. Her memory here functions in a dreamlike manner and events that happened at different phases of the expulsion of 'Arab al-Zubayd become intertwined. What binds them together is a single reality that extends from past to present: that of expulsion.

It is here, as she narrates expulsion, that Hamda mentions her Jewish friend, whom she calls Fifati. Fifati told Hamda that, in case of war, she would protect Hamda and her brother, if the Zionists were winning; she also asked Hamda to protect her, if the opposite were true. Hamda says she refused to go along with Fifati because she intended to follow her people; she also refused to protect her friend should the Arabs have prevailed. But the story of her relationship with Fifati is interrupted by a story of the massacre the Zionists committed against Kirad al-Baqqara:[5]

The Jews were already at al-Ku' al-Aswad road, it was right next to us. A guy from Safad was killed, and my relative's husband too, and someone from Kirad al-Baqqara, or was it Kirad al-Ghannama? That Kurdish guy from al-Baqqara could cross through this wall without leaving a trace behind him because he was as strong as a lion. There were 35 passengers on the al-Kuri bus. Al-Kuri was still in Safad, it was a bus from Safad, the people from Safad know about it. They packed them all in a bag, a soap bag. They filled a soap bag with all 30 passengers. My relative, my father's paternal cousin got a bullet in his neck and it came out the other side. He fell and remained there, we went to fetch him, his blood was pouring until there.

Hamda, appealing to God against the oppressor, says the Zionists would not let them bury her relative.

In this section of the interview, Hamda's stories become entangled; they appear as scenes that interrupt and cut into each other, and we can no longer be sure whether she is telling the story of expulsion, Palestinian resistance and *fida'iyin*, the Lebanese Civil War, the 1982 invasion of Beirut or the battles of the camps that followed. Something similar happens with Muhammad's story, although he tries harder to order his memory, as we will see.

The two narrators' confusion of different events from different periods of their lives tells us that what we remember is not what really happened in the past, but rather how we lived it, our experience of it, the changes it imposed and its enduring effects (both tangible and intangible) on our lives. In this way, multiple events from multiple time periods become confused and intertwined in our memory; the stories of different wars and battles that these two narrators lived through become tied together with the loss, destruction and displacement that they continue to entail.

MUHAMMAD'S NARRATIVE:
THE DISCOURSE OF A COLONISED BOURGEOIS

At the outset of his interview, Muhammad takes up a position detached from the Palestinians, bordering on what seems to be a process of othering: 'They are a simple people, with a good heart that renders them subject to manipulation.'

Although Muhammad did not belong to the Arab or Zionist elite in Haifa, he was aspirational and his life approximated that of an urban bourgeois. He worked in the army, attended a Jewish night school and lived in a house where all his neighbours were Jewish immigrants. Muhammad can enumerate every Jewish entertainment centre, club, café, cinema and tourist attraction in Haifa; drinking, dancing and courting Jewish women figure several times in his story. Whenever he feels compelled to condemn this lifestyle, he does so on the basis that such activities were a means of stripping people of their money. Muhammad proudly relates that he was declared a master of his craft by an English mechanics trainer; and that he managed to prove himself in the British Army.

In his urban, modernised, even if not really modern, mode of life, Muhammad is versed in the art of othering or what Frantz Fanon would describe as a colonised mode of racism.[6] Muhammad's constructed Other is, in the first instance, the *fellah*, who, being poor and oppressed by punitive British taxes, sold his land, only to be duped into losing his money to the Jewish immigrants who bought it. Muhammad also others Jews in some instances, mainly with reference to women and sexuality.[7] He states that Jewish men were lax when it came to their women and the latter's sexual conduct, and that Jewish women even used to swindle Arabs out of their money. The image of Jewish woman as Other, created by both fear and desire, emerges as the subject of seduction – she is not to be seduced but the seducer. He recalls how Jewish women attempted to seduce him and describes the advances of a neighbour who taught him Hebrew. When Muhammad tells us how a Jewish friend convinced him to go to the communist club, he uses a racist and sexist stereotype: 'You know the Arab man, always a victim to what's between his legs.' In telling this story, he deflects attention from his own position as a subjugated Other of the British and the Zionists, transferring his alienation onto the Jewish seductress.[8] Ironically, Muhammad went on to marry a Jewish woman, whom he 'others' not as seductress but as a rancorous person incapable of forgiveness. His narrative now opposes all people of her religion to Muslims and Christians, whom he views as having the ability to easily forget and forgive.

The memories Muhammad recounts here are of the final years of the Second World War, a time of economic prosperity in Haifa and Palestine as a whole.[9] Muhammad notes this affluence, explaining that there were lots of jobs with good salaries during the war and that the standard of living was improving. He himself worked in the army because the pay was high; as an independent mechanic, his salary would have been lower. While Muhammad is able to give a detailed description of entertainment and work in Haifa, he seems to take the position of an outsider when speaking of the 1936 revolt and six-month general strike:

> [In] the revolution people kill each other when someone leaks the land of another, they would shoot and kill him ... we never left the house [during the strike] ... they made all people wear the *kaffiyeh* from twelve years and up...[10]

Every instance of clashes between the Palestinians and the Zionists is understood by Muhammad to be planned by the British, in order to create conflict between Arabs and Jews.[11] He sees the perpetrators themselves – the Palestinian fighters and the Zionist gangs – as vagabonds paid by the British to kidnap and kill people from the other side. From the perspective of vulgar economic rationalism, people would only fight each other for immediate, clear financial gain. While Muhammad expresses interest in Zionist communism – he speaks of his Jewish communist friends – his ideological investments were limited and materialistic.[12] He is animated by the purported sexual libertarianism of communist clubs (which he depicts as brothels) but is also fearful of a British crackdown on Palestinian communists in particular.

Muhammad's account of the 1947 Partition Plan also echoes Zionist communist policy at the time. He clearly indicates that he was unable to understand the Arab position rejecting the resolution, which for him pointed to problems in the Arab mentality.

In his colonised, urban, bourgeois mode of being, Muhammad is a detached subject. His memories of Palestine are not ones of attachment or longing, and the question of Palestine is, for him, a question of revenge rather than right. Once he was confronted with the betrayal and ingratitude of an Arab-Jewish neighbour whose house was burnt down – and who took revenge on Muhammad's sister and her children, expelling them from their house at gun point – Muhammad could only conceive of relations with Zionists as a death struggle. At this point, he was willing to reject the civilising and humanitarian mission attributed to the colonising power by an American Diplomat, who asked Muhammad if he and his 'starving' and 'backward people' could reject the food and medicine Zionists were said to have distributed to them. But allusions to revenge do not reflect a change in Muhammad's position vis-à-vis Palestinians living as refugees in Lebanon following their forcible expulsion, to whom he transported international aid packages as an UNRWA employee in Lebanon.

Although Muhammad seems to attribute each and every act of violence to the British, blinding himself to the struggle over the land between Zionists and Palestinians, his ideological blindness is suspended at one instance – when he tells the story of a *fida'i* who was transporting weapons, and who had no option but to blow up his car upon finding his way blocked by Zionist militants. This incident of heroism suspends, for a brief moment, the calculating pragmatic rationalism with which Muhammad narrates the colonisation of Palestine.

A RELATION DEFINED BY OCCUPATION

Hamda describes how it became increasingly impossible to live with the settlers. Fear and distrust came between communities and, despite a history of neighbourly relations – whether in the case of 'Arab al-Zubayd or in the case of Haifa – and even despite gestures of solidarity at a time when people from both communities were being pulled apart, these were to be made individual instances that cannot influence 'the political'.[13] It is thus that when the battles started, when one party declared the land as theirs, no room was left for the other except either to fight or leave. Most often the Palestinians took both options but ended up displaced, and for many this displacement became an endless process, as in the case of Hamda moving from 'Arab al-Zubayd to Mallaha, to 'Alma, to Marun al-Ras, to 'Aytarun, to 'Ayn al-Hilweh camp...

During her internal displacement, Hamda tells us that settlers in the nearby settlement were willing to protect Palestinians' belongings and did return them. She is unable now to give us a detailed description of her relationship with Fifati, and what they shared and did together. The interview fragment in which Hamda describes Fifati is about the latter arriving on a horseback, on a bicycle or on a motorcycle, as if what matters most to be remembered is that Fifati was able to move easily between the two places.

Working and living with the Jewish immigrants, Muhammad describes them as neighbours and brothers with whom the Palestinians shared food and parties, and with whom they exchanged visits during the holidays of each community. Most of Muhammad's Jewish connections were Arab Jews who came from the Maghrib or from Syria, and with whom there was much in common, but not when it came to the Zionist project. Muhammad tells of a Jewish neighbour who was a mechanic and shared food with him, but saw their relationship in pure colonial terms, even when speaking about the two states proposed by the UN Partition Plan for Palestine: 'We are the mind, you are the arm, mind and arm work well together.'

The boundaries between Arab and Jewish communities also appear in Muhammad's story when he addresses mixed marriages, including his own. Different communities can be friends, neighbours and even like brothers, says Muhammad, but not when it comes to marriage. Although his wife's parents tried to set the British police against Muhammad and accused their daughter of theft (something that would sometimes occur in cases of mixed marriages, without this entailing animosity between different religious groups). Nevertheless, when the relation becomes one of annihilation, all other past connections and relations become null.

Hamda does not hate or blame her Jewish friend, she does not even feel disappointment or betrayal (as she does towards her relatives or Arab neighbours). However, relationships have material bases; they find their origins in a material reality of the shared and common in everyday practice. And when this material basis is dissolved by the dispossession and expulsion that started in 1947 and continues into the present, Hamda declares, there is no place for a question about a friendship that no longer exists. However, the past friendship itself becomes questionable in Hamda's present. Hamda uses the present tense to declare that she does not trust her Jewish friend to have protected her and her brother. Hamda even says that she cannot fathom why the Jewish woman was her friend: 'I do not know why she would befriend me, if she weren't as odious as I was, she would not have.' This is a judgement made in the present about the present, even if it takes the guise of the past.

Hamda Jumʿa
born in ʿArab al-Zubayd, Palestine
Interview with Bushra Mughrabi
Qasmiya gathering north of Sur, 2003

29'15"–30'18"

Hamda Jumʿa: [The Jews] started having cattle and goats and all, and we also had our own, *Alhamdulillah*. My father had 50 sheep … 100 sheep and 50 goats. We were hit by poverty. I became blind and I was stretching my hand out, asking this person and that person.

Bushra Mughrabi: *What other work did you do in Palestine, Hajjeh?*
Hamda Jumʿa: In Palestine, I worked at the Qadas airport.

How come?
The Qadas airport… […]

Who employed you at the airport? How come you found a job?
The British came, they said: 'We want to make an airport.' Where? Between us and Qadas. It was the same distance as between here and – God bless the Prophet Muhammad – how far was the airport … the same as between here and a bit further than the bridge, the Qasmiya Bridge.[14] I can describe it to you, because back then I could see. They started by digging trenches. The trench started here and it extended around this way until the other side, and turned again all the way until there, and went back again this way. These trenches were dug in Harrawi. They're still there. If someone could bring me to them, I would go to them. I can point the way. There were 40 or 50 of them, that was just the trenches. And the airport was so long … *Astagh-firullah*. From Harrawi until al-Nabi Yushaʿ, to give the airplane enough distance to land. We worked so much for the Jews, God what a dupe I was! Arabs are dupes. *Astaghfirullah*, record this so that Arabs can hear me say they're donkeys. We earned 25 lira, *25 lira*.

Per month?
No! 25 *qirsh* – our daily wage.

31'20"–40'19"

As for me, I was so big, like this, that when I stood up my sides would split and blood would come out, because I was so overweight. An Englishman

69

took a liking to me. He said, 'Ya chuku!' Chuku means little girl. I was a 15-year-old girl, maybe older. He'd tell me, 'You sit here.' Before I'd arrive, he'd bring along one of the girls who worked there and tell her, 'You go sit with her.' He would bring me inside with the girl. Then, he would bring the next girl to sit and wait by me before the first one even left. He would bring the second girl before the first girl left. I'd ask him why, he'd say. 'Chuku ... Ya zuzu' – he nicknamed me affectionately – 'so they don't say he's making zik-zik to her.' You know, immoral things. 'You are good, you are fine, you are (blows a kiss) good, good.' [...] Everyday, I would make 10 or 25 qirsh, I don't remember. And I worked there for one lunar year. Blida [women] started working with us – Blida, in Lebanon. Girls from Qadas came to work. All of them Matawliyyat. They would come visit al-Nabi Yusha',[15] God bless him. The Prophet Yusha' never allowed any other shrine on earth to be higher than his because he was so elevated. He was among the chain of prophets. The Jews like him and we like the Prophet Yusha' too. People visited him for the Ziyarat al-Nusf pilgrimage.[16] They came from Beirut to visit the shrine of al-Nabi Yusha' – all the way from Beirut to Palestine; from Safad to al-Nabi Yusha'. The visit lasted 15 days; it was called Ziyarat al-Nusf. What did we wear? Long dresses we called balashin, they don't have them anymore. We wore balashin and headdresses, and faramil made of jukh (points to legs), and faramil on our heads.[17] When the Matawleh danced the dabkeh, they would fall in love with the Bedouin women. They would say: 'Stay away from the path of jukh! Stay away!' Oh, how the dabkeh resonated! And the majawiz played! And the songs! What can I tell you, it was better than a wedding!

Where was this?
In al-Nabi Yusha', in Palestine ... where ... above the ... or below al-Nabi Yusha', it wasn't that far. The same as from here to the sea, even closer. That was the distance between us and al-Nabi Yusha'.

Hajjeh, when you worked at the airport, were you sleeping at your workplace or...
No! We came and went, our houses were nearby, the same as between here and the Qasmiya Bridge. Imagine the airport was here, we were as close as the bridge. We would come and go. We'd go up al-Ku' al-Aswad road, they built it because that's where the bus was burnt, the al-Kuri bus.[18] When we'd go up that road, the biggest of the girls would have to use her hands, just like you would going up a ladder. That was where the battle happened. By that time, we had left Palestine, the day that bus burnt. One Jewish sister

came to me – Fifati. She said, 'Ya Hamda, bring your brother. If the Arabs win, I'll stay at your place and you'll protect me.' I told her 'no'. She said, 'You bring your brother, and I'll protect you, if the Jews win.' I told her 'no, I'm following my people'. I didn't agree neither to go with her, nor for her to come with me. That was the same year we left. *Walla*, she predicted it: the Jews were already at al-Ku' al-Aswad road, it was right next to us. A guy from Safad was killed, and my relative's husband too, and someone from Kirad al-Baqqara, or was it Kirad al-Ghannama?[19] That Kurdish guy from al-Baqqara could cross through this wall without leaving a trace behind him because he was as strong as a lion. There were 35 passengers on the al-Kuri bus. Al-Kuri was still in Safad, it was a bus from Safad, the people from Safad know about it. They packed them all in a bag, a soap bag. They filled a soap bag with all 30 passengers. My relative, my father's paternal cousin, got a bullet in his neck and it came out the other side (she points to her neck). He fell and remained there, we went to fetch him, his blood was pouring until there … *La ilaha illallah, Muhammad rasulullah. Astaghfirullah al-'Azim.* May God condemn every oppressor … May God condemn every oppressor. I swear, we went to bury him, and the Jews surrounded us…

They kept saying, 'Zubayd, you should all leave. Zubayd, you should all leave.'

Who?
The *fida'iyin*, the guerrillas. The revolutionaries from the time my sister's husband, the poet, died.

Hajjeh, when you worked at the airport, was it around 1936 or after?
My dear, I tell you a he-goat and you tell me, 'Let's milk it!' And I'm a *taltamees* who can't even distinguish Friday from Thursday![20]

Hajjeh, I meant at the time of the British.
Yes, yes, with the British.

Ok, during that time, you told me there were revolutionaries…
Yes, there were revolutionaries. It was the day the almond harvest was destroyed and the Armenian workers were killed. So we left. The British entered and started mistreating us and mixing our wheat with our barley with our rice, and mixing everything together.

They did this to you Arabs?
Yes, to us Arabs. And whoever had a shop, they demolished it and gave away all the sweets. There were candied almonds and *ka 'k ban*, not like the sweets we have today. Each string of *ka 'k ban* was this big. And the candied almond had a hole in it, they used to call it *tiz al-habuba*, nobody was shy to say it. Those were our sweets. Dates, figs, candied almonds.

Why did the British do this? Were there any revolutionaries from your area?
From among us? It was during the time of al-Asbah.[21] They came the year my sister's husband was killed. You know Majd al-Krum? They established themselves there. What did I know? Barely anything, I was an ignorant, *'ayfa hali*. I had no idea why they attacked, nor who was a *fida 'i*, nor who was a traitor, my dear.

Did the British imprison or detain anyone from your people?
Before this revolution, my father was jailed, my uncle too and some of our people in Safad. They found a Jew – or maybe not a Jew – dead in Abu Zuwaytina. Abu Zuwaytina was as close as between here and this bridge.[22] They jailed them. My father was ... This guy used to hang braids. Each braid on my father and my uncle's head was this big. They tied them up from their braids and hung them from their heads and the top of my father's head was ripped out, and he became bald here (she points to top of her head). He was scalped; he lost the skin on his head. I was too young then. This jail story, I was too young to remember. But it was a real story – I would ask him what happened to his head and he would tell me, 'I was jailed with so and so.' I didn't know so and so either ... I wasn't aware of this story. I was born but I was still a little girl. I didn't know the difference between this or that.

And what about the Safad bus? Who attacked it and why? Was it the British or the Jews?
The Jews! The one who killed all the people I was telling you about was a girl.

A girl?
Yes, a girl. My sister took me to visit her grave, God bless your mother and bless her. I went up there and cried with her son, the hero. She only gave birth to a girl and a boy in Palestine. They told him, 'Mahmud, will you go and fight?' He said, 'Who do you want me to fight? It will either be my paternal cousin or my maternal cousin.' Even the most powerful Jew did not dare address him, over there in Palestine. He told them, 'I'm not going

anywhere. I don't want to go fight my brother or my cousin.' He was the only boy, he only had one sister. And he would help me because he was a nice person, kept taking me [places]. He died from a heart attack, poor guy. He used to lift weights; he didn't work. He used to do electrical repairs and lift weights.

41'20"–45'05"

Hajjeh, after they hit that bus, was your village scared?
They revolutionaries came and said: 'You need to leave this place.'

Hajjeh, were they revolutionaries or Jaysh al-Inqadh?
No. Jaysh al-Inqadh came and relocated us.

How?
For example: 'Today, so and so needs to leave al-Zubayd.' The village was called al-Zubayd. I was the last one to remain in our village. I had friends in ʿAlma, from the Abu Daʿas family. They provided me with five *dawab*. I had so much furniture and copper. We called it glass but nobody had actual glass nor did anybody know about glass. The cup we used to drink from was made of copper. He brought the *dawab* and sent me off. Who ended up riding with me? Jaysh al-Inqadh. Goddamn them as well, let them hear this. We took a road they called al-Haqura (unpaved path). A mountain! Full of trees, like the *suwayd*, and the *qandil* and – all the plants in the world were on this mountain. This person carried the mattress and that person carried the covers, and this one the pots and that one the *dist* with the *mansaf*. Until the mattress got stuck in a tree. One of the Jaysh al-Inqadh came to help me. My face was so red! My little brother was walking behind me, the father of this boy here. He said (air kiss). I told him, 'Hey!' – I ripped his shirt – 'Where did you come from, you idiots? Did you come to harm us or to help us? I swear I will report you to your superior!' 'For the love of your feet' – they spoke Arabic. 'For the love of your feet, please, you are my sister.' I said, 'Goddamn your father, and your sister's father, and the war! I wish I had stayed with Fifati instead of coming with you.' Before the Jews kicked me out, I met up with my maternal cousins on the road to Dayshum. The Jews were telling them: 'Turn back!' My maternal cousins said: 'We will not turn back.' They meant 'turn back' so that they could shoot them. They didn't want to turn back. They started walking backwards so that they wouldn't shoot them … The Jews started being more forceful. The Jews, I don't mean the British. They went and killed people from our neighbour-

ing village, a group of women from 'Almaniyya. They made them forage for mushrooms. Mushrooms that looked like nails; they used to come in boxes. Maybe you've seen these mushrooms in their boxes, maybe you haven't. They shot them and they died. They stopped going. I went back to 'Alma, its people had remained; they hadn't gone into exile. The people of 'Alma were exiled at the same time as Safad. I lived in 'Alma for a year. From then on, wherever my friends – people from 'Alma – left for, they took my younger brother and me along. We left for Marun al-Ras, from Marun al-Ras they brought me back to 'Alma, and from 'Alma they put me in 'Athroun[23] – may you not witness their *athra*.[24] We stayed in 'Athroun and the buses started coming, and they were saying: '*Yalla*. We want to send you to Lebanon.' In Palestine, I stayed in 'Athroun for eight days, then I went straight to 'Ayn al-Hilweh. Where did I stay? I stayed in the old refugee camp, near the roundabout. That's where I lived.

Muhammad Jamil ʿArabi
born 1923 in Haifa, Palestine
Interview with Mahmoud Zeidan
Mazbud, Iqlim al-Kharub, 2003

27'28"–41'40"

Mahmoud Zeidan: *How did you find these stories?*
Muhammad Jamil ʿArabi: Who told them to me? I lived them! And they happened in Lebanon!

No, let's stay in Palestine.
I'm telling you, these politics ... These were the politics they employed. How else would they create conflict between them so that they wouldn't like each other? These ones have their own organisations, and these other ones have theirs too. One time, the Jews built a building on top of the main British police station, and surrounded it with a three-metre-high walled checkpoint – three and a half metres! They built a scaffold on a truck. They got a barrel and filled it with explosives. The truck was driving towards them and when it arrived, they pulled it over at the station and it exploded. Jews! The Jew was authorised to do all of these things, what could one do? If an Arab man became a communist, they would beat him up and kill him. Not the Jew. It was a communist system, the Histadrut (Zionist Labour Federation) was a communist system. You had to pay the Histadrut a monthly fee and you would say what kind of job you were looking for, and they would enforce your employment, and would impose your salary amount on your workplace.

Who killed the Palestinian if he was found to be a communist?
The British! The government! It was prohibited!

Did it ever happen to someone in Haifa?
It happened to me! When I worked in the Jewish army, I had a friend who worked with me. They had a club, he would say, 'Come visit our club.' I would say I'd go and I wouldn't. One day, he said, 'Brother, why haven't you been coming? You're being difficult with me. I wait for you and you don't show up.' I told him, 'Brother, I work, you know.' He said, 'Brother ...' You know the Arab man: always a victim to what's between his legs. He said, 'We have girls, you show up, you come in and you choose the one you want, you go out with her and you deal with her.' I told him, 'You should have

said so earlier, I'm coming today.' I swear to God! I went. I discovered for the first time in my life that there were floors underground. I found him waiting for me. We went down one, two, three floors underground. What! The further down I went, the lower my heart sank – below my balls – until my knees. I went inside. There was an entrance like this, with a table and a guy sitting there. I went in … He dropped me off with the guy at the table and he kept going. He said, 'I'll be inside.' The other guy sat me down, 'Your name, *habibi*?' And I told him the first name that crossed my mind. Had he repeated the question, I swear I wouldn't know. Look at the inspiration! And it came out of me as if it were my real name – he said, 'Your name?' 'Trrruuuttt,' it came out. 'Where do you live?' I was living in Wadi al-Salib, I told him I lived in al-Halisa. He asked me a few questions; it went fine. Then he said, 'Where's your ID?' I said, 'What ID?' He said, 'So I can stamp it for you.' My ID was in my pocket! I said, 'I didn't bring my ID. Tomorrow I'll get you my ID, *ya sidi*. He didn't say to bring my ID so I didn't bring it along.' He said all right, bring it tomorrow. My ID was in my pocket but I had forgotten the name I'd given him! He registered it in his notebook; they have a notebook. He wrote it down. I went inside. There were seven or eight rooms. I went into the first room … Fucking hell, it was a brothel … Is it all right to say these things or not?

Yes.
Should I get comfortable?

Get comfortable.
I went to the second room and it was even more outrageous! In broad daylight. I went to another room … Disgusting! I turned around, got out and left. They cracked down on the headquarters exactly ten days later. Every single Arab whose name was registered was beaten up until he was split in two. The Jew told me himself. He said, 'What about you, nobody came for you?' I responded, 'Why?' He said, 'Every Arab whose name was registered there was taken and beaten up by the British. And you, nobody came to get you?' I told him, 'I never gave him my name!' Anyway, for them, it was authorised.

Why did the British take them and beat them up?
Because they wanted no communists.

So they found out that this club was for these communists?
No, it was a known communist club.

What was the name of this club?
I forgot my own self when I went there, I never even asked about its name or anything. I'm telling you, he took me three floors underground and by the time I got in, I was already shaking. He asked me, 'What's your name, *habibi*?' – *Khabibi*. I speak very good Hebrew, I learnt it properly. Our neighbour, she taught me. I knew Hebrew.

Did you learn it here or over there?
No, over there. She taught me there. She liked me. She taught me assuming I would become her boyfriend, but I didn't. I ate the bait and shat on the fishing rod. My uncle became her boyfriend.

What do you mean?
I ate the bait and I shat on the fishing rod, so my uncle asked her out. May he rest in peace. Anyway... But I never spoke Hebrew with them. I could understand their conversations but I never spoke. I spoke Arabic.

Your neighbour, where was she from?
Jewish from Egypt. She was married there. She came alone, and when the war broke out, her husband could no longer follow her. She made do with these people. She tried her luck with me and saw it was pointless, then my uncle caught her eye. Things turned out all right for her.

Were there lots of Jews in the neighbourhood you lived in?
Some of them still live in our building until today. A lot of people sold their houses. Not me. My building was all Jews. Arab Jews of course, from Halab.

How was the relationship with these Arab Jews?
We were like brothers and sisters, as if living together. There was one incident, but maybe it's a long story. A story that happened with our neighbours' cousin. He came from Halab; he was a young man. He arrived and stayed at their house, in our building, one floor above us – we lived under them. He was a worker but, while waiting to find a job, he worked in cement construction. Their buildings were all made of reinforced cement. The Jews built everything with reinforced cement. They used to pour concrete back then; there weren't machines like the ones they have today. They had concrete mixers but they hauled the mix in tin cans, on their shoulders. Those who hauled it upstairs in a tin can got 2 *gineh* a day. A regular worker got 1 *gineh*, and a worker who carried it upstairs got 2 *gineh*. So this guy worked for three months, carrying cement, until they gave him the ID card.

Until they gave it to him! As soon as they did, he entered the police force. And he got engaged to our neighbours' daughter, his paternal cousin. We were very close friends with them. For their marriage, I threw them an Arabic wedding.

He was Jewish, right?
Yes! Jewish from Halab. I threw a wedding for them, with cars, and horns and festivities. A wedding, just like an Arab family would throw one. And he got married. After that, when I got married, I left my sister in the house. After my father passed away and our aunt left us and all, I was living with my sister in the house. It was their house. Anyway, I got married, I left my sister in the house and I rented another house. Her husband used to work at the municipality. The municipality used to count a year as 14 months. They would give him two months' pay in November and in December as well. My brother-in-law got his paycheque, at the time, the partition had happened and the problems were starting. He went to the market and bought provisions for the house. May he rest in peace, he was from the Jabali family. He had built an attic especially for provisions, with shelves, and everything was stored in grain bags and crates and cans of oil or ghee or rice or sugar – a pantry. I said to him, 'Shafiq …' He was my paternal cousin. I said, 'Slow down, don't spend all your money.' All our life – and during revolutions – we were always in solidarity with each other. They went and built a wall between us and the Arab [Jews]. We had to go around in order to come down. He said, 'No! They are all our brothers!' I told him, 'This time is not like usual times.' I had an awareness or maybe a sixth sense. Anyway, Mister Shlomo, who I threw a wedding for, was living in a neighbourhood close to the Arabs. They attacked it and burnt his house down. He needed a house, so he came and took it out on my sister. He went over during the day, while her husband was at work (raises fists). Pulled out two guns to her face. '*Yi! Ya Shlomo?*' He said, 'Not a word.' She had a boy and a girl, Samir and Aida. He said, 'Get out, this minute. I want the house.' The neighbours came, they were his relatives, his cousins, from his uncle's house. He did not listen to anyone. They begged him so much that he said, 'Ok, take a few clothes for the kids.' She took a change of clothes for the kids and she left. So … My heart ached for her and I made a *nidr*. And I transmitted this *nidr* to Kissinger. They would send us people who were studying the Palestinian cause (winks). And I was at the UNRWA. And when you work at the UNRWA, the first thing you do is sign a document that forbids you to talk politics. A guy came who had supposedly graduated from university with honours, they had sent him here to al-Sharq al-Awsat to wander around at

our expense. UNRWA told me to, 'Go with him, take him and his people, wherever they want to go, take them.' Did he come to wander around in the camps? We visited the Shatila camp, and the Jisr al-Basha camp, and as we were going to Jisr al-Wati he stopped, and the people with him came down to take pictures. The guy put his arms on the window and said, 'Now, let me ask you this question.' I said that I was forbidden from talking politics and that it was not my business. I had signed so I wasn't allowed to speak about politics. He said, 'No, no, no, it's between me and you.' I said all right. Look how he asked his questions, 'Suppose you were sick, very sick, and there was no medication available, and you were going to die. And a Jew comes and tells you, here is some medication. Would you take it or not?' That was one of the questions. The next question was, 'Suppose you were hungry, very hungry, and there was no food. And a Jew brings you food, would you take it or not?' Each person gave a different answer and I asked him, 'Would I have to be extremely sick?' He said, 'Yes!' I said, 'I would tell him come closer, come, come, come, until he was close to me and I would strangle him. With whatever strength I had left over, either he would die or I would.' He said, 'Ooof! Is that so?' I told him, 'Yes!' He asked, 'Why?' I told him, 'You told me why. When I was in Haifa and I did this and that to this guy, and he did this and that to my sister. And I know that if I were to go back there, I wouldn't kill him even if I could. And I am Muslim. Do you know what Islam forbids us from doing?' He enumerated them to me. I told him, 'I know that if I were to go back there, I would open up his veins and drink his blood until his death.' And that's just one out of a million stories. Everyone has their own story. The cause was lost ... During the invasion, I was here in the UNDP, I stayed in Beirut and I didn't leave...

1h 42'44"–1h 47'55"

The Jews and the Arabs cohabitated a lot. The Jews who were from Arab families, whether from al-Mashriq or al-Maghrib, from Tunisia, or Algeria, or Halab, or Damascus or Lebanon ... They all lived there and spoke Arabic, and some of them didn't even know how to speak Hebrew; they would learn it in school. They lived like us, their weddings were like the Arabs', their celebrations were like the Arabs'. They threw weddings and sang, and everything. All those who sang for them were Arabs, and were my friends. They invited us and we would attend the wedding, and they would dance and sing and all. We blended together in a very lovely way.

When you went to these weddings, did they single you out because you were a Palestinian married to a Jewish woman?
It wasn't about being Palestinian; there wasn't a separation. It was either Arab or Jew.

Ok, would they single you out because you were an Arab, for example?
They would say *Aravi* and *Yehudi*.[25]

Would they single you out, because you were...
Not at all! On the contrary, they would invite me themselves. They would invite us because the majority of those who came from al-Mashriq and al-Maghrib lived in our neighbourhood as well. There was no separation. And during the matzah celebrations, they would bring us the matzah themselves and feed it to us. They would attend our holidays and we would attend theirs. There were no problems at all between us; it was all bullshit. But some of them were very fanatical. My father had borrowed 100 *gineh* with interest from a Jew, an Ashkenazi Jew, from those who curled their sideburns like this. And the guy liked my father a lot. When my father passed away, he came and hugged me and kissed me and cried. I did not know him. He said, 'I swear on my religion that I love your father more than I love my *kham*.' And the *kham* for them is sacred.[26] He came back again only to modify the terms of the loan. He told my mother, may she rest in peace, 'Madam, Misbah very much *habibi*. I change loan from his name – to the children's name and I don't want any interest, because I am becoming old and I might die, and I have three sisters who are not married. They will inherit from me and I am afraid they might cause you trouble.' They agreed. And then he died. So, some of them are decent. But those who were from Arab families lived among us. They ate from our plate and we ate from theirs; we ate the same things. We invited them to our weddings and we would attend theirs, and so on. But they brought the Falasha (Beta Israel) over and made them Jews. And they brought over whoever told them he was Jewish. Even if he wasn't Jewish, they would let him in. They taught them in the kibbutz, they showed them how to do this and that, and that was it. It was all bullshit. Because they could in fact cohabitate with us. But the Palestinians acted wrongly from the beginning. Had they formed a state from the start, just like Cyprus accepted the partition, there would have been a chance. There was no ... (he points to his head) none, whatsoever. The British government itself would place a bomb wherever it could cause a massacre. The police station in Haifa was here and the *hisbeh* was facing it. There was a junction on that road. They placed a bomb after which not

a soul survived; there was meat stuck on the *zinco*. Just a minute earlier, the police station guard had gone in and closed the door. And it blew up. What does it mean? They wanted to achieve this and they did. They succeeded. That's politics. Blasphemous! Whatever they wanted, they could do. So many stories, a lot of them.

Would you like to go back to Haifa?
What?

Would you like to go back to Haifa?
Of course, if I could, I would go back. I would go back but I would have to go back on foot. That was my *nidr*. I have a house there! We have a three-storey house there, each floor has three or four rooms, in the most beautiful area of Haifa. We can see [Ras] al-Naqura from our balcony.

4

Mandated Memory: The Schooling of Palestine in Nicola Ziadeh's and Anis Sayigh's Pre-1948 Recollections

Dyala Hamzah

Nicola Ziadeh (1907–2006) and Anis Sayigh (1931–2009) were ubiquitous Palestinian public intellectuals of the second half of the twentieth century, whose voices could be heard on the Arab world's major broadcasting networks,[1] whose pens defined or shaped the columns of its press,[2] and who devoted a lifetime to building the institutional pillars of Palestinian culture and, in equal measure, the Arab national project. They became fixtures of the Beiruti public sphere – at a time when Egypt, long the throbbing heart of the Nahda, was demanding that its intellectuals serve the Nasserite state – and of Palestinian resistance that came into its fold. They also bore witness to Lebanon's sectarian polarisation as it unravelled around the Palestinian Catastrophe: the Nakba, and the formidable societal, political and economic challenges it generated, found in post-Mandate Lebanon one of its major refugee harbours, and in Beirut the resources to channel its narratives.[3] Young graduates of Palestine's prize educational establishments converged there, often after completing doctoral studies in Europe, the United States or the Arab World. Many found employment at the American University of Beirut (AUB) or, after 1964, at the Beirut-headquartered cultural and political institutions of the Palestine Liberation Organization.

Born a generation apart, on opposite sides of the Ottoman demise, both Ziadeh and Sayigh identified as Palestinian Arabs of Greater Syria, though both had come of age after the territorial continuum of the imperial province of Beirut had ceased to exist. 'I have three roots', says Ziadeh, who was born to Nazarene parents, referring to his Damascene birth and childhood, his Jeninite and Jerusalemite youth, and his Beiruti post-expulsion adulthood. Sayigh likewise asserts: 'I am of a Syrian father whose origins were in Hawran (*jabal al-Duruz, jabal al-'Arab*), of a Palestinian mother from al-Bassa[4] and a Lebanese since my exile.' After completing doctorates in the UK, both became scholars of history and politics despite themselves, Ziadeh having favoured mathematics and Sayigh having dreamt of studying journalism.

Ziadeh, who lived to be almost 100, was trained at the Dar al-Muʿallimin (Teachers' [Training] College), established near established near Bab al-Zahra (Herod's Gate) in Jerusalem in 1918 and renamed the Arab College in 1927. One of two university preparatory government schools in Mandate Palestine, it eventually added two post-matriculation years to its curriculum in 1941.[5] Under the mentorship of Palestinian pan-Arab historian Darwish al-Miqdadi (1897–1961), who put words into practice by taking his student on a legendary trek through Greater Syria during the 1925 revolt against French colonial control, Ziadeh was inducted into Arab nationalism, which would prove a powerful determinant of his outlook and entire intellectual production. After a decade of teaching secondary school in Acre, a grant took him to London in 1935 on condition that he study for a BA in Roman and Greek history – a reflection of the Dar al-Muʿallimin curriculum as much as the Department of Education's proclivities.[6] After eight years of 'government' service at both the Rashidiyya College and the Arab College in Jerusalem, Ziadeh secured another grant in 1947, this time to write a PhD in Islamic history at the University of London's School of Oriental and African Studies. Upon graduating, he embarked on a lifelong career as a professor of Arab and Islamic history at AUB. His prolific oeuvre (42 books in Arabic, 6 in English and 14 English to Arabic translations) and his unique interest in North African history bear testimony to his espousal of Arab nationalism in which Palestine was but an inextricable part.[7]

Perhaps as a result of his enduring adherence to pan-Arabist ideas, Ziadeh never attained the popular renown of Sayigh, whose active political engagement made him the target of several Israeli assassination attempts. Briefly a member of the Syrian Social Nationalist Party, Sayigh demonstrated a lifelong commitment to Palestine and to Arab nationalism, from his early days throwing stones at Zionist settlers in mid-1940s Jerusalem to his appointment to the Palestine National Council.[8] One year shy of his death, Sayigh was still politically active as vice-president and spokesman of the 2008 Palestine National Conference, which called for a unified Palestinian rejection of the Annapolis Conference statement. The youngest and only Sayigh sibling to be born in Tiberias,[9] he was raised in the Scottish Protestant mission's vast rectory and attended the town's government school, before enrolling in Bishop Gobat School in Jerusalem, one year before the United Nations voted to partition Palestine. Upon his school's closure on 29 November 1947, he transferred to Sayda, where he finished his schooling at the Gerard Institute. After graduating from AUB with a political science degree in 1953, he obtained a PhD in Middle East Studies from Cambridge University in 1964. A writer, essayist, publisher and academic, Sayigh was also an institution builder. He chaired the PLO's Palestine Research Centre,[10] which he relentlessly worked to develop into a strictly academic establishment.[11] He launched the *Palestine Encyclopaedia* before joining its editorial board,[12] and supervised many prestigious journals and magazines published by Arab research centres throughout the region and by the Arab League.

As we turn to the interviews, probing memories of trauma and filtering them through our fact-checking, ethical considerations arise. Is it legitimate to intervene in these testimonies in order to apply contextual correctives? What are the repercussions of our interference as we time-code filmed interviews to excerpt this or that sequence? How do we not lose the voice and its tone, the gaze and its shades, the breath and its depth, as we prepare to slice into what is already a soundbite of a recollection, a memory prompted – mandated – by the interviewer's questions? And what to do with omissions or discrepancies between Ziadeh's and Sayigh's written memoirs and these oral interviews, captured at the end of their lives? I cannot begin to comprehensively address such questions here, except, perhaps, by inviting the reader to see for herself what is at stake. To that end, I shall draw attention to certain jarring testimonies, to inconsistencies between the life lived and its recollection, or between recollections themselves.

Among these interviews' most halting segments is Ziadeh's neutral recounting of his mother's snap announcement during the First World War: 'Nicola, your father is dead. Here are his clothes.'[13] In a very different way, Sayigh describes his swollen fingers as a schoolchild in Jerusalem, his anxieties lest the black ointment prescribed to heal them soil the sheets of his dormitory bed ... He waves his mutilated hand – the one that held the letter-bomb that exploded in his face in 1972 – at the camera with a casual, 'I had fingers at the time.'[14] The two intellectuals' testimonies also diverge with respect to communal life in post-Ottoman Palestine. Sayigh's passionate denial of sectarianism in Palestine, manifestly inflected with his later encounter with Lebanese sectarianism,[15] contradicts Ziadeh's recollection of protests against a prevalence of Christian teachers, which led the Tarshiha school where he was first appointed to close down. To be sure, this account is offset by countless positive depictions of communal coexistence, such as Ziadeh's privileged relationship with Shaykh Jarallah, who called him 'my son'.[16] At one point, however, Ziadeh interjects with a smile: 'We are *rum* orthodox, the original Christians of these lands!'[17] Sayigh, for his part, never once discusses the conditions under which his family converted to Protestantism.[18] Though both men were staunch secularists, their hints and omissions evince a matter self-censored or at least trivialised in the face of the Nakba, a catastrophe of existential proportions for Palestinians of all religious backgrounds. Another episode inviting disconcerting correctives is Ziadeh's lengthy elaboration on the circumstances of his early admission to Dar al-Mu'allimin at age 13 and a half (instead of 15). We *could* read anything from narcissism to dislike into his conspicuous neglect to mention 'Abd al-Latif Tibawi's admission at age 12, one year later;[19] however, what we *should* read is the ferocious, relentless competition that prevailed at the teachers' training college – the result of a selective education system that pitted all Palestine's top students against each other. 'They lived in a nightmare', says Sayigh of his brothers and their comrades, who were (un)lucky enough to make it into Dar al-Mu'allimin. And no testimony is more potent, none more revealing of the educational trauma visited on Palestine's elites-to-be than Sayigh's disclosure of life at the Arab College, in response to a question about Bishop Gobat School.

Sayigh and Ziadeh were trailblazers of the Mandate era, 'cultural aristocrats' from 'middle-class families hovering on the edge of poverty'.[20] Yet, who remembers them today, and how? Palestinian intellectuals' contributions continue to be sorely overlooked, both outside and sometimes within academic and political circles; and postcolonial assessments that ascribe this obfuscation to typical North–South asymmetries capture only half their story. By listening in on the school-day recollections of two luminaries from pre-1948 Palestine, these lines have striven to expose the mechanisms of their compounded erasure.[21] The translated excerpts below are not the most colourful segments of Ziadeh's and Sayigh's interviews. They have been selected because they narrate schoolboy memories of two of Mandatory Palestine's most important schools: the public Arab College (formerly Dar al-Mu'allimin), and the private Bishop Gobat School, also known as Madrasat Sahyun for its location atop Mount Zion in Jerusalem. As sites of vigorous yet heavily monitored Arab and Palestinian nationalism, these institutions produced the elites that staffed 'government' schools and tried haphazardly to organise national resistance from within.[22] As sites of a most egregious colonial obliteration, they are iconic of a Nakba ongoing, of a 'past continuous'.[23]

During the Mandate period, Bishop Gobat's diocesan school and orphanage, founded 1853 outside the walls of Jerusalem, 'became the main preparatory school for the Palestinian elite'.[24] Scores of activists, writers, politicians and artists graduated from Madrasat Sahyun, among them 'Abd al-Qadir al-Husayni, Ahmad Tuqan, Ahmad al-Shuqayri, Kamal Nasir, 'Izzat Tannus and Emile Habibi. Today, the school buildings still stand. Seized in 1948 by the Haganah, who used it to supply besieged Zionists in the old Jewish quarter of Jerusalem, the building found itself under Jordanian watch in no man's land after the 1949 Armistice Agreement was signed. During the Six-Day War of 1967, the Israelis conquered the premises – along with East Jerusalem, intra and extra muros – and eventually entered into a bitter ownership dispute with the Anglican Church over the school. The Church Mission Society fought hard to exempt the grounds and buildings, along with many of its other assets in Palestine, from the notorious Absentee Law that automatically transferred ownership to the State of Israel. Today, the building houses the Jerusalem University College (formerly, the Institute of Holy Land Studies), a self-described 'independent, degree-granting academic institution in Jerusalem' and 'extension campus for over 70 accredited Christian colleges, universities, and seminaries around the world'. Of its Ottoman and post-Ottoman Palestinian history, there is no trace in college publications. Compounding this erasure is the school's rather obscene motto: 'Read the land. See the Text. Live the Book'.

The story of the Arab College's erasure is just as violent. Founded in 1918, Dar al-Mu'allimin evolved into the Arab College in 1928. In 1934, it was relocated to Jabal al-Mukabbir, a neighbourhood south-east of the Old City that experienced the same fate as Mount Zion. While the college building was entrusted to the International Red Cross under Jordanian administration after the 1967 war, the surrounding area – formally under the purview of United Nations Truce Supervision Organization (UNTSO) – was occupied by Israel, and parts of the land confiscated to build the settlement of East Talpiot. In 1998, amidst the Oslo run-up to what were hoped to be 'final status negotiations', the Palestinian Authority was planning to revive the College.[25] Two years later, the Second Intifada erupted and the Sharon government embarked on its apartheid wall. Today, Jabal al-Mukabbir belongs to Palestinian towns and neighbourhoods under extreme duress. Ripped apart by the wall, its infrastructure is derelict and its growth stunted by the straitjacket of Jerusalem Municipality laws. Remembering these cornerstones of Palestinian identity by reading between the lines of their crafters is not so much a *devoir*, and even less a *lieu de mémoire*. It is the righting of an ongoing wrong. In this sense, too, it is mandated memory.

Nicola Ziadeh
born circa 1907 in Damascus, Syria
Interview with Mahmoud Zeidan
Beirut, 2004

3h 11'20"–3h 21'53"

Nicola Ziadeh: Let us talk about education in Palestine. The British administration supervised the education of Arabs while the education of Jews was
free and was affiliated with the Jewish Agency or the religious associations.
Here is what the Idarat al-Maʿarif (Department of Education) did: it gave
the Jews' share of the department's budget for schools to the Jewish spe-
cialists. There was a Jewish man working as an assistant to the department
director, the assistant had a lower rank than the deputy. He was Jewish.
His work consisted of ensuring that the money had been granted and to
provide statistics from the Jews on the state of schools and education. But
the department was not responsible for this. The education of Arabs was
conducted ... between themselves. The government of Palestine opened
schools in Palestine and they were good, despite what other people might
say. I taught in a village, at a high school and at al-Kulliyya al-ʿArabiyya
(the Arab College), and was knowledgeable about all the previous and suc-
cessive curricula. However, the education that was overseen by the Idarat
al-Maʿarif as concerns the education of Arabs ... was lacking. First, schools
in villages, with few exceptions like Tarshiha, al-Rama and Tubas in the
Nablus district, did not offer the full course of primary education. They
stopped in the middle, at third grade of primary school. Those who wanted
to further their education needed to go to the nearest city that had a secondary school ... that is, to finish primary school and start secondary
school. The secondary school I taught at in ʿAkka for ten years, and of
which there were a large number in Palestine's main centres – or let's say in
the district centres, in ʿAkka, al-Nasira, Haifa, Safad, Nablus and so on ...
these schools did not provide a full secondary school education, they only
completed primary school. There was a primary school in ʿAkka like the
ones you find in villages, so they provided four years of primary school and
only two years of secondary school. The education was good and the curricula were good. At first, naturally, the books came from all over but things
gradually became organised. Yet, schools were scarce. When the Mandate
ended in Palestine, the total number of schools that had been opened by
the Department of Education amounted to 400 or 500. A great number
of villages remained without schools – entirely – and those that did have

primary schools had limited means. The number of schools should have been much higher and it would have been possible but there was no intention to do this. Al-Kulliyya al-'Arabiyya, and al-Kulliyya al-Rashidiyya in its wake, only taught two years post-matric, which was the secondary school's final exam and the basis for admitting students as freshmen at the American University [of Beirut] or at British universities.

Mahmoud Zeidan: Were they government or private colleges?
Nicola Ziadeh: All of them were governmental. I am talking about government education. There was ... Let's finish talking about government education first. Government education was good but there wasn't much of it, it wasn't made available to people. Al-Kulliyya al-'Arabiyya, for instance, only offered two years after secondary school, meaning that it did not complete the required four years of university. This college was fine, the teachers were excellent, the administration was good ... but schools were neglected. None of the district schools or al-Quds' Rashidiyya had an assistant to the principal, a secretary of sorts who could correspond ... For this reason, Hasan 'Arafat, who was al-Rashidiyya's principal, delegated one of the young teachers who could use a typewriter to complete these tasks after school hours. An administration may not need much to function but there ought to have been one as a minimum. The principal should spend more time taking care of the school instead of having to deal with paperwork. But what is important is that schools were scarce.

So now, what were the other types of educational systems available to Arabs in Palestine? There were foreign schools from before and those remained; there were those that had opened during the British Mandate. For example, there was an English all-girls school in al-Quds that was called Miss Robertson – it was named such because its principal was called Robertson. That's how schools were named. There was a German school in al-Quds, there were Greek ... French schools – the Greeks, the Greeks, nobody was interested in them! French schools were mostly concentrated in al-Quds, Yafa and Haifa. Mostly, other areas didn't have such schools, though some did. These foreign schools at least completed high school education. There were national schools. Leaving aside the Quranic schools in villages – we are not concerned with those – we are talking about government schools in which students pass the matric state exams, there was: Madrasat al-Najah (al-Najah School) in Nablus, which is now al-Najah University and there was Rawdat al-Ma'arif in al-Quds, whose owner was 'Abd al-Latif al-Husayni. It was said that 'Abd al-Latif al-Husayni was helped by the Supreme Muslim Council, though I don't know. There were private schools but they were not able to match the government schools. There were also foreign missionary schools, the Frères had two schools in al-Quds ... In the last period, the number of private schools increased. Khalil al-Sakakini opened a school in al-Quds and others did as well but they were costly. Opening a school is not like opening a store. It wasn't just about having a teacher, students and a building. You needed laboratories, all these things ... a library! But despite all of that, the private schools had an important role in training Palestinian students and taking care of them.

What about the Russian schools?
Pardon?

What about the Russian missionary schools?
No, these were finished! They had shut down in 1914. These are ancient ... they're old news! When the Ottoman Empire fought with the Germans in the war, it became Russia's adversary so all of the Russian schools closed. There were schools that called themselves Orthodox and the like but they didn't gain any traction. The important thing is that there was a willingness to learn among the people and that was the reason why a lot of Palestinian students came to Lebanon. They used to go to the school in ʿAlayh...

5h 13'18"–5h 24'53"

During that time, I used to visit al-Quds where there was, since my time at Dar al-Muʿallimin (Teachers' College), a conference centre – the Young Men's Christian Association. I remember that, when I was at Dar al-Muʿallimin, we were invited to attend four lectures that were given by people about their respective religions. Shaykh Muhyi al-Din al-Mallah spoke about Islam, Pastor Elias Marmura spoke about Christianity, a Jewish man spoke about Judaism though I did not attend this one, and Husayn Ruhi, the Iranian Bahai who was an employee in the Department of Education, spoke about the Bahai faith ... There were similar cultural activities that continued. When I went in the summer, there weren't many conferences but there were events that I participated in. I went to bookshops, I borrowed and bought books. I specifically went to Maktabat Filastin al-ʿIlmiyya (the Palestine Scientific Bookshop), which was then owned by Bulus Saʿid, Edward Said's uncle.[26] I used to buy books and the ones they didn't have, they would order for me.

One day, as I was about to apply to the higher teaching exam ... There was no place to order books from in ʿAkka and I liked having all the books that I needed in front of me. I looked at the list of required books and found that it was very costly and I couldn't afford to buy all the books at once. So I went to al-Maktaba al-'Ilmiyya. The young man who worked there was called Wadi' Jalluq; he was a very nice young man. I told him, 'I have a special request from you.' I said I wanted all these books but as they cost up to 35 or 40 *gineh* I couldn't afford to buy them all at once or when they arrived. So I asked them, 'Would it be possible to place an order for these books and in return I will give you 2 *gineh* per month?' The young man replied, 'I don't have the authority to make such a decision in this case, let me see what my boss has to say.' So he went to Bulus Sa'id and told him that I was a customer there ... He told the young man to, 'bring him over so I can see who has requested this from us.' I went up to see him, a respectable man ... He asked me, 'What's the story?' I explained it to him, 'I am a customer of yours but these books are ... I can't buy them all at once but I need them, so if you could order them for me, and I will pay 2 *gineh* a month to cover their cost.' He thought to himself and said, 'Of course, you're most welcome.' He called Wadi' and told him to order my books. I reimbursed the cost of the books over a period of 15 or 16 months – 2 *gineh* each month. That's one thing, and it's important mind you!

The other thing was that I used to contact Khalil al-Sakakini because I knew him.[27] Is'af al-Nashashibi was difficult to get a hold of because he had his customers and whatnot. I didn't know too many people in al-Quds but I did know a few foreigners who worked in archaeology in Palestine. I used to ask them about archaeology because I had developed an interest in ancient history and Palestinian archaeology. One of them was called Mr Hammond; he was the director or president of the Kulliyyat al-Shabab in al-Quds. Hasan al-Karmi had gone there in his time.

Yes.

There were also others who worked at the museum. One of them was called Meyer, a Jewish man who worked in archaeology. I contacted him once and wrote to him with my questions, to which he responded. But there were few of them. The only Arab I knew in that period was Ahmad Samih al-Khalidi. In 1923, during the school year's last term, the president of Dar al-Mu'allimin travelled to England to learn about the organisation of training schools there. Khalil Totah was his name. He used to teach us psychology and civic education.[28] At that time, Ahmad Samih al-Khalidi was transferred from Yafa to the central administration. He became the central inspector there, which was a high position job. He used to work in education and was also interested in it, so Khalil Totah asked him to give lectures on his behalf on the history of education. Ahmad Samih was delighted because he was given the opportunity to do so. This was a scientific pursuit, a good thing! He came twice a week and gave us lectures. We all attended because the course was mandatory but the only one who tried to benefit truly from it was me. I used to ask him a few questions after the lectures. On a few occasions, he would tell me that he couldn't give me the answer on the spot and that he would bring it next time, which he did. I asked him, 'You talked to us once about Pestalozzi, the Italian pedagogue.[29] I would like to know more about her', to which he replied, 'I have a thesis about her, I'll bring it to you.' I am the only one who read the thesis. A friendship developed between us and, in 1925, the director Khalil Totah resigned from his position at Dar al-Mu'allimin and Ahmad Samih al-Khalidi was appointed as an interim director. He became the official director the next year. Because of our old friendship, I went to visit him when I went to al-Quds. Oftentimes, I used to accompany him on his visits. That was how I got to meet the amir 'Adil Arslan and how I got to know Ahmad's brother, Husayn Fakhri al-Khalidi. I met many others who used to frequent a British-style café in al-Quds called the Bristol. He took me with him. When I went to al-Quds, I had to...

Let's continue.
My visits to al-Quds were limited to these activities. I had a friend in Bayt Jala called 'Isa Atallah whom I befriended back when I was at Dar al-Mu'allimin. He was a principal at the school, I used to pay him a visit and spend a few days at his home. In Bayt Jala, I met the priest Iskandar al-Khuri ... Iskandar al-Baytjali ... Iskandar Haddad, who hailed from Marj'ayun in Lebanon. I also met Iskandar al-Khuri al-Baytjali once or twice...[30]

The poet?
The poet. However, there was not much going on as Bayt Jala was small. If I heard about a visitor coming, I would go and hear him speak. In those days, al-Quds had not yet become a cultural hub. Al-Qahira [Cairo] overshadowed Palestine. Everything came to us from al-Qahira. When I was in 'Akka, I read *al-Muqtataf* [*The Digest*] and *al-Hilal* [*The Crescent*], and subscribed to both of them. I also read *al-Siyasa al-Usbu'iyya* [*The Politics Weekly*] during the years it was published in, as well as *al-Muqattam*;[31] and the Palestinian newspapers I read were *Filastin* [*Palestine*], *al-Jami'a al-'Arabiyya* [*The Arab Union*] and when Faruqi created *al-Jami'a al-Islamiyya* [*The Muslim Union*], I read it as well. But I must admit that during that period, we were greatly influenced by what was going on in Cairo. For instance, I read every critique written about Taha Husayn's book *Fi al-Shi'r*

al-Jahili [*On Pre-Islamic Poetry*], whether it was published in books or magazines.[32] Such things used to come from there. The distance that separated us from Cairo, however, never prevented my cultural growth. The situation changed when I went to live in al-Quds. After I returned from England in 1939 and after teaching at al-Kulliyya al-'Arabiyya and al-Kulliyya al-Rashidiyya, al-Quds had become my centre. There was a greater opportunity to get in contact with people by then. My connection with Khalil al-Sakakini resumed to an even greater extent. I used to visit him at his home with Georges Khamis, who was my teacher at Dar al-Mu'allimin and later became my colleague at al-Kulliyya al-'Arabiyya. I used to attend lectures given at the YMCA and there were other clubs which organised lectures. It was an active period; there was the Young Men's Muslim Association and magazines were being published. They were being published before, of course, but I hadn't been aware of them. There was *al-Nafa'is al-'Asriyya* [*The Contemporary Poets*] magazine whose owner was Khalil Baydas. He was one of the first to have translated novels from the Russian because he studied in Russia. He was from al-Nasira, you know.

Yes.

I had become a part of the cultural milieu back then. My colleagues at al-Kulliyya al-'Arabiyya were 'Abd al-Rahman Bushnaq, Jamil 'Ali and so on but the person who became my friend was Ishaq Musa al-Husayni.[33] This friendship continued there and when I came back from England in 1959 ... 1949, Ishaq Musa al-Husayni was appointed to teach at the university and we became colleagues for a long time there.

Was it at the American University?
Pardon?

At the American University of Beirut.
Yes, yes, in any case it was the only one there...

Anis Sayigh
born 1931 in Tabariyya, Palestine
Interview with Mahmoud Zeidan
Beirut, 2003

20'–33'04"

Mahmoud Zeidan: Let us go back to the school system. Can you tell me about your experience at al-Tabariyya School? Can you describe the school to me?
Anis Sayigh: It was a government school. The most primary education among Arabs in Palestine was governmental. It was the opposite to here in Lebanon, or in other countries. Ninety per cent of Palestinian Arabs who were born in the 1920s, 1930s and 1940s studied in government schools. These had high standards and offered seven years of schooling, from first grade to seventh grade. There were no pre-schools; there were no kindergartens at the time. After seventh grade, students would go to al-Quds, Yafa or Haifa. Tabariyya … Secondary school started after I had already left, in 1946, and it lasted for one year until Tabariyya fell. In my days, and like most towns, Tabariyya only offered primary schooling. Seven years, seven grades, each year was divided into three terms: the first, the second and the third. At the end of each term, there were exams and the announcement of final grades. As a side note, during these seven years, there were 21 exams for 21 terms, and I came first in all 21 of them. And when I received my diploma at the end of the seventh year, at the end of school, the principal wrote – his name was Tal'at al-Sayfi, Mr Tal'at al-Sayfi, I'll tell you more about him in a bit – he wrote, 'This is the only student in all the government schools in Palestine as far as I know,' he made sure to be cautious, 'who came first of his class in all seven years, and every year in all three terms.' Tal'at al-Sayfi participated in the national movement in Yafa. He would write, deliver speeches and attend demonstrations, so the British detained him many times. They knew he was a man of science and education, so they exiled him to Tabariyya. His appointment to Tabariyya was a downgrade, since they had placed him in a small town. Instead of him becoming the principal of a secondary school in al-Quds or Yafa or Haifa, he became a primary school principal in Tabariyya. In that school, he practised his nationalism openly, even though it was frowned upon and he was under surveillance.

As for our education … the first three years were in Arabic. In the fourth year, we would study English as well. Mathematics and other subjects would start becoming more difficult in fourth grade. So the first three years were easy. In order to learn the Arabic language, we started with *sarf wa*

93

nahw.[34] I remember the very first day of the fourth year; we had a teacher whose name was Tawfiq Wahba, who was the Arabic language teacher. He wrote *al-bustanu jamilun* [The garden is beautiful] on the chalkboard. And then, *kana al-bustanu jamilan* [The garden was beautiful]; and *inna al-bustana jamilun* [The garden is beautiful indeed]. It all looked strange to us ... *Kana wa akhawatuha.*[35] How to decline *al-mubtada* [the subject] and *al-khabar* [the predicate]? *Inna wa akhawatuha*, who were the 'sisters'? *Inna, anna, lakinna, layta* and *la'alla* ... I still remember them! The fourth grade was the beginning of a serious education in *sarf wa nahw*, and it was the case with language class, English, history and geography, all of which interested me a lot. Although I was always weak in mathematics, I kept succeeding and I was top of my class. When I came to the American University [of Beirut], first-year students were not separated into either science or literature. Freshman year, the first year, offered the same education for everybody. The second, third and fourth years – after which you would get a BA – were split into a literary section and a scientific section, and I chose literature, of course. During my first year, freshman year, I was learning mathematics, physics and chemistry, and I always came last in all of them! I would get As in Arabic, English, history and geography, and sociology ... And I would get Fs in the sciences. That's why my average grade was not as high as when I was in Tabariyya.

Were there any girls in your school in Tabariyya?
No! There was the boys' school on one side and the girls' school on the other, and there was a distance of half a kilometre, or three-quarters of a kilometre, between them. It was very different back then, there were no mixed schools. Even in al-Quds, the Sahyun secondary school was not mixed. When I came to Sayda in February, it was not mixed. Only the American University was mixed, but even the first year there was not co-ed either. In our sophomore year, there were about 100 males and three females. The female presence was very limited.

Tell me about other difficulties you faced in school.
In Tabariyya, there were no difficulties because I was at the top of my class even in the scientific subjects. In al-Quds, my biggest problem was the weather. Tabariyya is a very warm city. In al-Quds, you could wake up in the morning and suddenly find snow on the street. I was not mentally prepared for cold weather. And I had a disease in my fingers – I had fingers at the time (he points to his maimed left-hand fingers), they would get swollen. The doctor back then, it was in 1946 or 1947, prescribed a black ointment

and that I should bandage my hands; I kept trying to avoid touching my bed sheet so that it would not become black. So I greatly suffered from the weather, as well as from physical education class. I have never been sporty in my life and I am still not. In Tabariyya, we didn't have sports classes, so it wasn't a problem. In al-Quds, I had to play soccer and basketball and so forth, and it was my most hated thing. So I would ask my mother for a medical note, which she would get the doctor to sign, saying that my health did not permit me to play sports. The teachers found it surprising! And when I came to Sayda, it was the same. The biggest problem was when we had to play soccer on days when the weather was nice. And I dislike soccer. I dislike all kinds of sports.

What was the name of your school in al-Quds?
In al-Quds, Bishop Gobat. Bishop: B-I-S-H-O-P – you know, *mutran*. Gobat: G-O-B-A-T. The school of *mutran* Gobat, which was established in 1860 or 1870, was among the first secondary schools in Palestine. As for Arabic, there was the Sahyun school, located in Jabal Sahyun, south of al-Quds, between al-Quds and Bethlehem. So if you were going to Bethlehem, you would drive by it, although the school was on top of a mountain and the road was in the valley. From the school, around the end of 1946, 1947, when the Arab–Zionist conflict began, we would carry stones on us and whenever we saw Jewish cars, we knew they were Jewish – they were not that far below – from the drivers' faces … We would throw stones at them. Those were my first contributions to national agitation, if you can call it that.

Could anybody from Tabariyya attend that school?
No. In the 1920s, the Palestinian government founded Dar al-Mu'allimin (Teachers' College) in al-Quds. A few years later, its name changed to al-Kulliyya al-'Arabiyya (the Arab College). It was the highest-ranking secondary institute in Palestine, and probably in the whole Arab world. This institute only accepted top primary students from governmental primary schools. Being from a governmental school, as well as a top student, guaranteed one's attendance at al-Kulliyya al-'Arabiyya, which had a total of 90 students only. So, in the first year, 30 students were accepted, and not more. The institute prepared them for the matriculation exam, the matriculation diploma at the end of the fourth year. Not one student failed the matriculation exam from the year the institute was established until 1948. The last exams were taken in 1947, or at the beginning of 1948, and no student ever failed the exam because they were all top students. The competition was fierce, there was the top student from Tabariyya, and the top student

from al-Nasira, and the top one from Safad, and from al-Quds, and from Bi'r-as-Sab' who all attended the institute; they were all in the same class. So the competition was intense among the top students who excelled, the elite, so to speak. And they were truly an elite, in that about 20 students from that school became professors at the American University, after 1948 – 20 students from the same institute! At the moment, Dr Muhammad Yusif Najm is writing a book about the Kulliyya, and how this elite school functioned. My brother Tawfiq, who was the top student in Tabariyya, was accepted to the Kulliyya. Four years later, when my brother Munir, who was first in Tabariyya, applied, they said they did not accept brothers. However, they made him take the exam and enrolled him, even though my brother Tawfiq had graduated from there. They don't usually take brothers, in order to leave room, for a greater number. When I graduated, they said, 'A third brother, no way'. In the whole history of al-Kulliyya al-'Arabiyya, only three brothers were ever permitted to graduate: Muhammad Yusif Najm and two of his older brothers. They were all top students, and some political circumstances allowed for the British to enrol them. No three brothers ever attended again. So, when they asked that I enter the college, the doors were closed to me since two of my brothers had attended, Tawfiq and then Munir, who was still a student there when I went to al-Quds, he was still a student at al-Kulliyya al-'Arabiyya. I was very happy I wasn't accepted because I knew from my brother Tawfiq and my brother Munir how very strict the College was, in its regulations and practices. Because everyone was a top student, they were prohibited from staying up late, prohibited, prohibited … there was a whole list of restrictions. You had to be the first and stay the first, and succeed in the matriculation. They lived inside a nightmare. So I was happy they had not accepted me.

Another side story: the school I attended required me to wear a green jacket and grey trousers, a 'uniform', they called it; all British schools required it. And because Tawfiq was always telling us how his studies were so intense and the regulations so strict, and because Munir after him said the same things, I developed a complex about school. The school emblem and the jacket were green, so I developed a complex about the colour green. Since the 1940s until this very minute, I cannot stand the colour green…

(He laughs) I'm not wearing green…
I'm not wearing my glasses at the moment … I've been married for 45 years and there is no way that anything green could ever enter our house. If a bouquet has green, ok, it would be normal. But it would be impossible for a jacket, a tie, my wife's dress or any household object to ever be green, impossible.

Figure 4   ʿAbdullah Husayn in front of Ranana Police Office,
Palestine, circa 1945. Courtesy of the Nakba Archive.

PART II

The British Mandate and Palestinian and Arab Resistance

5

Motivations and Tensions of Palestinian Police Service Under British Rule

Alex Winder

The Palestine Police was established in 1920, as Britain's post-First World War military administration of Palestine (via the Occupied Enemy Territory Administration or OETA) transitioned to a civilian administration, granted as a Mandate by the League of Nations but colonial in all but name. Over the force's nearly three decades of existence, it expanded massively, transformed in structure and became increasingly central to debates over the goals and effectiveness of British administration in Palestine. It was originally structured along the lines of other British colonial police forces, with a small British officer corps commanding locally recruited officers and other ranks. By the end of 1921, for example, 38 British officers oversaw a force of 54 local (Muslim, Christian and Jewish) officers and 1,133 local lower ranks, about 90 per cent of whom were Palestinian Muslims and Christians.[1] Palestinian discontent with the Mandate, which committed British support to establishing a Jewish national home in Palestine, periodically erupted into anti-colonial unrest and intercommunal violence, prompting massive increases in British personnel and the incorporation of Zionist paramilitary groups into police auxiliary units.[2]

The Palestine Police thus became less representative, and more repressive, of the population among which it operated. This transformation is most apparent during the 1936–39 revolt, when Britons surpassed Palestinian Arabs as the force's largest demographic component. From the end of 1935 to the end of 1938, the number of Palestinian Arab policemen remained steady (hovering at around 1,500), while the number of Jewish policemen more than doubled (from over 300 to over 700) and the number of British police more than tripled (from nearly 800 to nearly 2,500). The police brass marginalised Arab policemen and mobilised British and Jewish policemen and auxiliaries to crush the Palestinian uprising.[3] By 1939, some

16,000 Jewish colonists had been recruited into the Jewish Settlement Police, paramilitary units largely acknowledged as a front for the Haganah.[4]

After brutally suppressing the Palestinian revolt in 1939, Britain's priorities were redirected by the outbreak of the Second World War. The Palestine Police supported the British military in Palestine, guarding infrastructure (railroads, ports, pipelines), patrolling borders and monitoring potential 'enemies' (including Germans and Italians, as well as Arabs who hoped the war would diminish Britain), among other tasks. In the war's wake, the police became embroiled in the tense, often brutal, conflict between British security forces and Zionist organisations, especially the more radical Irgun and Lehi.[5] The number of British policemen increased further, consistently topping 3,700 in the Mandate's final years, as did the number of Palestinian Arabs, which hovered around 2,500 in this period. The number of Jewish regular policemen ranged from 650–750, supplemented by 13,000–15,000 Jewish Settlement Police.

When Britain announced its intention to leave Palestine in 1948, the Palestine Police were drawn into the conflict for Palestine's future. The roles of Palestine's policemen in this period, and their post-1948 trajectories, reflect the fractured nature of the force and the divergent futures of its different parts. British policemen protected British citizens and property in anticipation of retreat and, after 1948, were transferred across the British Empire to quell liberation struggles from Malaya to Kenya.[6] Jewish policemen supplied intelligence, materiel and manpower to Zionist militias, and formed the core of the Israel Police after 1948. Many Palestinian policemen joined Arab efforts to defend Palestine in 1948, some in leadership positions.[7] With the failure of these efforts, the dismemberment of the Palestinian body politic and forced displacement of hundreds of thousands of Palestine's Arab inhabitants was a catastrophe that Palestinian policemen experienced alongside their compatriots from other walks of life.

The geographic and professional dispersal of these Palestinian policemen may explain the relatively meagre scholarly attention they have received. The Palestine Police's Britons figure in histories of empire and decolonisation, and its Jewish police exemplify Israeli narratives of institution building and state formation. Employed by an institution best known for its repression of the 1936–39 revolt, however, Palestinian Arab policemen do not fit comfortably within nationalist or anti-imperialist Palestinian historiographies.[8] Oral histories of former Palestine Policemen offer insights into the experiences of tens of thousands of Palestinians who served during the Mandate period, providing nuanced portraits of Arab police service frequently reduced to mere statistics or characterised alternatively as acquiescent (in Palestinian nationalist narratives) or obstructive (in dominant British and Israeli narratives) to imperial or Zionist objectives. They help answer basic, but crucial, questions: Who were the Palestinians that served in the Mandate police? What were their backgrounds and why did they join? How did they understand their work? And how did it figure into their social, professional and national identification?

Palestinians from various social classes served in the Palestine Police. For members of notable families and educated elites, police service was an opportunity to advance within a quasi-state infrastructure – whether to the top echelons of the Palestine Police or by using police service as a stepping stone towards more prestigious or better paying positions.[9] The majority of the Palestinian Arabs in the Palestine Police's lower ranks, meanwhile, came from working-class and agrarian backgrounds, seeking a steady pay cheque in times of economic turmoil and insecurity. These paths to police service are in many ways exemplified by Ahmad Agha and 'Umar Shihada, whose histories appear here. Ahmad Agha – interviewed in a suit and tie and a dapper fedora – came from a landowning family in Tarshiha, north-east of Acre, and was educated at the prestigious St Luke's School in Haifa. He had been preparing to become a lawyer but, after seeing youths from Tarshiha undergoing police training, was moved by their virility and enlisted in the Palestine Mobile Force ('out of love for masculinity', as he puts it). 'Umar Shihada – interviewed in a robe and headdress – describes growing up in Qabba'a village, north-east of Safad, where agricultural labour – tough work for meagre pay – predominated. After the 1936–39 revolt, Shihada found employment with the British military and, after the Second World War, like many Palestinians likewise employed (as drivers, cooks, messengers and other non-combat roles), he transitioned into the Palestine Police. 'There was no work back home, then,' Shihada recalls.

'It was better to be employed and gain a salary than to remain in the fields throughout the year … We used to make 33 lira and 3 mils in the police. We took 6 lira per week in the army. We were surviving. That's how it was then.

Police records from the close of the Mandate indicate that the most common former profession of Palestinian policemen was farmer or *fellah*; the second most common single prior 'profession' recorded was 'student', and nearly 10 per cent of the records show previous employment attached in some capacity to the military or police.[10] There may not be a singular 'typical' profile of a Palestinian policeman – recruits hailed from across geographic Palestine and fit varying socio-economic profiles – but Agha and Shihada are far from outliers. Indeed, the Palestine Police was one of the few public institutions that brought together such a diverse cross-section of Mandate Palestine society, including not only Britons, Jews and Arabs, but also rural and urban Palestinians of different social statuses and degrees of education.

Despite deep frustration with the British administration and its support for Zionism, Palestinians in the police tended to see their role as one that combined personal improvement, community service and national duty. As an avenue for social mobility on an individual scale, the Palestine Police offered training and education, including physical drills that instilled the kind of masculine discipline that Ahmad Agha found attractive, as well as instruction in English – both Agha and Shihada pepper their oral histories with words or snippets of dialogue in English, as if describing their service returned them to a bilingual state of being – and law.[11] On a communal and national scale, however, it is difficult to disentangle the Palestine Police, like other imperial police forces, from issues of political control and suppression of movements for national liberation. This may be particularly true for Palestine, where such struggles are ongoing.

Most Palestinian policemen, however, saw no contradiction between their police service and their commitment to their communities or nation. Arab policemen could incur their compatriots' wrath or disdain if perceived as overzealous in pursuit of Palestinian patriots, or as unduly servile to British or Jewish officers.[12] Police service in and of itself, however, was not universally reviled. Ahmad Agha dismisses suggestions that other Palestinians might look askance at Palestinian policemen: 'What was there to say? They were employees. They didn't accuse them of treason.' 'Umar Shihada, moreover, describes how Palestinian policemen could use their position to advocate for their countrymen or spare them certain injustices. Shihada describes several cases in which he saved Palestinians from the three-year sentence for firearm possession. He clearly takes pride in helping a suspect surreptitiously dispose of a pistol via a teapot, recounting the anecdote as evidence of both patriotism and cleverness. 'What's the use of taking him and imprisoning him,' he asks, referring to the suspect. 'Of what use is he to me? He's an Arab with a gun; he's a young man. That was also one good deed I did.'

Despite the role of the Palestine Police in crushing the 1936–39 revolt, Palestinians like Shihada and Agha had no difficulty squaring their police service with admiration for the revolt and its leaders. (Shihada even joined the revolt as a teen.) This was made easier by the contentious relationship between the British administration and the Zionist movement in the Mandate's final years. Agha, for example, speaks at length about police patrols to halt unlawful Jewish immigration into Palestine. 'They didn't have documents or anything of the sort,' Agha recalls. 'You just saw a rented boat full of people stuck at the [Haifa] port. We often turned them away, returning Jews on the same boat back to Cyprus.' However ineffective, the police were undertaking practical steps to counter Zionism. When Britain announced its plan to leave Palestine, and the looming battle between Zionist and Arab forces began to materialise, Palestinian policemen were central to local and national defence efforts. A number assumed prominent roles in armed forces like Jaysh al-Jihad al-Muqadas (Holy War Army) led by 'Abd al-Qadir al-Husayni; many more took their service weapons and returned to their homes to defend their families, neighbours and countrymen from Zionist armed forces.[13]

It is hardly naïve, nor does it assume naiveté on the part of Palestinian policemen, to see the Palestine Police as something more than the coercive arm of the British imperial state, or even to imagine it as an institution that, in certain regards, served Palestine's Arab communities. Enlistment often had immediate personal motivations – economic and social mobility foremost among them – but police service was never only an individual act. Training, patrols and service forged shared professional identifications among police, and interactions with the public – complainants, witnesses, lawbreakers, victims and bystanders – shaped popular understandings and expectations of justice and good governance. Oral histories of former members of the Palestine Police help illuminate these complex processes, which are so crucial to understanding Palestinian society during and after the Mandate period.

Ahmad Agha
born 1930 in Tarshiha, Palestine
Interview with Bushra Mughrabi
Burj al-Barajneh, Beirut, 2004

14'10"–27'14"

Bushra Mughrabi: *What were the subjects that you learned in school?*
Ahmad Agha: Arabic, English, maths, everything … Those who graduated from the Tarshiha school were cultured. As my time at the Tarshiha
school came to an end, I started thinking about how I was going to build
myself a future. I was young when the agricultural crisis and its difficulties hit, so my mother suggested taking me to stay with my cousin, who
was a brilliant lawyer in Haifa back then, thinking he'd set me up there. So I
stayed with him. My cousin asked me, 'What do you want?' I told him, 'Any
job.' 'What do you want to learn, my boy? Do you want to go wash dishes?'
He was a generous man. He took me in as you would a child and gave me
a job at his office while I studied at St Luke's, at St Luke's School in Haifa,
which was one of the best and most important schools in northern Palestine. It was a private school, just like the American University [of Beirut]. I
stayed there until year three of secondary school, when I was 16 years old,
I think. Back then you used to ask for permission to go home during Eid
or other holidays. Once, I was coming back, carrying my backpack and
books, wearing shorts, a school uniform and I stumbled upon a gathering
of youths from Tarshiha. 'What's going on?' I asked them and they told me
that there was a military training. I stood among them, talking to them …
The recruiting officer picked me out of the group and asked me, 'Would
you like to join the army?' I told him, 'Yes, I am prepared to be a man.' He
replied, 'Ok, the next meeting will be in Nazareth.' In al-Nasira. So we went,
and once there, he said, 'You'll go to your training school in Bisan.' So we
did the training school. What's the name of the group I was telling you
about? The group that the British created to fight against Jewish terrorism.
This group was called PMF, Palestine Mobile Force. After that, we graduated and they transferred us to the perilous regions. They briefly took me to
Haifa where I settled, and later, they moved me to Jenin.

Were you all Arab students at the training school?
Yes, Arabs. The training there consisted of a foot drill – meaning exercises
– then armed drill, then musketry, then tactics. It was a very good training.
A person would come out of it equipped to handle many situations.

How many years were you there for?

It was six months of training, from the early morning ... You'd wake up and do sports until the evening, then rest and eat in the afternoon. They transferred me to Jenin, to the headquarters of the Palestinian Defence Force.

This Force, this school you enrolled in, did you go so you could train for a career or was it just on a whim?

Out of love for masculinity. In anticipation of the situation. I was studying to become a lawyer under the direction of my cousin Jamal Hamid, who was like a father to me. I loved him very much. But I found myself financially dependent on him, among other things, and our financial situation in Tarshiha did not help so I preferred it. In the end, they transferred us to Sarona camp in Tel Aviv, where I was a soldier for some time.[14] I became an officer in charge as well as the military camp's translator in Sarona camp. That's where the painful tragedies happened.

We would go on night patrols against the cowardly Jews. The Jews were cowards; we would catch them in the streets sending women to seduce us. They would stand at the door of the camp and throw bombs at us. We would set out to capture them ... on a few occasions. That's war for you; ours was against Jewish terrorism. There was a guy, Menachem Begin, at one point when I was in the camp with the British.[15] There were 16 British men in the section with me. A fellow wearing a policeman's uniform was in a P.T. car, the one with the telephone, and it was parked.[16] He asked, 'Does anybody speak English in here?' I answered, 'Me, what's wrong?' He said, 'We're going to park the car here,' and I replied, 'That's not for me to decide. It's forbidden, there is another man who is responsible for this place, you have to see him.' He went to a British officer who gave them permission to park, the English guy allowed them to park in the camp. Menachem Begin asked me, 'Are you Arab, or British, or what?' He was short and I didn't know who he was, I thought he was part of security.

Was he in the same camp as you?

In the same camp, inside. He was with P.T. but I thought he was part of security coming with the mail, and we suddenly lost sight of him, we couldn't find him anymore. The Jew had left the camp. A British officer came and said to me, 'What are you doing there?' I said, 'Nothing, Sir.' 'Get inside,' he told me. He outranked me. I wanted to walk into the camp and there was a tap where I wanted to wash my hands. And suddenly, the whole camp shook. It was destroyed. All 16 British men who stayed in the room with me were killed and 20 buildings were demolished.[17] Trutwein, the British officer that I told you about, was on the third floor. He was also killed and his feet dangled from the roof. They rescued me from among the dead and wounded; I was considered dead, under the rubble. They put me in the medical inspection room. I woke up and found myself among a number of dead men. This was a tragedy.

Was the explosion caused by a bomb that someone had placed?
It was an explosive device, a car bomb.

Was it the same car that you said they wanted to park in there?
That was the one that did it, that one flew, it was booby-trapped. They came and asked, 'Any damage in here?' With the telephone, for example. I told them we didn't have any. So they went and got permission from someone else – not me – a British officer, and he allowed them to park it, so 16 people perished … no, 20.

Were they British?
There were camps all over and the Sarona camp was German.

I meant the ones who died, were they British or Arab?
They were British; they were all British. Those who died in the room with me were all British, the only Arab among them was me and I survived. I survived but I was wounded.

What was the British men's reaction when they found out?
You know the British hubbub. The British went out on patrols, there was chaos; they sent out tanks, patrols and generals; that was what happened. And after a while, they settled down, I don't know why – conspiracy, or silence or reconciliation.

Do you know the names of some of the people who died? The British men who died in the camp?
There was a man called Johnson, I don't remember all those names.

During your service, how were your relations as an Arab with the British officers in charge?
Very good. I treated them well, like brothers. When I went to the cafeteria, they'd say, 'Here comes the generous man.' At some point, I found they acted in one way and then in another. How did the Jews trick them? By way of women. The officers who came out of the camp with me were bribed by

the Jews with temptations; they would corrupt them, to the point where if someone was your friend 100 per cent until then, he might no longer be. These were the Jewish tactics...

How long did you stay at the job?
Two years from when I was 16 years old. They disbanded the group around that time. They disbanded the PMF that I was telling you about. I was still at Sarona camp. They picked me with eight other Arabs. They told us, 'You are being transferred to Haifa but not as a mobile force. You'll join as an additional police force, immigration, and you'll go as additional police,' where? On ships, against Jewish immigration.

So we went to Haifa for two, three months or more after they disbanded the group and we boarded the small boats and undertook searches for illegal Jewish immigrants. This one time, a Jewish man asked me while I was on a boat, 'Where are the explosions coming from?' And I told him they were coming from that area that belongs to the Jews. Another one, Jewish, named Musa, who pretended to be a friend, he was a captain in the British army with me, told me...

Musa what?
Oh, I don't know. So he told me, 'Listen, I'll crush you and the biggest British man with my boot. This is not your time or the British's time. Tell the truth, the explosions are coming from the Arab regions, in Wadi Rush-miyya or whatever, or else you can spend the night in the sea,' meaning that he would cut me up and throw me into the sea. I stayed until the group was disbanded. I was very cautious especially when I went to receive my severance pay. I didn't want to go by land to Tarshiha because I didn't know if they had blocked the roads, so I decided to go by sea, going from 'Akka to Haifa to receive my severance pay from the British in a boat.

Did you quit or did they let you go?
They let me go – a while before the British left.

How much did they pay you?
I was paid 22 Palestinian lira.

What did people say about those who served in the British army?
That they're earning a living. What was there to say? They were employees. They didn't accuse them of treason.

Did they accept the idea that someone…
Of course. They were employees. They're British … Where would you work? Let's take somebody well educated – he was either a schoolteacher or an officer. No, he wasn't accused of treason. So we came back to Tarshiha after some time; that was the tragedy.

1h 11'51"– 1h 14'15"

You told me earlier that when you were employed by the British, you would go to the port and seek out the Jewish immigrants who had arrived. Did you ever send immigrants back to where they came from?
When I was asked, 'Where are we and why are we here?' I would explain to them, 'They are attacking the others, they are thieves more than people, it's not their land.' I used to explain to them, I had the guts, so I was almost put on the Jews' blacklist. They were the aggressors in the port.

What kind of documents did they have with them?
They didn't have any documents or anything of the sort. You just saw a rented boat full of people stuck at the port. We often turned them away, returning Jews on the same boat back to Cyprus. They set up camps to continue the procedures, the British would complete their procedures as immigrants and provide them with papers and send them again legally. But it was arbitrary at first.

What was the document they gave them?
They would give them a Palestinian passport.

Palestinian?
Yes.

So that they are considered residents of Palestine?
Yes, residents of the region.

Did you have the power to send people back?
Never. We gave our notes on that. We only gave our remarks, we would say, 'It's not regular.'

Were there any clashes between you and the British when they noticed that you were becoming aware of this?
There was nothing we could do. We had no say. We were bound by silence and there was nothing more we could do.

Didn't they replace you with British officers for example? Did they push you away as Arabs?
No. As I said, this was a six-month transitional period. News of our release came suddenly. We were stationed at the Haifa port and we weren't allowed to go to town because it had been demolished. When we went there, it was as if we were crying over ruins.

What year was this?
In the beginning of 1948.

'**Umar Shihada**
born 1922 in Qabba'a, Palestine
Interview with Mahmoud Zeidan
Tal'abaya, al-Biqa', 2004

9'04"–11'45"

Mahmoud Zeidan: *Was there anyone from Qabba'a who had completed his education and later received a higher diploma elsewhere? Who finished their education and left?*
'**Umar Shihada**: There was one among us, his name was Husayn 'Ali al-Rifa'i … His father took him to Safad, where he received an education. He went as far as his baccalaureate, as the brevet … I mean the baccalaureate, sixth grade. That's it. He spoke English. Other than him, there was nobody.

What did he work in later?
He worked as a policeman. He went to the police in the end. There was no work back home, then. It was better to be employed and gain a salary than to remain in the fields throughout the year. The season did not yield anything. It didn't make you money. So you had to go and get a job for 10, 20, 30 lira … We used to make 33 lira and 3 mils in the police. We took 6 lira per week in the army. We were surviving. That's how it was then. We took care of the reaping and harvesting, that work. We baled the hay in the barn. My father would take us down to the *rawzana* to stack the hay and we'd come out suffocating. And if you didn't go, you'd get spanked and you'd work. That's the peasant's way. We fed the cows at night; we covered the hay late at night and we fed them dinner. We herded them during the day in time for dinner. You had to wake up early to herd them, too. That's another thing. People used to leave this job. And the British didn't have any jobs for us, no factories, nothing in the country. That was Palestine. When I turned 13 years old, the 1936 revolution happened. I took a rifle and went to the revolution. I caught up with the revolution and told myself that it was easier than working with hay or in the fields. I joined the revolution with 'Abdallah al-Asbah, Mahmud al-'Uthman Abu Sultan, Abu 'Atif al-Mughrabi, he was a leader against the British in our region. Against the Jews, that is. We prevented the Jews from farming for six years … In six years, not one court opened for them to complain. We ran our own courts. The revolution tried criminals, traitors and collaborators, and executed them.

Let us talk about this some more. I want you to tell me what kind of work there was in Qabba'a?
There were only peasants, no one else.

Do you mean no one else worked there?
A merchant, you mean? No, there was none. There a [slurred] ... and an olive press. Those who came at the end of the year for the olive curing, worked at the press and were paid in oil.

29'21"–31'31"

Did you benefit from the training at the time?
I benefitted from the arms training, being a driver and handling weapons. I received a military training. We saw the bombs being dropped by planes; we saw it. This was different from the revolt; it was more intense. We used to wear masks; they gave us masks, and gave us whatever weapons were available. They used to give us decent food and decent clothing. The soldier was precious to them. The machine or the tank could be blown up, as long as the soldier was still alive. The soldier was more precious to them than a plane or a tank.

At the end, when we finished, they took us from Port Sa'id to Rishon [LeZion] near Tel Aviv to rest. We stayed in Rishon for one year. In Rishon, they told us, 'The war is over, it's over, go back to your homes.'

They gave each one of us a civilian suit, with a tie, a trench coat, a hat and a ticket fare. 'Where are you from? Going to Qabba'a, Safad? Here's an Egged bus ticket, it will take you home.'

They gave each of us 15 lira of pocket money. After a while, they called for us to get our severance. I went to Safad and got my severance. He asked me: 'What do you want to work in now that you've finished the army?' and I said, 'I want to go to the police. I don't want to go back home.'

'Do you want to work with the police?' he asked and I said, 'yes'. They wrote my name down, gave me a piece of paper and sent me to Haifa. Once there, I went to the police headquarters on al-Muluk Street. We had already served in the army, but they taught us about the law. We had served and received arms training, but the legal training taught us how to engage with civilians and how to deal with them. So we did a training session and I became a corporal with two stripes.

41'55"–55'50"

You told me that when the war ended, they trained you in the law...
In the law, they trained us in the law.

Tell me about what you were taught about the law.
The law, for example, how when we entered a town and found two people fighting, we were meant to gather them and take them to the *mukhtar*, and make them reconcile. Or if someone was wanted by the state, we'd go and bring him in.

Our trainer in al-Quds was Sulayman Sa'id who was from Nablus and head of the police force. He said, 'If you were taking someone for an execution and found another drowning in the sea, the river, what would you do? There is no tree around'. We told him, 'If there's a tree, we'll tie the one we're taking to be executed to the tree.' He said, 'There are no trees. You're on a land where there are no trees, nothing. What do you do?' So I replied, 'We release the one to be executed and save the one who is dying.'

'Why?' he asked.

I told him, 'Because the one who is still alive is more important than the one who is dead. Wherever the prisoner would go, at the end of the day we'd catch him. The state will capture and bring him in, but the one dying we can't bring back.'

He gave me a ribbon for it and told me, 'Yes, that's correct. Your answer is correct.'

Where would the wanted man go? We need to save the other one from dying. I told them, 'We release the wanted prisoner, he has nowhere to go, the state will capture him.'

I served in al-Khalil, Bayt Jibrin and Gaza. They placed us there, those of us from the northern regions, and those who came from there in the north; we didn't serve in our own areas. When I was in al-Khalil towards the end, we were told that it was over in 1948; the British said they were leaving, Britain was leaving.

'Where will you go?'

'Each one to his village.' They gave us each a rifle and took us to al-Ja'una near Rosh Pina. Only a few metres separated us from Rosh Pina.

But before your work was over … Tell me more about what the police like you did about the army.
The police.

Tell me, what did they also train you in? Like these questions, for example, and...
The law ... questions about the law.

What were the questions?
How to deal with people. How to deal with ... the government. How to deal with ... traffic laws. If there was a driver who violated the law, you'd write him a ticket. And that was it; we left afterwards.

When you went to arrest someone, for instance...,
When we went to fetch a wanted person, we used to search houses and take the *mukhtar* with us. We took the *mukhtar* with us, that was our law. We went with the *mukhtar*, searched the house and after we were done search-ing the house, we asked the owner to write down that nothing was missing and he would sign with us. The *mukhtar* would then sign and stamp the sig-nature. If the owner complained and said that we had taken gold or money or something, our papers would be already signed.

If someone refused to comply or go with you, did they teach you how to bring them in?
By force! By force! We handcuffed and beat him. Refuse? He couldn't refuse. This was an order from the military police, the police. You had to bring him in. It was like the police are now; they beat the person who doesn't comply. He'd be beaten and we'd shoot him in the foot, not his chest. It had to be in the foot, it was not about killing him.

What else did they teach you that you benefitted from while working in the police force, like the law, for instance?
With regard to the law, for instance, we learned how to treat people well and with morals. If someone was drunk, you shouldn't beat him. Bring him in and give him coffee to sober him up, afterwards take him to court and try him. You couldn't beat him up. Beating up someone who was drunk or high in the cafés was forbidden. We would approach them at restaurants and shops in a humane way. We would sweet-talk him before we brought him in. If he did anything to resist, we'd beat him up. If he did not comply or if he held up a knife, we'd beat him up as well. We'd bring the whip out and that was that.

Do you remember an incident taking place in a city or village when you were sent out to bring someone in and the whole thing got out of hand?

No one ever said anything when the police came to the villages. People didn't say a word. They all feared the British. We used to be seven or eight men in the car, not just one or two.

What was your role back then?
I was a corporal with two stripes.

Did anything happen in the cities?
No, nothing happened in the cities; we went on patrol. They brought us to Haifa where we patrolled the cafés. We didn't have to pay at the café; we used to drink coffee for free. We went to the movies and rode the bus for free. No one dared to take money from us. It was forbidden not to pay, the law said that we had to pay, but they never took any money from us.

Were there any amusing incidents in the villages or cities during your time at the police? Were there funny moments or funny situations that happened to you while you were out there?
No, nothing like that happened to us. The police went to the *mukhtar*. We used to drink coffee with him and ask him if he had encountered any problems. He gave us names of people and we went to fetch them. The *mukhtar* would tell us he was looking for so-and-so and the watchman would come with us to locate his house and we'd bring the person in. As for funny moments, there weren't any.

What I meant was if there was something that happened by mistake, for example. Did you ever arrest someone by mistake?
No, we never brought in anyone by mistake; it was only by the *mukhtar*'s orders.

Did anyone pull any pranks for example?
If a man was wanted, his name would be registered at the police station for us to fetch him. For instance, if we went to the *mukhtar* and said, 'Mukhtar, we are looking for the son of al-Zaghmut,' he would tell us where the wanted man lived and come along with us to bring him back to the police station to hand him over to the sergeant who would interrogate him. The arrested man would then be transferred to court and, if he wasn't found guilty, he'd be released and be free to go. All we had to do was bring him in. There was an officer at the police station who would interrogate him and who had the authority to transfer him to court or arrest and jail him.

Was he British or Arab?
He was British.

Who was the officer you worked with?
His name was Mr Zlotnik. Mr Zlotnik was his name, and Imray. They were officers. There was someone there who translated for him when he spoke. If anyone came in with a charge, they'd arrest that person and put him in prison for 24 or 48 hours, after which he would be transferred to court. It was forbidden for us to keep him for more than 48 hours at the police post. He would be transferred to court where he would be either charged or found innocent. That's all I know.

Were there any Jews in the police with you?
No, they had their own and we had our own. There were a few, but they didn't come with us. We'd go on patrol with the British and the Jews would go with the British. A British sergeant or British officer would accompany us. There were Arab Jews with us. Some of them used to come in uniform, too, but they were Arab Jews, they were patriotic. The problem solving and coordination, however, was the officer's responsibility, not ours.

Did you resolve any problems in the Jewish neighbourhoods, for example?
We'd go to the Jews. If someone had received a traffic ticket, we would go to the Jewish neighbourhoods. They respected us and everything. The Jewish *mukhtar* used to send the watchman with us, which they called the *shomer* in Hebrew. He'd locate the house of someone who had a ticket and we'd bring him in and collect the payment.

Do you remember what most of the problems were about?
There was a Jew who had a traffic ticket, so we went to the Jewish neighbourhood and informed the *mukhtar*. We went to his house before going to the *mukhtar* and found an old Jewish man there.

Was this in Rishon?
In Rehovot, [no,] near Hadera, in Netanya. I told him we were looking for someone called Pinhas, who was Jewish. He told me he didn't know where his house was and to go to the *mukhtar* who could locate it for us. We went to see the *mukhtar*, who sent the *shomer*, or the watchman, with us. We all went to his house. I saw the old man I found earlier and said we had already asked Abu Dumit; he told me he had nothing to say. He took his daughter to the *shomer* – look how cunning the enemy was. He refused to tell us where

his house was or what his name was. 'It's not in my interest,' he said. When you went to the Arab regions, a hundred people told you who the person was, whose son he was, what he looked like. They always told us where people's houses were, the Arabs.

Were there other incidents such as these?
In al-Khalil, someone from Bayt Jibrin came in to inform on his father. He told us, 'My father has a rifle.' He told me specifically, 'My father has a rifle; it's in the haystack.' I asked him, 'Well what type of rifle is it?' and he said, 'British.' I told him that we would go and bring it in and told him to go away. I informed his father to take the rifle out of the haystack. He took it out and changed its hiding place. We went and searched. The father wanted to give me 10 Palestinian lira. I told him, 'No, my brother.' He replied, 'Are you from Safad?' I told him that I was. He told me, 'You are honourable people.'

What were the 10 Palestinian lira for?
To bribe me. He thought he'd bribe me, because possessing a rifle had a penalty of three years in prison. He wanted to bribe me because I told him to hide the rifle, to move its hiding place. I didn't tell him that his son had told us about it.

Why did his son tell on him?
His father oppressed him. He wanted to marry someone and his father wouldn't allow him to. Those were the Arabs; they were like this. They would tell on each other.

What year was this?
This was in 1943 …1947, 1946 actually. In Bayt Jibrin. They used to tell on each other there.

Were there other stories like these that you remember from your time with the police? Were there other incidents that happened between people?
I was once in Hadera, just sitting there. I was police, a corporal, but it was also normal for me to dress as a civilian. I gardened and planted flowers and things like that. I was sitting outside. The British army drove in … with workers from the region. There was an old man, but the agent accompanying the workers told him to go away, and that there was no work for him today. On the first day I saw him, I was sitting outside, he was turned away. And the same happened on the second day. They kicked him out. So I called out to the old man, I was dressed as a civilian, and I said: 'Come here.'

'What do you want from me, what do you want from me?!' he said.

I told him: 'Let me tell you something...'

So he came towards me, and I said: 'Why did the agent turn you away?'

'My friend, this man is a prick. He wants my daughter and I don't want to give her to him. He is a prick who turns me away and I have four daughters at home, I need to feed them.'

'Bring your food with you tomorrow morning, and I'll let you work.'

'Really?'

'Yes and here's a Palestinian lira from me.'

He came the next day. The other guy said to him, 'Didn't I tell you not to come?'

So I told him, 'No, he's coming.'

'What's it to you?' he replied.

I was dressed as a civilian and I was planting roses at the station. He must have told himself that I was a worker. I told him that he was coming.

'Come here,' I said, 'come here.'

'I don't want to,' he replied.

I called the two soldiers from inside the police station: 'Bring him over,' and they did.

'At your orders, corporal.'

When he heard the word corporal, he was stunned and said: 'At your orders, Sir,' and looked down to the ground.

'You prick, you want his daughter by force and you prevent him from working for four days. Give him four lira.'

He gave him four lira and got a few slaps from me and said, 'I won't ever talk to him again.'

That is one good deed that I did in my life. This thing happened to me, I did a good thing.

The second time, one guy came telling on another guy who was apparently housing two outlaws from Bayt Jibrin.

What do you mean by outlaw?

Revolutionaries who were wanted by the state, they were in his house ... He housed them. The British police chief came at two in the morning and said, 'We are going on a night patrol.' 'Where to?' He said that there were two wanted men we needed to arrest. They were to be executed and were wanted by the state and they were in so-and-so's house. The house was far from town. It was an isolated village house near the fields. It was two in the morning and it started to rain, we left. There were eight of us and when we arrived the light in the house was on, which meant that there were people in it. We arrived and surrounded the house from the outside. It was still raining.

He said: 'Corporal, you open the door.'

The first person to enter was more exposed to danger because the person inside could shoot. A wanted person carries a weapon, right? We busted the door open and we went in. I found an old man sitting there with two young men drinking tea. They had a big yellow teapot on the fire. I told him, 'Police! Don't move!' One of the young men took out his hand from his side, he was holding a gun, he placed it in the teapot. We went inside and surrounded them. 'There's no one here you motherfucker,' I told the British guy. 'Listen here you motherfucker!' I told him, 'Let's wrap this up, it's late and it's muddy, where are the outlaws? It's just an old man and his sons, up late, who don't have work in the morning.'

I held the teapot in my hand and turned towards the son who threw out his gun, 'Take this and make tea for us. Wash it and make us tea, move it!' I said that so he would take the gun outside. He went, took out the pistol and brought back the teapot.

The next day, his father sent me a gift of ghee and honey, and things like that. 'What for?' I asked him. 'Because you saved us from three years of prison,' the young man said. What's the use of taking him and imprisoning him, of what use is he to me? He's an Arab with a gun; he's a young man. That was also one good deed I did. Only God knows.

6

Storying the Great Arab Revolt: Narratives of Resistance During 1936–39

Jacob Norris

The individual testimonies of Salih al-Nasir, Maryam Sabha, Rif'at al-Nimir and 'Abd al-Rahman Sa'ad al-Din remind us just how indispensable oral history is in documenting moments of collective resistance. These accounts both enrich and disrupt our understandings of the Great Arab Revolt of 1936–39, pushing us to ask new questions about the uprising and reminding us to listen to ordinary Palestinians as makers of their own histories.

The four testimonies presented here are emblematic of collective Palestinian memory of the 1936–39 uprising. As living memory of those years begins to fade, established plot lines of this revolutionary episode are passed from generation to generation, reinforced by its central position within the Palestinian collective story. The uprising, known to Palestinians as *al-thawra al-kubra* (the Great Revolution or Revolt), was the first time Palestinians rose up in an organised mass national movement to throw off the British and Zionist colonial occupation. It is not surprising that it has often been referred to as the 'First Intifada', not least when we consider the *thawra's* importance in establishing some of Palestine's most potent national symbolism. The *hata* or *kafiyyeh* checked scarf emerged for the first time during 1936–39 as a symbol of Palestinian resistance, reflecting a specifically rural, peasant identity which had gained control of the uprising by 1937. So, too, did the brutal British repression of the *thawra* establish a precedent by which Palestinians began to be subjected to specific forms of colonial violence that persist to this day – most notably collective punishment and torture, as well as spatial control via a comprehensive system of checkpoints, watchtowers, border walls and militarised zones.

These plot lines can be found in the four oral testimonies presented here, all of which are related by people who lived in rural communities in the 1930s, and who emphasise the uprising as a seminal moment in Palestine's national history. Most strikingly, they all testify to the brutality of British repression of the uprising. Maryam Sabha and ʿAbd al-Rahman Saʿad al-Din, both from the village of al-Zib on the northern coast of Palestine, give us a picture of a British regime prepared to stop at nothing in its efforts to crush the resistance. In Maryam's account, British checkpoints or 'barriers' (*hawajiz*) loom large, hemming in the residents of her village between the mountains and the sea. 'They would kill whoever crossed them [the checkpoints]', she recalls, going on to describe the well-documented British tactic of placing Palestinian prisoners in trucks and trains that were then driven through suspected mine fields – something reinforced by ʿAbd al-Rahman. Maryam describes in poignant detail how ten people from her village were killed and a further ten wounded in one such episode.

ʿAbd al-Rahman's account adds graphic detail to this picture of endemic British violence in and around al-Zib. Many of the grotesque methods of torture and collective punishment he describes have already been reported by historians using various kinds of documentary archives. Waterboarding, foot-whipping, the running of 'gauntlets' between British soldiers administering blows with canes and rifle butts, and the wanton destruction of families' vital supplies of grain and olive oil – all are by now well known to us. But it is only in these harrowing personal accounts that we begin to understand the immense physical and mental suffering they inflicted. By extension, we gain a strong sense of how Palestinians themselves were drawn into a cycle of violence in which acts of brutality become normalised. ʿAbd al-Rahman is quite open about his willingness to administer severe beatings to the Egyptian translator who worked as an informant for the British, as well as his involvement in the laying of mines that killed numerous British soldiers. Given the military imbalance between the two sides, the cycle could only end in disaster for the villagers of al-Zib. There is a harrowing inevitability to ʿAbd al-Rahman's account of how British troops eventually burnt down the entire village, leaving the houses looking like 'a charcoal factory'.

Alongside trauma and destruction, there is a strong sense in these testimonies of the uprising's status as a formative and heroic episode of resistance within the longer Palestinian story. All of the interviewees describe the uprising as *al-thawra* – a word usually translated into English as 'revolution', thus inscribing the events of 1936–39 with greater historical significance and legitimacy than the most commonly used words in English: 'revolt', 'rebellion' or 'disturbances'. In a similar vein, all the confrontations between revolutionaries and the British are remembered as specific 'battles' ('the battle of ʿArrabat al-Batuf', 'the battle of Wadi al-Tufah', etc.), and thereby commemorated as part of a collective historical record rather than simply memories of the past.

These accounts not only confirm certain popular narratives but also speak to recent trends in academic writing on the uprising. In keeping with the broader 'transnational turn', many recent histories of the *thawra* focus on the ways in which fighters, supplies and ideas flowed across the borders of the newly created Mandate jurisdictions.[1] In the interviews, we find examples of families and individuals taking refuge in French-ruled Syria, seeking hospital treatment in Damascus and receiving arms and military training in Transjordan. Historians of the Palestine Mandate have also noted the growth of scouting and athletic associations whose colonial origins were subverted by the local population to create vehicles for national resistance.[2] Rif'at al-Nimir confirms this trend as he describes how scouting was used as a cover for popular military training: 'there was a teacher at the al-Najah school, professor Mamdu al-Sukhun, who would sometimes gather us under the guise of scouts, to go gun training.'

In addition, these accounts are powerful reminders of oral history's ability to open different windows onto the past. One obvious example is the way oral testimony can reveal cracks in national narratives. In his influential book, *Memories of Revolt*, Ted Swedenburg was less interested in using oral sources to determine empirical truths about the uprising of 1936–39, and more concerned with what they can teach us about how national myths and symbols are constructed and reconstructed.[3] For Swedenburg, Palestinian oral testimonies of 1936–39 reveal some of the key internal struggles that have taken place *within* the forging of collective Palestinian memory – in particular those relating to class, gender and 'collaborators'. What exactly were revolutionaries fighting for in 1936–39, and why did some Palestinians choose to collaborate with the British?

It should come as little surprise, then, that the following interview excerpts echo such inconsistencies in the national narrative. Most notably, Rif'at al-Nimir describes how a series of doctors in Nablus refused to treat a wounded man he and his comrades were carrying, due to a British pronouncement that any doctor found to be assisting the resistance would have their license revoked. In the end, Rif'at and his fellow fighters had to force a doctor to help the wounded man at gunpoint, uttering the words, 'Either you treat him or I fire my gun at you.' This is clearly not a straightforward case of 'collaboration' with the British regime: the reluctance of the Nabulsi doctors was the product of external British pressure. Nevertheless, Rif'at's account of the episode highlights a reality deeply unsettling to any national narrative: some members of the population chose self-preservation over commitment to the national cause.

Oral accounts such as these, then, help us arrive at more nuanced understandings of the pressures placed on populations during anti-colonial insurgencies. But if our only interest is to pick holes in nationalist narratives, then we surely miss so much of oral history's potential value. For me, the most fascinating part of listening and watching these accounts is the way the interviewees employ certain words, intonations and body language to express themselves. Paying close attention to these kinds of details (enabled by video footage in the Nakba Archive) allows us to ask different types of questions that have little to do with the verification of nationalist claims. How do Palestinians of a certain generation construct narratives about the past? What kind of temporal and spatial categories do they employ? And what role does the interviewer play in facilitating or restricting certain types of responses? Dynamics of insider/outsider and proximity/distance work in interesting and complex ways here. One of the emphases of the Nakba Archive was to embed members of Palestinian refugee communities in Lebanon in the whole process of devising, recording and cataloguing interviews, in a way that ensures knowledge is shared and disseminated across generations. The interviewers themselves tend to start the recordings by stating their particular village of origin in Palestine, as well as affirming their status as part of a group of 'independent researchers'. Tracing the effect of these attempts to create bonds of solidarity and common purpose therefore becomes an important part of how we 'read' these interviews.

In this context, each interviewee should be viewed as a storyteller in their own right. When they agreed to take part in interviews intended for publication and dissemination, they took an active decision to relate their experiences to an external audience: primarily the interviewer, but also to a series of imagined wider publics that could variously be described as Palestinian, Lebanese and perhaps global. At first glance, some seem more comfortable than others in this role. Maryam Sabha, for example, gives the following response when asked for the exact date of the British massacre of her fellow villagers in the mine explosion: 'I can't guess it for you, I mean, one is not [implying, I am not] educated. Education is worth a lot, it plays a great role.' In her modesty and self-effacement, Maryam seems to be reflecting a prevailing view of 'history' as a distinctly masculine field of knowledge off-limits to a woman like her. But once she moves beyond the interviewer's attempts to elicit specific factual information, she seems to grow in confidence, becoming more comfortable in her role as storyteller. She describes the explosion of the truck in visceral detail, and provides the names and professions of those killed in the blast. At the rhetorical level, she punctuates her account with frequent exhortations to the listener, God or the Prophet Muhammad, reflecting well-established techniques of Palestinian storytelling and in the process betraying her confidence in narrating certain aspects of the past.[4] At one point, she even talks the listener through her choice of words for the sake of narrative effect and humour: 'There's Muhammad 'Ataya as well, they call him Muhammad Issa, Muhammad 'Ataya. He also passed away, so we don't keep repeating "died". He passed away.' These are the words of a woman fully cognisant of her role as narrator.

Equally revealing are the silences in the interviews. Salih al-Nasir uses the metaphor of 'heavy clouds' to describe his life during the *thawra* – something reflected in his facial expressions and body language when he talks about the hardships he suffered. Upon recounting his torture at the hands of the British, he exclaims, 'May God disfigure them. May God curse them and their supporters.' But he chooses not to go into the darkest recesses of these memories, preferring instead to elaborate other details of his life at the time – the various places between which he was forced to move, and his particular roles within his unit of the resistance forces. More than once in the interview, he pauses when his recollections arrive at an experience of torture or emotional distress, then changes topic. We should not be surprised at people's reluctance to discuss painful memories in the context of a formal, filmed interview. But it can be useful for the oral historian to interrogate these silences, or simply leave them hanging in the air as eloquent reminders of the limits of historical knowledge, and the ethical dilemmas of trying to reach the so-called 'inner worlds' of people who have lived through such trauma.

Rather than view these interviews as mere sources of factual knowledge, we should carefully listen to them as dynamic and interactive *processes* – processes in which both interviewer and interviewee are engaged in a creative act of making history. Once we do, we can glimpse different types of temporal and spatial conceptualisations of the *thawra*. It is striking how the interviewees do not frame the *thawra* as a discrete event that can be neatly contained within the years 1936–39. Rather, it appears as an open-ended process with no specific end date, and, implicitly, is understood to be ongoing. Maryam's testimony jumps to and fro between the 1930s and 1940s, suggesting a longer view of the late Mandate period as a time of continuous violence, upheaval and hardship for Palestinians. On the other hand, 1936 often constitutes a definitive starting point in these accounts: the moment in which many people decided 'enough was enough' and took up arms against the British. But even these types of descriptions unsettle standard academic accounts, which hold the initial phases of the rebellion in 1936 to be a largely urban campaign of civil disobedience. By contrast, these rural recollections show us the extent to which peasants resorted to violence from the earliest stages of the uprising, in their desperation to rid Palestine of its colonial masters.

Above all, the enduring appeal of these oral testimonies lies in their ability to help us see Palestinians as fully rounded, complex historical subjects. Everyday acts of kindness – the offering of cheese and eggs, for example, by a Bedouin community in Rif'at al-Nimir's testimony – punctuate narratives of violence and trauma. So, too, do very personal affairs that had no direct connection to the *thawra*, but were inevitably disrupted by it. Maryam Sabha was engaged when the uprising broke out in 1936, but her marriage was put on hold due to her fiancé's involvement with the resistance. Salih al-Nasir, meanwhile, relates how his wife was heavily pregnant by the time he was released from prison. Barred from returning to his home village of Saffuriyya, Salih went into hiding with his wife to evade the ever-tightening military grip Britain had imposed on their country. As he describes in broad brush strokes how they moved between Palestine, Lebanon and Iraq, we listeners are left to imagine how they overcame the challenges of childbirth and starting a new family in such dislocating circumstances. In many ways, we can read this as the Palestinian story writ large: resilience in the face of enduring colonial oppression, dispossession and exile. Yet, it is precisely because they allow us to move beyond faceless grand narratives that these oral testimonies hold such power. Each one of these individuals is a storyteller, weaving their own personalised account into the great tapestry of Palestinian experience. Together they remind us of the power of oral history to document episodes of anti-colonial resistance in all their complexity.

Salih al-Nasir
born 1912 in Saffuriyya, Palestine
Interview with Mahmoud Zeidan
'Ayn al-Hilweh camp, Sayda, 2003

28'09"–36'36"

Mahmoud Zeidan: *You were saying that after 1936, you could compare your life to heavy clouds. Please clarify what happened to you.*
Salih al-Nasir: 19 April 1936 ... The revolution started. The revolution – started. I was one of its members. I worked for a bit, while my family was in the village. Each day passed and they were asking for it. Every single day. I was arrested after a battle we were involved in, in 'Arrabat al-Batuf. Me and another guy were arrested because we were bringing a wounded person over to Damascus to get him treated. We were arrested there. The army had surrounded the area and they were searching for people, and so on and so forth. We were arrested. They took us to Tabariyya, and from there to Saffuriyya, and then to 'Akka, and from there to al-Quds. We endured four months of torture. Four months where they made us taste bitterness. May God disfigure them. May God curse them and their supporters (he sighs heavily). After these four months, we got out on the condition that I would be denied residence in Saffuriyya. I would have to live in al-Nasira. I would have to prove my presence every day, three times a day. And the police would need to find me home any time they wanted to raid it. At the time, I didn't really care about these restrictions...

I got out of there and I found one of the cars from the revolution waiting to pick me up at the prison door. It arrived by coincidence. The person who was driving it was a guy from our village called Salim al-Ahmad. They called him Salim al-Ahmad al-Khushfi. I told him I needed to go to Saffuriyya right now: 'I want to go to Saffuriyya in order to get my family.' He said, 'Yalla.' We took the car and left, we parked it between the olive trees and I stepped out. I took a road and kept going until I reached our home. I took my family – I kidnapped them actually. They were invited at our relatives' and I was scared of the sanctions. And from there, we took the road between the olives until we reached the car, we got in and we kept driving south. We ate dinner in al-Kabri ... We ate dinner in al-Kabri and, in the evening, I told the leader of the faction – I was the one responsible for the weapons, and for the revolutionaries' clothing, and for guard duty, I was responsible for all of these. So, I told the leader of the al-Kabri faction: 'Bring me the faction and bring me the leader of the faction, so he can help us escape and take us to Lebanon.' He brought me armed men from his village, and they took us, and I took with me ... They got us horses for my wife. My wife was pregnant with my son Muhammad, and so we went to Lebanon. And we continued to work with the revolution, and my wife was in Lebanon. And we were living in al-Midan neighbourhood in Damascus. The French were in the country; they were in Syria and in Lebanon. At the time, in Syria and in Lebanon, they would turn a blind eye to us, a little bit. Not out of love for us! One must know a friend from a foe ... Not out of love for us. In 1925 and in 1926, the revolution in Syria was on. The British had opened the doors of Palestine out of regional ambitions. Because of their regional ambitions, they were turning a blind eye to the revolutionaries who were coming to Palestine. In 1926, the revolution ended in Syria. The French were not stupid, they knew. They were seeing that revolutionaries were coming and going to Palestine without any objection, without any surveillance, without anything. In 1936, it was payback time. The French started turning a blind eye to us, a little bit. In 1939, the Second World War happened with Germany and Hitler and all that. The British and the French formed an alliance – against Germany obviously, which was backed by Italy. Everyone knows the story (a heavy sigh). They made a deal. And then, they began gathering and imprisoning those they managed to arrest among us – 40, 50 people. The railroad was closed off. They sent them directly to Palestine, and handed them over to Palestine. The British government didn't waste any time. Tribunals, an execution here, a life sentence there, 15 days for this one, and I don't know what for that one ... That's how it happened. What are we supposed to do in this situation? This is the point we reached. What could we have done? What was the solution? Should we have gone to Jordan? We would have been in the same situation, and a bit worse. Should we have gone to Egypt? God forbid! On the one hand ... and on the other hand, there were 80,000 British soldiers at the canal in Egypt. Where were we supposed to go? Should we have gone to Turkey? The Turkish ... These people are not our people. We had no other choice than to go to Iraq. We were forced to go to Iraq. We stayed in Iraq; I stayed there for about five years.

Maryam Mahmud Sabha
born 1920 in al-Zib, Palestine
Interview with Mahmoud Zeidan
al-Maʿshuq, Sur, 2003

33'46"–38'53"

Mahmoud Zeidan: Tell me about 1936, what did you see? Were you already married?[5]
Maryam Mahmud Sabha: No, I wasn't married in 1936, I was engaged. When we left, he was on his way to Lebanon to buy a rifle and he went with those who left.

Before you left ... I want you to tell me more about what he used to do in 1936. Did he tell you? How did you perceive the British when they arrived in the village?
They would go up to the mountains, outside the village, and they would put up their checkpoints. And they would kill whoever crossed them, and whoever escaped, escaped. They made checkpoints for those who came from Tel Aviv, and those who came from the port and wherever else they came from, they would put up checkpoints and kill them left and right. As they say, each to his destiny.

And about what you were telling me before, were they your relatives in that bus?
No, none of the people in the bus were my relatives. They were my cousin's relatives. My husband's relatives. Poor them. One of them, his wife recognised him from his shirt. That time the mine exploded on them...

Tell me what happened, tell me the story.
I told you already, when they took them up to that B'rith camp,[6] they put them in the big truck they got from the village ... It was the al-Saʿda family truck; they used it for trips to Haifa. They put them in that truck and they made them go twice or three times over the mine they planted for them, but it didn't blow up. On the last trip, it exploded and it killed a lot of people.

Do you remember the year and the date it happened?
I really don't know. Maybe 1948. No. Maybe 1947, or ... 1946, something like that, I don't know. I can't guess it for you, I mean, one is not educated. Education is worth a lot, – it plays a great role.

How many of them were in the truck?
They put in about 20 of them. Ten of them died and ten wounded remained.
Those that were over there, in front … The big truck swayed forward, and
those who were in the back, they all died. Ten died.

Can you tell me the names of those who died and those who were wounded,
if you recall any?
There is Yunis al-Shaykh Taha, he died. There is Yusif al-'Alwani, he died.
God pray upon the Prophet Muhammad … There's Muhammad 'Ataya as
well, they call him Muhammad Issa, Muhammad 'Ataya. He also passed
away, so we don't keep repeating 'died'. He passed away. There is … God
pray be upon the Prophet Muhammad. There was al-Shaykh Taha, he was
wounded. You know … some were killed and some were wounded.

How old were they approximately? What was their profession?
Some of them were 25, some were 30. One of them, they used to call …
There was al-Shaykh Taha, he was 25. Muhammad Issa was barely 22. That's
how old they were, you know. There were other older ones. Yunis al-Shaykh
Taha as well, he was older than 30. These men died. There was Yusif al-'Al-
wani, he was also 30.

What was their profession? Yusif al-'Alwani, for example, what did he work
in?
They had orchards, they all had orchards. And they worked in their orchards
and made a living out of this work. They worked for their own sustenance.
It wasn't a job at a company, or a position in the army, no. It was their sustenance. The people of al-Zib did not have jobs. Very few of them were
dressed in military uniforms, very few.

Rif'at al-Nimir (Abu Rami)
born 1918 in Nablus, Palestine
Interview with Mahmud Zeidan
Beirut, 2003

10'06"–17'35"

Rif'at al-Nimir: In 1936, let's talk about 1936 ... In 1936, when we were students, the revolution was happening and we decided to take part in it. However, prior to the beginning of this revolution, there was a teacher at Madrasat al-Najah (al-Najah School), Professor Mamduh al-Sukhun, who would sometimes gather us under the guise of scouts, to go gun training.

Mahmud Zeidan: Firearm training?
Rif'at al-Nimir: Firearm training, which was later moved to al-Zarqa. And at the time, there was in al-Zarqa...

In Jordan?
In Jordan. There was ... I think, if I remember correctly, his name was 'Ahad al-Sukhun. He was a well-known officer who undertook our training. However, in the first stage of our training so to speak, we would go as scouts and spend a day or two ... Under the excuse of being scouts – boy scouts were not forbidden – so we would go. And so Professor Mamduh al-Sukhun would train us for the struggle. I took part in the revolution in the year of 1936, based on the encouragement of Professor Mamduh al-Sukhun and Dr Farid Zayn al-Din, who became the director of Madrasat al-Najah. A doctor. He was a Lebanese, from here.

A Lebanese?
A graduate of the American University [of Beirut], and then I don't know where he got his doctorate from. So we joined ... I personally joined the revolution, and I remember once – as an example related to the revolution – I took part in a battle that happened in Nablus, in Wadi al-Tufah, at the entrance of Nablus. And one of the fighters who was with us was wounded, he was one of the villagers we were with. And when he was wounded, we carried him to the doctors in order to get him treatment. This incident is very important. So we went to three or four doctors. They refused to treat him, because at the time, the British government had issued an announcement saying: 'Any doctor who treats a revolutionary shall get his permit revoked and shall be prohibited from practising.' In the end, there was a

doctor called Dr Ahmad al-Tahir from Nablus. If you go to Nablus, you'll find the al-Tahir family there. Dr Ahmad al-Tahir had a small hospital, I remember clearly. And he was from 'Asira al-Shamaliyya. The wounded guy ... 'Asira al-Shamaliyya, which is above Nablus. Jabal Jarizim. So we went to get him treated and he apologised, again same story. Until one of my classmates – who also became a doctor later on, Dr 'Abdallah Salah – pointed his gun at him and told him: 'Either you treat him or I fire my gun at you.' I swear, that's the story. He said, 'Ok, I'll treat him, but don't go saying that you brought him to me.'

Of course, naturally, since we were the ones bringing him, there was no way we would speak about the matter. So ... As for me, I participated in another battle...

Can you give us a bit more detail about this battle of Wadi al-Tufah?
Nothing. We were present ... This battle happened against the British ... The British army was the army that was present at the time. There was a military convoy and we were highly experienced with altitude defence, and there was an exchange of gunfire between us and them. And it resulted in the wounding of this person, and he was treated in...

Were there any casualties on the British side?
No. Not as far as I could tell, or at least, we did not see any during that specific battle. However, we did see some during the battle of Dayr Sharaf.

What year was Dayr Sharaf?
They all happened in 1936.

Can you tell us a bit about the battle of Dayr Sharaf?
During the battle of Dayr Sharaf, there was a man with me named Kamal Yasin ... Kamal Yasin. He was a relative, first of all. Second of all, I joined the fighter 'Abd al-Rahim al-Hajj Muhammad, Abu Kamal...

Who happens to be your maternal uncle.
It's a coincidence, him being my maternal uncle, but we joined him at the time. And I remember when the battle of the village of Dayr Sharaf ended, it was sunset, we met and we climbed mountains and walked all night long ... to the point of exhaustion. Until we reached Wadi al-Far'a in the morning, and we were starving to death because we hadn't eaten the previous day nor on the previous evening and we had been walking the whole night. And I will always remember, I went up to Kamal and asked him, 'How much

money do you have?' And he told me, 'I have three piastres.' Or four piasters
… And I had one piastre and a half or three, we said great, we can buy
ourselves a loaf of bread and a piece of cheese and eat. So there, we met
someone – we were in the wilderness, in al-Fara – someone who had made
a small tent, and next to it were chickens and a woman who was making
milk or something of the sort … or butter. I mean she had it in a…

Milk churner?
She was churning the milk. We went up to him, *as-salamu 'alaykum wa
'alaykum as-salam.*[7] He responds, 'Ya hala!' Really, the guy said to us, 'Ya
hala, ya hala, most welcome guests.' Sure, God bless him. We told him we
wanted to have a bite and they prepared us butter, from that churning …
And she made eggs and all, and we ate. When we came to settle the bill he
said, 'Really? Shame on you for asking.' So we ate, and we saved my one
piastre and a half and the three piastres of my fellow fighter.

'Abd al-Rahman Sa'ad al-Din
born 1915 in al-Zib, Palestine
Interview with Mahmud Zeidan
Beirut, 2003

1h 3'00"–1h 18'46"

Mahmud Zeidan: *Were the British destroying houses?*
'Abd al-Rahman Sa'ad al-Din: Isn't burning destruction?

What happened in your village?
When they came to surround the village ... Should I tell you it to you from the beginning?

Yes.
When they came to surround the village, the revolutionaries were keeping watch on Ma'souba, a settler village called Ma'souba.[8] They planted a mine against the British Army. At midnight, the British Army left the camp to do the rounds. They stepped on the mine, the mine blew them up and seven others. They were gone. The tank was completely gone, no more tank. They had placed a 6-metre long pipe full of heavily compacted explosive material, inside it were six detonators. This mine had been sent by the revolutionaries to someone in Jenin, I don't remember his name but he used to be an important leader. They sent it, but they did not know how to use it or operate it, they could not figure it out. They returned the pipe from Jenin to Tarshiha, and from Tarshiha to our village, see? When they brought it to our village, they told the fishermen, 'You guys figure it out.' The fishermen got a piece of wood, six metres long, and the pipe was carved with six holes, and on each hole they hammered a piece of wood and the nail went into that wood, see? Inside that hole. And they filled it with explosive material and placed the detonators inside it, and they put it in the ground. At midnight, the tank began moving from Ma'souba. There were men from Tarshiha, from al-Kabri, from al-Humayma, from al-Zib, from al-Bassa, a total of 20 or 30 young men or more, on the lookout and waiting for the moment the tank would come out. Once the tank drove out over the mine, it blew up and the tank was thrown over, and all the people were gone. There's a saying, 'Even the mischievous are afraid'. And I was sitting at home and they told me, 'The army has arrived in al-Bassa.' People left their homes to see what was happening. There was burning in al-Bassa, there were killings in al-Bassa, they did horrors in al-Bassa.[9] A man came and told them, 'Who

put that thing there?' They said, 'The people of al-Zib, not us.' They came over to our village. They surrounded the village and they got everyone out. Muhammad and 'Ali were visiting me at the time. They took us to Iqrit ... and beat and tortured us. They foot-whipped each guy the way he would be at the shaykh's. They would put the rifle between his legs and hit him. Ten, twelve cane beatings each. They would hit him over and over and throw water on him, and throw him in the thorny bushes. Immense torture. People were tortured a lot. I said to a guy called Abu Sulayman, 'Abu Sulayman, I swear I want to leave, I am scared.' Who was I scared of? The Egyptian translator. This Egyptian translator used to come to our village and intimidate us. He'd bully us in our own village, for example, he went to my cousin, slapped him on the face and took a lira from him. And he took from others as well. He came for me once, but some people objected and didn't let him. We went, Hayat the *hajjeh* and I, to the *bayyara* for a haul, and here come Fayad 'Alayan and 'Ali al-'Abid and Faisal Sarhan with many others, about seven or eight of them, asking what had happened. We told them. And the 'Ataya family was insisting on accusing so and so. I told them, 'I don't know this so and so.' One of the 'Atayas who used to work with the British government said, 'I swear, Hayat, I can secure an engine room for you and...' I told him, 'Why would you do this for me? If I die, what use would this be to me? I did not see anything nor do I know anything!' He told me, 'I swear I will cook you like fried chicken.' He threatened me.

The 'Ataya son?
Yes. And while we were on our way, a tracker came with the British military to investigate the tracks that were left behind when they entered the village. I went to see someone called Hasan Sahyun, he was a tracker with the British Army. A Bedouin. I know him, and him and my sister's husband were together, he was known as Husayn Masri. I went and stood near him, and said, "Abu Muhammad, the problem is this and that.' He said, 'Just go and don't worry. I'll take care of it.' He walked briefly around the scene of the explosion and told me, 'All traces are gone.' As soon as he said these words, we received the news that the brother of the guy who threatened me had just passed away at Haifa Hospital. So the guy went to the hospital and forgot about me.

When the British surrounded the village and entered it, do you remember the scene? Do you remember what they did?
The scene? They surrounded the village and what? Did the village resist? There was no resistance. No resistance at all. When they got to a home,

they kicked everyone out: the man, the woman, the child. They spoiled kerosene, wheat, barley, bedding, full gallons of oil that they broke and spilled on the ground. I'm telling you the whole village was blackened like a charcoal factory, like coal that had burnt. I swear, it was completely charred.

They burnt it?
They burnt the village; nothing was left. Me, my wife and my kids, all we had left were the clothes we were wearing. I swear to God. And the whole house was a charcoal factory. A real charcoal factory...

What did you feel when they burnt your homes?
I was at the hospital. I went from detention to the hospital.

What happened, so that you had to go to the hospital?
My legs were broken, this leg here, and this one was cracked, and my jaw injured here, and my head was bruised, and my spine was fractured, and my ribs were broken. I was three-quarters dead. Nobody could say that I was...

I meant how did this happen to you?
It happened because the Egyptian guy ... When he hit my cousin ... One day, on our way to the orchard, we found the Egyptian up on the mulberry tree – up on the sycamore tree – eating sycamore figs, and his rifle was where? On the ground. As soon as I saw him up on the sycamore tree, I ran towards the rifle. I took it, I loaded it and I told my cousin, 'Go cut some sticks.' Pomegranate branches are known to make good sticks. I told him to cut them, and we kept beating him until he was finished. And we took the rifle from him. Although I was scared of him, I swear, as soon as I saw that he was the translator, I was afraid of him...

What was his role, this Egyptian, what did he do?
A translator.

For who?
For the British. A translator, and he would identify, 'This person is so and so, that person is so and so.'

So he would indicate to...
Yes, yes. He would come up to you and tell you, 'Hey you, where are you from?' I told him, 'I'm from Saffuriyya.' He would continue beating you and telling you, 'Where are you from, boy?' 'From Saffuriyya.' Until you said to

him, 'Ya sidi, I am from Saffuriyya.' 'Ya sidi', the words 'ya sidi'. If you said the words 'ya sidi' to him, he would let you go. If you did not say 'ya sidi', he would not let you go –at all.

And when they detained you all in Iqrit, what happened to you?
They took people to investigate them and they beat them. As I told you, they foot-whipped them, beat them, and threw water on them. When someone came back from investigation, he wasn't returning walking on his feet. He was crawling on his knees. His feet were swollen like bread coming out of an oven, from the beating. They would beat him over and over, and throw water on him. Then give him a break, and then beat him again. They would beat him without any mercy or pity. There were three or four guys with canes, taking turns. Some canes were this thick. They'd keep beating him and beating him ... I swear to God, I took so much beating, they slayed me whole.

And then, what did they do to you all, when the Egyptian identified you?
They surrounded us and they took us, and put us in a camp. I'm telling you, it was a huge camp, people came from all over 'Akka and Haifa regions, that's how big the camp was. There were people from our village and your village and other villages. We were many from Saffuriyya, ten or twelve guys. They took us to Iqrit and beat us, and during the investigation they triaged us. The Egyptian guy sorted us apart from each other. You know how women *dabkeh* dancers form a circle? He arranged all the men in a circle. The major came, and the officers, and the army men, and the translator and the informant.

As I told you, he would ask you, 'Where are you from?' and you'd say, 'I'm from Saffuriyya' and he wouldn't leave you alone until you said 'ya sidi'. As soon as you said 'ya sidi, I am from Saffuriyya', he would leave you alone. But without you calling him 'ya sidi', he would not leave you.

He triaged you?
He triaged us, 23 men, and he told the prison, everyone in the prison and around it – they had established other camps and high lookout points to keep an eye on it. Prisoners slept on the ground, with no tarps above their heads, and the British Army stayed on the upper levels where they had their *kouseh*, one of those big 1,000, 2,000 *kouseh*.[10] So they triaged us, and they said, 'If someone comes to you and you hide him, we will kill all of you.' We sat and began thinking and there was a guy, his name was al-Fadl, God bless his soul. I told him we were going towards death, but how our death would

happen was unknown. It was the middle of the night when the British Army came inside the camp. People were asleep. They attacked them in every way possible, in their faces, in their backs, in their chests, and they tied their legs to the bus while they were sleeping. They brought us out by foot, the 23 of us, and in the ground there was a pole here and a pole there, and a rope between the two poles so that your leg would slide under the rope and you would fall over. You know what I mean? With all the beatings, we made it down and there was Hasan al-Sambu, the driver...

Hasan?
Hasan al-Sambu. Sambu. I told him, 'Hasan, why are you crying, what's wrong?' He said, 'I'm crying over myself and you all.' The bus was divided in two parts. One part was for passengers, 20 passengers sitting in front, and another part was for transporting things. Al-Fadl came and said to me, 'Come, let's sleep in the front, on the cushions.' Usually, the ones they triaged slept in the bus overnight and then they would bring them. I told him, 'I don't want to sleep inside.' So I leant my back on the divider between the passenger side and the transportation side. I was sitting there with a guy. They brought us from here to there to everywhere until the beginning of the day. The gas station was located close to al-Bassa. The army had placed it there. The petrol station was for the army. The Jews, I mean. He asked, 'Do you need to fill up some gas?' He replied, 'No I don't need to.' He said, 'Go on, fill it up for him, fill up the whole tank.' He filled it up and we drove through al-Bassa, they let us cross through. The bus was closed, tied up with ropes, and it was going at 45 kilometres per hour, very slowly. Behind it was the army, 100, 150, 200 of them, I don't know how much. There were so many cars, as far as your eyes could see. We arrived at al-Bassa and we went up to al-Bassa and we arrived at Marj Banna, they call it Marj Banna, below Iqrit. That's where the mine was planted. There was a bridge, the mine was there, next to it.

They had planted a mine against you, along the road?
Yes, along the road between two trenches. They would measure the width of the road and dig a trench for water on one side and another one on the other side, and the pipe was in between...

You mean the Arabs planted a mine against you?
The Jews. The British put it there.

The British planted a mine against you?
Yes.

STORYING THE GREAT ARAB REVOLT

How did you know that it was the British who planted the mine?
They took us to Dabuya in ʿAkka,[11] we were the ones who got the explosive material from there.

You, as in the people in the bus?
Yes. We hauled it from the British warehouses, with the pipe, and we brought it over. Three containers of explosive material. The pipe required three containers.

Three containers of gunpowder.
Yes, each container was this big.

Did you also fabricate it?
No, they did. As for us, they took us, they made us carry it, and we brought it to the car. They didn't place the mine on our side, they placed it on theirs. And when the mine exploded, they began investigating.

7

Songs of Resistance

Ted Swedenburg

Memories of the Palestinian revolt of 1936–39 have been kept alive, in part, through songs, poems and stories passed down through the generations. Those recounted by Fatima 'Abdallah and Husayn Lubani are examples, showing both the strong virtues of that memory and its limitations. Both elders are of a village background: Lubani from al-Damun, located east of 'Akka, born in 1939; and 'Abdallah from Sa'sa', located north-west of Safad, date of birth unknown. Neither is old enough to remember the events of the revolt. 'Abdallah, a woman of limited education who memorised passages of the Qur'an, is a keeper of songs and stories from the Mandate era, a repository of oral memory. Lubani, by contrast, is well educated. A former teacher with UNRWA, he is the author and editor of several books, and here he reads from a manuscript that includes some poems published in his book, *Dictionary of Popular Palestinian Songs*, which appeared in 2007, after the interview was conducted.[1]

As Lubani notes when he begins his remarks, modern Palestinian history can be seen as a 'sequence of linked revolutions'. And so, when it comes to memories of the revolt, it is very common for Palestinians to assimilate and mix accounts from other eras. When Fatima 'Abdallah is asked about songs sung against the British, she goes back to a very old one, probably dating from the early 1920s: 'O dear, O my dear/Faisal has left Paris/Ottoman rule has gone/British rule is here.' The poem refers to Prince Faisal's departure for Syria after the Paris Peace Conference in 1919, and to the British occupation of Palestine after the expulsion of the Ottomans in 1917–18. The English translation fails to capture the simplicity and catchiness of the Arabic verse, the rhyming of 'aziz' (dear), 'Bariz' (Paris) and 'Ingliz' (English), which serve as mnemonic devices. (Amusingly, after these lines, the song shifts from the political into metaphorical expressions of love).

Ya aziz, ya aziz
Faysal rawah min Bariz
Rah hukm al-Usmanli
Ija hukm al-Ingliz

When Lubani is asked about the revolt, he turns first to a famous song that pre-dates the rebellion, one known both as 'Min Sijn ʿAkka' ('From Acre Prison') and 'Al-Thalathat al-Hamra'' ('The Bloody Three'). It memorialises three Palestinians executed by the British authorities for their role in what is known as the Buraq Uprising of 1929. Lubani sings a section that begins: 'A funeral procession...' The poem was authored by the famous poet-singer Nuh Ibrahim, and became renowned in the Palestinian community of the 1970s and 1980s after Damascus-based Palestinian folkloric music group Firqat Aghani al-ʿAshiqin (Songs of the Lovers Ensemble), recorded a beautiful version that circulated widely on cassette. The song has helped make the executed men – Fuʾad Hijazi, ʿAta al-Zir and Muhammad Jamjum – into national heroes. All three were tried and convicted for their roles in the killing of 133 Orthodox Jews in Safad and Hebron, who, contrary to the lyrics of the song, were not armed with guns, and were mostly indigenous and Arabic-speaking. In the immediate wake of the 1929 killings, the Palestinian national leadership disavowed any responsibility for these events; but within a year or two, especially after their public execution, the three men began to be depicted as nationalist symbols.[2] Nuh Ibrahim's song mentions no concrete details of the three men's actions, instead presenting them as noble strugglers symbolic of all Palestinians martyred in the battles against Zionism and colonialism.

Nuh Ibrahim is probably the most celebrated popular poet and singer of the 1936–39 revolt, and the likely author of all the poems Lubani reads before turning to verses by Farhan Salam. Born in 1913, Ibrahim grew up in a working-class environment in Haifa, and became a well-known singer and poet as a young man, performing for social clubs and labour unions. Eventually, he made several recordings on vinyl and also performed in cities outside Palestine, including Beirut, Cairo and Damascus. It would seem that in the early 1930s he was also recruited to join the underground organisation of Shaykh ʿIzz al-Din al-Qassam. Ibrahim was arrested for his political activities and incarcerated at Acre Prison for five months in 1937. There, he came into close contact with other prisoners from peasant villages, and so, upon his release, he began to produce poetry rooted in rural traditions, much simpler and more direct than his earlier poems.[3] After leaving prison, Ibrahim joined the revolutionary forces as a fighter-poet, and appears to

have served under the command of Khalil Muhammad 'Isa, known as Abu
Ibrahim al-Kabir, a Qassamite and regional commander for the Galilee.
On 28 October 1938, Ibrahim was on his way to visit some of his relatives
in Majd al-Krum together with three fellow fighters, when the group was
spotted by British forces conducting a regional cordon and search operation – what Palestinians at the time referred to as a *tawq*. A fire fight ensued
and Ibrahim and his three comrades were killed near the village of Tamra.[4]
Although Nuh Ibrahim's career as poet and singer was relatively short, he
left behind an impressive, and influential, volume of poetry.[5] It is of interest
here that he describes the situation in Palestine, in a poem written between
1935 and 1938, as a *nakba* or catastrophe, well before the occurrence of the
Nakba.

Lubani reads from another poem composed by Nuh Ibrahim, about
Shaykh 'Izz al-Din Qassam and his martyrdom in battle with the British
in November 1935 in Ya'bad Forest. Qassam was born in Syria, educated
at al-Azhar University, and was a leader of the Syrian revolt against French
occupation in 1919–20. Condemned to death by the French, he took refuge
in Palestine. He served as a teacher and preacher to the poor and labouring
classes of Haifa and, in the mid-1920s, began to organise an underground
network of cells, in Haifa and surrounding villages, with the aim of launching an armed struggle. In November 1935, Qassam took to the hills with
several of his men to initiate guerrilla war against the occupation, but they
were spotted and hunted down by the British after only a few days in the
maquis. The battle at Ya'bad and the brave example of Qassam were, nonetheless, important precipitants of the revolt of 1936–39, in which several of
Qassam's surviving lieutenants played a leading role.[6]

Lubani reads a segment of a Nuh Ibrahim poem titled 'Lamentation (fi
ritha') for 'Izz al-Din al-Qassam'. In the Arabic, verse, rhyme scheme and
metre are simple, direct and powerful. The first three lines of each stanza
rhyme, while the fourth line always rhymes with the last word of the responsorial refrain, "Izz al-Din: ya khisara, ya 'Izz al-Din' (O what a loss, O 'Izz
al-Din). The very form of the poem thereby elicits collective participation.
The poet – or any reciter or singer of the poem – signals to the audience
with the fourth line of each stanza that the responsorial refrain (known as
a *lazama*) is coming, encouraging the crowd to join in at the end of each
stanza, with 'Ya khisara, ya 'Izz al-Din':

'Izz al-Din, ya marhum	'Izz al-Din, O deceased
Sawtak daris lil-'amum	Your death is a lesson for all
Ah, law kunit adum	O had you remained

Ya kabir al-mujahideen   You'd have become a leader of the *mujahideen*
Ya khisara, ya 'Izz al-Din   O what a loss, O 'Izz al-Din

Lubani reads these lines in an order somewhat different to that in which they appear in other published versions, but this is oral poetry, so a poem's verses can be shifted around by anyone who recites them.

Lubani reminds us that the revolt of 1936–39 – which began as a six-month-long general strike – evolved into an armed insurgency, waged by fighters based in the countryside. He reads from another Ibrahim poem that commemorates the battle of Bal'a, also known as the battle of al-Mintar. It took place near Bal'a village, located 9 kilometres from Tulkarm, close by the highway linking Tulkarm and Nablus. Jabal al-Mintar is a mountain overlooking Tulkarm, situated between the village and the city.

The battle of Bal'a, on 2–3 September 1936, was one of three major engagements that Palestinian revolutionaries fought under the leadership of Fawzi al-Din al-Qawuqji.[7] Qawuqji, a Syrian and pan-Arabist, was an Ottoman army officer who fought on King Faisal's side against the French occupation of Syria in 1919–20, and then joined the Syrian Legion created by the French Mandate authorities before deserting to fight French colonialism once again in the Great Syrian Revolt of 1925–27. In the late 1920s and early 1930s, Qawuqji helped train King Ibn Saud's army in Saudi Arabia. In 1932, he relocated to Baghdad, where he worked as a trainer in the Iraqi Military Academy. Along with volunteers from Syria and Iraq, Qawuqji entered Palestine in late August 1936 to join the armed revolt, and declared himself its commander. He quickly imposed a unified and centralised structure over the armed Palestinian resistance fighters, whose military effectiveness was soon improved.

The battle of Bal'a commenced when Qawuqji's joint Palestinian, Syrian and Iraqi forces ambushed a British military unit travelling the Tulkarm–Nablus Highway. The colonial unit called in reinforcements from the British base in Nablus, and when tanks, artillery and aircraft entered the battle, they were able to chase off Qawuqji's forces. Although the British claimed victory in the battle, their reports noted that their opponents had acquitted themselves quite well militarily. Qawuqji and the Palestinians also claimed a win at Bal'a, based in particular on their success in shooting down two British warplanes – an impressive feat – and withdrawing their forces from the field to fight another day.[8]

After the battle at Bal'a, Qawuqji's tenure as commander lasted only five weeks, during which he prosecuted two more important campaigns. His arrival in Palestine, and the fact that his intervention raised the anti-colonial forces' military proficiency were cause for great celebration among Palestinians; and many popular poems and songs were written about him and his battles. But despite breakthroughs for the armed Palestinian resistance, the Arab Higher Committee – the Palestinian national leadership – called off the strike in October 1936, and had Fawzi al-Din and his volunteers withdraw from Palestine.[9]

Nuh Ibrahim's poem about Bal'a is composed of simple, direct, easily memorisable rhymes:

Bayn Bal'a wa al-Layyeh	Between Bal'a and al-Layyeh[10]
Tisma' al-Mauser dayyeh	You could hear the Mauser thundering
Bayn Bal'a wa al-Mintar	Between Bal'a and al-Mintar
Sar ishi' 'umru ma sar	Something happened as never before
Bayn Bal'a wa al-Mintar	Between Bal'a and al-Mintar
Dhabahna jaysh al-kufar	We slaughtered the army of unbelievers

Lubani reads another poem that praises Sa'id al-'As, a friend and comrade-in-arms of Qawuqji, who helped recruit Syrian and Iraqi volunteers to fight in Palestine. Al-'As had served as an officer in the Ottoman army, fought on the side of King Faisal in Syria, and led anti-colonial fighters during the Great Syrian Revolt of 1925–27. When that insurrection was put down, al-'As went into exile in Amman; expelled from Jordan by the British, he joined his old comrade Qawuqji in Saudi Arabia. Lubani claims that al-'As was a friend of Qassam's, and he may have been, as both men fought the French in 1919–20. Lubani is correct in stating that Qassam was from Jabla in Syria but not that al-'As was from near Jabla, as the latter was born and raised in Hama. Al-'As did not serve in the region where Qawuqji fought his battles, in the 'Triangle', the mountainous area between Jenin, Tulkarm and Nablus known to the British as the 'Triangle of Terror'. Sa'id al-'As instead helped organise the armed resistance in the hills south of Jerusalem, in the area of Bethlehem and Hebron. After his forces engaged the British near Halhul on 24 September 1936, the British launched a search and cordon operation in the area. Al-'As and a small band of his regular fighters were spotted, on 6 October, by British aircraft, and then ambushed at the village of al-Khidr, near Bethlehem. Al-'As met his death in battle, while his lieutenant, the Palestinian 'Abd al-Qadir al-Husayni, was wounded.[11]

Both Lubani and 'Abdallah mention the mufti, Hajj Amin al-Husayni, the president of the Supreme Muslim Council, and head of the Arab Higher Committee (AHC), the body formed in 1936 to lead the national resistance against colonial occupation. The British banned the AHC in September

1937, and the mufti fled to Lebanon to escape arrest. The poem (presumably by Ibrahim) that Lubani reads addresses the mufti in exile: the 'mufti of the Arabs/calls out from the mountains of Lebanon'. It is noteworthy that Hajj Amin is referred to as the mufti of the Arabs, not just of the Palestinians, and that the poem calls for Arabs to 'save Palestine from the grip of its enemies'. It was Hajj Amin who requested that Qawuqji help the AHC organise and wage the revolt, although the two later fell out. That Qawuqji, al-'As, and other volunteers from Syria and Iraq joined in the revolt is testimony to how the struggle in Palestine roused solidarity throughout the Arab world during the 1930s. The line from the poem that begins with 'All the Arabs gathered/from the Gulf until Tetouan [Morocco]', is no exaggeration, as there are reports dating from 1929 that calls for Arab and Muslim solidarity with the Palestinian struggle were concerning French colonial authorities in North Africa.

'Abdallah, for her part, mentions the mufti in a story about Hajj Amin visiting her village of Sa'sa' for a wedding. It is hard to make sense of the events she describes, which seem to have nothing to do with the revolt. She tells of a dispute between people from her village of Sa'sa' and people from Dayr (probably Dayr al-Qasi, a village just west of Sa'sa'). Of significance is her account of travelling troubadours, the popular poets who, like Nuh Ibrahim and Farhan Salam, used to perform at weddings. Two poets were hired for the event she describes, along with their *hadayeh* – entourages who would accompany poet-singers, join in the singing on the chorus, and clap along. As was common at such events, the troubadours compete with one another, and both praise the mufti.

Lubani also reads from poems by Farhan Salam, another popular poet from the village of al-Mujaydil, near Nazareth. Born in 1917, he was educated in a Christian school in the village, went on to join the Palestine Police and then enlisted in the revolt, in which he served both as fighter and poet. Although Nuh Ibrahim is far better remembered today than Salam, the latter is probably the second most important popular poet of the 1936–39 revolt. After the rebellion ended, Salam lived in exile for a time in Transjordan, before returning to his village. In 1948 – when Zionist forces occupied al-Mujaydil, emptied the village of its inhabitants, and razed all its buildings (save the church) to the ground – Salam fled to Syria, where he lived in Yarmuk camp on the outskirts of Damascus. According to Lubani, Salam's songs were broadcast by Palestinian resistance radio after the PLO was founded. Salam passed away in Abu Dhabi in 1999.[12]

Among the important themes Salam raises in one poem Lubani reads is a reminder that Palestine is the 'cradle of Jesus'. The poet refers to the Church of the Nativity in Bethlehem, where both Christians and Muslims lived (at the time, the town's population was around 85 per cent Christian and 15 per cent Muslim). Nuh Ibrahim similarly stresses Palestine's multi-faith character in his 'O, Arabs' poem. There is no difference, the poet states, between Muslims and Christians; and, 'the Druze are our honoured brothers in faith'. Nuh Ibrahim distinguishes here between 'Muslim' and 'Druze', but at the same time affirms respect for Druze beliefs and proclaims that all religious sects were engaged in a common national struggle. Although sectarian tensions did at times develop during the revolt, villages in the north of Palestine in particular had a significant Christian minority, and a number of Christians participated actively in the armed insurrection, some in leadership positions. The issue of the Druze role in the revolt is somewhat more fraught. Druze fighters were indeed involved, most notably Druze volunteers from Syria who fought with Qawuqji's forces. Hamad Sa'b, a Druze from Mount Lebanon who had seen battle alongside Qawuqji in the Syrian revolt of 1925–27, assumed command of the Druze company that was one of the four main units of Qawuqji's resistance forces, and Druze fighters were among the martyrs at the Bal'a battle. During the later stages of the revolt, however, several Palestinian Druze leaders either took a position of neutrality or defected from the rebellion, and some groups of fighters launched violent attacks on Druze communities.[13]

The last poem that Lubani reads is a dialogue written by Farhan Salam. It belongs to a poetic form known as a *muhawara*, a kind of staged, performative debate, in this case between the Mufti Hajj Amin and Chaim Weizmann, who headed the World Zionist Organization. Nuh Ibrahim was equally renowned for composing poems of this sort. The *muhawara* belonged to the poetry genre of *zajal*, based on the common practice at Palestinian life-cycle celebrations, where poets or singers would compete with each other by improvising within prescribed rhyme schemes. Fatima 'Abdallah tells of one such artistic duel, where a poet from Hittin village competed with another from Safad to sing improvised praises to the mufti using the *'ataba* form (a Palestinian folk musical form with a fixed rhyme scheme, but usually an unfixed metre).

Salam's *muhawara* of Weizmann and the Mufti revolves around the question of partition, to which Weizmann urges Hajj Amin to accede. This dates the poem to the aftermath of the issuance of the Peel Report – the conclusions and recommendations of the Royal Commission of Inquiry launched by British government in November 1936, after the AHC called off the insurrection. Issued in July 1937, the Peel Report recommended that Palestine be partitioned into Arab and Jewish states. Palestinian Arab opinion was infuriated, especially because the plan called for most of the Galilee, overwhelmingly populated by Arabs, to be included in the Jewish state. In September, Palestinian gunmen assassinated the district commissioner for the Galilee, and the British retaliated by banning the AHC and arresting or deporting hundreds of nationalist activists and leaders. A new phase of the Palestinian armed revolt was launched in fall 1937. In Salam's poem, Hajj Amin asserts that partition will not occur because of the opposition of the Arab kings, whom he describes as 'lions'. Lubani mocks this descriptor. Even at the time of the revolt, any notion that the kings were leonine was false. The monarchs of Saudi Arabia, Transjordan and Iraq had pushed the AHC to end the revolt in October 1937, just when Qawuqji's rebel forces were gaining traction. If the Saudi and Iraqi kings opposed the Peel proposal for partition, Transjordan's King 'Abdullah expressed his support. Of course, the Arab kings' abysmal failure to impede partition in 1948 is probably the strongest grounds for Lubani's scorn.

The revolt reached its apogee in the summer and fall of 1938, when insurgents gained control, for a time, of most of the highlands and many Arab urban centres. The British responded with a vigorous counter-offensive, deploying some 20,000 troops, vastly superior firepower and brutal counter-insurgency tactics. By 1938, the resistance was not united as it had been under Qawuqji, and guerrillas committed a number of errors, brutalities and abuses. Nonetheless, they forced the most powerful colonial power in the world to commit substantial forces to wiping out a rebellion mobilised mostly by peasants. And although some resistance commanders perpetrated criminal acts, many other commanders, as well as everyday fighters, were motivated by high patriotic values and acted accordingly. It is curious, then, that none of the names of those Palestinian commanders are memorialised in the poems and tales recounted here. Instead, these folk accounts celebrate three leading Syrian resistance fighters, Qassam, Qawuqji and al-'As, as well as the Palestinian civilian head of the national movement, Hajj Amin. On the basis of a review of some of the sources of Palestinian popular song (and pending thorough investigation), my sense is that these interviews are symptomatic of how popular memory of the revolt has been shaped by the existing, and especially written, cultural archive. The names of the three Palestinian men executed at Acre Prison are probably better recalled than the name of any Palestinian commander of the revolt, with the possible exception of 'Abd al-Qadir al-Husayni – who is primarily remembered for his role and martyrdom in the resistance of 1948, rather than any of his actions in 1936–39. Nuh Ibrahim seems to have left behind no poems memorialising notable Palestinian resistance figures from his period of involvement in the armed struggle, from autumn 1937 to October 1938, perhaps because their activity was clandestine. And if such poems of this sort do exist in the archive of Farhan Salam, they are not the verses for which he is remembered.

During the mid-1980s, when Sonia Nimr and I interviewed elderly villagers and former fighters about the 1936–39 rebellion, the revolt commander most often held up as an exemplary figure – as one whose actions symbolised all that was noble, nationalist and honourable about the revolt – was 'Abd al-Rahim al-Hajj Muhammad, from the village of Dhunaba near Tulkarm. These are precisely the sorts of principles that Lubani and 'Abdallah are concerned with promoting as central to the resistance struggle. 'Abd al-Rahim was a regional commander, who at one point assumed the title of Commander-in-Chief, and who operated in the 'Triangle' area. He was besieged and killed by British forces on 26 March 1939 at Sanur, a village south-west of Jenin.[14]

'Abd al-Rahim al-Hajj Muhammad certainly deserves to be better remembered in the collective memory. According to Sonia Nimr, writing in 2012, elders in the Tulkarm area did sing songs about the man and his actions and character. It is hoped that these verses will be circulated and documented, and become better known; and that songs and poems celebrating other honourable Palestinian actors in the revolt can be located and archived. Fatima 'Abdallah's and Husayn Lubani's interviews are valuable in that they represent the resistance of 1936–39 as a popular struggle, one characterised by great sacrifice and bravery on the part of its participants, and by strong efforts to promote national unity across religious and sectarian lines. Their memories remind us of the solidarity that the Palestinian resistance already inspired across the Arab world, and the long record of Arab 'leaders' who betrayed the Palestinians. Finally, 'Abdallah's and Lubani's accounts are exemplary in their great reverence and appreciation for Palestinian popular culture, a tradition that continues to play a critical role in preserving the history of Palestinian struggles. They are sure to inspire further research on this invaluable oral archive.

Husayn Lubani
born in 1939 in al-Damun, Palestine
Interview with Mahmoud Zeidan
Trablus, Lebanon, 2004

1h 23'23" – 1h 39'46"

Mahmoud Zeidan: *Let us talk about the repertoire of protest songs in Palestine during the British Mandate, during the Great Revolt especially. I would like to know what you remember of other poets or songs, specifically ones by the well-known popular poet Nuh Ibrahim.*
Husayn Lubani: *Bismillah il-Rahman il-Rahim.* Palestine went through numerous consecutive revolutions. Modern Palestinian history could almost be seen as a sequence of linked revolutions that began in 1920, with skirmishes between the original people of the land, the Palestinians, and the expatriate Zionist and Jewish groups to our land, our beloved land, the land of Palestine. Poets were never absent from these very important events; they were continuously present. They took it upon themselves to urge the people and incite audiences to hold on to the land, and to refrain from selling their plots. These speeches were directed at a number of people, and it was mainly non-Palestinians who went ahead and sold some of their lands. The poets, specifically, were much more revolutionary and nationalistic in their public addresses than the writers, the teachers, the speakers and the broadcasters. Their poems urged their audiences to resist and to stand up against Jewish terrorist groups, who had perpetrated many massacres. So they resisted against the British who were collaborating with the Jews to invade the land of the Palestinians, beginning with the first High Commissioner, Herbert Samuel who was a Jew, a British Jew.[15] During the famous 1929 Buraq Uprising, three of our finest Palestinian youth were martyred. Their ages ranged between 25 and 27 years old, and one of them was Fu'ad Hijazi…

You mean they were executed…
They were executed … They were killed of course … Martyred … Executed at the 'Akka prison on 3 June 1930.[16] And that's the story, the event that the famous great Palestinian poet Ibrahim Tuqan recounted.

Al-Thulatha'…
Al-Thulatha' al-Hamra', yes. Many others like Ibrahim Tuqan wrote about that major event. Al-Thulatha' al-Hamra' in 1929, these three men were

martyred and their names were Fu'ad Hijazi, 'Ata al-Zir, and Muhammad
Jamjum.

I think the last two were from the al-Khalil region. The popular poet says:

> Revolution happened in al-Quds, it did
> The throne's roosters called out to the sky
> Arab men woke up to it
> Drawing their daggers on the Zionists
> Revolution happened in Bab al-Khalil
> The Zionists' blood flows on the ground
> Young Arab men! Pick up the Martini[17]
> Protect our homeland from the Zionists
> Mother, O Mother, don't you worry
> I sacrificed my blood, a ransom for the homeland
> Along with my relatives and my cousins
> We are the homeland's young men, do not worry.

Our relatives recited this poem on the day the three martyrs were killed,
and they kept repeating it until 1948. When we began seeking refuge, we
were singing it in our school plays:

> A funeral procession through the doors of 'Akka
> Jamjum and 'Ata and Fu'ad Hijazi
> God punish the High Commissioner
> And make his women weep over his death
> The three died as lions
> Do not mock them, you Jew
> They held a stick while you held a rifle
> But you kept complaining, Goddamn you
> Visit the cemeteries on holy days
> Go to 'Akka and visit the glorious ones
> 'Ata and Fu'ad, the martyred ones
> Do not fear death

People sang a song the day the Syrian-Palestinian hero, 'Izz al-Din al-Qassam, was martyred. He loved Palestine so much that he left Syria with the
French, lived in Haifa and found work at the Haifa mosque. God greeted
him as a martyr in Ya'bad in 1935, it was an unfair battle against the British
enemy – tanks and aviation ... People said:

'Izz al-Din, O deceased one
Your death is a lesson for everyone
O, if only you'd remained, oh leader of the freedom fighters
'Izz al-Din, what a loss
A martyr for your people
Who could deny your chivalry?
O leader of the freedom fighters
You established a group to fight
For the liberation of the nation
Saving it from the idiot Zionists and colonialists
The game of treason is a game
Thus the disaster befell us
And blood flowed up to our knees
But you never yielded or surrendered.

This was a very famous account and it was a popular Palestinian folk song during the 1930s.

During the 1936 revolution, following the strike that lasted six months and six days, the longest strike in modern history indeed ... There were battles between the mujahideen, who were known as 'Bin Mujahideen' or as 'the Revolutionaries', who sought refuge in the mountains, valleys and forests, and were vanquishing the British Mandate ruling the country at the time. There was a famous incident in the region of Nimrin, in which the fighters were clearly and visibly victorious. The popular poet, Nuh Ibrahim, says:

O bird, have you no knowledge
Of a battle that happened up north?
It ensnared after 'Asr prayer
Only darkness could untie it
Between Bal'a and Bayt Nimrin
You could hear the strikes of the *qayazeen*
Between Bal'a and al-Layyeh
You could hear the Mauser thundering
Between Bal'a and al-Mintar
Something happened as never before
Between Bal'a and al-Mintar
We slaughtered the army of sinners
You Zionist, take your people and leave!
This land is our land

You Zionist, you do not scare us
Our flag floats above the clouds
Commissioner, go tell your country
London is our horse stall.

That was the revolution in 1937; it went on from 1936 and became stronger in 1937. Nuh Ibrahim also used to recite a type of popular *zajal*, called *muthamman*.

Palestine the afflicted
Is the most noble and beloved spot
Its fight against colonisation
Makes us proud to be Arabs
The original mother of the ancient world
It built the countries of Prophets
It holds great value in the world
Of which celestial writings hold proof
Britain, the damned
Sold it to the Zionists
The house of God, now plunder?
What a topsy-turvy world
This patient homeland
Cradle of love and peace
Cradle of Christ, the victorious
And first qibla of Islam
Cradle of Christ, the pure
Cradle of the dignified prophets
Is now the house of many dangers
With this mandated state
It holds many Arab heroes
Who never falter or fear
No matter how big the horrors
They never abandon their purpose
They know no humiliation
And if they put them in the cannon
They would strike as shining examples
Of beloved chivalry in the world

This poem used to be sung, and it was broadcast on the radio:

All the Arabs gathered
From al-Khalij until Tetouan
Standing under its soil
Women and elders and youngsters
You Zionist, where do you flee?
If we Arabs made a pact
Al-Sharq would be your grave
You son of a damned nation
Admire the revolutionary army
As it carries out its attacks
Slaughtering the colonising army
Seizing its weapons and machinery
The revolutionary jumps into the fire
And fears not for his life
Long live young free men
And the flaming rifles.

I have a poem here in my notes that follows the *murabba'* style, not the *muthamman* one.

You Zionist, leave us alone
This homeland is our homeland
I don't think you'll enjoy yourself
In the lands of Palestine
You Zionist, you cheater
In our country, you have no wage
You thought you could own for free
In our own country, you evil one?
Palestine, do not feel humiliated
Your men will not leave
And al-Aqsa is chanting
For your young men, O Palestine
Here comes Sa'id al-'As, shepherding our zeal and enthusiasm
His men are shooting bullets at the armies of sinners.

Sa'id al-'As was a friend of 'Izz al-Din al-Qassam, and both of them were from Syria. One of them was from Jabla and the other was from the vicinity of Jabla:

Sa'id, the leader, the hero
Does not fear firing bullets
O, brothers of the revolution, shout
'Come, let us attack the sinners!'
To die on the day of *jihad*
Is the highest honour, O generous ones
That we may protect our country
From the grip of colonisers
Sa'id, the most glorious fighter
Never retreats from his purpose
He was martyred on the land of al-Khadr
In your name, O Palestine.

He was martyred in 1936. At the time, there were even a number of Lebanese men who participated in the revolution, during the period when the delegation of Fawzi al-Qawuqji arrived. During that time, the Lebanese who arrived were among the *qawaleen*, so they were influenced by the general atmosphere, by the flames of the revolution. One of them said:

O, son of Palestine
Your voice rattles the valleys
Calling for our Kings to answer it.

This is the *shuruqi* style.

O, Arabs
Arabs, ignite and liberate the homelands
Save Palestine from the grip of its enemies
Let go of the past
And patrol the field
Roam the battles
And their four corners
This matter will not be resolved
If countries are massacred and blood flows on their shorelines
The mufti of the Arabs
Calls out from the mountains of Lebanon
'Do not let the enemy possess their lands'
There is no difference between Muslims and Christians
And the Druze are our honoured brothers in faith
It is our duty to all be united
To crush and erase the armies of Zion.

It is by Farhan Salam, a great poet who sang for the revolution and passed away in Damascus. He sang many revolutionary and popular songs, which were broadcast on the radio, of the revolution, from its early days – the revolution that happened after the Nakba. The poet tells the story of a battle that happened in the woods of al-Nabi Salih, in the jurisdiction of Ramallah.

> I called out, in the name of the One, the Judge
> The mention of this name made the devils flee

This one is also sung in the *shuruqi* style.

> In the cradle of Jesus and the Isra' of the Prophet Adnan[18]
> O West, our volcanoes have erupted from your oppressions
> O West, we are Arabs, from the people of al-Qahtan[19]
> Our history will teach you the circumstances of our past
> O church of the cradle, who was greedy over you?
> Around you could be found Christians and Muslims
> On the day of hate, lions, who do not accept defeat
> When the wolf strikes, the Arabs protect their fields

Et cetera.

> And if Balfour ignores the value of our homelands[20]
> It is with our souls that we serve our lands
> O, Jerusalem rock! Be satisfied and safe
> And if we ever abandon you, complain about us to al-Rahman
> And around you, you will find brave and courageous men
> Who can serve your enemies *Zaqqum* and gasoline.[21]

There was another song they sang for the leader. It was about a dialogue between the leader of Palestine, the deceased hajj and mufti Muhammad Amin al-Husayni, and Weizmann, who was one of the founders of the Jewish state ... May it disappear, insha' Allah. He says:

Weizmann told Hajj Amin: 'Here are four million, for you'
The mufti answered: 'Should you die trying, you will never own Palestine'
Weizmann told him: 'Hajj, I implore you,
Please sign this document for me, and we would be forever grateful'
The hajj told him: 'Doctor! Do not take pride in your wealth
Forget Balfour's promise and live among us as a *dhimmi*.

He responded:

> 'O Hajj, do not embarrass me
> We have fermented the dough
> Write down the partition
> And all of us will be in accord.'

He responded:

> 'As long as Arabs exist
> The partition is rejected
> The Arab kings, the lions
> Do not agree with this partition.'

Arab kings are lions … Yes, true lions, *Alhamdulillah.*

Fatima ʿAbdallah
born in Saʿsaʿ, Palestine
Interview with Muhammad al-Masri
Mar Elias camp, 2004

39'19"–52'54"

Muhammad al-Masri: *What songs were sung by the revolutionaries against the British?*
Fatima ʿAbdallah: (Singing) Ya Aziz, Ya Aziz, [King] Faisal has left Paris. The Ottoman rule is gone. The British rule is here. Ya Aziz, my love, my dear, your wish is my command. Atop my cheek is a garden, full of home-grown apples and apricots.

Are there any other songs specifically against the British?
What? You want me to sing some more?

Against the British … If there were other songs against the British…
Songs? There were many!

Against the British.
Should I sing?

The ones they used to sing … against the British (at this point, we understand she is hard of hearing).
For the British?

Yes.
For the British … God bless the Prophet … Me, I did not mix with the British. And they did not sing for the British. Nobody sang for the British. People did sing for Turkey … Since it's Muslim.

What would they sing for Turkey?
Many songs were sung about Turkey … I cannot really remember them … The days go by … The days go by. If it weren't for God, this God right here, I wouldn't be here talking. Right? (she breaks into song):

Oh *Zlut*,[22] we bid you inform your government that we have taken over
  its forts

Oh *Zlut*, we bid you inform your government that we have taken over
    its forts
Oh our country, we wish you prosperity, and their forts will never deter
    us
Oh we wish their country laid waste, with owls crying above it
Plant the flags on the mountain, blessed is our country
Oh our country, we wish you prosperity, and their forts will never deter
    us
Oh we wish their country laid waste, with owls crying above it.

This song was sung against the British.

Are there any more songs like this one?
When one wishes to remember something, He said (recites from the
Qur'an):

> So remind, if the reminder should benefit;
> He who fears [Allah] will be reminded.
> But the wretched one will avoid it –
> [He] who will [enter and] burn in the greatest Fire,
> Neither dying therein nor living.
> He has certainly succeeded who purifies himself,
> And mentions the name of his Lord and prays.
> But you prefer the worldly life,
> While the Hereafter is better and more enduring.
> Indeed, this is in the former scriptures,
> The scriptures of Abraham and Moses.[23]

Oh Allah, bless the Prophet.

When the foreigners went to visit the Ka'ba, this sura was revealed to
these sinners, right? Which *aya* (verse) was revealed to the sinners? He said
(she recites from the Qur'an):

> Have you not considered, [O Muhammad], how your Lord dealt with
>   the companions of the elephant?
> Did He not make their plan into misguidance?
> And He sent against them birds in flocks,
> Striking them with stones of hard clay,
> And He made them like eaten straw.

What is the story behind this sura? One of them told his elder sinner, 'I want my things.' The elder asked: 'Do you want your herd, or do you prefer the Kaʿba?' He responded, 'No, the Kaʿba already has God as protection.' He made the sinners ride the elephants and they all went to demolish the Kaʿba.

Hajjeh, when a visitor would come to your house, and you would sing to him to welcome him, what would you say to him?
Welcome and warm greetings, my dear (she sings):

See ʿAkka's bounty, and how everyone fights over it.
What is your request, dear horse riders, dear family?
We do not need any rain from you, we do not need any money from
    you, nor any of your brides riding on camels' backs.
Welcome and warm greetings, my dear.
This is the bounty of ʿAkka, and everybody fights over it. What is your
    request, dear horse riders, dear family?
We do not need any rain from you, nor do we need your charity, we do
    not need any of your brides riding on horses' backs.

This is what we used to tell them.

... Tell me what happened.
When they invited the mufti ... Not Abdulmajid, but the mufti ... Abdulmajid had already been killed. When they invited the mufti, is when they took over our village, and they took over all the villages. Unlike us, Dayr did not have the traditions we had. We had traditions where we would prepare celebrations for the bride and the groom to be. Dayr did not have these wedding rituals, so they took the mufti and they went to our village, but the Safadiyya (people of Safad) used to stay in our village ... They came to our village and wanted to prepare the wedding celebrations of Dayr's wedded couple. They went to the end of the village and asked the Dayr people to leave, but they did not want to. Since they didn't want to leave, they attacked them. They attacked with sticks and guns and wreaked havoc. So the mufti said 'Let's go to the fields of Saʿsaʿ, let's move the wedding there'. They brought the meat and the home-cooked food and everything they could possibly get and went to the fields. The women went to cook in the fields, and the wedding party, *al-sahja*, from the fields of Dar Hbus to the fields of Dar al-Saʿid ... The *hadayeh* came down ... They had not only

one *hada*, but two *hadayeh*. One of them was from Safad and the other one from Hittin. The *hadayeh* started singing poems. The one from Hittin said: 'I am a Hittini and I am blind in my right eye. Hey you, Sa'id al-Safadi, I raised you with my own hands. Once you grew up and became a man, you became arrogant towards me.' He continued: 'Oh Lord of the Supreme Throne,[24] O Abu Fu'ad, may I witness your lasting happiness, and in the *diwan* you spread your carpet, until the land of al-Sham, and your great reputation is known from Dayr to Hawran and Lajat.'

This *'ataba* verse was improvised by the Hittini poet and dedicated to the mufti. The mufti said: 'Here, give a *bakhsheesh* in exchange in exchange for the *'ataba* verse.' People used to give *bakhsheesh* back then. The poet kissed the money, brought it to his forehead, and said: 'You who brings this *bakhsheesh*, return it. To the generous and good ones, give it back. And if Abu Fu'ad draws his sword, he does not put it back, and his left arm doesn't anticipate.' These two *'ataba* verses were dedicated to Abu Fu'ad, to the mufti.

Hajjeh, what other songs do you know? Were there any sung for the mufti al-Hajj Amin, or any mohawraba for him?
No, I cannot recall any songs for Hajj Amin ... For the mufti, they sang: 'For you, our mufti, this trip I shall endure.' This was a song by Sa'id al-Safadi ... 'For you, our mufti, this trip I shall endure. I swear to God, I will not walk on the paths of Sa'sa'.' This wedding was for the mufti. All of this cooking and havoc and wedding, it was for the mufti.

Did the mufti visit Sa'sa'?
Of course, these were the effendi's family ... The Abdulmajid family and his people. They are from Safad.

Hajjeh, do you remember the songs people used to sing for the revolutionaries? When they used to see them fighting the Jews or the British?
I do not recall any of them anymore, I will not lie to you. People used to sing so many songs for the revolutionaries.

What about in 1936? Do you remember any songs for the revolutionaries then?
In 1936 ... God bless the Prophet ... I truly can't recall ... No, I cannot recall ... People sang indeed for the revolutionaries, and when the young men would come through our village, in Palestine, the women would come

out and sing for Abu Ammar (Yasser Arafat's *kunya*), they would sing: 'Abu Ammar, O strong and high wall, O Damask rose...'

In 1936, Hajjeh, I meant in 1936.
In 1936 ... 1936 ... 1936 ... I don't remember these bygone days ... My dear, God have mercy on you, God bless you. I mean ... Go around the whole neighbourhood, I dare you to find a woman like me, and as old as me.

Figure 5   Kamil Ahmed Balʿawi, Palestine, 1949.
Courtesy of Balʿawi family and the Nakba Archive.

PART III

War and Ethnic Cleansing

8

The Roots of the Nakba

Salman Abu Sitta

While the idea of al-Nakba – the idea of depopulating Palestine – germinated in the minds of European fundamentalist Christians and Jews in the nineteenth century, only after the First World War was it converted into an action plan on the soil of Palestine. The myth promoted during the nineteenth century that Palestine was 'a land without people' was just that – a myth – and its fabricators knew it. Rather, they planned to make it so – to make Palestine a land without people by depopulating it, destroying its villages and erasing its record from history and geography.

This plan took root in Palestine upon the issuance of the British government's infamous Balfour Declaration, the implementation of which started with the appointment of Zionist politician Herbert Samuel as first High Commissioner of Palestine in 1920. Under the British Mandate, Samuel oversaw the enactment of over 100 ordinances to facilitate the transfer of land to incoming Jewish immigrants and to build separate Jewish institutions including an embryonic army, which were the foundation for the future state of Israel.[1] But there were not many Jewish citizens for the projected state at the time. Thus, the British opened the gates of Palestine for Jewish immigration.

The flood of Jewish European settlers to Palestine reached its peak in the mid-1930s. By the end of 1936, the total Jewish immigrant population had risen to 384,000 or 28 per cent of the whole population (from 9 per cent at the beginning of the Mandate).[2] Alarmed at this influx, which threatened their existence in their country, the Palestinian people revolted against British policy and Jewish immigration in what is known as the Arab Revolt, from 1936–39.

The revolt was met with utmost British brutality. For the first time, Palestinian villages were bombed by air. Villagers' houses were demolished in the first occurrence of collective punishment. British forces attacked villages using tanks and artillery, destroyed communities' supplies and held men in cages for two days without food or water. Collective punishment was widespread. Political parties were dissolved. Leaders were imprisoned or deported. Archival research has brought to light British and Israeli files that document the extent of British repression and Jewish collusion in colonial military operations.[3] Husayn Mustafa Taha, who was born in Mi'ar in 1921, witnessed this indiscriminate clampdown on Palestinian political activity first-hand: 'The British came to our village and blew up our houses, suspecting that rebels (*thuwar*) were among the village people.'

The Palestinians were left defenceless. 'Anyone who had a rifle was sentenced to death,' Taha says. 'One of our people was accused of having a rifle. He was taken to prison. We got lawyers, Ahmad Shukayri and Hana Asfur, to defend him. After months in prison, he was found innocent.' Others were unable to hire a lawyer and were hanged.

In contrast, Jewish immigrants were trained in night combat by a British officer, Orde Wingate, who formed the Special Night Squads.[4] 'The British gave the Jews ammunition and we had none,' Taha says. British support also included training, protection and uniforms. The Jews, in return, provided intelligence information and translated Arabic pamphlets into English.[5] Jewish armed forces – notably 20,000 Jewish policemen, supernumeraries and settlement guards – frequently assisted British troops (which amounted to between 25,000 and 50,000 soldiers).

A minimum estimate of Palestinian casualties: 5,000 killed, 15,000 wounded and a similar number jailed. More than 100 men were executed, including leaders such as the 80-year-old shaykh Farhan al-Sa'di, who was hanged while fasting in Ramadan on 22 November 1937. Thus, about 50 per cent of all male adults in the mountainous region of Palestine – corresponding roughly to the West Bank today, and where the revolt was particularly active – had been wounded or jailed by the British, like Taliba's father.

By 1939, Palestinian society was dismembered, defenceless and leaderless. The year 1939 can be identified as the year of the British-inflicted Nakba. Ben Gurion found this to be a prime opportunity for pouncing on Palestine and prepared what he thought would be a long-term plan. At the first big Zionist conference in the United States, held at the Biltmore hotel in May 1942 and attended by 600 Zionist leaders, Ben Gurion announced the formation of 'a Jewish Commonwealth' in Palestine.

This would require the depopulation of 1,200 Palestinian towns and villages. Ben Gurion instructed the Haganah to start the 'Village Files' project, which created spies' groups disguised as Boy Scouts recording every minute detail about each village: its population, economy, routes, military training, political affiliation and so on.

After the Second World War, with the Palestinians utterly decimated, the only obstacle hampering Zionist objectives was the continuing British military presence in Palestine, as Taha notes.

ZIONISTS ATTACKING BRITAIN

At the conclusion of the Second World War, Zionists settlers rewarded Britain for its support by launching a terror campaign against their erstwhile benefactors. They bombed British headquarters, hanged British soldiers and kidnapped British judges.[6] In 1945, Britain had to fly the 6th Airborne Division to Palestine to fight Zionist terrorism. Its aim was not to defend Palestine against Zionist attacks but to save British soldiers from them.

Zionists also assassinated Count Folke Bernadotte, the UN mediator appointed to bring peace to Palestine. Jewish actions were described as 'terrorism' by the UN Security Council in Resolution 57 of 1948. In the final six weeks of the Mandate, Zionists attacked and depopulated 220 Palestinians villages and committed 25 massacres. The League of Nations mandate compelled British authorities to protect Palestinian life and property, but they did not intervene. They did not intervene when massacres were committed against Palestinian villages. Dayr Yasin was the most notorious; the British Chief of Police in Jerusalem was a few kilometres away, but he did nothing. The British assisted in the expulsion of Palestinians from Tiberias by providing transport. Rather than defend civilians during the massive evacuation of Haifa's Palestinian population, British forces facilitated their departure.

A handwritten book of signals exchanged between British patrols along the Jaffa–Jerusalem axis and Force Headquarters in Jerusalem in the critical period of April–May 1948 provides a damning record of the British collusion and failure to honour their obligations.[7] In Wireless Log No. 129 of Duty Troops (April and May 1948), frequent entries detail the British Army's refusal to rescue Palestinian villagers when the latter were attacked by Jews. The army was ordered to watch, report and not interfere. When Jews asked for help, the troops were ordered to rescue them.

Britain's unceremonious departure from Palestine was disgraceful, leaving the country in the hands of European Jewish settlers whom British imperial forces had admitted, trained and armed.

Mi'ar, like many Palestinian villages, was left defenceless. The community had 40 fighters to defend itself against Zionist attacks. Husayn Mustafa Taha witnessed these events. 'What could we do in the face of Jews who had

Howitzers? They had planes, planes all the time ... chasing us when we left Mi'ar; we left everything behind. We sought refuge in Suhmata, the planes followed us. We went to Dayr al-Qasi, the planes went after us,' Taha recalls.

From the British planes in 1936 to the Jewish planes in 1948, al-Nakba was the fate of at least 500 cities and villages. Not only was the rural countryside – the core of the people – depopulated and emptied of the Palestine landscape, the main Palestinian cities, the urban centres of commerce, culture and polities were also emptied. The fear of imminent death, broadcast on loudspeakers by Zionist fighters, led villagers to seek safety in nearby villages. Both host and guest sought safety when both were attacked.

Why such fear? This mass exodus was prompted by a premeditated scheme of massacres. Upon close observation of the location and timing of massacres within Israeli military operations to conquer Palestine, it becomes clear that massacres were a weapon of ethnic cleansing. The Haganah forces – comprised 120,000 soldiers in nine brigades, led by Second World War veteran officers – committed at least 50 massacres, concurrently with the 31 military operations they conducted.

The same strategy was deployed across Palestine. Each village was surrounded from all sides, leaving one side to escape. Scores of young men were killed and the remaining men taken to concentration camps. Some survivors were allowed to escape, to tell their story as a warning to others.

The scale of the calamity was too much to comprehend. All refugees thought that this upheaval could not last and they would soon return: Taha left with only four blankets and a sack of wheat, with his four children in tow. As he relates, they moved from one village to another, never reaching their final destination in Lebanon in a single journey. The massive depopulation of Palestine could not have happened as a consequence of military operations alone, which could have subsided, permitting people to return. It happened as a result of ethnic cleansing, propelled by massacres.

Taliba Muhammad Fuda, born in Suhmata in 1929, witnessed the Majd al-Krum massacre as a little girl. She relates,

They called us to the square. They separated men aside and women and children in a corner. They lined up a dozen young men and sprayed them with machine guns. Then they lined another dozen. A Jewish man speaking fluent Arabic called for Haj Abid [who was apparently targeted in a 'Village Files' list]. They killed him and burnt his house. They loaded us women and children in a bus. The old men in another bus. They took us to a Jewish colony where the crowd spat on us, laughing and gesturing. They ordered us to walk, shouting, 'go to King 'Abdullah', shooting over our heads.

The UN Truce Observers investigated this massacre half-heartedly. Their reports can be found in UN file 'Atrocities'.[8] They ceased to do similar investigations as there were 'too many and they had no time to investigate'.

According to the International Committee of the Red Cross (ICRC) records and my published research, the male survivors of the massacres were taken to several concentration and forced labour camps, where they remained for up to two years. When their villages were attacked, many refugees saved their lives by crossing the border into Lebanon. When some tried to return home to bring back some old relatives or valuable possessions, the Israelis were waiting for them and shot them dead as 'infiltrators'. The irony, of course, is that a Palestinian returning home is called an 'infiltrator' by an armed Polish settler who arrived from the *shtetl* to the shores of Palestine in the dead of night in a smuggler's ship.

Britain's position was one of extreme opportunism. Zionist terrorists committed atrocities against them, yet they did nothing to retaliate. That was a contrast to their brutality towards the Palestinians. Moreover, after the Israeli conquest, their Legation continued to function in Tel Aviv, and the British Consul continued to operate in Haifa. His presence there provides us with crucial information about the situation faced by Palestinians who remained at home. Tucked away in British archives, we get a damning picture of Israeli brutality, which met with no British action, not even a slap on the wrist.

Mr Ezard, the British Consul in Haifa, wrote a detailed report on the circumstances of Palestinians who remained under the new government of Israel. The 60-page report, dated 12 July 1950, details the brutality of Israelis and the theft, looting and plunder of Palestinian property under the guise of the newly crafted Absentee Property Law.[9] Of the Israeli brutality, the Consul stated in his report:

Only this week Archbishop Hakim told me that three weeks ago he had watched from his Nazareth orphanage window the treatment meted out to a party of 20 Arab infiltrees who were being kept in a tent a few yards away. From 7.00 to 9.30 in the morning these Arabs were made to run round [sic], carrying against their chests heavy stones weighing, the Bishop estimated, 20 to 25 kilograms each. The men were kept on the move until they collapsed.

Palestinians escaping massacres in Lebanon frequently attempted to return. Israelis waiting at the border shot and killed them. Those who made it and returned home were not safe either. Taliba recounts the story of a young man who had escaped to Lebanon. 'He heard that his wife, childless for twelve years, was about to have a baby. He returned to see her. On the second day, the Jews knew about it and came, shot and killed him.'

Israel turned British Mandate laws to its advantage. The Absentee Property Law of 1950, used to rob Palestinians of their property, is based on the British Enemy Property Act, devised to confiscate German property in the Second World War.

The Defence (Emergency) Regulations enacted by British authorities in Mandatory Palestine in 1945, which were designed to combat Jewish terrorism, were subsequently turned against Palestinians remaining in their country. These regulations were applied against Palestinians until 1966, when military rule was replaced by permanent apartheid laws.

CONCLUSIONS

The idea of depopulating Palestine and replacing its population with European Jews in the nineteenth century became a reality in the twentieth century. This was made possible by British policy during the Mandate period, when the institutional structure for the state of Israel was created. British colonial power enabled Jewish settlers to try out ways of strengthening their project, to test their methods and to create physical centres from which to conquer Palestine in 1948.

Although they used British tools, Jewish settlers far exceeded their mentors in brutality, efficiency and extent. Geographically, they expanded over Palestine into Egypt, Syria, Lebanon and Jordan (through conquest of the West Bank, Baqura and al-Ghamr). Time wise, they have exceeded 70 years of occupation – twice as long as the Mandate period. Legally, while the British were bound by the League of Nations' terms, the Israelis have violated dozens of UN resolutions and articles of international law. One has only to consider the collective punishment, home demolitions and expulsion under any guise that Palestinians face today to see that racist and apartheid practices are still ongoing.

All this means that al-Nakba is still ongoing.

Husayn Mustafa Taha
born 1921 in Mi'ar, Palestine
Interview with Mahmoud Zeidan
Miye wa Miye, Sayda, 2003

19'38"–25'10"

Mahmoud Zeidan: Do you remember the names of some of the people who came to Mi'ar during the revolution?
Husayn Mustafa Taha: There was a leader called Abu Ahmad, and there were people from Saffuriyya – I have forgotten their names. I forget, I forget, I forget. This illness has made me forget. There were leaders who came to the village, they said: 'The Jews are coming to take your land, to kick you out' – to kick us out of our land, and to seize it with the help of the British.

What did the village people do when they heard these words?
What did you want them to do? They took up arms and they created troops. Among them was my paternal uncle Ahmad al-Husayn. He was the leader of a troop and he had armed men, they would come and go. They left when [the Jews] came and blew up our village. There was a British or a Jewish Jeep, I don't know, that came from 'Akka. They blew it up before it reached the village. The Jeep exploded and the people in it died. They used contact bombs that reached Mi'ar – those who blew up the Jeep were from Mi'ar. They came and blew up the whole village. A part of it. They blew up our homes – us, the Taha family, and the 'Akariya family – they blew up our homes. A few houses were left standing next to them, we started sleeping at their house, we reclaimed our homes all over again, they blew up our homes.

Why did they blow up your home – the Taha family home?
I don't know, maybe it was targeted? Why did they blow it up ... Maybe because my uncle was the leader of a troop and they knew that information, that he led a troop against them.

So they blew up the houses of the entire family?
Yes, they did.

Your paternal uncle's and your father's and ...
All of us, all of us. Our entire family. They blew up all the Taha family houses.

Can you describe to us what you were doing when they came and blew up the house? Was it during the day or at night?
I told you they took us during the day, they gathered us and took us to the outskirts of the village. They detained us and they took us to the outskirts of the village. In the meantime, they blew up the village and then they kicked us out. They took us to the outskirts of the village in order to blow it up. They did not keep us inside the village. They gathered the men and the women, and all of us. They gathered us and they took us outside the village at a distance of five kilometres. No, not even five kilometres. Two or three kilometres away from the village, and then they exploded it.

How did people react after their homes were blown up? When they came back and found their houses destroyed, what did the people of Mi'ar do?
They began rebuilding it and they started working for the revolution, joining the revolution, attacking the Jews, attacking the British. Nakba.

Did they detain anybody from your family, any of your relatives? Apart from the fact that they took you away to the village outskirts and blew up the homes, were they detaining people?
They detained a man called Husayn Abdul-Hadi. They found a rifle in his house. When they were searching homes, they found a rifle at his place. They took him and put him in prison, and he was going to be executed. The people of the village, we all got together, and gathered some funds and got him a lawyer, Ahmad al-Shuqayri. And this other lawyer, what's his name? I'm confused. I can't fully remember.

After you mobilised the lawyer's help, al-Shuqayri, did they release the man that was jailed?
Yes, they released him. They released him. They took the rifle and they released him. They took the weapon and they released him. Hana 'Asfur, that's the other lawyer, his name is Hana 'Asfur. We sent him the lawyers Ahmad al-Shuqayri and Hana 'Asfur, until he was discharged. They said that someone had put [the rifle] in his house. They made up an excuse in order to get him out.

If someone was caught with a rifle and couldn't get a lawyer?
They would hang him.

Did it ever happen to anyone in the village? Did they hang anyone?
No, nobody from our village. It never happened. This man was the first to ever get caught with a rifle at home.

During that time, the confrontation was with the British. When did the confrontation start with the Jews? When did the friction start between you and the Jews? What was the date and how did it start?
I'm not sure exactly ... In 1948, in 1947, I don't remember properly.

26'14"–32'30"

Do you remember how the Jews attacked Mi'ar?
When they arrived, they attacked and began shooting at us. They fired cannons; they placed mines; they kicked us out and displaced us.

Was there any resistance? Was anybody from Mi'ar fighting?
They were defeated. The people of Mi'ar were fighting them and shooting at them, but the others beat them because their ammunition was stronger. The British gave them ammunition and their ammunition was more powerful than that of Mi'ar's people. They arrived at the village, they invaded the village, and they kicked us out of the village.

How many fighters from Mi'ar were there?
There were about 40 of them.

Forty of them?
Yes.

And how many rifles were there in the village, approximately?
I don't know, about 30 or 40 rifles – 50 rifles, I don't know. There were about 40 rifles. But the others started bringing out the cannons, and – what do you call the other thing – the B7, that B7, the B7. It has a name, I'm forgetting it. What's it called – *hashkad, hawz, hawj, kawhawz?* I don't know its name.

(Bystander interjects) Schmeisser.[10]

Did a battle take place in Mi'ar?
That was the battle that happened between us – between us and the Jews. They came from the west of Mi'ar, and they started shooting at us and we were shooting at them. They defeated us with their ammunition; they reached Mi'ar and they kicked us out. They reached Mi'ar and they defeated us.

What did you do when they defeated you? Did you stay in the village or did you leave?
We left. We left.

Where did you go?
I went to ... we went to ... We were dispersed. We were dispersed and we left our *tarsh* behind, and we left everything we owned, furniture and all, we left everything. I went to a village called Suhmata and I lived there.

Did Jaysh al-Inqadh come to your village? To Mi'ar?
No they didn't. Jaysh al-Inqadh did not come. If they came after we left, I wouldn't know about it. Jaysh al-Inqadh did not come.

Do you remember the date you left for Suhmata?
It was the month of July 1948. We left, we went to Suhmata and we stayed during July, August and September. In September, my daughter named Amina was born in Suhmata. And they started bombing Tarshiha with airplanes, and Suhmata too, they were bombing it with their planes, so they drove us out of Suhmata. And we left. We went to a village called Dayr al-Qasi. And from Dayr al-Qasi, they kept following us, and bombing with planes, and planes circling over us throwing bombs, and throwing barrel bombs. And then they took us to a village called Rumaysh. We reached a village called Rumaysh. They went after us until they drove us outside the edges of Palestine. With airplanes. They went after us with airplanes.

So you couldn't stay in either Dayr al-Qasi or Suhmata?
No, I couldn't. Because we were stripped of our weapons. We had no more weapons. We couldn't stay. We went to Rumaysh, to a village called Rumaysh. It's in Lebanon.

What did you take with you when you left Mi'ar?
What did I take with me ... All I took was a mule, can you believe it? I took a female donkey and four blankets with me. Four blankets, and I left with my children. With my children, I had three children. Two children: Fatma and Muhammad – it was hard on me. I had a female donkey and four blankets, and two bags of flour. We used to eat barley flour in Suhmata. We'd grind the barley and eat it. And this is the last of what I have to say.

No, I want to ask you one more question. When your wife gave birth in Suhmata, did she leave right away, or did she have time to rest – when she was pregnant with your daughter?
She rested for a bit – not right away. She left 20 days after the girl was born. They started bombing Tarshiha with airplanes, and they bombed Suhmata until they kicked us out.

What did you feel when you first left Mi'ar? And later on, when you left Suhmata, how did you feel?
It was a feeling of desperation and subjugation. What feeling? A feeling of joy? No, a feeling of desperation, and a feeling of subjugation, and a feeling that the British and the Jews defeated us. And a feeling of lack of power to resist against them! That was the feeling.

35'33"–39'20"

Who did you leave with, when you got out of the village? And which of your relatives stayed there?
I left with my children. I took my children and my siblings. My son Muhammad, and Fatma – they were young. They were two or three years old, and I got them out. My father and my mother stayed there. They stayed there, in Palestine. They stayed in the village. The elders stayed in the village. But the young men, they kicked them out, they told them: 'You're not staying. Either you go, or we massacre you all.'

Who said these words?
The Jews.

So they gathered you all and told you to leave?
Yes. They gathered us and said: 'Go, leave. You can choose – either you die, or you leave the village.'

What about your father, until when did he stay there?
He passed away.

Did he pass away over there?
I had a sister there; he stayed with her. A sister in Majd al-Krum. My mother and my father went to her house. She took them in, and she took care of them, and fed them and looked after them. They passed away at her house. They died in 1962 and in 1964. My mother died in 1962 and my father died in 1964 – they died...

And you did not get the chance to call them or to see them.
Never. Never. I did not get the chance.

I want to ask you, do you have any hope that we'll return to Palestine?
We have hope, Insha' Allah. Insha' Allah, nothing is far from God. Nothing is far from God. If God Almighty wishes, Insha' Allah these arrogant oppressors who kicked us out by force, Allah will send them someone who will take revenge on them, and return us home. We will return by force, Insha' Allah, we shall return to Palestine, and to Mi'ar, and to Safsaf, and to 'Akkbara, and to al-Damun, and to all Palestinian villages – and to Shafa 'Amr, and to all villages, Insha' Allah. We have hope. I am not losing hope. Even if it's the last day of my life I'm not losing hope, Insha' Allah.

What do you predict the future will hold?
God knows. God knows. I cannot prophesise what the future will hold.

Let's say you could choose an alternative to Palestine – Lebanon, or Europe for example, or a compensation – or if they could bring you back to Palestine, what would you choose?
I would return to Palestine. I would want to return to Palestine. I would not accept any compensation or any money. I would not accept anything. Not even *tawteen* in Lebanon. Not even *tawteen*.

I want to thank you very much, ya 'amm, for agreeing to sit with me although you are ill.
Yes, truly, I'm ill. If I weren't ill, I would have given you more time.

Is there anything I forgot to ask you about, that you would like to say?
Like what?

Anything you would like to say before we end?
I say Insha' Allah. I ask God Almighty to grant us victory and to bring us good fortune, and that we return to Palestine. This is my very last request – that we return to Palestine while I'm alive. That I return with my children. And that all Palestinians in Lebanon, and in Syria and in Jordan – that they all return to Palestine. And that we create a state in Palestine. Insha' Allah, Insha' Allah, Insha' Allah.

Insha' Allah.

Taliba Muhammad Fuda
born 1929 in Suhmata, Palestine
Interview with Amira Ahmad 'Alwan
2003

45'10"–48'46"

Amira Ahmad 'Alwan: *Did you witness the 1936 revolt?*
Taliba Muhammad Fuda: Yes, I remember it.

Were there any political parties in the village that confronted the revolution?
No, this I don't remember. I remember that the British entered when the revolutionaries left, they wrecked homes and searched them. When the revolutionaries were back, every seven or eight men would go to a villager's home and have lunch, or dinner or sleep. They would stop the kids and tell them: 'Could you please keep an eye on Ras al-'Aqaba in case the army shows up?' And the kids would say, 'The clouds are coming in!' so the revolutionaries would leave. I don't remember there being any parties in our village. Maybe they had them in cities like 'Akka or Haifa, but I don't remember there being any in our village. I was just a 14-year-old girl when I left.

You told me your father was detained by the British.
Yes, by the British. He was detained in 'Atlit, and he was detained in 'Akka, in al-Raml prison, that's what they called it.

Why was he detained?
He was with the revolutionaries and, at the time, those who were ... were accused of ... They accused him of ... Someone from Sa'sa'.

Who told them he was among the revolutionaries?
His wife. When he knocked at the door – but I don't want this to put me in trouble. Would it be wrong of me to say more?

No, no.
A leader would come, for example, Abu Raba, Abu Khidr, Abu Ibrahim, like the ones in charge here. He would give orders to a soldier or a revolutionary and say, 'Go fetch so-and-so for us', and he'd go and fetch them. So he knocked on the door. She asked him, 'Who are you?' He responded, 'I am Abu Talib'. She told [her husband], 'Don't go, *ya zalameh*, don't go with

him.' He said, 'No, it's Abu Talib, I want to go with him. I will not come back home.' When they came, she went and they complained. My father was absent for about a year. He stayed here in Melehma, in Syria. When they said that the Arabs got their demands, and I don't know what – I remember this moment – women started trilling because the British had supposedly withdrawn from the villages. They came and denounced him. He came back, truly, he came back and stayed. My mother was bringing the mattress over to him. During the day, she took it back, and at night she brought it to him on a piece of land they called Khalt al-Njas. He would sleep in it, over there. At sunset, she would bring the mattress and the cover to him and, in the morning, she would take them back. Every single day. One day, he was sitting at Shaykh 'Abdallah's place, may he rest in peace, Ahmad al-Salamun's father. He used to sleep there as well; he wouldn't dare sleep at home. He slept at his house. A guy came … Corruption has been around since the beginning of time … He denounced him in Tarshiha, so they came and took him. I was about seven years old at the time. He was not well behaved nor did he ever become well behaved. 'My father is in jail, my father was jailed! The British took him, the British took him!' That's what I said. I was aware at the time.

54'35"–1h 11'44"

Were there any Jewish settlements or kubbaniyat *next to your village?*
Yes, the closest one to us was Nahariyya. I know there was Nahariyya. We used to go there to get medical treatment sometimes, at the beginning. If [a woman] wanted to get her children seen by a doctor, or if she needed anything else, we would go to Nahariyya. I went there myself and got medical treatment.

Is Nahariyya close to Sha'b or to Suhmata?
No, Nahariyya is close to 'Akka. From 'Akka, it's even further north. Around al-Kabri, around al-Bassa, on that same road. On the coast.

How did the Jewish settlers treat you?
We never saw them, nor would they come. Sometimes, about 20 or 30 of them would come and walk street by street with a map, and sing songs in their jargon, they would sing their songs. And they'd go up to the mountains and walk around, they followed a piece of paper they had on them.

Did you ever deal with them? Did you work with them?
No, not at all. They would not even enter the village. They wouldn't enter. As far as I can remember, they wouldn't enter.

Did a Jew ever buy anything from your land?
No.

When the Jews attacked the village, what did the villagers do?
You mean Majd al-Krum? When people left the village? As I told you, at first, we left to Dayr and al-Bi'na, and from there, we fled. Then Majd al-Krum surrendered. So they stayed. We came back. They gathered the young men and lined them up at the *hannaneh*;[11] they call it *hannaneh* over there, the *hannaneh* of Majd al-Krum. Am I saying anything I shouldn't? Should I tell you everything?

Yes, tell us.
They lined up seven or eight of them, or maybe ten, I don't remember. They lined them up at the *hannaneh*. They blindfolded them, they turned their faces towards the wall of the *hannaneh* and they sprayed them with bullets. We saw this from the mosque window ... Imagine how humiliating, how atrocious it was to see young men collapsing before our eyes. They moved them here and there and lined up another row. They blindfolded them. A second later, a whistle blew. He raised his hand up like this – the guy inside the car. A car arrived – a Land or a Jeep, I don't know. It just arrived. It was roofless. He raised his hand up, he stopped. One of them came out of the car. He started talking in their jargon – I have no idea what he said, I can't tell you. He looked at them and began removing their blindfolds, it seemed he told them to remove their blindfolds. There was a guy called Hajj 'Abid, from Majd al-Krum. It turned out he knew him, that's what it looked like. He was hugging him and saying, '*Khabibi* Hajj 'Abid! *Habibi*! You die, Hajj 'Abid? No die, Hajj 'Abid.' He hugged him so tightly! They had blown up his house – he was one of the leaders of the revolution – along with other revolutionaries' houses, one of them was Abu Ma'luf. The revolutionaries used to refer to his house as the people's refuge, even Jaysh al-Inqadh (the Arab Liberation Army) would have lunch there. As soon as the Jews entered, they blew up his house. Then they killed him, they sprayed him with those who were sprayed with bullets. They put him at the *hannaneh*, and they sprayed Abu Ma'luf with those who were sprayed with bullets. He was from Majd al-Krum itself. They burnt his house; they blew it up. He had a garden in his house; they burnt it. The

sheep were still in there, they went in and the sheep were there. But all the armed men had left with their weapons that day, they all fled the village. As for us, you know, people stayed put, some people came, some people went. We began to go to Sha'b secretly, to bring back things. Did we leave with anything? No, we left with nothing. We only had the mattress and the cover left, and a change of clothes, that's it. We hid everything in the hay, supposedly until our return. All our furniture was hidden in the hay. We went there for one last run. My son was already dead, but we would go there and pick the olives from our own olive trees – from the olive trees that belonged to us. We would go there and they would make us pick them, and then give us wage money. They gave us wage money. We would walk the same distance as between here and the port. But the way up was very steep, just like between here and up to Jabal Turbul. The valley was here, you'd take the road up and then there was a descent. We picked olives for the Jews! Not for us. But they would give us five *qurush*. One day, we went there, we wanted to get a few things and we wanted to put our clothes away – we were hoping to get our cupboard. My own cupboard. I carried a cupboard shelf; it had two drawers at the top.

The minute we entered the village, it was surrounded. We stayed there for a bit, I told you the guy came and all. We came out when they said they were gathering the men. They started calling the unmarried men and they gathered them all. They stopped some buses and started asking unmarried men to raise their hands. They would go up to them and say: 'Are you unmarried?' If he said yes, he would tell him: 'Get in the bus.' 'Are you single or married?' 'No, I am single', and he would say: 'Get in the bus.' 'Get in the bus.' They got all the single men into the bus. Everyone who was single started saying they were married. So that … They did not even know why or how … He would just come up to a guy and say, 'Are you married?' He would say yes. He would respond: 'Sit over there.' You're married? Sit over there.' 'You're married? Sit over there.' 'Do you have a family?' He would say yes. He would tell him: 'Sit over there.' We had no idea about anything. They were Arab Jews; they spoke Arabic. The guy who was asking spoke Arabic.

The Jews who were in 'Akka and Haifa spoke Arabic just like us. The nationalist Jews. Yes, most of them spoke Arabic, just like us. I lived in Haifa, I stayed in Haifa, I used to go to Haifa, I went to Hadera,[12] I went to Wadi Rushmiyya, because my brothers-in-law and my sister-in-law were there, so we would go and take their things to them, and we would stay with them. The people living one floor above them were Jews, she would tell him, '*Yi*, why are you talking to him? *Yi*, he talks like Muslim people talk' –

whenever he said a bad word or whenever he swore. She would say, 'You're talking like Muslim people talk.' They spoke Arabic, just like us!

He would say to him, 'Come. You go.' He would send a Jew with him and tell him: 'Go bring your family and come here. *Yalla!*' He would go and bring his family and come. All the married people, anyone who said: 'We are married.' Some were from Mi'ar, others were from Sha'b, from Majd al-Krum, from al-Birwa, from somewhere. I swear, there was a guy from al-Birwa, he asked him: 'Are you married?' He said yes ... When the people of al-Birwa were leaving, he came and rented from us, in Sha'b. We had a room upstairs and a room downstairs, we had space. He came and rented – no, stayed – with us. He came and said, 'Can I rent from you?' He responded, 'No, I don't rent. Rent? No. Stay. Stay with us until God grants deliverance Insha' Allah.' He stayed with us, in our house, in our home, with us, with our family, in our own home. When we left, when people had to leave and they kicked him out, [the Jews] said: 'You bring family and come.' He had three children: a month-old boy in a swaddle, in his mother's arms, a two-year-old boy and a five-year-old boy. They gathered these people, and they came to my uncle. I was standing right there. They came to my uncle's – we were waiting to see what they were going to do to these people. He asked him: 'Are you married?' He said, 'yes'. 'Do you have a family?' He said, 'yes'. He said: 'Go bring family and come.' So I ran and I beat them to the house. I went in and they went in right after. He told her, 'Khazna! *Yalla*, you have to come with me.' My sister-in-law was living with us. She had three girls. And my brother-in-law was there, he was eleven or twelve years old. His name was Fayad. They clung to their mother: '*Ya mama*, we don't want you to leave! We don't want you to leave!' He turned around and saw me, and said: 'You go with *khawaja*.'[13] I said: 'No, he is not *khawaja*!' He said: 'You go with *khawaja*!' He loaded his gun in front of me. My mother-in-law came and said, 'Go with your father-in-law, go.'

We had no idea where they were taking us! No idea where they were – but I thought, whatever I did, it was better than picking olives. I did want to go. They took us and we left in the night; they made us ride in the buses. They made the elders ride in a truck, I swear, and they drove in front. Men and women were separated, and the buses were on their way. Anytime we reached a Jewish *kubbaniyya* ... The sun had set in al-Layyat, before we reached the coast – between al-Birwa and Majd al-Krum, there was a plain called al-Layyat. We drove through the night. There were buses driving in front of us, the truck was in front of us, and there were more cars in front of the truck that was carrying the elders. And it was so cold! It was around January. We kept going, and every time we came close to a Jewish *kub-*

baniyya or a plain inhabited by Jews, they would stop, blow a whistle and they would come out. They would applaud and spit on us, while we were inside the bus. This woman moaned, that woman cried, another woman – we left it up to God, we had no idea where they were taking us. They took us until ... I don't know these other lands very well. The buses stopped, and they said: 'Yalla! Go Down. Yalla, go to King 'Abdullah.' The first one ... King 'Abdullah at the time, not this one – his grandfather! 'Yalla! To King 'Abdullah.' And we walked as they were shooting at us. When they began shooting, the woman who was with me, the one who was renting from us, the poor woman from al-Birwa ... She was holding her son firmly with one hand, and on her head, she was carrying a bundle of clothes – their change of clothes – I don't know, I don't remember what was on her head, she was carrying something on her head. She let go of the boy's hand, and she firmly clasped the clothes on her head and grasped the infant in her arms. And we started running. She forgot the boy. She forgot her son, a two-year-old boy or maybe he was three, he was just starting to walk. And we started running, with bullets shooting behind us. We walked the same distance as between here and the dome, and even further. When we arrived, each one started calling their relative's names. They said, 'Stop. Let some people go call the Jordanian Army' – that's what they used to call the army of al-Difa – 'so that they don't think it's a descent, and start shooting at us.' They told us to stay. That guy was looking for his wife. He didn't find the boy: 'Woman, where is the boy?' She said, 'I don't know.' 'How do you not know?' She said, 'I don't know, when they started shooting, he was holding my hand, I cannot recall where...' She had let him slip away.

They backtracked and they found him. They went back, they were behind us, they found him crying and shouting. They took him and brought him to Majd al-Krum, to the *hannaneh*, where they – to the square, and they called the *mukhtar*. They said, 'We found this child, he was left behind'. It seemed like there were people who knew him ... His aunts, his father's sisters had not left with him. The only ones who left were his wife and children. His aunts were young, maybe [their brother] didn't want them to leave, I don't know – they didn't leave. Who recognised him? His aunts. They collected him. Some witnesses confirmed that he was indeed their nephew. They took him. As for us, we arrived all the way there, and the Jordanian Army came and took us. They put us in a plain called Khirbat Umm al-Fahm, it was a *khirbeh*.[14] We stayed there, they brought us firewood and kindled it for us until we were warm. We had to wear so many layers because of the cold! Until the next morning, when they made us walk the same distance as between here and the reservoirs, by foot. They sat us under the olive trees and they brought us breakfast – bread and dates and I don't know what, and before sunset they took us up to a village called 'Ara and 'Ar'ara. They were two neighbouring villages; they were only separated by a valley. They looked close to each other. They said, 'This village is called 'Ara and this one is 'Ar'ara.' They placed us in mosques. They took the men over to one plain and they took us to another plain. We stayed there for about three days, in that village, in the mosque. Then, they made us ride in a – I don't remember, maybe a truck, not a bus. That's all I remember, a truck. They took us to Jenin. They said, 'This is Jenin.' They took us to Jenin, to a hotel, or I don't know what, with a *hammam*. And that poor woman, her one-month-old boy died, the one she was holding in her arm – the woman who lost her son. The one-month-old infant who was in her arm died as well. She said, '*Ya wayli*. I had three and I have only one left?' She cried so much. We stayed in Jenin for about eight days. We went and found the tents ready for us in Nablus. Between the Nablus fountain and the pitched tents, there were barely 100 metres – 100 *dhira*', and the main road joined them. They put every 12 or 13 people in a tent. We stayed there for about three months. At that time, we had braided hairdos, we called them *lirat* or *jahadiyat*; they served as ornaments – we had no money! We left without any money or anything. They would bring us bread and cheese and things like that, they would go to the villages and bring us olive oil – my uncle and the men who were there. We would forage for herbs, like chard and spinach. There were gardens around us. One day, there was a guy with us whose son was in al-Ghabisiyya – he was an old man named Sa'id al-Mahmud, Abu Muhammad. His son had sent someone from al-Ghabisiyya to pick him up, when he found out we were in Nablus. Sa'id al-Mahmud was also my uncle's relative; he was his paternal cousin. My uncle said to him, 'I want to leave with you.' So we did some paperwork, I sold the gold I was carrying on my belt, and we did some paperwork and paid a fee, and we travelled from Nablus, to Jordan, to Damascus, until we came to 'Anjar. And that is our story.

9
Four Villages, Four Stories: Ethnic Cleansing Massacres in al-Jalil*
Saleh Abdel Jawad

'The sheer terror of the crime makes the killers, who profess their own inno-cence, more readily believed than the victims, who are telling the truth.
– Hannah Arendt[1]

This is the story of four Palestinian villages in different parts of al-Jalil (Galilee): Saliha, al-Husayniyya, Safsaf and ʿAylut. The story is based on the testimony of four women who experienced the occupation of their villages first-hand, as young girls during the war of 1948. One of the villages (al-Husayniyya, in al-Hula plain north of Lake Tiberias) was occupied by the Jewish military organisation Haganah in mid-March 1948, that is to say, prior to the formation of the Israeli Army in late May 1948. ʿAylut, which sits directly west of al-Nasira (Nazareth), was occupied by the Israeli Army in mid-July of the same year. Meanwhile, Saliha and Safsaf, both situated near the border with Lebanon, were taken late in the 1948 war. If we compare events in al-Husayniyya with the other three villages, we can see that even after its formation, the Israeli Army continued the legacy of terror established by Jewish paramilitary organisations. This was despite, or perhaps owing to, the level of discipline enforced in the Israeli Army.

In the minutes or hours that followed the occupation of each of these villages, family homes would be destroyed and massacres carried out in which entire households – mothers, fathers, sons, brothers, sisters, husbands – were killed. Such indiscriminate and brutal murder constituted the norm, and not the exception, as we shall see in the following pages. It would be followed by a mass expulsion of the village, over the border and into Lebanon.

In the somewhat unusual case of ʿAylut, only some of the families, who had taken refuge in al-Nasira, were able to return to their village and stay there after it had been completely evacuated.[2] When they did return, a year after being displaced, the tragedy of single families torn apart was laid bare,

* This chapter was translated from the Arabic by Lindsay Munford.

186

and it became clear who had left and who remained: a brother or son in 'Aylut, and a brother or son in Lebanon; a husband here and a wife over there. All of them grew up and the majority died without ever meeting again, even once. They did not even hear about their loved ones – except on the radio![3]

In two of the four cases (al-Husayniyya and Saliha), the girls sustained heavy injuries and lost their fingers. In the first case, it was from rubble that hit the girl when her house was blown up with her and members of her family inside.[4] In the second, it was flying debris that struck her when the houses in Saliha were destroyed en masse, engulfing families that were gathered in the public square. As a result, the two girls required months of intensive treatment in Lebanon.

However, the injury that did not and will never respond to any kind of treatment is the trauma of the massacre. Even dozens of years after the Nakba, Kamila Al-'Abd Tahir, from Saliha, is still deeply traumatised. Anyone who watches and listens to the video interview recorded with Kamila, who was then in her eighties, will see from her body language, the hard look in her eye, and her plaintive, grief-stricken tone that the events of the massacre and the loss of her romantic childhood are engraved on her mind as if set in stone. It will also be evident that since then and until she dies, she will never escape the image of dozens of handsome innocent youths being slaughtered like sheep. 'Have you seen sheep all laid out? The young men were strewn out on the ground like sheep. I remember the massacre, it devastates me, and the fire engulfs me.'

The image that really stays with her is of being seriously injured and holding her brother, who had critical injuries and was bleeding out in silence. Both had been hit by flying debris when the houses of Saliha village were destroyed. Then there was the execution of young people who had been rounded up in one place for the purpose. After the execution, the army pulled out of the village.

According to Kamila, 'After the army withdrew on the first day of the massacre, no one was rescued and no one got buried'. Earlier, the terrified residents who still lived (the vast majority of whom were women, and a few elderly men) had just about managed to move the dead and injured to the village's only mosque. There was neither first aid nor doctors in the village, and the injured were dying in silence. The terrified and traumatised women were simply incapable of burying dozens of men and boys.

Fortunately for Kamila, she and her brother had been moved to a house on the edge of the village, where they were joined by their mother. If not for that, the three of them may well have died in the fire or the blast, a fate which befell those who had been moved to the village mosque:

> On the second day, the army troops returned to the village, poured petrol over the bodies and set them on fire in the mosque before blowing it up, never mind who was inside it – dead or wounded. Then they told the few people left in the village, 'Get out of here or we'll burn you alive!' Kamila and the remaining villagers were convinced that the troops would carry out their threat, and it frightened them. 'The dead were dead. What could they do for a dead man? But if they burn someone alive?'

Avoiding death by burning or explosion was by no means the end of Kamila's personal tragedy. In the isolated house where she had been holed up with her mother and brother on the outskirts of the village, the two women, feeling utterly helpless, watched over their boy: Kamila over her brother, and Kamila's mother over her son (and favourite child), as he took his last breath. All Kamila could do was to hold him and cry. 'I held him in my arms, completely soaked in the blood of my brother, Kamil. Blood was seeping out of his whole body'. The young man was very upset as he felt his end draw near and declared, sobbing, that he did not want to die so soon. For two days, the two women clung on to his dead body, in a state of denial and distress. His mother wept and whispered to him, as if he was listening to her, 'Kamil! My kind, affectionate Kamil. It's your mama. We're not going anywhere. We'll stay here and weep'. Eventually, the two women fled the village. This proved difficult because of Kamila's wound, which hampered her movement. During the shooting, she had been injured by a bullet that lodged itself near to her spine, and was not discovered until decades later, when an X-ray was taken in Lebanon due to pain she was feeling in this region of her body. They left Kamil's body behind without burying it, like everyone else.

The massacre in the village of Saliha was no exception. The official Zionist narrative had acknowledged the Dayr Yasin massacre in April 1948, yet this atrocity was acknowledged as an exception, a one-off that ran counter to the general rule that emphasised the 'Purity of Jewish Arms'.[5] In any case, Dayr Yasin was a massacre committed by dissident members of two organisations: Etzel and Lehi. Until the early 1990s, Palestinians themselves concentrated on a couple of massacres only: Dayr Yasin and al-Dawayima. In the early 1990s, I began my work as director of the Research Centre at the University of Birzeit, looking at Palestinian villages that had been destroyed by Israel and whose inhabitants had been forced to flee. The massacres were never the core focus of the project. For our study, my research team and I selected ten villages at random, based on the availability of witnesses and for logistical reasons. The team's work revealed a bombshell: we discovered that massacres had taken place in five of the ten villages. This inspired me to write a paper that was published in 1996 in *Al Ayyam* newspaper (produced in Ramallah) with the title, 'The Dayr Yasin massacre: The Rule, and Not the Exception'. After that, I embarked on a separate, personal project on the massacres. By 2003, I had managed to categorically and decisively document 68 massacres that had been committed in 68 Palestinian villages (of the 531 villages that Israel had occupied and destroyed, and whose people were forcibly expelled).[6]

Based on new information available since 2003, we can now say that no less than 100 massacres were committed in Palestinian towns and villages that were occupied and whose inhabitants were forced to flee. This means that, on average, a massacre was committed in one in every five villages whose residents were displaced. The proportion could have been as high as one in three or one in two if one considers that the only reason dozens of villages did not witness a massacre is that their inhabitants had already fled in terror before the Israeli forces arrived. In those cases, news of massacres in other villages had preceded the Israeli troops' arrival, meaning that there was no need for a massacre. The figure of 100 suggests that massacres took place on a large scale, something previously unknown to researchers and experts. The massacres were used as a tool of ethnic cleansing. Yet, for various reasons, this high figure is in fact a conservative estimate. There are geographical areas for which my data is still minimal and on which I have not been able to gather any information at all, such as the villages of south Palestine and Bedouin camps in the Negev region. The reason for this is that although there are survivors in the Gaza Strip, I have not been able to visit since 1995. I expect that a significant concentration of war crimes were committed in these areas because they were, just as Gaza remains today, less frequently (or not at all) covered by the press or international monitors, as compared with the rest of Palestine. In addition, the people living there were less well educated and open to the media, and less inclined to talk about what had happened to them. Furthermore, there will almost certainly have been secret massacres that will never come to light because none of the survivors live on to bear witness to what took place.

Another fact that has escaped the notice of Western researchers is that when we talk about the dispossession and destruction of 531 Palestinian villages during the 'Nakba', such a figure may seem modest to a French researcher, say, who may be comparing it to the number of villages in his or her country. However, the scale of the tragedy wrought by ethnic cleansing in Palestine would be apparent if that same researcher were to learn that those 531 villages comprise over 80 per cent of the Arab villages that were subjugated by Israeli forces and that fell within the borders of the new state.

The massacres committed in the four Arab villages in this study were carried out as part of the systematic destruction of Palestinian society, and constituted gross violations of the international laws and customs of war in that:

1. They were perpetrated in the absence of any military imperative;
2. In cold blood, and not in the heat of battle;
3. Against civilians, after the village had surrendered and combatants had thrown down their weapons; and
4. After the Israeli forces had taken full control over the village. At this point, they became 'occupying forces' according to the international laws of war, and thereby responsible for the security of the citizens of the village even though they were resisting the occupation, as per the Hague Convention (Section 3) of 1907, and subsequently the Fourth Geneva Convention.

Typically, a village would be surrounded on three sides and then shelled in order to compel its people to flee. To that end, a safe passage or corridor would be left open, leading to the Arab areas that remained (in central Palestine, the passage was to the east in the direction of the West Bank; in Western and Central al-Jalil, it was to the north towards Lebanon; and in Eastern al-Jalil, it was westwards towards Syria). Those who stayed behind and had not fled by the time the Israeli troops arrived were harassed until they did so. For the most part, such harassment would involve killing a select group of young men – a clear 'message' needing no further clarification. You had two choices in front of you; there was no third: either you die or you leave.

Even though, in most of the massacres, Israeli forces targeted young and adult men of fighting age (16–50) and excluded women and children, a significant number of elderly people, women and children were killed in some villages. This occurred particularly, but not exclusively, when the Israeli forces used explosives to destroy homes, blowing them up with everyone inside, without differentiating between village elders, men, women or even babies.

This is the case for al-Husayniyya compared to the other three villages. Al-Husayniyya was attacked as its people slept, at one o'clock in the morning.[7] This was the preferred time for the Israeli forces, who had the edge when it came to night combat, and qualitative and numerical superiority in other respects. The village *mukhtar*, 'Uthman, was the father of our witness Maryam and a close friend of the Jews. I believe that part of the shock experienced by these young women stemmed from the close relationship they had with their Jewish neighbours. Speaking with shame and sadness, in a faint, broken voice, Maryam – even 60 years after the dispossession – still recalls the names of all the Jewish children who would play with her and her siblings in her family home. She remembers her mother teaching the wife of a Jewish friend of her husband's how to cook popular Palestinian dishes like *mujadara*, and the name of the skilled Jewish doctor who would treat her and the people of her village. She also recalls the names of her father's Jewish friends who would enjoy 'proper Arab hospitality' in his home.

On the one hand, she feels slightly embarrassed, even ashamed of these human relationships, which were actually commonplace before the Nakba. On the other hand, the massacre was perpetrated by the Jews, who, in her innocent mind, were only human. She even felt that some of them were 'friends', who stabbed her community in the back. Israeli sources follow a clear narrative about the killing of her father, the village *mukhtar*. According to the Israeli record, the *mukhtar* begged the attackers for his life and, although armed, was friendly towards them. However, Maryam makes no mention of this account of events. According to her, the attackers entered the courtyard and set about killing their three cows. Then, as they laid explosives around the house, she saw that they had spotted her. A Jewish man yelled at her to go back into the house to die with the rest of her family and then came the explosion. 'We stayed where we were in the early hours, buried under the house, until by dawn the villagers began to panic and got us out from under the rubble. Both of my legs swelled up until I looked like a barrel. On the second day, blood was running from my nose and mouth [it transpired that she had internal haemorrhaging], and it was six months before I was able to walk again.'

The close relationship between al-Husayniyya village and its Jewish settler neighbours is not an isolated story. The same was true in 'Aylut, as village girl Amina 'Abd al-Karim Al-Wakid explains. This fact is crucial as it goes against the myth of an ancient deep-rooted enmity between Arabs and Jews, which has served to justify the use of brutality against 'the Other'. It is a myth promoted by Zionist propaganda and, with repetition and the passage of time, blood has been spilled continuously as a result ever since 1948. The concept has leached into the Arab consciousness and come to dominate thinking on both sides. From this perspective, al-Husayniyya and 'Aylut – just like dozens of other Palestinian villages that got on well and peacefully coexisted with their Jewish neighbours – expose the efforts by Jewish settlers to chase out and kill Palestinians, regardless of the latter's positive attitude towards them.

Still, the concept of an ancient deep-rooted enmity was not sufficient to allow a Jewish killer to murder a young man or woman while looking them directly in the eye. Other ideas and mechanisms took care of that: the dehumanisation of Palestinians, the repudiation of every human attribute that brings two communities together and cultural distance. These are the same tried and tested mechanisms that are used by oppressors anywhere, anytime, to facilitate murder: by German Nazi troops against Jews, Russians and Gypsies; and by North American settler troops against Indigenous Peoples, Filipinos and, finally, Iraqis.

The four witnesses have something in common that has never before been discussed. Unlike perpetrators of many massacres committed around the world, the Israeli forces have been completely unwilling to bury their victims, even in mass graves. This was the case in al-Husayniyya and in Saliha, Safsaf and 'Aylut. Sometimes soldiers would leave dead bodies out in the open. More often than not, terrorised survivors, escaping to save their skin, did not have the chance to bury the dead. Occasionally, families would be given the opportunity to bury their children, as in the town of Lydda. This was so that the Israeli troops who remained in the town did not become sick. In villages where people were killed in great numbers, such as Saliha, Safsaf and al-Dawayima, the dead were assembled with some of the living in a house or mosque in the village. This was then blown up with survivors and the dead inside, turning the destroyed house or mosque into a mass grave. There were mass cremations, too. This is how 28 elderly people who were being evacuated from the village of Tirat Haifa died, as they got off the bus that was transporting them. Bodies would also be thrown into wells, which was the case in Safsaf, Dayr Yasin and al-Dawayima. In 'Aylut, Saliha and Safsaf, the carnage ensued in several phases. At each stage, women survivors would witness – with an agony that lingers – their loved ones, left out in the open or buried just below ground level, being ravaged by dogs and wild animals.

WALL OF SILENCE

How did the Zionists get away with it? Their heinous actions were shrouded in silence and forgotten for dozens of years. Not only did they revel in their astonishing ability to cover up the truth but they also showed unprecedented brazenness in comparison to other colonisers that had committed similar acts. They opted to avoid engaging in the matter and put up a wall of total silence that allowed them to insist to this day on the purity of Jewish arms, which became one of the Zionist myths of the 1948 war. The tragedy is that the victim herself would sometimes be complicit in this 'game of silence', since for many complex reasons, she chose not to disclose her story. These reasons include the fact that Arab regimes did not want to raise an issue that would cause unrest or turmoil among their citizens. Another reason is that some victims still fear that they would be killed if they spoke out. There is also the sense of there being no justice in the world, and that talking about things will not make an ounce of difference.

CONCLUSION

The massacres of the 1948 war were a foregone conclusion from the moment the Zionist movement resolved to settle the Jewish Question by establishing an exclusively Jewish, ethnically and culturally homogenous state in Palestine, along the lines of a modern European nation state. Although Zionism is not inherently bloodthirsty, like any displacement-settlement colonisation project in history, its architects resorted to violence when they felt that no matter what efforts and tactics they employed, they would neither succeed in capturing all Palestinian territory, nor in ousting the original population – who remained in the majority – by non-violent means. Unlike earlier settler colonial projects, the Israeli occupation took place in the mid-twentieth century: after the advent of mass media, in the wake of the Nuremberg trials and amid the final stages of concerted campaigning for international laws to define and prohibit genocide (which culminated in the adoption of the UN Genocide Convention on 9 December 1948). While these factors may have modulated Zionist forces' strategy, the well-planned, carefully orchestrated practice of massacres and terror was central to the systematic ethnic cleansing of Palestine they perpetuated.

In these pages, thanks to the witness accounts recorded, we are given a new perspective on the massacres, a humane one consisting of flesh and blood and raw emotion, which does not simply reel off information as if by rote.

Most Israeli historians are aware that their leadership planned and executed some of the most appalling ethnic cleansing in history. They know, too, that numerous atrocities have been and continue to be committed against the Palestinian people in a Nakba that has continued unabated since 1948. Many of those historians have developed mechanisms for denial. Some of these mechanisms are unique, yet most are implemented as part and parcel of any displacement-settlement colonial project. Have the above pages succeeded in eliciting their compassion? I doubt it, as from its inception the Zionist movement has stripped Palestinians and Arabs of their humanity. Though their reflex will likely be to ignore these pages, as they have previous studies, the facts of the Nakba have become increasingly difficult to ignore.

Close attention to oral testimonies, and other empirical evidence these corroborate, is essential as we continue to struggle against colonial narratives that legitimise inhuman injustice, past and present.

Kamila al-ʿAbd Tahir
born circa 1933 in Saliha, Palestine
Interview with Bushra Mughrabi
al-Murayja, Beirut, 2004

6'06"–16'16"

Bushra Mughrabi: *When you were young, what did you think of the Jews? How did you feel about them?*
Kamila al-ʿAbd Tahir: What do you mean, when we were young? The Jews have always been scary! When we were little, when my younger siblings would go outside of the house, we would say: 'The Jew is after you.' My sister would jump and scream: 'Aaah! They scared me!' These are the things that happened when we were kids! What else could happen?

Why would you tell them: 'The Jew is after you'? What did he represent in your mind? How did you imagine him to be?
We used to hear people say: 'The Jews are treacherous', 'The Jews are killers', 'The Jews...' That sort of thing. And they were treacherous indeed because when the massacre happened ... Listen, I want to be able to tell you everything I forgot when I was younger. But when the massacre happened, those are tragedies that can never be forgotten. They can never be forgotten. What can I tell you ... It's not ... What can I possibly say?

How did the massacre happen? What happened to you?
As I told you, we were leaving Saliha. We left, my brother and I, and everyone was saying, 'Ya ʿammi, this is going to happen, that is going to happen.' So they sent the Circassians their way, so they could surrender since the Jews would not speak to anyone.[8] This person said this to that person who said it to the other, and everyone was erratic. Some ran away, others said the Jews weren't trustworthy. As for us, we got out and left. We went to get the wheat so we could leave. As we were carrying it, the Jews began bombing Saliha. They arrived and the village people were ... Those who entered the village spoke Arabic: 'If you are in the village, surrender.' Some people surrendered and others did not surrender. My sister ... My two nephews, one of them – their father was hugging them, their mother had passed away a long time ago. Their father was hugging them, one in this arm and the other in that arm. When they shot them ... Every time someone came they would tell him: 'Sit.' When they shot them, he fell back like this, with the children in his arms. One boy in this arm and the other boy in that arm. They were

little, Ismail and Yusif. Anyway, they came, people said, 'The Jews are here,' and that they called for people to surrender, and I don't know what, and that they wouldn't speak to anyone, they wouldn't attack anyone or anything. I was with my brother, he said, 'Sister, you go to the Shamali house, to your aunt's, and we'll go and see what happens.' I told him 'no, it's night outside,' I said: 'No, I don't dare to go. What if a Jew finds me, what if he says something, what would I say to him?' I kept clinging to him, he pushed me, and I kept saying no, I'm not going anywhere. We arrived – there were armoured vehicles lined up in front of a house. We arrived there. They searched my brother and his friend before letting them in. When they finished searching them, he came closer and was about to lay his hand on me. I yelled and ran to my brother. The Jew, goddamn him, said to me: '*Ruh, yalla, ruh*.'[9] They were taking them away, basically. He was trying to speak but didn't know how: '*Ruh!*' I said, 'I can't, I don't want to leave.' '*Ruh!*' He kept telling me to go and I wasn't leaving. At the end, he grabbed me and yelled: '*YALLA!*' – like this, with his hand. He pushed me, with my brother and his friend. We went inside and sat where they had people gathered. Every time someone arrived, they told him: 'Saliha *zeft*. Saliha not good.' They didn't say 'Saliha.' They said: 'Not good. Saliha *zeft*.' They came and started saying there was a rifle in the village, that there were arms. People started – people were naive, really naive – those who had weapons were handing them to the Jews. The people of my village – because people were so naive – whenever a Jew died in front of their eyes, they would go to Khirbat … Whatever that village is called, in al-Malikiyya, Qadas, where battles were happening – my brother was among the first ones to go – they would retrieve the rifles. He told them, 'Bring the rifles and surrender.' Every time a rifle came, they would hand it over to the Jews. They collected the rifles for the Jews. They would recognise them. 'Saliha *zeft*,' that's what they started saying. Every time someone came, they would search him and say: '*Yalla. Yalla!*' They kicked everyone out. These young men would go, young men and women … Actually, there were no girls at all, not one girl, to tell you the truth. They sat everyone down, and said: 'Where is the *mukhtar*'s house?' One guy said: 'I think it's this one.' It wasn't my uncle's house; it was the wrong house. They blew it up and the rocks flew out to the pond. There was a guy called Mustafa 'Abbas; they went and blew up his house. They surrounded the houses before they destroyed them. We were sitting there and thinking: 'Dear God …' – we didn't expect to be so frightened. We thought they might even expel us, or they might leave us and nobody would talk to us. Letters came that said: 'Surrender and raise the white flag.' It was all just talk. Whoever tells you the opposite, tell him … Because I remember every single thing.

Where did the letters come from, Hajjeh?
From the Circassians. They said that – I don't know. The people were not –
some said yes, some said no. Some said, 'It's impossible ... These Jews can
never be trusted'. At the end, they lined all these people up. They lined them
all up, so many young men – each one of them was ... Some were two or
three siblings. They lined them all up and sat them down and said: '*Yalla!*
On the ground'. They didn't even let one of them stand. All of them sat on
the ground; I was looking at them. There was something like ... and *yalla*,
they started (gestures bullets spraying) at these people. This one got it in his
head, this one got it in his heart, this one ... The rest of them picked up and
left immediately. We stayed, those of us still alive stayed. They moved those
who had been killed inside the mosque. The next day, the Jews came and
blew up the mosque ... Burnt the mosque.

Who moved the killed ones, Hajjeh?
Village people! From our village. You think the Jews would have picked
up the killed ones? People picked them up and put them in the mosque.
They came and burnt the mosque and blew it up. Its stones flew out and
landed in the Saliha pond. Its stones flew out. As for my brother and I, they
took us and put us in a secluded house at the edge of the village. A woman
came along, she was wailing for her children lost in the massacre. I called
out to her, 'Would you please go tell my mother – who is in Harat al-Shar-
qiyya (the Eastern Quarter), at my uncle's house – tell her your children
were lined up and shot.' The woman left. She told my mother, who came –
you know how a mother is. My brother was a young man and I was ... She
started wailing and crying. They took us and put us in a room. The next
day, the Jew came. He said: 'After – ', so they gave us a deadline before they
would come and burn us. I stayed with my brother for four days, with my
wounds open and my brother had been dead for two days; he died two days
before I got out. And for two days and two nights, I was next to his dead
body – my head by my brother's head. I did not abandon my brother.

You were sleeping next to his dead body?
Yes, I slept next to his dead body. Do not say he was dead!

Martyred.
Martyred. Don't ever say 'dead'! I stayed next to him. In the end, my
mother panicked. She said, 'They'll come burn us alive, I want you to get
out.' I told her, 'Let me die here.' There were covers, a piece of cover and
she tied it around my waist, like a belt. I had been without food or water

for four days. If someone were to give me water, they would have said, 'She might die if we gave her water.' My mother got me out, she tied a belt around me and my sister had gotten my maternal aunt out. But I stayed, so my mother tied the belt around me [to carry me], and we walked – I don't know where to. There was a location between Yarun and Saliha. Israeli soldiers were on their way: they were coming from far. They stopped their truck, got out and started running our way. I told my mother, 'Ya Allah! You brought me all the way here to die? You should have let me die over there, instead of getting eaten by monsters.' Truly! She said, 'This is your destiny, my daughter.'

19'04"–22'42"

What can I tell you, the killed were … have you ever seen sheep just lying there? They were sheep just lying there, young men, all of them – some old, some middle-aged, some … All of them … The Jews left, they had no idea about anything. Every time one came, he would spit at Saliha, he would say: '*Hayda zeft. Saliha zeft*' because they uncovered their weapons. Because the people were from Saliha, their weapons were – when there was a battle, for example, in al-Nabi Yusha' or al-Malikiyya, the Jews would invade the whole territory. The people of Saliha would go. It was full of young men, they were excited, they had weapons. They didn't need much to take up arms and *yalla*. What can I say, my dear … so many examples. Since then, believe me, whenever I tell these stories, blood boils over from my heart. If you knew my brother … My brother was among those rare men! When he was younger, he used to always stay in Haifa. When I saw his tall body just lying there, I told my mother, 'Mother, what a tragedy he had to die this way.' And I stroked his hair, like this. And we wept, all we could do was weep. What do you want me to tell you – about Palestine and about Saliha … The Saliha days. Saliha is full of worries. It is, my dear.

The woman who was from Tarshiha, was she among the wounded like you? What did she work in?
Yes, she was among the wounded, they took her out from under the rubble. From under the rubble, they took her out…

Hajjeh, when they gathered you in the village, how long did you stay together before they started shooting at you?
Before they sprayed us?

Yes.

Maybe half an hour, by the time they went and blew up some homes, and surrounded some houses and demolished them, and then they came. They started going around the village. Every two seconds, my brother was telling me, 'Why didn't you go and stay at your aunt's?' I said, 'I don't want to go, what if someone found me in the middle of the night, what would I tell him?' He stayed silent, and then said, 'You're the one who's going to get me killed. What if someone said something to you in front of me, what if someone hurt you?' What would anyone say to me? I told him, 'This is how things turned out, *khalas.*'

Did they search homes, did they catch young men?
Yes, they caught many of them – they were entering homes! The next day, around morning, the Jews had swarmed the village. The following day – they swarmed the village! My mother is the one who told me – I didn't see any of it, I was at home. She said, 'The village is filled with Jews.' My mother would leave the house; she'd come and go. She'd tell me the village was filled with Jews. They didn't call it Israel at the time, they said 'the Jews'.

So they had you gathered in the village?
(She nods).

Did anybody ever come to talk to the Jews or to act as a mediator between you?
Yes, there was a guy called Na'im Ismail. He went and spoke to them and said, 'We'll surrender, and we'll find whoever is not surrendering and we'll make them surrender,' and all that. [The Jew] said: 'No! I can invade a hundred villages like this one in a day. I'm not waiting or anything.' He was so puffed up with his own words. He said he wouldn't wait.

23'00"–24'47"

Other than you – who stayed in the village – were there people who left the village?
Yes, so many people. Many people left, my dear, so many people – only very few stayed. My uncle came over and told my brother, as we were standing outside – he said, 'Kamil, my nephew, take your sister and leave!' My brother said, (she throws back her hand dismissively). None of them were scared. I was terrified! One guy came, his name was Na'im Ismail, he said, 'Kamil, obey me and leave.' He had stayed in the village, his father was in the village

and all. 'Obey me, take your sister and leave.' My brother said, 'I have no idea why these people are so scared, better leave it up to God. Where should we go? We don't even know anyone. Which village should we go to?' Na'im Ismail said: 'Leave! The land of God is vast.' We got out and we came back again. Our destiny was to come back and to suffer this terror.

Where did you go to?
First, we went to Yarun. Then we came back to Marun because my maternal cousin had married someone from Marun.[10] And my family knew her family from a long time ago – they passed away. They knew them from a long time ago, so we went over to them. They said, 'Will you take what you need, take any sustenance you need with you.' The donkeys, when we left them, they were loaded. We left them, loaded with supplies, in the house. We did not untie them or anything. Then we went – and we left everything there.

34'04"–35'55"

Did [the Jews] kill any young men? You said they were standing at the Saliha border. Did they kill any of the young men who were getting out from inside the village?
Those who got out were leaving at night; they didn't let anybody see them. *Hayat* Na'im Ismail, may he rest in peace, and Ibrahim Qasira. Na'im Ismail's father placed him inside the room and the other guy picked his son up – he had a son. His name was Mahmud Qasira. He picked him up and put him inside the room as well, and they both left. They left, and I kept calling him – 'I beg you Abu Sa'id, give me water.' He said, '*Ya* Abu Sa'id' – no, I mean Ibrahim Qasira. He said, '*Ya* Ibrahim Qasira, I want to know who this girl from the massacre is, the one who is screaming.' He got closer and closer, and I told him, 'Please, Abu Sa'id, give me water, I'm so thirsty! Pick me up and throw me in the pond like this *yam*.' Might as well just throw me whole! He said, '*Ya 'ammi*, I can't –' He said, '*Wallah, ya* Ibrahim Qasira, nothing broke my back more than this girl screaming between the martyrs.' 'Between the dead', is what he said that day. A bit later, as he was leaving with Ibrahim Qasira and before they arrived in Lebanon, they killed them in Saliha, while they were on their way out. They massacred them. Not even a bird could cross through.

So they weren't among the wounded?
No! They were not wounded. They were neutral and standing on the side, and they sprayed everyone with bullets, but they were on the other side, so they weren't shot and nothing happened to them. When they got out, they died on the way. Both of them died on the way.

Maryam ʿUthman
born circa 1937 in al-Husayniyya, Palestine
Interview with Bushra Mughrabi
Burj al-Shamali, Sur, 2004

5'09"–9'20"

Bushra Mughrabi: *Did you use to buy from the Jewish settlers?*
Maryam ʿUthman: No, but the village I was telling you about, Harat Zubayd,[11] used to buy vegetables from them and anything they needed, and also they used to come visit us; they were very kind. But in that other village [Hulata],[12] if anyone needed to go to the doctor, they would deny them entry at the gate. If the person was an Arab, if they spoke Arabic, the others wouldn't speak Arabic at all. The village had two gates only, the southern gate and the northern gate. They had someone assigned at each gate. If they saw you were an Arab, they made only one doctor available for you. He was a very bright doctor, his cabinet was among lots of trees. All the Arabs would get treated by him, they paid.

Did [the Jews] make a point of visiting you because they knew you, or were they random visits?
If they knew you, they would just pay you a short, symbolic visit and leave.

Did you use to visit them?
Very rarely, but as I said, the Arab Jews would come, and Arabs would go to them and our young men would work their lands, water their *bayyarat*, till their soil and plant it. The other ones never let an Arab work for them, ever.

Do you remember any names of Jews who used to visit you?
I remember the doctor's name, and there was a guy who worked as a guard on their farms, his name was Ishaq Burukh, and the doctor's name was Raymond. I know only their names. He would bring his wife with him, as well as his kids, in the afternoon. He had a small car. Not every day; every 15 or 20 days, or every month. They would come in his small car, visit us for a bit – him, his wife and their kids – and then leave. And the guard who kept an eye on the farms would swing by. We had neighbouring lands, the Jew's plot was here and the Arab's plot was right next to it. He would come over for a cup of coffee, we would exchange news and then he'd leave.

Were his kids your age?
No, they were older. He had three girls and two boys.

Did you play together?
No, we rarely visited them. If they came for a visit, we would play together.

Did you play together in your house?
Yes, we did play in our house … But they spoke good Arabic. Other than that, there wasn't much mixing.

Do you recall their names?
Yes. The older one was called Rina. The middle one was called Khaba. The youngest one was called Duira. They were like Arabs, they cooked in their homes just like we cooked. They ate and drank just like us. They milked cows and had an oven in their house in which they baked their bread. We were the same. He had two boys. The older one was Shimon and the other one, Nakhum, who was a little younger. One time, we went to visit them and I found his daughter kneading, just like we knead. She had the dough and she was squatting and kneading. Then, they lit the oven and she went to bake the bread. They buried it just like you would with a *taboun*. And her mother was cooking *mujadara*. When I used to visit her, she would say to me: 'Your *mujadara* is tastier; you cook it better than ours. We don't make very good *mujadara*.'

You told me your father was the village mukhtar.
Yes, he was.

When a guest came to al-Husayniyya, where would they stay?
There were the ʿatawiya – or I don't know what they call them – a village committee. Some people hosted them in their homes, others would tell them, 'The *mukhtar*'s house is over there.' They came, stayed over, ate, drank, had lunch. There was also a government patrol, with one British guy and two young Arab men. They would also come over in the morning, have breakfast, stay for an hour or so and leave. Then they would come back at noon and have lunch, and they would feed their horses.

9'45"–10'29"

When did you start noticing problems between you and the Jews?
When the British began to withdraw. The British started withdrawing and handing things over to the Jews. The Jews started hating us; they could no

longer look at an Arab. The day they completely withdrew, we began seeing them train every single day, outside the village – young men and women, at dawn, training outside. What did people say? They said, 'These are tourists, they're here for a breath of fresh air.' They trained girls as well as boys. A short while later, they started taking revenge on the Arabs. Wherever they found an Arab, they pulled him over – or whenever an Arab went to them. They began hating the Arabs.

13'15"–17'16"

They surrounded the village from the east, from the *qibla* and from the west.[13] The northern side remained open for a bit. Where were we to go? The village itself was tiny, barely half the size of this one. The village guards who died, died when they ran out of bullets, and those of them who found a place to hide were safe. They stayed until they blew all the houses up and whatever was inside them, and then picked up and left. They even killed one of the revolutionaries, among the few who were sleeping at Husayn Ja'far's house. They say he was kicked out and they took him along with them. That's what I heard; I didn't see any of it. I wasn't awake but that's just what I heard. As soon as they entered, I woke up; I heard gunshots, I heard cries, I heard it all. They came in at around one in the morning.

So there was a guard who was awake, and they clashed with him...
Yes! They clashed for about half an hour, or an hour, and you could see bullets falling like raindrops. My father left and my mother asked him where he was going. 'I want to see what all these gunshots are about.' When he came back, he told us the Jews had invaded the village. She said, 'Then let's get these children out, let's go somewhere else.' He said, 'There is no road, where do you want to leave from? Just stay home, hopefully nothing will happen.' Barely had he stepped into the house when the Jews were already in our yard. We had three cows in our yard, they killed them as well. They were dead. When they entered the house – there was a gas lamp on in that corner there, he said, 'We should turn this light off, in case they see us.' The door was sort of hidden. He had a small gun, he pressed himself against the door and began shooting at them. My mother started scream-ing at him. She said, '*Ya zalameh*, you'll bring calamity upon us!' What was he supposed to do? It was raining bullets outside. He said, 'It's only death. Let me just die.' The Jews were digging a hole near the door. Near the door! They wanted to place a mine there. Do you know what they did so no one would see them? They started throwing sonic bombs that exploded inside

the house, but the smoke that came out of them blinded you. I was awake at that moment. [My father] came and told her, 'Ya mara, they're about to blow up the house on us. You're going to be martyrs, you're going to die. We're all going to die tonight.' He pulled out the mattresses for us, all the way over there and brought two covers, and he put them on Ahmad and I, and Rasmiya. We were sleeping. He covered us with them fearing the bullets would hit us, and thinking that if they did, the covers would protect us. Thinking that if a bullet were to go through the wool, it wouldn't reach the person. He had barely finished that when the whole house blew up. We had no idea what had happened, nor what hadn't happened. We stayed there until the morning, until the villagers came, from al-Shum,[14] from Marus, from 'Ammuqa. The neighbouring village also came and asked whether we were dead or alive. I was not really conscious; I didn't know where to go. I sat there and I saw Ahmad, they pulled him out dead, and they were still working on getting Rasmiya out, you know her. They kept pulling on her body, from among the wood and the metal. Here (she points to her leg), they tore it all and her bones showed. They pulled out one girl; she was about eight months old. My mother was holding her and breastfeeding her, a rock fell on her mouth – the girl died. My mother was completely disfigured, and her father was hit by many bullets (she points to her head), his hair was completely entangled. There was my father's cousin, who also lived with us, along with his daughter. They died at the door. He placed a mine at our door – he was digging a hole for it and she was standing near the door. She told him: 'Wallah ya khawaja, we are women, there are no men among us. There aren't any men or – '. 'Ok. Ok.' Her and her daughter turned into meat, they brought them all the way back from the bayadir. Their bodies were torn into two or three pieces. They blew up her and the house.

What is her name?
The girl's name is Fatma ... And her mother's name is 'A'isha. And her sister's name is Samira, she was about eight months old. They all died. They made us leave in the morning and they started moving us in small groups to different villages. They took us to Marus and we stayed there for about two months.

21'50"–22'06"

Did people stay inside their homes when they started bombing them?
Some of those who were in the north fled to the valley, after they left the house. They knew it would get hit, so they left for the valley. They were safe.

205

Everyone who stayed inside died. God extended the lives of those who left, only.

26'00"–26'37"

Were you aware that you had been hit?
When they got me out, I was unconscious until noon and I didn't know anyone or anything – until the afternoon, when I was able to see a little. I remember, they put me in a house at the edge of the village and they left me, and they got busy with the dead and the wounded. Nobody came to see me, except for an old man, I remember. I told him, '*Ammo*, I need water.' 'Abdallah Qasim, you know him. He said, 'I am ill, I cannot give you any water.' I kept fainting and waking up, again and again. It took a week until I was able to see properly again.

Khalidiya Mahmud Yunis and Jabr Muhammad Yunis
born circa 1924 and 1922 in Safsaf, Palestine
Interview with Mahmoud Zeidan
ʿAyn al-Hilweh camp, Sayda, 2003

19'30"–29'10"

Mahmoud Zeidan: *Which army came to your village, to Safsaf?*
Jabr Yunis: The Syrian army. They sent Jaysh al-Inqadh [the Arab Liberation Army].

How was your relationship with them? Did they give you weapons, for example?
Jabr: No, not at all.

Did you serve with them?
Jabr: No, no. They never gave us one bullet.
Khalidiya: They entered the village like monsters…
Jabr: The village people left. It was April 1948, when all of Safad fell. The people of Safsaf left the village and went to Lebanon. We stayed there for 10 or 15 days, then the Jews left and went back to their postings. People started coming back to collect their harvest and their lentils, and all … You know, they were farmers. They came back to the village and harvested all their crops until the end. Olive season came, so they began picking the olives, and that's how the Jews attacked the whole village, during olive harvest. They attacked the whole region, not just our village. All of Safad.
Khalidiya: That was the beginning of it all – the first time the Jews came in.
Jabr: They attacked them and the battle lasted two days. No, one day, one night only. The Jews entered the village and they devastated everything in their path. So, next question?

When they entered the village, were the inhabitants still inside or –
Jabr: Yes. Yes. Yes – in the village.

What did they do to the people who were in the village?
Jabr: What did they do to the people?

Yes.
Jabr: What do you mean, what did they do to the people?

You said they entered the village.
Jabr: The Jews entered the village.

Khalidiya: They invaded it.

Jabr: They invaded it. When they invaded it, they entered people's homes and picked out the men and lined them up and fired shots at them. That's what happened. I was one of them. I'm not lying, I was one of them.

I see.

Jabr: Here – two bullets (he points to his leg). They went in through here and came out through there.

Let me see, can you raise your hand a little?
(He raises his elbow to reveal a deep scar).
Khalidiya: He fell hard on his head.

The shot in your leg, is it visible? Can you raise your trousers?
Jabr: I'm not sure they go high enough.
Khalidiya: Here it is. Look, this is where the bullets entered. Let him see (she points to her husband's knee). Here it is, look. There … It's huge.
Jabr: Here it is.
Khalidiya: They hit him here and went up his leg, there.
Jabr: They got stuck and my sister took them out with a needle.

How many bullets?
Jabr and Khalidiya: Two.
Khalidiya: And another one brushed his side.

Please describe how it happened – when they killed them. How did it start?
Khalidiya: When will I ever get to talk…
Jabr: It started when they invaded the village and part of its inhabitants left. When the Jews entered, they opened the road for the villagers to leave. Some Jews told them to leave and some Jews asked them to stay. Those of us they brought back returned to the village and went to Shaykh Ismail al-Nasra's house, al-Zamur. We stayed at his house for a bit. The Jews came: 'Leave! Come out!' They kicked us out. 'You, you and you', they picked us out from among the women and took us to another place, another house further away. Picture a diwan here, for the guests. Over there, between this door and that spot, there was a wall with a door, it was the women's house. They took us under the mulberry tree, there was a mulberry tree facing the house. 'Come here! Come here!' We went there. They said: 'What do you have?' They searched us and found nothing. What could we have? Those of us who were doing the rounds on the mountain, what were they supposed

to have? They took us, searched us and didn't find anything. 'Stand over there!' they ordered us until the last one. About 22 young men. They made us face the door and they stood behind us. My sister's son looked back at them and said, 'By God, have mercy.' They said: 'Look away, you *khamorim*! You dogs!'.

Khalidiya: Abu Fawzi's brother.

Jabr: They shot us; they sprayed bullets at us.

Khalidiya: And his brother was there.

Jabr: Pardon?

Khalidiya: The *Hajj*'s brother. You are two siblings.

Jabr: They sprayed us. And when they did, all the men fell at once.

Khalidiya: Oh, the sorrow…

Jabr: I fell but I got hit by two bullets only, here (he points to his elbow). When I fell, I moved my leg, I was lying among the dead. A Jew said to another in Hebrew: 'He's still alive. Shoot him again.' He shot two bullets at me, they went into my thigh, here. Two bullets. He fired them and the two bullets stayed here. I stayed there, lying under the dead bodies, from morning until sunset. God saved me. When night fell, I wondered whether I should stay under the dead bodies. I went into the house, I looked for drinking water but I didn't find any. I went up on the *mastabeh*, you know how they used to make them. I went up there looking and there were olives and dried figs. I pulled the cover off the mattress, I went inside, I covered myself with it and slept. And my sister was outside, calling me. Fatma.

How long had you been lying among the dead bodies, before you got up?

Jabr: I was lying with the dead bodies from sunrise until sunset – God is our saviour. I left and I went looking for water but didn't find any. I went to the *mastabeh*, I found dried figs, and olives laid out for pressing. I sat on the olives; I placed a mat on top of them. I laid on the mat and covered myself with a sheet and stayed. A few moments later, my son 'Ali calls out for me. He was six years old. Muhammad. '*Ya ba! Ya ba!*' I said, 'I'm here, son.' He was calling me from outside and I could hear him. I told him to come in; he came in. I said, 'Did you bring me water?' He said, 'There is no water.' I was still lying there. I asked him, 'Who's in the house?' He said, 'My aunt Fatma is there, and my aunt Hishma,' and I don't know who…

Khalidiya: And his mother, his mother.

Jabr: And his mother. I told him, 'Let them bring me a drop of water, even if they have to buy it.' There was no water, no nothing in the middle of the night. So I kept lying there, and soon after my sister Fatma arrived – 'Ya Jabr! Ya Jabr!' – I said, 'I'm here, sister, come in.' She came in and said, '*Yalla,* get up.' I said, 'Where do you want me to go, I'm unable to walk.' She had no idea what had happened to me. 'I can't walk.' She said, 'I'll take you to the women's side, maybe God can save you for your kids' sake.' God is our saviour … She brought me inside the house, into the women's space.

Khalidiya: It was a short distance…

Jabr: It was a short distance; it wasn't far. You just had to enter from here and walk straight. So I stayed there for a bit and suddenly the Jews showed up: 'What's happening? Why are you here?' They told him, 'He's dying of hunger and thirst.' There was no food or anything. They said, 'Ok, go inside, go back to your spaces'. They let the women enter … No, actually, I'm getting ahead of myself. They got the women out and I told my wife, or I don't know who…

Khalidiya: Your sister.

Jabr: I told my sister Fatma, 'Before the Jews come in, tell them there are wounded people. If they ask you for the names of the wounded, tell them they were inside the house and got shot inside the house.' We had a house near the well, it had herds of sheep and goats and cows. That's where we were. When the bombs hit the house, they killed 50 goats and 4 cows. I barely had time to say, 'God is our saviour', than it killed them. We stayed there and when the bombings intensified, we went up to village. The houses we were in were located below the village, on the west side, not in the residential areas. We went back to the village and in my uncle's house, Mar'i al-Hasun's house. Do you know where it is? We went inside and stayed there until the Jews entered the village. 'Come out! Come out!' We did, the Jews were there and there was nobody else in our village. The Jews had remained and the people of the village had taken off. We left and took the al-Ras al-Ahmar road. We went to see Nayif al-Mahmud, the son of Mahmud al-Nasra. He asked us, 'Where are you going?' We said, 'We want to leave, where are the people?' He said, 'They are all at Ismail al-Nasra's house, at my uncle's house.' We left once more and headed to Ismail's house. We went in and the house was full. We went inside and suddenly the Jews showed up. When they let us enter, we did, then the Jews came and said: 'Come out, everyone! Come out!' They made us go out. They chose one man, two, three, four … 'You, you, you, you.' They took the young men outside, over to the other house. When we got to the house, they said: 'What do you have? Bring here, *yalla*.' What were we supposed to have? Those who were doing rounds or staying in a house, what else were they doing? We didn't answer him. One by one, they picked and searched every person, and said: 'Go here, go there, go there', until we were all up. They came and stood behind us and sprayed us all with bullets.

Amina ʿAbd al-Karim al-Wakid
born in ʿAylut, Palestine
Interview with Bushra Mughrabi
al-Bus camp, Sur, 2003

43'05"–44'02"

Bushra Mughrabi: *Hajjeh, were there any Jews around you at the time?*
Amina ʿAbd al-Karim al-Wakid: Yes, the Jews were close to us. The Jews were close to us … They used to come over to our houses and our men would go visit them. They used to wear the *hata* and the *ʿigal* and the *ʿajam-iyya* and they used to visit my in-laws' house.

Would their wives come over as well?
No, their wives wouldn't come. They were Jews.

Which colony were they from?
They used to call it Karkur; it was close to us. They called it Karkur. It's a small colony, next to our village, close to us. They used to ride horses and come over to visit us. They spoke Arabic.

There weren't any problems between you, right?
No! There were no problems before. There weren't any problems, they happened around the end. They stopped coming after the conflicts, since they became our enemies.

51'33"–55'05"

We stayed in al-Nasira. In al-Nasira, the men left at night and our *tarsh* were outside. They came and surrounded the village, and took 18 men. They lined them up … and the Jews were the ones who shot them. They shot some of them. They told us, 'If you want them, you have to bury them. If we come back at five in the afternoon and find someone still here, we won't shoot you, we'll put you in the shops and we'll blow up the shops and everything inside.' We picked them up and put them in the mosque. We put them in the mosque and left for al-Nasira. We came back the next morning to bury them but the dogs were burrowing through them and eating them. We picked up their remains, as much as we could, and buried them like you would a corpse. This lasted five or six days, until they came and surrounded the village. I was telling you about my cousin on my father's side, he was simple-minded. He was tall and skinny. He was taken away from the village by four or five men and they killed him. Nobody knew whether he was still alive or dead. Eleven or twelve days later, he was found eaten by birds and dogs. They went, picked him up, brought him back and buried him. This was my cousin, his name is Dib. That's all I know ... and my uncle Salih was there, I was forgetting about my uncle Salih. So they surrounded him. Abu 'Ali went to hide. I hid my brother-in-law and his wife in the *khawabi*. We had *khawabi* which we called *qawayir*. Back then, we called them *quwwara*. We hid him behind the *quwwara* and all the women left. They blew up our house and my brother-in-law was inside the house. And they blew up Abu 'Ali's uncle's house, and his other uncles' houses, and three of the Abu 'Ayash family shops, and the *mukhtar's* house. They blew them up. When they blew them up, us ladies started yelling: 'This is our house! This is our house!' They called the concierge. Whoever they found in the house, whether in the house, or in the shop, or in the room, they would blow up the place and everything inside it. The whole house blew up on Ahmad, Abu 'Ali's brother. We went to rescue him and he responded: 'I am alive! I am alive! Get me out!' We searched and we got his brother out and he was still alive. He's still in Palestine. We got him out. Abu 'Ali came, he was hiding in a cave near the house. When he came out of the cave, they pointed their weapons towards the village and began firing at the village with their cannons. Whoever escaped escaped and whoever stayed in the village stayed. As for us, we went to al-Nasira – me, my sister-in-law, my mother-in-law and my father-in-law. My husband and his brother Ahmad, who's still in Palestine, left. They slept outside ... The next day, they took their weapons and their *tarsh* and they left. Until Abu 'Ali reached Bint Jubayl, here.

10

Remembering the Fight

Laila Parsons

The final volume of 'Arif al-'Arif's monumental six-volume history of the Nakba, titled *Sijill al-Khulud* or *Register of Everlasting Life*, is a record of the Arab fighters who fell in battle during the 1948 war. The first 126 pages list the Palestinian war dead. Al-'Arif carefully documents their names, where they were from and where they died. The remaining 170 pages are devoted to listing the dead from the Arab armies, including the Syrian, Egyptian, Jordanian, Iraqi and Lebanese armies, as well as Jaysh al-Inqadh (the Arab Liberation Army), the volunteer army raised by the Arab League. Also listed are volunteers who travelled independently to Palestine to fight and died there far from their homes in Saudi Arabia, Yemen, Sudan, Libya, Morocco, Algeria and Tunisia. 'Arif al-'Arif wrote *al-Nakba* in the years immediately following the war when the events of 1947–49 were still fresh. Devoting the final volume of *al-Nakba* to a record of war dead, marked the respect he felt was due to those men and women who struggled to save Palestine from Zionist conquest and who paid for that struggle with their lives.

Watching closely the videoed accounts of Kamil Ahmed Bal'awi, Muhammad Abu Raqaba and Mahmud Abu al-Hayja, I found myself drawn to 'Arif al-'Arif's canonical chronicle of the Nakba to help me better understand the words of these three men. The respect for soldiers contained in al-'Arif's history, and the closeness of his account to the events in both time and space, help us understand the effort that all three men exert in the videos to tell things as they were. Some of that effort is conveyed through signs such as facial expressions, hand gestures and tone that could only be detectable in a videotaped interview. Their words are also elicited in response to the interviewer's questions. But this dialogic frame only intensifies their need to communicate in detail the historical truth of events they experienced. This is partly because many of the interviewer's questions emerge from a much later understanding of the Nakba. All three men struggle to redirect the questions away from current portrayals of the Nakba and insist on their lived experience of the catastrophe.

Many of the Palestinians who died fighting against Jewish forces fell in the summer of 1948. Between April and July, Jewish forces conquered the major Palestinian cities and towns of Haifa, 'Akka, Yafa, al-Nasira and Safad. Battles in al-Jalil were particularly fierce as Palestinians fought for their cities, towns and villages with sporadic support from Jaysh al-Inqadh, which was stationed for much of the summer in Tarshiha in the northern al-Jalil. The extracts below from interviews with Abu Raqaba, Bal'awi and Abu al-Hayja revolve around the events of summer 1948 and their aftermath. Abu Raqaba, who came from a well-to-do family in 'Akka, joined Jaysh al-Inqadh soon after the fighting between Jews and Arabs began in December 1947. Because he had a secondary school education, he was sent to Qatana Camp in Syria to train as an officer.

While thousands of volunteers joined the ranks of Jaysh al-Inqadh in the winter of 1947–48, only a small number of trained officers were at hand to lead the volunteers – a structural weakness that hampered Jaysh al-Inqadh's operations throughout the war. When Abu Raqaba's hometown of 'Akka fell to Jewish forces on 17–18 May, he was still in Qatana, only halfway through his training. When he and his fellow Palestinian cadets realised their cities were rapidly falling to Jewish forces, they tried to return to Palestine to fight; however, Hajj Amin al-Husayni himself instructed them to stay and complete their officer training. Bal'awi fought in the villages around Safad as an ordinary soldier in Jaysh al-Inqadh. After Haifa fell on 22–23 April, Abu al-Hayja left for the village of Sha'ab located on the main road between 'Akka and Safad. There he joined an independent unit, largely comprising villagers from Sha'ab and the surrounding areas, which occasionally benefitted from Jaysh al-Inqadh reinforcements. He took part in the fighting and grippingly recounts how the village of Birwa was recaptured from Jewish forces in June 1948.

All three men are at pains to convey the chaos of that summer and the lack of effective communications in the field. The Jewish forces' superior weaponry also looms large in their accounts. Abu Raqaba describes how the Haganah attacked al-Jalil by air and – 'bam bam bam' – instantly killed fighters who had no anti-aircraft defences. Abu al-Hayja relates how Jewish fighters had a 'deadly' abundance of machine guns and ammunition at their disposal, whereas Palestinian villagers had to 'sell an entire olive grove' to buy a single rifle. The three men also carefully describe those weapons they did possess. Bal'awi tells of safely delivering the heavy muzzle of his unit's mortar gun to his commanding officer, after hauling it over miles of rough terrain along with his own rifle, blanket and other supplies. Abu al-Hayja distinctly recalls the British-manufactured Bren machine guns, and, most importantly, the anti-tank rifles procured by Abu ʿAsaf, a well-known village commander who had a reputation as a fighter during the 1936–39 revolt.

Concern for family also permeates these men's accounts. Abu Raqaba had no idea what had become of his relatives for months after ʿAkka fell. When he eventually found them months later, living in a tent in Burj al-Barajneh Camp near Beirut, he was able to move them into a small apartment nearby on his officer's salary from the Jaysh al-Inqadh. Balʿawi similarly knew nothing of his family's fate until he made his way to Lebanon towards the end of the war, and found them living in an orchard of fig trees in Bint al-Jubayl, with nothing to eat and having to pay for access to water. In the video, he shows the interviewer a photograph of his family in this orchard. Food and other resources were equally scarce in Palestine. Abu al-Hayja recounts his and his friends' fear they would lose the summer's harvest and starve, and how his unit joined forces with villagers to liberate Birwa after Israeli soldiers had occupied the village in early June. Armed with old Ottoman rifles, shovels and sticks, they retook Birwa and successfully reclaimed the surrounding fields, before the Israeli army launched another attack and reasserted control over the village towards the end of June.

All three men's careful descriptions – of weapons, anxieties about family, villages taken, liberated and then lost again, and food scarcity – accentuate the chaos and confusion of events as they unfolded. Yet their younger interviewers pose questions that sometimes draw the men away from details of their direct experience, and encourage them to speak instead to overarching narratives of the Nakba. Broad themes such as the betrayal of Palestinians by Arab armies, massacres in particular villages and the mass flight of people from their homes are central to the narrative structure of the Nakba as it is understood today by generations who have grown up in exile.

The dissonance between these accounts of those who lived through the Nakba and their interviewers' questions reveals a generational gap. For example, Balʿawi's interview includes a description of his involvement in the fighting that took place in Safad and the surrounding villages during the lead-up to the fall of Safad on 10 May 1948. He does not give specific dates, but if we cross check his account with ʿArif al-ʿArif's detailed history, it is clear that Balʿawi is referring to events that occurred in the first week of May. He describes the local command of Jaysh al-Inqadh ordering his unit to leave their base in Tarshiha and retreat northwards to the village of Raʾs al-Ahmar near the Lebanese border. Midway through his account, the interviewer suddenly interjects with a question about the village of Safsaf, which Balʿawi had mentioned briefly a few minutes earlier, as a village he passed by on the journey north. The interviewer likely asks him this question because Safsaf is well known today as one of the Palestinian villages in which a massacre took place. But the massacre in Safsaf did not occur until the end of October, several months after the events that Bal'awi is describing. So the interviewer collapses time when she asks, 'Did you find out what happened in Safsaf after you left?' Confused, Bal'awi tries to explain why he did not: 'There was no war there at the time. The Jews hadn't gone to Safsaf or any of these villages. Inhabitants were still in their villages.' Moments later, the interviewer returns in frustration to the question of Safsaf: 'Have you heard about the massacres that went on in Palestine?' Seconds later she insists again, 'The massacres, the massacres!' to which he responds, 'Oh, the massacres were far from us in the Jerusalem districts and those parts, the massacres happened there first.' Since Bal'awi's focus is on events in al-Jalil in early May, he is clearly referring here to the massacre in Dayr Yasin, which took place on 9 April. Exasperated, the interviewer changes the subject to enquire about Bal'awi's parents.

Watching this exchange closely on video, I was struck by the distance between interviewer and interviewee: Bal'awi is trying to bring his younger interlocutor into the lived experience of the Nakba. For the interviewer, it doesn't really matter whether the massacre at Safsaf happened in May or October. But the date matters a great deal to Bal'awi, who knows he did not leave villagers behind only to be massacred a few days later. At one point the interviewer asks bluntly, 'Did you feel like people were committed to fighting? Were you and the Arabs with you serious about fighting?' Bal'awi meets her question with a brief moment of tired silence.

Abu al-Hayja is less taciturn than Bal'awi. He tells his story with pathos. His account of the fall of Safad begins with a hortatory 'Let us go back in time.' After a long pause, to allow for that shift in time to occur, he recounts his participation in a battle near Majd al-Krum, which lay on the main 'Akka–Safad road near the village of Sha'ab. Palestinians fought on that road in order to block Jewish forces from reaching Safad in early May 1948. Abu al-Hayja then describes how they were ordered to retreat from the Safad area by the High Command of al-Jami'a al-'Arabiyya (the Arab League). Like Bal'awi, he stresses that he and his friends were ordered to retreat and had no say in the matter. But he refuses to offer an opinion on why this order was given. Instead, looking directly at his interviewer he says, 'Analyse this for me, was this patriotism or treason? You are an educated young man and I assume you have done your research.' He implies that there may well have been treachery on the part of Arab League leaders, but he shifts responsibility for verifying that hypothesis to the interviewer,

who – through his research – would have a more systematic and comprehensive grasp on history than Abu al-Hayja, who experienced history from
the ground up, as an ordinary fighter, without the panoramic perspective
of an educated researcher analysing events with the benefit of hindsight.

Abu Raqaba also tries to explain to the interviewer the distance that
separated him from the decision makers much higher up. When the interviewer starts to ask, 'did you sense the seriousness of the [Arab] League's
intention to fight or did you feel...?', Abu Raqaba quickly jumps in: 'We
were very young back then. We were not seasoned politicians, so when
they said they were going to create the Jaysh al-Inqadh [Arab Liberation
Army], we believed them and we went to train on that basis.' Unlike Bal'awi
and Abu al-Hayja, however, Abu Raqaba was an officer-in-training, and
thus closer to the central command of Jaysh al-Inqadh. When the interviewer asks him why he did not cut short his training in order to return to
Palestine and fight, once he had understood that large cities and villages
were falling to Jewish forces, Abu Raqaba patiently explains the constraints
on Jaysh al-Inqadh, and the harsh reality of the balance of forces on the
ground. He describes how the Jewish forces, with their greater numbers and
superior weapons, made it impossible for the Arab army to mount an effective campaign to retake Palestinian towns and cities. Jaysh al-Inqadh, he
says, 'couldn't have tipped the scales of battle in our favour with the humble
weapons at hand'.

All three accounts reveal a certain weariness from years of bearing the
burden of having to account for the catastrophe of 1948. All three men
are valued as witnesses to events they experienced. At the same time,
their interviewers sometimes push them to explain the Nakba according
to the national-historiographical conventions forged long after the events
took place. Paying close attention to the interview form itself, and to the
'dialogic' moments captured on the videos, allows us to better understand
the complex intergenerational dynamics at work in these exchanges. This
in turn enriches our understanding of the Nakba, an event whose meaning
continues to evolve across generations. I encourage readers to read the
extracts below with respect for the lived experiences they convey, and to
bear in mind what Abu al-Hayja says to his interviewer after describing,
with tears in his eyes, the return of the village of Birwa to Zionist control at
the end of June 1948: 'Al-tarikh la yarham'. History is merciless.

Kamil Ahmad Bal'awi
born 1928 in Shafa 'Amr, Palestine
Interview with Amira 'Alwan
Badawi camp, North Lebanon, 2003

1h 10'50"–1h 25'40"

Amira 'Alwan: *Where did you go after you trained in Tarshiha?*
Kamil Ahmad Bal'awi: We went back to a village called al-Ra's al-Ahmar, near their village (he gestures to someone off-screen). It was called al-Ra's al-Ahmar. We stayed there for a while. An order came in telling us 'Get dressed! Get dressed!' so we got dressed, took our things, passed through their village and went to a village called Safsaf.[1] I think our friend here comes from Safsaf (he points behind the camera). We had dinner there and later went by foot to Safad, and we passed through an area called Wadi al-Laymun, a valley near the western part of the village. The Jewish neighbourhood was located in the western part of the village, in the direction of the *qibla*,[2] and the Arabs were over on this side. We fought the Jews, but some were visible to us and others weren't. They bombed us and we bombed them. After some time, our officer Hisham al-'Azm said we had to form a line of defence behind our frontline positions. We took our bombs and our mortar, we had one of those. We took it and placed behind in order to have a line of defence in case we needed to retreat. The whole operation took two hours, with us transporting things and getting settled, and then we were finally positioned. As day broke, we found out that people had retreated, so we asked what we should do. They told us to do as our fellow soldiers had done, so we retreated. We headed towards the hospital in Safad, by-passed it and went down into Wadi al-Laymun, where we had left through. Once we got to Wadi al-Laymun, Adib al-Shishakli bombed the Jewish neighbourhood from the western point with the cannon aiming at a village called Mirun, which was almost opposite Safad.[3] It was a useless attempt. When we arrived at Wadi al-Laymun, we found our commanders inside an abandoned British police station. I was carrying the mortar's muzzle on my shoulder although I was also carrying my blanket, a rifle, equipment and other things; until I personally handed it back to the officer, Muhammad al-Saraj. He started to ask me about the people of his village, the people of Hama – 'How is so-and-so? What happened to so-and-so?' – so I told him, 'This person died, the other was injured'. He knew I was with them and then he told me, 'You will now receive a raise in your salary and become a corporal'.

He gave me two stripes – it's there in the photograph – because I handed in the part of the mortar. We used to get paid 70 Syrian or Lebanese liras at the time, I don't know, and they started giving me 90.

Who gave you all these orders to retreat from Tarshiha?
Our commander! That guy ... al-Shishakli. Adib al-Shishakli.

Why?
Because ... Who do you want us to fight, the walls? The Jews got in and disappeared inside. No one was visible anymore and it was night-time. He ordered for us to retreat and we retreated. We came to Tarshiha, we had supper in Tarshiha, and we continued retreating in the night all the way back to al-Ra's al-Ahmar.

When you retreated from Tarshiha, did the young men stay in the village to fight?
Of course they did. They stayed there; it's their village.

Didn't they ask you why you left them?
No, they didn't ask us because they said they were guarding the village so that nobody would enter, and they stayed. We told the village *mukhtar* that we were going to retreat. We did, and we headed back to al-Ra's al-Ahmar, where we stayed.

How did you feel about going there to protect and defend people, and having to leave them suddenly as you retreated?
Soldiers couldn't do much in this situation. The officer was in charge of them. When the officer ordered them to retreat, they had to do so. They couldn't disobey their officer's orders.

Did you feel like it was a betrayal?
No. Soldiers like us didn't feel that way. Betrayal can only result from the high commanders, the very highly ranked officers. We didn't feel that way. However, when the Jews, village residents and the Druze army fought in our village, I heard – while I was there – that a high-ranking Druze officer went to the village I was telling you about, to [Khirbat] al-Kasayir, and was given money by a Jew who was sent to him. He gave him money and they retreated from Shafa 'Amr and went to Lebanon, to the villages.[4]

Did you feel like people were committed to fighting? Were you, and the Arabs fighting with you, serious about the fighting? Did you feel like the orders you received to leave Tarshiha were serious or was there a scheme being prepared?
No, we didn't feel like there was anything like that. They told us to advance but we didn't know where we were advancing to. It was night-time. In the morning, we advanced to our positions and they told us to station in these spots until an unspecified time. The informant told the commanders when the plane was coming and when the Jews would come out of the castle. Soldiers didn't know anything. They told us to get dressed and to prepare ourselves, so we obeyed: we got dressed, got our things and left. Informants went to the command; we knew nothing of such things.

How were your experiences in Safsaf and al-Ra's al-Ahmar?
Well, we stayed in al-Ra's al-Ahmar for a while. We went to Safad, passed by Safsaf and kept on going.

Did you cooperate with the residents of al-Ra's al-Ahmar?
The people there were good to us. They gave us houses to sleep in and everything but our food was provided by the army.

Did the young men of al-Ra's al-Ahmar cooperate with you? Did they defend their village?
How could they cooperate? There was no war in al-Ra's al-Ahmar, there were no Jews there, they were far away. Our command stationed us in al-Ra's al-Ahmar because they were sure it was a safe place. After al-Ra's al-Ahmar, we went to Safad and it fell, so we went to the borders with Lebanon, to Palestine's borders. Some people slept outside, others inside. The troops were dispersed and some people remained besieged in Safad until the next day! They broke a window, brought the blankets – ours, the ones from our military camp – tore them up, knotted them together and threw them out the window to escape. They went down the blankets and landed on the ground on the other side, and fled. They didn't come until the next day. We were in Blida, a small village in Lebanon. Our regiment's meeting point was there. When the regiment was complete and almost all the soldiers were back, we rode to Bint Jubayl and headed to Mirun, to Yarun. So we went to Yarun and Bint Jubayl, we stayed in the cars and reached Sayda, then to Damascus. We drove on the Damascus road and arrived in al-Maza.

Did you find out what happened in Safsaf when you left?
No. There was no war there at the time. The Jews hadn't gone to Safsaf or any of those villages. The inhabitants were still in their villages.

Do you know what they called the Jaysh al-Inqadh in the villages?
Pardon?

The Jaysh al-Inqadh, what did they call it in the village?
They called it the army, the Liberation Army.

Didn't it have another name?
(No answer was provided).

Why did they call it Liberation Army?
Because it is supposed to ... to save the Arabs from the Jews, to protect them from the Jews.

Why did they later start calling it the 'fleeing army'?
Because it was defeated and because it had no strength, like the strength of the Jewish forces. It could neither defend nor fulfil its duties, so it retreated, and when it did, they called it the 'fleeing army'.

Had you heard about the massacres that went on in Palestine?
Like what?

The massacres that were perpetrated in the nearby villages.
You know, there were problems in all the villages...

The massacres, the massacres!
Oh, the massacres were far from us, in the districts of al-Quds and those parts. The massacres happened there first. They would tell us, 'They attacked this village, killed its women, boys and children.' Later the Jews started to move from one village to the next. When they came to Sa'sa' in the Safad district, they raided three or four houses. The Jews surrounded the villages; they raided them and fled. But Safsaf, al-Ra's al-Ahmar and Jish, all these villages were still there. This was considered to be a terror tactic to scare Arabs away and force them to flee. They did this to people in other villages as well.

How did you get news from your parents while you were away in the Jaysh al-Inqadh?
When my parents fled, especially my mother-in-law, the head of my family, I was in Blida. I was telling you about this village named Blida, and its inhabitants *al-Matawleh*. I went to Bint Jubayl; I had heard that Palestinians

were coming to Bint Jubayl and living under the trees and things like that. I went there and I had been recently paid 90 liras. I told myself that if I found them, I would give them the money or buy them whatever they wanted. I went there and found them sitting under fig trees. Under fig trees ... If they wanted to fetch a sip of water, they had to fight with the owners of the water and with money no less. I took this photograph in Bint Jubayl. There. When I went to them, I got this photo taken in Bint Jubayl. I returned to Blida for a few days after which we received an order to leave. We got in the cars and they brought us to Damascus.

Muhammad Abu Raqaba
born 1929 in ʿAkka, Palestine
Interview with Mahmoud Zeidan
Beirut, 2003

22'30"–29'34"

Mahmoud Zeidan: What did you do after graduating from school in al-Quds? Did you work?
Muhammad Abu Raqaba: I worked as a teacher for three and half months at *Al-Ahliyya* Secondary School in ʿAkka. There was an *ahliyya* school there but it wasn't a government school. I read an advertisement in the newspapers saying that the League of Arab States' General Volunteer Inspectorate had decided to organise training for Palestinian officers after the Partition Plan for Palestine was issued. The training was open to those who had either completed their matriculation, or completed the fourth level of secondary school. I had applied to study medicine at al-Jamiʿa al-Qahira (Cairo University), and I was accepted because my grades in matriculation were good – we had sent copies of them, of course. At the time, I hesitated between studying medicine in al-Qahira or joining the national service. We thought that the national service was going to be temporary and last six months to a year; that we would liberate Palestine and go back to our studies. For some reason, I chose to enrol. My entire family stayed in ʿAkka when I left it. Back then, Palestinians, particularly the youth, were not allowed to leave without a permit. The Palestinian leadership, headed by Hajj Amin, issued an order to all the National Committees preventing anyone from leaving unless they had a written permit citing one of three reasons: to join the jihad, to pursue higher education or in the case of an acute illness that could not be treated in Palestine. I applied to the National Committee,[5] which was issuing permits, and they gave me one. We also waited for the exam committee, because this body had appointed a committee that toured all the Palestinian cities to select students who would later become officers. The committee covered all of Palestine but did not come to ʿAkka, because the road from Haifa to ʿAkka had been blocked. The committee went to Yafa, al-Difa al-Gharbiyya, Haifa and then back to al-Quds, and finally to Damascus. It couldn't come to ʿAkka. My late friend Zuhayr Brum, God rest his soul, and I took the permits, left ʿAkka and went directly to Damascus, to the chief of staff. We told them that we were there to volunteer because the committee hadn't come to us. They told us, 'It's a good thing you came. We need a contingent from ʿAkka.' Because they had taken

students from all the Palestinians cities, within both 1948 and 1967. They took us in right away and transferred us to Qatana.[6] There, I encountered a few of my friends from my time at Jami'a al-Najah al-Wataniyya (An-Najah National University) in Nablus. They had also volunteered. So-and-so was from Haifa, another from al-Khalil, another from al-Quds, and another from Nablus ... It was quite a group. One of them, for example, was Subhi al-Jabi, who later became commander of the Jaysh al-Tahrir al-Filastini (Palestine Liberation Army) during [Ahmad] al-Shuqayri's leadership.[7] He was my friend both during the course and in Nablus. Another was 'Ali Bushnaq, who was Ahmad Jibril's relative and mentor; he also preceded him as a leader in al-Jabha al-Sha'biyya.[8] There was Ibrahim Tawfiq, the only one among our friends who is in Beirut, where he climbed the ranks and became Abu Rami's assistant at the bank. This place used to be a bank and his room was right over there. There was also Misbah al-Budayri, who was a commander in the Jaysh al-Tahrir, 'Uthman Ja'far Hadad from Gaza, who also became a commander in the Jaysh al-Tahrir al-Filastini, or rather he was chief-of-staff of the Jaysh al-Tahrir al-Filastini. We came from all the Palestinian cities and met in Qatana, and we went through an intensive military training in order to fight. The story goes that during this training, it was our first time meeting or seeing Hajj Amin, because in April, May and June, Palestinian cities began to fall at the hands of the enemy.

What year was that?
This was in 1948. In '48. We had a meeting at the military training and asked ourselves, 'What are we doing here while our cities are falling?' I was from 'Akka, which fell on 18 May, and I didn't know where my parents were! People started to worry. Those from Haifa, Yafa, Safad or Tabariyya ... All of these cities fell during our training. So we organised a strike, and we held a meeting and told them that we wanted to stop training and join the battle ... as soldiers. At the time, the training was funded by the League of Arab States, which was based in Syria and its director was Hazim al-Khalidi, God rest his soul, who was from al-Quds but who also was an officer in the British Army. His assistant was Wajih al-Madani, who later became Major General Wajih al-Madani, the first commander-in-chief of the Palestine Liberation Army – not the chief-of-staff but the first commander during al-Shuqayri's leadership. All of them were annoyed because we only had three to four months left to graduate. In any case, we were all surprised when one day Hajj Amin came to Qatana. Hazim al-Khalidi knew him; he was apparently in Damascus at the time. Al-Khalidi went to him and told him, 'Please, we have problem and we need you to resolve it'. So

Hajj Amin al-Husayni arrived – and I have a photograph of him inspecting us, and of course, we had a lot of respect for him. We paraded in front of him and he gave us a speech. As I recall, he said, 'We have a lot of soldiers but we need officers. You are lucky to have the League of Arab States committed to graduating you as officers. You have completed more than half of the training, be patient and finish it.' And the third thing he said was, 'The struggle against the Jews is long' – it's not like it ended after 1948 and that's it – 'and since this struggle is going to be long, we need officers with a proper military education.' So we were convinced and we continued our training until we graduated…

54'58"–1h 02'13"

Let's go back to our discussion about the Jaysh al-Inqadh; you told me that when you volunteered, and before you graduated, they took you to South Lebanon when al-Jalil al-A 'la had not yet fallen…
Yes.

Why didn't you go into battle then?
There was no battle…

Or rather, why didn't you go into battle since half of the villages or main cities had fallen?
We were 64 Palestinian officers on a training mission. If we had wanted to go on a combat mission, we would have needed to take 4,000 soldiers; each officer would have taken 30 soldiers, to lead them into battle. The Jaysh al-Inqadh we were affiliated with could not make such decisions. Adib al-Shishakli, Wasfi al-Tal and the commander Shawkat Shuqayr each led a defensive battalion in order to defend the region they were in, and they barely could.[9] There was a gap between us and the Jews with regard to the number of arms and the quality of training. They had no clue about an attack strategy for any region, to free it. For example, al-Zib fell and 'Akka fell. There was no idea to form a force – there was no force to begin with! – strong enough for us to attack and to reclaim 'Akka. I remember that we followed specific tactics until we arrived at the heights of Tarshiha, where the troops there followed defensive tactics. Poor things, they could barely anticipate or fend off a real attack by the Jews, and that's what happened. When the Jews attacked the region, they came with planes and bam bam bam, killed the fighters, who didn't have anti-aircraft defence. Then they sent tanks. There was a guy called Hamdi al-Salih, who was one of the

fighters in Tarshiha; he wrote a book where he described in detail the battles that took place. The Arab states had no intention of attacking; the most they could wish for was to be able to defend and preserve the territories that were still in their possession, and yet, unfortunately, they weren't able to. So the Jews carried out the attack with planes, tanks and foot soldiers and most of our troops had to flee their villages and retreat to Lebanon.

During this training, did you sense the seriousness of the League of Arab States' intention to fight or did you feel...
We were very young back then. We weren't seasoned politicians, so when they said that they were going to create the Jaysh al-Inqadh, we believed them and went to train on that basis. We were part of the Jaysh al-Inqadh and our training, itself part of the League of Arab States, was conducted under the auspices of the Jaysh al-Inqadh. And at the same time, in Qatana, training sessions for wireless communication and nursing for Palestinians were taking place. There were also up to 3,000 ordinary soldiers training. All of them were in Qatana during that time. But even if all of them had turned into fighters, they couldn't have tipped the scales of battle in our favour with the humble weapons at hand.

You weren't able to return to 'Akka afterwards because the whole of Palestine fell at the hands of the Jews when you were abroad?
I think the last time I saw 'Akka was when I went to Tarshiha. We went up to the high fortifications and behold! There was 'Akka, you could see it from afar. One of the funny things at the time was I knew that there was a mosque in 'Akka called al-Jazar with a tall minaret and I couldn't see it, darn it! I cried so hard, 'They even destroyed the minaret!' You see? I could see 'Akka but there was no minaret! It was very moving, I was incredibly affected. And then the tour ended. We had stayed ten to twelve days on our tour in al-Jalil, and we went back to complete our training and graduation. We weren't officers yet, you see, we were still officers in training.

How did you join or reunite with your family later on? And what happened to your parents, why did they leave 'Akka? They must have told you about their displacement.
Yes, of course. The fall of Haifa, then later Tabariyya and Safad meant that the defence forces and ammunition were weakened in 'Akka, which led most of its residents to flee. Among them were my parents; they fled without my knowing where they went. Later on, when we graduated from Qatana, I requested a leave of absence and came to Lebanon. They told me

they were in Sayda, so I went there and they told me, 'No, the people of 'Akka are in Burj al-Barajneh.' I went to Burj al-Barajneh and they told me they were in the camp, and indeed they were living in a tent in Burj al-Ba-rajneh camp. I stayed with them for two days, I was wearing my military uniform, and I took advantage of that time to … The weather was like today's, it was autumn and a bit rainy, so I fixed their tent for them, and I put many heavy stones on the pegs, and I dug a trench around the tent thinking that would make it better. The rest of my family, my uncles and aunts, had taken an apartment so I went to visit them as well, and I was surprised to learn that my paternal aunt, whom I loved very much, had died. She came from 'Akka, she was the last one to leave, and barely spent 10 or 15 days in Lebanon, then passed away. With my humble salary at the time – I was a candidate to become an officer, we weren't full officers yet – I told my parents, 'Take a room.' Instead of the camp, a room. Indeed, they moved from the camp into a room with a bathroom and kitchen in al-Siba'i building neighbouring the camp. I came back a second time on a different occasion when I was on leave, and was transferred to Hums afterwards. I presented a request to the command there to bring my family over, I gave them all the details and they said I could bring them. I moved my father, mother, sister and two unmarried brothers to Hums. We took a modest apartment in Hums because my military salary at the time, which consisted of 230 Syrian lira, had to provide for everyone. We came across a nicer apartment later, a military one, which was the same rent, so we moved into it. My parents stayed in Hums for six or seven years.

Mahmud Abu al-Hayja
born circa 1928 in Haifa, Palestine
Interview with Mahmoud Zeidan
Burj al-Barajneh, Beirut, 2003

59'17"–1h 20'25"

Mahmoud Zeidan: *Please tell me why you left Haifa.*
Mahmud Abu al-Hayja: The battles in Haifa had intensified. Their weaponry was heavy duty. The British had retreated and had given their weapons to the Jews, from tanks to cannons and so much more ... And what did we own? Barely a single rifle. And what is it good for? So we left and Haifa fell.[10]

Do you remember the last moments before you exited Haifa? Where were you and what did you do? Tell me what you saw before you left your home in Haifa.
Before I left my home in Haifa, we entered into more than one battle against the Zionist enemy, and we fought, and some of us were killed, and we killed some of them. Except that when a battle is not equal, one of the two sides will undoubtedly vanquish. The Jewish weaponry was deadly. From machine guns, to hand grenades, to ammunitions and so on ... Whereas, in our case, say you wanted to buy a rifle for 100 *gineh*, you had to sell an entire olive grove. A huge olive grove, or a big parcel of land, in order to buy a single rifle. 100 *gineh*! This equals 10, 15, 20,000 dollars, which is not an easy amount to come up with.

Who were the young men fighting with you? Do you know...
I do remember a man, God bless his soul, named Muhammad al-'Amayati who died in Haifa. Another one called 'Abid Rashid, God bless his soul, he passed away in Beirut. There was a man named Hasan Mustafa Husayn who died in Damascus.

Do you remember anyone from your resistance days together, who might still be alive?
To tell you the truth, the names ... Honestly, it's been 50, 60 years. If only the diaries were still available, but unfortunately ... When Haifa fell, some of the armed men sought refuge in 'Akka, and many battles went on there. The operation commander ... I do have names but they're upstairs ... There were two of them: one was martyred at the police station in 'Akka, in front

of the al-Jazar mosque. The other one was martyred at the citadel. When
the Jews first arrived at 'Akka, they came in from the sea. Our young men
blocked them and sent them back. Then they came back from the sea and
Nahariyya, and they were blocked again. And then, they came back a third
time from the sea, Nahariyya road, and a road called Tal 'Akka.

In that time, where did you go after you left Haifa?
To Sha'b.

You left from Haifa to Sha'b directly?
Yes, to Sha'b.

Do you remember the date?
(No answer was given).

*Ok, tell me how the people of Sha'b reacted when they saw you coming from
'Akka as refugees? What was the situation like for their young men and their
people?*
The young men, the town of Sha'b as a whole, owned about 10 or 15 rifles
– 20 – maximum. Most of them were left over from the First and Second
World Wars, there were less than 20 rifles. We took turns guarding the town
with them.

*When you arrived in Sha'b, how was the weather? Did you arrive in the
summer, in the winter?*
In the summer.

And in that time, the people of Sha'b were organising neighbourhood watches?
(He nods).

*I would like you to tell me more about the people of Sha'b. You said there were
only 15 young men.*
That was the number of rifles.

*Who were these men? Tell me their names, and who was coordinating you all
in Sha'b?*
There was a man called Ibrahim al-Hajj 'Ali, who was nicknamed Abu Is'af
because his son's name was Is'af. He was from the people of the 1936 revolution and a great man. He was outside of Sha'b. When things started
stirring, he came back to Sha'b.[11] He brought with him four or five rifles,

one Bren British machine gun and one FM German machine gun. He also brought two weapons, their length went from this door here to that door there, and they were called [anti-]tank rifles. These were missiles used for tanks, their bullets were bigger than the 500 Doshka (DShK), equivalent to the 800 Doshka. Huge ... and a small cannon, 40, maybe 60 calibre? Yes, 60.

There was a village named Qal'at Jiddin,[12] near Tarshiha, close to the borders with Lebanon. These areas were besieged by the villagers. They wanted to bring in supplies, but there was no other road than through the town of Nahariyya – al-Kabri. If you go past it and past Tarshiha, you get to Qal'at Jiddin. There were small roads that led to the villages, and the people of al-Kabri were blocking them. In Palestine, you had what was called *faza'a*. An example of that was when the village of Safsaf entered into a battle, the men from most surrounding villages came to the rescue. In this battle, they were able to kill more than 100 Israeli soldiers who had tanks. And until today, in that same area, you can find a statue that the Jews placed in memory of that battle. It's still there. One time, in 1948, we went in during a Palestinian operation and we blew it up. They built it back. And they kept what was left of the burnt cars and tanks in that spot, all collected into one pile as a memorial. That happened in none other than Safad. So the Jaysh al-Inqadh left, on 15 May ... Weren't we going to talk about Jaysh al-Inqadh?

I wanted to know if they came to Sha'b, let's stay in Sha'b.
But in order to get to Sha'b, we must talk about Shaykh Mahmud al-Tabari and his meeting with King 'Abdullah.
All right.

When Shaykh Mahmud brought the villagers together, they told him, 'Whatever you decide on, we will follow you. We have always obeyed your orders.' He said to me: 'I am confused. I am worried they might do the opposite and accuse me of being a traitor. I told [the villagers], King 'Abdullah is my friend, let me ask him for his advice. I had previously studied with him when the Jami'a al-'Arabiyya still existed. I went to Amman and met with Prince 'Abdullah at the time, or King 'Abdullah.' It had been a good year, the olive trees were carrying so much that their branches were touching the ground. The wheat was this tall ... A man walking through the cornfields would disappear into them. It was truly a good year. So, Shaykh Mahmud met with King 'Abdullah and told him: 'Your highness the King, the Jews are saying so and so.' The King said, 'Nonsense, Shaykh Mahmud, 15 May is upon us.'[13] The shaykh replied: 'Your highness, the wheat is about to get harvested.'[14] The King said: 'If [the Jews] harvest it, they won't have time to thresh it, and if they thresh it they won't even have time to winnow it. The Arab armies are arriving in Palestine.' I am telling it how it is. Shaykh Mahmud said, 'Your Highness, give us a few rifles so that we can defend ourselves until 15 May.' The King replied: 'Shaykh Mahmud, go back home and rest assured, 15 May is imminent. In only a few days, you will see things you never would have dreamt of seeing.' Shaykh Mahmud was smart indeed, but who could contradict the King? He went back to the village, gathered the elders and told them: 'Brothers, the conspiracy is greater than Palestine. I will ask my relatives in the village of Sha'b to prepare a few houses for me. I shall leave and whoever wants to accompany me there is most welcome.' I remember that some of his Circassian friends went with him to Sha'b. He stayed in the village until it fell.

Let's go back in time … During the battle of Safad, the Jaysh al-Inqadh was present, and those among them who were fighting the Jews were winning. So the Jews had to find their way to Safad. They had to go through the 'Akka road, then Majd al-Krum, al-Ramya, al-Farradiyya and so on, in order to get to Safad. They were blocked by the people of Majd al-Krum, if you've heard of it. It's a town near Sha'b. Of course, the *faza'a* happened and we all took part in it, and we fought the Jews. We burnt them in that battle and killed a great number of them; it was not too bad. They were not able to get to Safad. But orders came from the General Commander at the Arab League, who was his Highness the King, for us to retreat from Safad. Analyse this for me, was this patriotism or treason? You are a young educated man and I assume you have done your research. So, Safad was invaded once more by the Jews.

We stayed in Sha'b … in a village before Sha'b, between Majd al-Krum and 'Akka, called al-Birwa. The Jews had invaded it and, as I told you, the crops were this high. It had been a good year. The Jewish bulldozers went to harvest and what about our farmers? They had been waiting for this moment … We had placed a group of young men, one of whom was Kayid Abu al-Hayja, my relative, I named my grandson after him for his courage. One of my sons who died was called Kayid, God bless his soul, his picture is right here. My other son had a boy and named him Kayid after him. Kayid Abu al-Hayja was the Guard Commander in the region that was controlled by Sha'b. The battle started and our armed men got dispersed. Upon hearing the order 'Allahu Akbar', we darted through the cornfields, until we arrived at the top of al-Birwa. We got into an extremely fierce battle and we conquered the village. We killed a great number of them and took their weapons and ammunitions, as well as two machine guns made in Belgium. We also took a mortar. Some of the *faza'a* were also there, they had come from Saffuriyya, and from here and there, and they helped us fight, I can't deny it. One night, the Jews counter-attacked us and were able to occupy part of the village. In the morning, the battle intensified, and we won again and made considerable gains. We killed a great many of them and liberated the village again. We kept battling until the evening.

A group of soldiers, part of Jaysh al-Inqadh, was stationed in the village of Majd al-Krum, and the leader of that region was an Iraqi man with the rank of captain, named Jabir. And he was under the command of Adib al-Shishakli. You remember those names.

In the evening, or rather before the evening and after 'Asr, Jabir came to us and said, 'God bless you, people of Sha'b. You accomplished more than you needed to. You have been battling for 48 hours, you should rest. Go back to the village and rest, and we will stay here.' Truly, they were tired. During that battle, those who did not own a rifle had fought with sticks, axes, shovels. The women were running between the men, ululating and carrying water buckets. They were ululating, these women of Sha'b (he sighs). We went back to the village, to Sha'b. Two hours later, bombings started coming from al-Birwa, they were directed against us. They handed over the village to them. General Commander's orders, of course. History is merciless ... I do not fear for my life, I am 79 years old and I have lived long enough. My wish is to be a martyr. And by God, I wish our base were in the south, so that we could penetrate into Palestine through the borders. But unfortunately, you know, the protectors of borders, there's no need to name names (he sighs). We went back to the village and we began guarding it.

Figure 6 Said Otruk, departure from 'Akka, April 1948.
Courtesy of Said Otruk and the Nakba Archive.

PART IV

Flight and Exile

11

The Dispossession of Lydda

Lena Jayyusi

The conquest of Lydda and its sister town Ramla, and the forced exodus of their people between 10 and 14 July 1948, saw the largest single instance of depopulation during the Palestinian Nakba. Jaffa had fallen two months earlier (on 13 May), and many of the people of Jaffa and its surrounding villages had taken refuge in Lydda. Estimates of the total number of people expelled from the two towns, including those who had taken refuge there, range from 50,000 to 70,000.[1] Lydda's fate, in particular, is marked as a turning point in many of the stories told by, or about, prominent Palestinian figures, including Ismail Shammout, the renowned Palestinian painter featured here,[2] and George Habash, founder of the Popular Front for the Liberation of Palestine.[3]

Lydda and Ramla were targeted in Operation Dani, the offensive launched on Ben Gurion's order on 9 July at the end of the first truce of the 1948 Palestine War.[4] Their fall was particularly emblematic in that both had been designated as part of the Palestinian Arab state outlined in the United Nations Partition Plan, adopted on 29 November 1947.[5] As the excerpt from Shammout's narrative indicates, this UN resolution shaped – perhaps critically – the local population's expectations.[6]

Ismail Shammout was born and raised in Lydda until the age of 18, when he was forced out with his family and community on that fateful July day. Renée Kutih was born and raised in Ramla. She married a well-off man from Haifa and left Palestine after the fall of Haifa on 22 April 1948, before the fall of Lydda and Ramla. Both recall a life of plenitude, Shammout's memories focusing on collective scenes, Kutih's detailing private life; through both testimonies the texture of an established, abundant way of life that was taken for granted comes through poignantly – though with a clear distinction emergent perhaps from their respective class locations and gender.

For Shammout, it was the sounds and colours of the lively communal gatherings (feasts, holiday celebrations and markets) that left an indelible mark on him, and which he expressed in his paintings, as he notes in the longer interview (not included in the present excerpt). He tries to communicate the joyful vibrancy of these occasions, which for him spoke of a rooted, diverse and integrated community, and a fullness of life in sharp contrast to the days after the Nakba, when simply getting bread, 'specifically bread', was a great issue.

For Kutih, it is the traditions and fullness of a prosperous bourgeois life whose horizons were open and expanding that are vividly remembered. Her father and uncles had owned a lucrative bus line operating between Jaffa, Ramla and Lydda, in addition to land, shops and businesses. Her bridegroom had worked at Spinneys in Haifa and was so well-to-do that he took her on a six-week luxury honeymoon in Europe, from where she shipped back 14 packages of merchandise and gifts for friends and family. She refers repeatedly to the rich contents of her parents' home – the fine bed linen that her mother had prepared and stored to give to each of her four children on their wedding days; the sets of handmade brass pots labelled with their names. She also talks of the lavish festivities surrounding her brother's graduation from medical school in Beirut, and of her own wedding in Haifa. Her narrative, at the same time, illuminates informal obligations, traditionally carried by the wealthier Palestinian classes towards those in their immediate community who were less fortunate – a notable feature of the weave of communal life in those days.

As with so many Nakba narratives, irrespective of class lines, a haunted phrase returns in one form or another: 'We took nothing with us.' Here is the subtle expression of the trauma of *complete and sudden dispossession*. In this context, Shammout quietly celebrates the fact that he managed to keep his passport and a few family photographs with him at the checkpoint set up by the Jewish forces, who were intent on stripping everyone of their possessions as they passed through. However, Shammout's and Kutih's narratives make visible divergent trajectories of dispossession. For Shammout, the exodus from Lydda is clearly narrated as a purposeful and violent expulsion of a population against both their expectation and will. In his first person account of the events, he does not refer to the infamous massacre at the hands of Jewish forces in Lydda's Dahmash mosque on 11 July, which left 176 people dead,[7] many of them splattered 'on the walls'.[8] He and his family had remained in their home for the first three days after Jewish forces entered the city. The massacre was a demonstration of the fate of anyone who resisted Jewish conquest. Shammout nevertheless describes in detail the way Jewish troops drove people out of their homes and city at gunpoint on 13 July, and speaks of corpses littering the streets of Lydda (426 men, women and children according to Pappe).[9] Stripped of their valuables and belongings, families were relentlessly forced to continue moving on and out. Jewish troops even denied expellees access to water on their long trek in the burning July sun. Shammout talks of seeing many drop dead, and of the families compelled to leave them unburied on the road. An estimated 350 people died on the trek.[10] Shammout ultimately ended up with his family in Gaza. He was later to produce a memorable series of paintings representing that forced and catastrophic exodus.

Kutih's departure, on the other hand, was partly anticipatory, arising from the fear generated by prior events, such as the Dayr Yasin massacre on 9 April,[11] and the fall of Haifa on 22 April. She had gone with her husband one weekend to make her first official visit to her parents' home after her marriage (a traditional rite), when they suddenly learned that her brother had had surgery in Beirut. Her worried parents decided to visit him then and there, and left her in charge of the family home, while her husband returned to work in Haifa. When Haifa fell, her parents declined to return home. A protracted period of anxiety and confusion ensued, as Kutih fretted over how to get out and join her family. Once a passport had been secured for her by her husband, and delivered by the British Army, she left for Beirut, with her younger siblings and their maid, via Lydda airport. Kutih says, 'Everyone was thinking about emigrating.' This stands in stark contrast to the perspective Shammout articulates.

This divergence speaks to class location and the different choices, opportunities and affinities it affords. Such differences are not specific to the Palestinian experience but are visible in all societies subjected to war or attack. The point here is not only that many members of the upper middle classes left prior to the height of the attacks and expulsions, and that they had the means to leave and to find opportunity to prosper afterwards. What is more interesting than the difference in mode and timing of departure is the difference in the assessment and perception of events. Class location would have shaped people's perceptions of what was happening, what was possible and who was doing what. Whereas multiple other Palestinian testimonies of 1948 describe the struggles, the battles, the hanging on until the last minute, the defence preparations, Kutih suggests there was no concrete trouble or violence in Ramla, only people attempting to 'stir things up' and frighten people by spreading stories of impending attacks. She does mention a large explosion on the edge of Ramla, which she locates right after her parents' departure for Beirut. In fact, on the night of 4 April, there was a Jewish attack – part of Operation Nachson[12] – on the headquarters, just outside Ramla, of Shaykh Hasan Salama, regional commander for al-Jihad al-Muqadas.[13] There had been attacks on Ramla earlier in the year,[14] beginning in February, when the Irgun had detonated a bomb in the town's market.[15] Multiple battles involving men from Ramla also took place in the surrounding countryside and Jewish attacks on the town resumed in earnest in mid-May, though most were repelled.[16] Kutih may have been out of town when some of these events took place, yet one might expect to hear some awareness of them. First person narratives usually touch on issues and events of concern to the narrator's community, as she demonstrates when speaking of other matters.

Shammout, by contrast, tells of public meetings and the neighbourhood defence groups in which he participated. He also talks with pride of the day the people of Lydda built a 10-kilometre protective trench around the western part of the city, in a project of profound communal solidarity and unity. He specifically refers to the women of the town bringing food and drink to the men as they worked, narrating a relational and concrete awareness, on the women's part, of the events and stakes of the conflict. Thus, gender alone does not explain the absences in Kutih's account, though it would certainly have shaped her vision of the world around her. Her larger frame of reference, however, is clearly bound by the upper middle class world she grew up and lived in, which would have shielded her from many of the experiences and processes that people in (very) different social and class positions would have been aware of, encountered or engaged.

Whereas Shammout talks critically of the British support for Zionism, and terms their clear facilitation of the Zionist project a 'conspiracy', Kutih speaks more than once of her family and husband's affinity with the 'English'. Nevertheless, a shadow of disquiet colours her narrative: at several points she refers to cars with loudspeakers roaming the streets of Ramla, telling people to leave temporarily for safety, as one of the reasons for departure. Asked who was behind the messages, she says: 'the British government'. She also talks of the British helping people onto trucks leaving town, a recurrent theme in Nakba narratives. Yet she still maintains that life under British rule had been 'very happy', and everything had been 'going right'. In evidence here is the paradoxical location where class and national belonging can coexist within the colonial context in a tense and sometimes contradictory relationship. Indeed, the listener can perhaps detect a sense of betrayal in Kutih's tone and hesitant words.

Shammout's narrative is threaded through with tropes of trust betrayed. The townspeople had been assured by the nearby Jewish settlement of Beit Shemen to the east of Lydda that the settlers wanted peace and would not attack. So they dug the trench on the west side, from where they expected to be attacked. But the attack did come from the east, and from troops gathered in Beit Shemen. Betrayal also came from supposed Arab allies: the Jordanian battalion that was supposed to be defending Lydda withdrew – inexplicably by Shammout's account – on the eve of the attack. In fact, the Jordanian Legionnaires were given the order to withdraw by Glubb Pasha, the British Commander of the force.[17] Perhaps most cruelly, the people of Lydda were betrayed, as Shammout notes, by their own habits of expectation, their trust in others' decisions and declarations – by their own naivety.

Holding Kutih's and Shammout's narrative side by side, we are given an insight into the multi-pronged strategy that effected the dispossession of the Palestinians in 1948. On the one hand, there were the direct attacks, mass killings and violent expulsions. Both Lydda and Ramla were bombed by air prior to the ground assault[18] and Moshe Dayan rushed through Lydda in his jeep, firing his machine gun indiscriminately, on the first day of the attack.[19] On the other hand, there was intimidation by threat, rumour and alarmist warnings – methods of psychological warfare – as indicated by Kutih's reference to people 'stirring things up'. Was this a continuation of the 'whispering campaigns' that Yigal Allon launched with Plan Dalet in the spring of 1948?[20] Direct attacks, of course, gave substance to psychological tactics.

A question comes to mind when viewing these testimonies. It pertains to the ethics of memory and remembering. How is it that only a few years after the darkest period in Jewish history, when Jews were rounded up and subjected to the ultimate evil, how is it that Jewish men and women (some of whom had recently arrived from Europe) could proceed to strip Palestinian men, women and children, so cruelly, of belongings and belonging as they herded them out of home and country? How does the 'memory' of trauma obscure the humanity of another people? How does the lesson of trauma resolve in a way that is so radically exclusionary? That remains the necessary question.

Ismail Shammout
born 1930 in Lydda, Palestine
Interview with Mahmoud Zeidan
Mala'ab al-Baladi, Beirut, 2003

12'03"–18'35"

Ismail Shammout: One of the most famous *mawasim* was the *mawsim* of al-Nabi Salih, in the city of Ramla.[21] People came in groups from the areas of Lydda and Ramla, as well as from neighbouring villages, and were led by teams carrying colourful flags, chanting or singing specific religious songs. They gathered in the square of the minaret of al-Jami' al-Abyad (the White Mosque), which exists to this day and whose architectural design was very beautiful. I saw it again seven years ago, in 1997, when we had the opportunity to visit Palestine ... a beautiful architectural piece. Although the mosque had been destroyed by earthquakes more than 100 years ago, the minaret is still in that square. People gathered there to sing, dance *dabkeh*, compete in horseback riding and all sorts of activities. It was a well-known *mawsim* where they also sold a white, walnut-flavoured *halawa* in clay pots. Those who participated in al-Nabi Salih, the Nabi Salih *mawsim* – which lasted two, three days or perhaps more, I don't remember – would always return home with this *halawa*.

Another *mawsim* was al-Nabi Rubin, which took place south of Yafa, between al-Majdal and Yafa. It was one of the most famous *mawasim* in central Palestine. It was essentially a summer resort for families from the region of Yafa, Lydda, Ramla and its villages. People stayed there for a month, a month and a half or two, and pitched tents, opened markets, opened theatres and cafés. It was truly a place for recreation and joy. Some tents were decorated with photographs, drawings and motifs, and some people made small huts out of straw mats and lived in them during the period. Incidentally, the Rubin area was covered by sand dunes and the most famous dune was called Tal al-Sukar, because its sand was bright white, so much that they compared it to sugar. We were very happy during these *mawasim*. There were also other *mawasim*, for example, in spring, I remember our family always going to Wadi Jindas. Families spent an entire day there; it was not a simple stroll but a collective outing, not just a family by itself, no, everyone would go, especially the women and children. We would go and spend the day there. The valley still had some water running through it; it rained heavily during the winter, but after winter there would always be some water left. But springtime, it would be flourishing. Spring in our country was very beautiful.

Another *mawsim* that we celebrated and rejoiced in was the harvest *mawsim*, when they harvested wheat and barley crops. People celebrated this occasion and considered it an Eid. They participated in all kinds of joyful activities on that day. Another Eid that I will never forget in Lydda is the Lydda Eid, this is what it was called, and it was celebrated by our Christian brothers. There is a famous church in Palestine called the church of al-Qidis al-Khadr. In English, they call it Saint George's Church, and it is believed that Saint George or al-Khadr is buried in that church. So on that day, which is called the Lydda Eid, almost all of Palestine's Christians came to Lydda to celebrate this *mawsim*, this occasion. It was also a joyful celebration, which started at the church and then people moved outside to the olive grove. They spent an entire day dancing and doing the *dabkeh*, and singing, and racing, and food and drinks. All of the colours that one could imagine were present in the traditional Palestinian costumes, those of our women from the villages of Palestine, especially when they came from a diversity of places, so accordingly the costumes that were present on those occasions were varied. That's what I remember.

51'42"–1h 15'22"

What I do remember is that after the United Nations Partition Plan for Palestine, people started becoming restless because something was different. Groups began to be formed to fight against this plan. What people would be drawn to was the news they would hear on the radio. At the time, radios in Palestine, and particularly in Lydda, were big and functioned on battery, a battery just like car batteries. People congregated in cafés, because each café had a radio, to listen to the latest news. So there was a popular interest among the people. As I told you, there were Palestinian organisations at the time, whether they were two, less or more, I'm not very sure, but there was something called the Arab Higher Committee, and there was something called the Istiqlal Party.[22] There wasn't much competition in the sense that the catastrophe was going to hit us all, we all felt it, so committees started forming to build the resistance. I remember these committees being called national committees. Why they called them that, I don't know. Ok, so the question was, what should we do? They would meet. I was a young man, so I did not attend these meetings but they said that we had to guard the area or the neighbourhood at night. Ok, so what was being asked of us? We were asked to stand guard on a street in groups of two or three men. In fear of what? I don't know what we were afraid of. So we stayed up until a certain time and people from the neighbourhoods took turns.

Mahmoud Zeidan: Were you also a guard?
I was one of them. Afterwards we also took up arms. These arms existed before the British left Palestine, so before 15 May 1948. The British had crates of weapons, of British rifles as we called them. The wooden crate would be cut in half using oxygen and its contents would be sold as scrap iron. The weapons were then brought to town, to Lydda and other villages, and sold as scrap iron. The rifle would be cut in half with oxygen; people bought it and went to blacksmiths or welders who used oxygen and tried welding the scraps together, but it was disastrous because if they weren't welded together with great precision, it caused problems for those who used the rifles later on. Other people used rifles as decoys.

I was a guard during that period. They used to give us pieces of weapons, but I didn't know how to use them. Or was scared to, but I felt proud of doing my duty just like the others, while being 16 or 17 years old. One of the most important events that happened during that period was when the people of Lydda and Ramla decided to dig a 10-kilometre trench around their western edges, because there weren't any settlements near the eastern edges aside from the one I told you about earlier, which was located near the north-eastern part of Lydda and was called Beit Shemen. This settlement was cut off because it was established in an Arab area. The closest city was Tel Aviv and there was a distance between them. This settlement sent its representatives to the people of the region – among them were the people of Lydda – saying, 'We are peaceful, and here we are raising white flags, nobody harm us, we will not harm anybody either.' They considered that these people were indeed sincere; we've always been easily duped. Anyway, we therefore always expected danger to strike from the western area. One day, we were called to dig a trench and the people of Lydda and Ramla came out, men, teenagers, boys, children and women, each with their own tool: *touriya, fas, krayk, qazma* – the women of course helped us with drinks and food – and we dug a trench in a single day! Its length was approximately 10 kilometres. It was great day. You could feel the people's rallying and unity, their sense of a common danger, and their sense of security; that they had to do this. It's one of those images that I could never forget. I remember that every neighbourhood had a *marja '*. If anything happened, we would relay it to this *marja '*. Whatever happened and could happen. It's well known that Yafa fell almost three months before Lydda and Ramla. It fell towards the end of April. While Lydda and Ramla were confident that they weren't in great danger, I should add that both were considered to be part of the Arab area according to the partition. And so was Yafa, although it was situated in the middle of the Jewish area; Yafa, the city, was an Arab city according to the partition. But Yafa fell. The Jordanian Army arrived to Lydda and Ramla and was supposed to protect this area but one day – and this happened at the beginning of July 1948 – one or two days, or perhaps hours, before Lydda fell, orders came to retreat. So, danger was expected from the western area, Yafa fell at the end of April, and a few hours before Lydda and Ramla fell, the Jordanian army, or Jordanian garrison, brigade, battalion, or whatever it was, retreated. They received an order to retreat. Why? We don't know.

The situation in both Lydda and Ramla was destabilised and a state of fear gripped the people there. What was going on? The Jews entered then from the northern area, from Yafa and Tel Aviv, until they reached Lydda Airport. They managed to arrive at the airport and occupied it. From there, they managed to sneak into the Beit Shemen settlement, which flew the white flags. A large number of Jewish forces assembled in this settlement and, as I recall, waged a war against Lydda and Ramla from both eastern and western areas, which was not expected. The east had been established as an open route to the Arabs. However, that is what happened ... a conspiracy. Like what happened in 1967, we expected them to come from the west and they came from the east or vice versa, same story. Anyway, the Israeli forces entered through the regions of Lydda and Ramla, at that time also populated by many others, because the number of people in Lydda and Ramla then was no less than 100,000 people. To be exact, it was between 80,000 and 100,000 people. They were not only inhabitants of Lydda or Ramla but also displaced people from Yafa or from the villages of the district of Yafa or from those between Lydda, Ramla and Yafa. Both cities fell after a battle that, according to my information, killed at least 1,000 martyrs from Lydda and a similar number of martyrs from Ramla. They closed in from the west and the east and both cities fell.

We were at home of course; I had an older brother, who was two or three years older, as well as my father, my mother and my younger siblings. We were seven siblings along with my father and my mother. We were hearing the bullets and the battles from here and there, and were sleep-deprived for days or even weeks before that. We couldn't find sleep at night because we would hear the fierce battles at the border. We could hear them within normal hearing ranges, and we began to be able to make out the different sounds of a Bren gun, a Sten gun, a Tommy gun and others. You know, that's how it was. Anyway, when the two cities fell, we stayed at home. There weren't any means of communication and telephones were not widespread in homes. The only possible means of communication was to tell your neighbour, who would tell his neighbour, and so on.

The next day, on 10 July – Lydda and Ramla fell on 9 July – the Israelis knocked on our door, came in and saw my older brother. They took him. They took him by force. My father said to them, 'What do you want from him?' but of course there was no room for discussion and my brother disappeared for one or two days, and then he came back home. We lived in terrible fear, we didn't know … We tried to imagine what was coming, we didn't know. My brother came back a day and a half later and told us that they had taken him and other young men of his age to fill sandbags in order to produce fortifications for the Israelis on the roads, and sometimes to take furniture from homes to use as obstacles on streets, to prevent any potential traffic. In those two days, bullets were fired and even clashes happened without us knowing where – we had no radio, we had no telephone, we were completely isolated.

On the last day, which was 13 July 1948, we felt a rumbling of people walking outside. There were so many people walking. We were scared! We peered through the window and saw the streets filled with people. Moments later, our door was knocked on with rifle butts. Israeli soldiers. We opened the door and they said, 'Out. All out. All out.' Where, out? 'All out', they made us go out. We left our homes and joined the torrential river of people walking towards a large square called Sahat al-Nawa'ir in Lydda. People remembered, and we too, that this operation was not different than similar operations carried out by the British during the Mandate and during the intensification of skirmishes with the Palestinian revolutionaries in the years 1936–39 or afterwards. People would be required to … Not with soldiers knocking on people's homes with their rifles, but with a crier in the streets who announced a curfew, and ordered people to assemble in this or that square. People thought this operation was going to be similar in that we would remain in this square, the Israelis or Jews would enter our homes and search for arms and revolutionaries like the British used to do, and at the end of the day, they would tell people, 'Go back to your houses.' But this time, it was not the same. This time, after they grouped us in more than one square in Lydda, they opened a specified path – of course, we were surrounded by armed Zionists – and ordered these multitudes to start heading east.

Naturally, July is hot. There was no water. It was Ramadan. Children started screaming and crying because this one was thirsty and this one was tired, and people walked down the path that was designated for them, heading east. We passed through the centre of Lydda and I saw with my own eyes the stores that were broken into and violated; they were opened with axes and everything in there was turned upside down. While we walked, we found martyrs, killed, a corpse here, a corpse there. It got hotter … It was around ten in the morning when we started walking. As we were beginning to leave Lydda, there was an orchard belonging to the Hasuna family. My younger siblings were thirsty so I told my father and mother that I was going to try bringing water from there. There were soldiers standing along the road but there were 20 metres or so between each one so I snuck between them and got to a big pond of water, in the orchard. I found a faucet and struggled to open it, until water started running from it, so I found a bucket or something and filled it with water. People saw me and they all ran towards me because everyone wanted water. As I finished filling the bucket and headed to join my parents, I saw a jeep driving fast and it stopped right at my feet. An officer came down and put a gun against my head. He told me, 'Throw water, throw water, throw water!' What do you mean throw water? A guy had a gun to my head, you forget about water and you forget everything. Of course, I threw the water. I thanked God that he didn't shoot me. He kicked me out, so I went back to my parents and siblings and I continued walking with them.

This was a difficult day. It was a day neither I nor the people who walked along this road will ever forget. The exhaustion, the fear, the panic, the terror, the loss, not knowing where we're going and for how long … We left with just the clothes on our backs. No one brought anything because we hadn't anticipated this; we were all taken by surprise by people ordering us to leave by force. Not to mention the thirst and the hunger. The road we were forced to take wasn't even a road, it was mountains. In the summer, our mountains are yellow and arid, dry, rugged; there is no water, no wells, nothing. I personally saw people dying of thirst with my own eyes. Children, or women, or elderly people. Their families would leave them there, place some straw over them and keep on walking. I saw with my own eyes people tearing out patches of grass from the ground to suck on, to wet their lips with a drip of water from the root of the plant.

After three, four or five hours, at three or four o'clock in the afternoon, we found a place that was known for its natural wells, where water would gather and remain even throughout the summer. Indeed, we found a few of those wells; they were natural and not man-made. A bit of water was left in these wells, it was red and mixed with clay at the bottom. Hundreds of people rushed to them. Some found ropes or tore their shirts or ties or anything of the sort to knot them together and lower whatever recepta-

cles they had and fill them with water. And of course, while they pulled
them up they would shove one another and half the water would spill. I
was able to get some water ... red water. I ran with it, people followed me,
children. I didn't care about anyone, I only cared about my mother, father
and siblings, until I got there and they were able to drink it. It was fresh
water even though it was dirty and red – God knows what was in it – but
our thirst was so extreme that we drank anything.

There was a man from the Harun family that I'll never forget. He was
in charge of turning the water on for people in Lydda, because they used
to open faucets at specific hours during the day. This man was thirsty and
riding a mule that was almost dying – I don't even know where he got it
from. He started yelling, 'Folks! People of Lydda! I spent 40 years giving you
water, a sip of water for the love of God, a sip of water for the love of God.'

We kept on walking until there were no more Jews around and we felt
like it was a safe area, an Arab area. We kept walking until we arrived to
the outskirts of a town called Ni'lin. The people of Ni'lin rushed to our aid
with whatever they could; whoever had an animal gave a ride, whoever had
some bread or a jar of water saved whoever they could save. We slept on the
ground under an olive tree, with the sky as our blanket, as they say. It was
after midnight and some people kept on walking. We were woken up by
sunlight the next day; we overslept from the exhaustion. Jordanian military
cars drove us from Ni'lin to Ramallah. They filled the cars, as one does with
bricks, with as many as they could fit. In Ramallah, we were dispatched to
schools and other places. Our fate was to go to a school, I don't remember
its name anymore, but it was an all-girls high school in Ramallah. I saw it
again and I remembered it, of course, when I visited Palestine in 1997. We
were crammed in one room with 30 or 40 other people. There was no room
to stretch; we could only squat. Hunger struck and we wondered how we
could find bread. They brought in emergency relief food: bread, specifically, bread ... Let's stop here.

Renée Kutih
born 1925 in Ramla, Palestine
Interview with Mahmoud Zeidan
Verdun, Beirut, 2011

22'46"–34'12"

Renée Kutih: Our house was one of the most beautiful houses, our house was in what they call here 'downtown', inside the market, but it was a house like a castle, with a downstairs and an upstairs, that's a story in itself. When they first built it, the downstairs was for my grandfather, my father's father. He was a wheat merchant you see, and every day – it was a must – the least we had was five, if not six men come back home with him for lunch, but there weren't dining tables like today with tablecloths and things like that. They had something like trestles, do you know what a trestle is? We had about six, seven, ten of these, God knows, and the wood came on top and then they would put a plastic cloth over that, and however many men would come with him, it didn't matter to my grandmother, meaning my father's mother. She had a woman, her name was Khadija, come especially to help her, because it was expected that every day, every day, people would come and eat at our place, there was no escaping that. My grandfather and *Teta* would sleep and live downstairs. Downstairs there was a garden, and bedrooms, rooms, rooms, very large rooms, beautiful, refreshing, and an Arabic bath made to work on wood of course, in the garden they had cupboards in the walls, especially to bring us the wood from the orchard, and in it we would stack the wood, chopped to the size of the geyser, you know how they used to place it inside the boiler. My mother, she was very, very generous, more than you can imagine, I mean, her mind and her religion were people, that's it, all she cared for in life was other people, we had God's plenty, he had provided us, she could not put a morsel in her mouth before giving to someone. For example, we would cook, the pots we had ... They were all, you know, made of brass, and grandmother's kitchen was like a counter, a big stove, with hollowed places where the pot could rest, we would put the coal there, and the pot on top, I mean six, seven pots would sit there on the stove. After lunch, after they were done eating, the neighbours would come – their situation was a little fragile – we would give them the pots and my mother would tell them, 'Take what's inside, wash them and return them to me.'

This is one of the many stories we tell about my folks. Everyday, all kinds of produce would come from the orchards, we planted not only oranges, but oranges in all their varieties, I mean all shapes and colours. As well as *mulukhiyya*, and ... They would raise chickens and young pigeons. Everyday, out of all these provisions, they would send us whatever we wanted – bags, cartons – and my mother would distribute. She would keep some for us and distribute. My paternal uncle's family was living with us in the house, my uncle who is a pharmacist ... Alex Kutih, if you know him, near Jeanne d'Arc [street], he owns a pharmacy there. Ask him and you will hear the same story I am telling you ... They lived with us, with my mother, for 13 years, we lived in the same house. Imagine how patient my mother was, she lived with her mother-in-law, a long time ago mothers-in-law were different than today, never did my mother answer her back, can you believe this? To the point that when my *Teta* was dying – we had in those days the Feast of the Annunciation, and my mother and the women around her were making *ka'k*, at the time we would make *ka'k* with dates, and poor *Teta* was dying upstairs – my uncle the pharmacist would go up to see what she wanted. He'd say to her, 'What do you want mother?' She would tell him, 'I don't want anything, all I want is for Fadwa to come up and answer me back.' She wanted my mother to answer her back if only one time. Look what an upbringing [my mother] had, she loved family, she loved respect, she loved all these things.

After my grandfather and *Teta* died, my mother saw how much abundance there was, so why should she have to keep paying attention to who took the oranges, who took the lemons, who took any of these things? She had no patience for this, she was preoccupied with tending to the house. The floor we had upstairs was of a different order, it had parlours and a dining room. If you were going upstairs from our gate, you'd enter our house through an iron gate. Its key was this large, this large! So when you went up the stairs midway, we had made, pardon me, like a room, a toilet and a washbasin, so that if a guest came and he needed, he would not go up directly to our own bathrooms. What did my father think, poor guy, he kept turning around and around in his head, 'What should I do with the property below, what should I do with it?' Can you guess what he did with it? He changed it, he turned it all into stores, shops. He said, I will rent them out to whoever wants to rent them, I don't want to leave the house below unattended, with people coming and going. My mother thought, 'As they like, let them do what they want', how could she keep up, we were four children, although she had a maid just for her, Armenian, she lived with us for 17 years, and she came with us.

So he rented them out, dear sir, on the basis that he did not wish to get rent from them. Why? This was new. The first guy, the one who got the smallest store, was a tinker – why did dad want him? Because we used to pickle the cucumbers in tins, back then, not in tiny pressure jars (laughs), and everything, as I'm telling you, was abundant, we had plenty. Back then, we didn't have gas, right? We had the *babor*; you needed a tinker daily to repair the *babor*. The *babor* went out, and the *babor* broke down, and the *babor* … The other thing is, he told the man, 'Look, I don't want any rent money. You just manage the household jobs for me, and if you have left over money … For example, say I give you 10 *gineh* per year, you see what the household upstairs uses up, and if any of it is left over, you'll make us brass pots with it.' See how they used to think back then? He made brass pots, for me and my brother, who I told you is a doctor, and my sister, I also have a sister in the United States, and also a brother who died, may you not see ill, he made each one of us pots, from the smallest one for heating milk, to the one that fits a whole sheep, and our names were engraved on them, I swear to God…

There was a man who used to sell fabric. Back then, they would re-upholster the bedding, there wasn't Sleep Comfort or any of these things, there was tulle from which they would make the quilt cover, and tents, all these things … He was a fabric vendor. [My father] told him, 'You go upstairs' – to my mother, her name was Fadwa – 'You go upstairs and ask her what she wants and you bring it upstairs to her'; he would bring linen upstairs to make bed sheets, pillowcases, and bring this and that upstairs, 'And I don't want any rent from you either.' Each person who rented, we would benefit from his trade. It was a nice idea.

But there were neighbours who had a delicate situation, my mother liked them a lot, she would tell dad, 'Let us give them a monthly wage.' Despite all his wealth, and he had a lot of money and everything, he disliked anything mandatory. He would tell her, 'Look, every time they're in need, I'll give to them, every feast, every special occasion, every time you feel…' – she had seven kids, that woman – 'Just tell me, I will give to them, but to impose an obligation on me, each, say, first of the month, to go give them whatever it is, I am not going to agree with you.' My mother was intelligent, look what she did, she started bringing *athwab*, this linen *thawb* … The neighbour was a good woman, neat, tidy, balanced, her name was even 'Adla.[23] Imagine, I met her kids in Toronto, two or three years ago. A beautiful upbringing is of great benefit if the parents don't spoil the kids, so mum said to her, 'I am not going to give you money on a monthly basis, Umm' – I don't know what her name was, Umm Basim maybe – 'But I am going to give you a job that will entertain you and from which you will benefit.' She started bringing her all that she wanted made, she would bring her boxes of threads for hem embroidering, so it was that instead of her feeling as if she was begging from my mother, or bothering us, she would be doing something for us, she would be happy and entertained, and on our side, what my father had an obligation to give – you know, like the *zakat* you have for Eid, the gifts, and that stuff – he would not fail them, not to mention what they would receive each and every day from the orchard's harvest, of all shapes and sizes. We used to plant every single thing, anything you can think of, we would plant...

1h 20'22"–1h 25'08"

My parents travelled and I stayed at their house. A very big explosion went off in Ramla that day, and neither my husband nor my parents were there. Just me and the girl, the maid. Her name was Badr, from Jizin, from here. They did not come back, my parents. Two days and Haifa fell, and the situation deteriorated with incredible speed! They didn't come back. And I stayed at my father's home and didn't go back to my own. I had not brought anything with me! I had brought only one nightgown and some underwear because I had not meant to stay ... I had not meant to stay. This is the only thing that I brought with me from my house in Palestine. The whole situation lasted a long time, my father hadn't taken anything with him, not his papers, or money, nothing ... Nothing. They stayed with my uncle who has the pharmacy now. They had rented an apartment in al-Mazr'a from the Azan family. There were letters, talks and phone calls: what are we to do? The first issue was that my sister was still at boarding school. As for me, I was alone in the family home; my parents were here and my husband was in Haifa. We were all in different places, and there was no way for us to communicate with each other. There was talk, talk, talk. First, my father shattered our hopes of being able to return to Palestine in that situation. He said that he would return if things calmed down, 'Those who are there are fleeing, how am I to return?' He never returned.

My uncle the pharmacist and his family had already left. Before this explosion had occurred, they had left Ramla, they said no, we don't want to stay. They brought a truck, loaded it with all their furniture and things and moved to Lebanon. They took an apartment in al-Mazr'a, as I said, and stayed there. After numerous discussions and talks, we understood that there was no way my father and mother would come back, but what was to become of me and my sister? She was sent to me by her school in Ramallah, and I stayed, awaiting God's mercy, what was to become of my husband Fawzi in Haifa? How was I to leave? I didn't have a passport, I didn't have a passport ... I needed a passport if I wanted to go to Lebanon later and I didn't have one. He did everything he could and when he found out that Spinneys company was moving to Lebanon, he managed to send me a passport with the army. I then took my sister and my other brother who was staying with us, boarded the plane from Lydda, and left my father's home. I didn't bring anything with me. I brought the domestic servant with me. My uncle's family in Yafa – where there were more troubles than in Ramla – came to live in our house. They were shocked. They would open the closets, see all the stuff stacked there ... I told you how my mother used to make linen sheets for all of us. Each of us had six sheets, pillows, quilts. She prepared everything for our future. And all the pots and pans, the store-room, the silverware ... You know, all of this I'm talking about is secondary, it's the house itself, the property and the bus company – we had all these buses, sixty-eight of them working for us, in partnership with the Dalal family, if you have heard of them here, and others. It was a proper company, and it was called the Ramla–Lydda–Yafa Bus Company. We didn't bring anything with us.

1h 27'45"–1h 30'33"

Mahmoud Zeidan: *I'd like you to describe the situation in Ramla in general; what was happening outside the house?*
The situation was not at all comfortable. Everyone was exhausted, especially after the Dayr Yasin massacre happened. All of the men who had women and girls were ready to leave everything behind to get them out of the country. No one made any visits or went out, there was nothing of the sort. We were at home waiting. Everyone was thinking about emigrating. They no longer thought about staying in Palestine, in their homes. They managed for my sister and I to take the plane to Lebanon, and my uncle in Yafa – I had a second uncle – assured us that he would come to live in our house together with a doctor from the military hospital called Sami Bishara. They took over the house – because it was fully equipped – and they fled from Yafa because Yafa and Tel Aviv, you know ... But my uncle in Yafa managed to get a truck and transport all of their belongings.

How did you learn about the news of Dayr Yasin before you left?
The news spread around town. I forget now if the radio broadcast or not but people circulated such news. The massacre of Dayr Yasin was an historical event. It was very important news, a lot of people died and it was very ugly. They would cut the women's stomachs; they would be pregnant. And some

they would rape them and these shameless ways they had. That's why no one wanted photographs or chairs or the house, they just wanted to leave, but they didn't know how. Cars drove around calling out: 'Leave just for 15 days and you will all return.' They broadcast it over loudspeakers: 'Leave just for a short time then everything will go back to normal.'

Did you hear this?
I heard this. I heard this just as I am seeing you now in front of me. Everyone started to want only to leave.

Who were the people who called out from the cars?
It was the British government who was doing this, with the help of, in agreement with the Jews, that's for sure.

1h 44'49"–1h 46'30"

You told me that you took the plane; did you run into some trouble on the way?
No. It was a short distance.

Did you see any Jews on your way to Lydda, for example?
No.

Were the people of Lydda still there or had they already left?
At that time you couldn't tell who left, who didn't, who was hiding, or who was scared to leave their house. Yes, you saw some people in the streets, of course but ... I told you earlier, there weren't any killings or beatings as much as persons stirring things up ... Stirring things up ... Let's say you live here and someone would come roaming about saying, 'Folks, today Lydda is going to attack you,' and so on and so forth. Those who got scared ran away, but they did so thinking they would return. They never thought they wouldn't return. The houses were emptied and they occupied them. This was the simple plan that even a small child could dupe you with.

Who were the people who stirred things up?
We heard that it was the British government who did; you can never know how true ... you could never tell. We were very happy under British rule, we were very happy, because everything was going right, but ... When the Balfour Declaration happened, and the number of Jews increased abroad, they didn't have a place to put them in, and no one wanted them, so they sent them to Palestine according to what Balfour had promised them.

12

Scars of the Mind: Trauma, Gender and Counter-Memories of the Nakba

Ruba Salih

Safsaf, the village 7 kilometres northwest of Safad where Subhiya Salama found refuge, was attacked early in the morning of Friday, 30 October 1948, by Haganah, Stern and Irgun Zionist paramilitary units. Arab armies refrained from joining the exiguous local resistance and fighters retreated too, leaving villagers to defend themselves.[1] The village was encircled from all sides. That night, between 50 and 70 men were shot and buried in a ditch, and several women raped and killed. Subhiya survived this massacre.

Some time earlier, she had escaped her hometown along with many others seeking safety from the fury of war, as Jewish forces were attacking the surrounding villages one after another. Today, we know most villagers left out of grave fear. One terror tactic wielded by Zionist military organisations was to broadcast ghastly sounds of sirens, fire, moans, shrieks and wailing women – forewarnings of what could happen should Palestinians stay put.

Safsaf seemed safe, and Subhiya and her family were generously welcomed and offered shelter for what they thought would be a temporary stay. Yet Jewish armies would soon reach Safsaf. Amidst chaos and horror, Subhiya attempts to run from the imminent carnage, but the Jaysh al-Inqadh (Arab Liberation Army) is patrolling the area and sending villagers back. Subhiya's sister-in-law, Nazha, is returning from the fields, unaware Safsaf has been attacked. She will lose her leg to a landmine planted around the village. Subhiya's memory is fixed on this moment: she is carrying Nazha on her shoulders, she needs to get her away from the shelling and shooting, fast. But Subhiya is young, barely more than a child. She cannot bear the weight of her sister-in-law's wounded body. In this fraught moment, Nazha begs Subhiya to leave her behind and save the children, who are trapped in the house with no defence. Subhiya is thus confronted with a dramatic choice: should she remain with Nahza or run to the children's rescue? 'Israel' – Subhiya recalls the Jewish militias as one with the state they would beget on the ruins of Palestinian villages and cities – was fast approaching and time was running out. Subhiya remembers leaving her sister-in-law languishing injured on the ground alone and running to the children. She turns back to see Jewish forces stabbing Nazha in cold blood before the eyes of her mother, who 'dies of sorrow' on the spot.

How does a survivor apprehend and remember the scale of violence, loss and erasure that Palestinians experienced during the Nakba, and continued to experience in its aftermath? And what lenses and approaches can the listener apply to such dramatic recollections of the 1948 war? In *The Drowned and the Saved*, Primo Levi reminds us that any reliving and retelling of traumatic memories is susceptible to fraud. Yet, where perpetrators' unconscious desire for exculpation provides incentive to deceive, victims are absolved: 'Anyone who suffers an injustice or an injury does not need to elaborate lies to exculpate himself of a guilt he does not have.'[2] Still, victims' recollections can go adrift in other ways. Reminiscences of trauma can seem numb and unconvincing when treating the most cruel, excruciating events; yet richly detailed in regard to what might appear as bizarre or ordinary moments. Equally, we tend to willingly forget the most gruesome details of illnesses from which we have recovered.

It is against this backdrop – specifically as far as questions of recovery and memory are concerned – that I shall situate the memories of Subhiya Salama and Amina Banat. The events these women witnessed and survived can be fully remembered only at the cost of reliving unbearable pain; and yet they cannot, and must not, be forgotten. As Palestinians, they have not only endured violent mass expulsion and witnessed ferocious massacres but also erasure from a history that privileges the perpetrators' point of view – a history of fraud and omission. As refugees, their plight is ongoing and their wound still open. There has been no recovery. I would like to suggest that these should be read as traumatic memories rather than through the canon of oral histories of the Nakba.

The phenomenon of trauma, as it emerges in personal recollections of the Nakba, invites close analysis because it both exceeds and confirms our habitual methods of historical enquiry. Trauma, Cathy Caruth reminds us, 'does not simply serve as record of the past but precisely registers the force of an experience that is not yet fully owned.' Recollecting trauma paradoxically elicits 'absolutely accurate and precise' images that are 'largely inaccessible to conscious recall and control.'[3] To become a narrative memory – a conscious and active form of recalling that feeds the canons of historical validity – trauma must be verbalised and integrated into a larger existing discourse around historical events. In the case of the Nakba, this knowledge is framed in nationalist terms often oblivious to gendered micro-histories, and to the individual and hollow aspects of traumatic events. The argument here is that if the collective story of the Palestinian expulsion has gained increasingly widespread legitimacy, the subjective dimensions of this collective trauma remain obscure.

Alessandro Portelli suggests that oral history differs from other forms of remembering in that it tells us less about facts and more about their meaning. The factual interest of oral records lies in the narrator's subjectivity: what she believes has happened, and the meaning she ascribes to events, constitute historical facts.[4] The singular stories of Palestinian refugee women express not merely individual experiences of collective loss – of land, of home, of loved ones, of identity – but also personal traumas unfolding in a context where violent war and patriarchal oppression are variously intertwined. Their subjective memories engender a particular and oppositional narrative that enmeshes and juxtaposes private and public spheres.

Subhiya and Amina bring to light a hidden history of female courage, physical resilience and creativity. When her husband makes for the border when fighting breaks out, leaving her stranded with their two small daughters, she pays Druze men to escort her to the Lebanese border on the backs of a donkey and camel, with the few belongings she could salvage. Amina astutely hides her valuables – two gold swing bracelets – in her baby's pillow; and later bargains with Jewish soldiers who demand her gold in exchange for crossing the border and securing water for her crying, thirsty infant. Men are nowhere remembered as heroic actors protecting women and children; rather, those not killed are tragic cowards running for their own safety (her husband), barring the path to families attempting to escape the carnage (the Arab army) or refusing water to thirsty children (a man at the border). Along the way, Amina looks out on a barren landscape of death and decay. She renders the carcass of a rotting animal with chilling precision, vividly likening worms to 'boiling rice' in dirty, blood-stained well water too deep to reach and yet so precious. Her own resourcefulness prompts her to plunge her *mandil* into the bottom of the well and squeeze some water onto her hands.

Amina's experience of motherhood is a sequence of losses, paralysing grief, sheer loneliness and waiting. Her two baby girls die in her arms, of unnamed illnesses, on the interminable, years-long journey in and out of temporary shelters. We assume she is eventually, somehow reunited with her husband in exile. Two years on, she gives birth to the first of five baby boys, four of whom will 'disappear' in the Israeli carpet-bombing of Lebanon in 1982, their bodies never to be found. This suffering is too painful to remember as more than a series of flashbacks, but Amina's body remembers; she finds herself repeating gestures made 71 years ago, when caring for her ill children. A linear account of these events proves impossible to articulate; while the visceral, frightful snapshot of her husband's brain splattered on the walls remains impressed upon her memory. Another sensory metaphor: Amina relates the multiple losses and separations which have marked her life as physical disappearances: 'They died, I did not see them.' Subhiya's ways of bringing certain images into words also demonstrates that her body has kept score of what she cannot process at a psychic level: we grasp the heaviness of the body Subhiya had to carry, the food that was eaten, the thirst and loud cries of the children.

Amina's painting of life in Palestine before 1948 is a lively one in pastel colours, and far from mythical or romanticised. Her early years appear as fully-fledged oral testimony, providing access not only to facts and events but also to the meaning they held in her eyes. Her extraordinary memories of communal life in Shaykh Dannun have been clearly processed and integrated in a narrative that compares the past to the present. Amina explains, 'We were living the natural way [...] living a slow life.' Human temporality was harmonised with the rhythms of the natural world, and human and non-human life enmeshed such that cacti and watermelons were cared for like babies in wombs. Subhiya's re-enactment of the Safsaf massacre is similarly interspersed with vivid memories of the rhythms and demands of peasant life, detailing ordinary chores to be attended to, even as villages were being erased with bloodshed and wanton violence across Palestine. Subhiya remembers her family harvesting olives – she even specifies the number of gallons produced – and cracking wheat.

Amina was 18 years old when her village, Shaykh Dannun, was attacked, and only 14 when her parents gave her away in marriage to her maternal cousin. She guides us through her anguish: at the sight of the family coming to bring an end to her childhood, she runs away to hide in shock and shame. Nobody is interested in the little girl's feelings or desires: 'You won't get away with this!' her mother angrily retorts. Her cousin wants her and the marriage is non-negotiable. Overwhelmed and possibly traumatised, Amina retreats to her childhood world with her friends, play-acting the domestic life soon to consign her to real motherhood and responsibilities. Amina makes sense of the abrupt extirpation of her childhood in a manner akin to a traumatic experience. Unable or unwilling to understand the reason for her predicament, she finds relief in the knowledge that it could be God's will.

After the war, Subhiya's and Amina's oral testimonies blur into traumatic memories. These emerge as a sequence of flashbacks, their words still numb, as if uttered in the immediate aftermath of the attacks. In Amina's flashbacks, war is intertwined with forced marriage, as if personal trauma both anticipates and is transposed into collective trauma. The marriage marks a premature and harrowing end of her childhood, while the Nakba is the destruction of her entire world. In light of Primo Levi's insight that trauma can only be apprehended once a framework exists that can give meaning to the experiences – or, to use the metaphor of the illness, once recovery is completed – it is clear that the atrocities these women experienced have yet to be fully processed. Indeed, Amina's and Subhiya's oral accounts testify to injuries that are ongoing in their present lives, or wounds which still await recognition and reparation. The existing historical canvas, imbued with nationalist meanings, is what they are offered to inscribe and process the meaning of what they went through, but this canvas is both inadequate and unfinished. The ongoing actuality of the Palestinian tragedy entails not only the impossibility of curing the trauma by narrating or forgetting, but also the effacement of women's gendered and subjective traumatic experiences, which are subsumed under the more imperative narratives of collective, national catastrophe.

However, read in their own terms, as traumatic memories rather than simply as oral histories narrating subjective experiences of war events, Subhiya's and Amina's accounts disrupt not only hegemonic Israeli renditions of 1948, but also a collective (and androcentric) rendition of Palestinian national history, with its focus on the collective dimension of displacement and dispossession. In these unprocessed traumatic memories, we find seeds of what could be seen as counter-histories. Both Subhiya and Amina resist making their trauma legible through the trope of martyrdom. In a reversal of the nationalist convention that renders the national trauma – the loss of the country – as the paradigm according to which individual histories acquire or lose meaning, and to which they can never compare, Amina asserts that nothing can compare to or compensate for the excruciating pain of a mother who has violently lost her child. In her own poetic and political lyrics:

If I told you that my country could compare to my children, I would be lying. A child is more precious than one's own soul. A mother is not more important than her child. As they say, '*I'd rather wish for death to have me and to spare my child.*' As for my country, I could never forget it, and it remains in my thoughts, but not as much as my children. Even my husband who was martyred, not as much as my children. Not even my sister, not as much as my children. Nor my brother, not as much as my children. My older brother who died, not as much as my children. And my sister died, and they all died, but none of them compare to my children. My children were born from my heart.

Subhiya Salama
born in al-Zahiriyya, Palestine
Interview with Bushra Mughrabi
ʿAyn al-Hilweh camp, Sayda, 2006

4'30"–6'33"

Bushra Mughrabi: *Before the hostility began between you, were you friends with the Jews?*
Subhiya Salama: We were very close friends with them. We would visit each other and share meals together, and there were no problems between us at all. We were such close friends with them, but when the enmities started between us, it was over.

In what way were you friends? Did you have any Jewish friends?
No, I was not personally friends with them. It was the adults who were friends, like my uncle, for example, who was friends with them. We kids did not get involved with them, but my uncle, bless his soul, was very good friends with them. He would bring basil and sell it to them, the plants with a stem and triangular leaves. He became very good friends with them.

Would you offer good wishes or visit each other on important occasions?
The adults would, not us younger kids. My older uncle would see them on important occasions, his children, who were older than us, would go as well. But there was no intermingling between us children.

At that time, did you feel there was hostility between you?
Yes, we did. There was this young Jewish boy who said us, 'Soon, you'll see.' The Jews would say: 'We are ready to put down money to kill a Muslim.'

Where would they pay?
Jews collectively raised money through organisations. We had a feeling that that sort of thing would happen.

Because they were collecting money?
Yes, they collected money because they knew a war would break out. They knew, but we didn't. We had no idea anything like this would happen, but they knew.

22'17"–27'11"

Who took you all [away from the town and the fighting]?
Our extended family did. The men in my family and my brother-in-law, all
of us. Each one of us moved his own family. The fighting went on all night
between the Jews and Safad. At dawn, entire crowds of people were suddenly
fleeing Safad, some were barefoot, some women were still in their nightgowns. Nobody went through the regular roads; we had to cross through the
ditches. We escaped with those who were fleeing and we arrived to Jish. As
soon as we arrived, a plane bombed Jish and people got dispersed. We kept
running until we arrived to Kafr Bir'im, where we stayed at a man's house,
God bless him. We spent 15 days at his house in Kafr Bir'im, just our family,
not the rest of al-Zahiriyya. And then we moved to Yarun, here in Lebanon.
Kafr Bir'im is at the border, but Yarun is in Lebanon. We stayed there about
15 days as well, and then people started saying, 'Let's go back', and everyone
wanted to go back. We took the bumpy roads back and we stayed under the
fig trees in Safsaf. Then we moved from under the fig trees in Safsaf, into
a house, with the help of the people from Safsaf, who called us '*akhwalna*'.

Whose house?
We stayed at the house of the Yunis family. My sister-in-law, who was very
strong, and my husband. I was still young, so I was scared to go back to
our village. They would go out and harvest a bit of wheat and crack it. And
when olive season came, they would go pick and press the olives. They harvested about 30 or 40 oil gallons and they were still not done, so they stored
the gallons where I was living in Safsaf and went back to picking. When
Safsaf fell, I was taking care of the children. Four of them were my brother-
in-law's children, another four were my sister-in-law's children. All of them,
and my mother-in-law, my sister-in-law and I were in Safsaf, and they had
gone to al-Farradiyya. They had left the place where they were bringing
back the olives and the oil from, and had gone from al-Farradiyya to Bint
Jubayl. I stayed in Safsaf. My sister-in-law came back home with a mutilated
leg. She was attempting to go back to the village when her leg got blown off.
My mother-in-law is an older woman, and my brother-in-law's children
and my sister-in-law's children were all young. My sister-in-law's son was
young like a basil stem. They took him from among us. So I had to carry my
sister-in-law on my shoulders, but I was so young and small, and she was
big-boned and heavy; I carried her for so long that my clothes got torn off.
I tried to run here or there and they would say, 'Israel is coming this way'.
At the beginning, I carried her on my back so that we could run away with

everyone who was fleeing, but Jaysh al-Inqadh did not let us leave. They said it was forbidden. So we went back to the initial house where we were staying and it got hit; we got out through the window. We left and we found women sitting around with men and children, and sat with them. The fighting went on all night long. I said to my cousin's son, 'Sa'id, please go, leave. Maybe you can escape and we'll be all right staying here.' The boy didn't move, he was 18 years old. They showed up and took people away, that time they took 40 men and lined them up and killed them. They took him and my sister-in-law's son as well – he was another one from our family.

What were their names?
One of them was Sa'id and the other one, Salih.

Salama?
Yes, Salama. No, they were Shahin. Sa'id Shahin. Not from our family name, but his mother was one of us, she was my cousin. Sa'id Shahin. The other one was Salama. Salih Salama. So we left and stayed at that house for seven days, and two of the men they had shot were still alive, and they came crawling back to stay among us women. They were wounded.

28'55"–33'54"

How did the Jews enter Safsaf? How did you know these were Jews entering your village?
They just showed up. Just like you showed up here, at my doorstep, they showed up at our doorstep. When my sister-in-law saw them, while I was carrying her on my back, she said, 'Please just throw me here and leave, go and be safe with the children.' They showed up in front of us, just like that. So I dropped her off right there, and they came and killed her. As soon as I turned around, I saw them stabbing her with knives.

They were stabbing the woman with knives?
They stabbed her with knives. No shooting or anything, and my mother-in-law was standing right there and looking like this, she was standing in front of her. She died of sorrow for her daughter.

What was her daughter's name?
Her name was Nazha.

Nazha Salama?
Nazha Salama.

But why did they kill her with knives?
Because of her leg ... They assumed she was a fighter.

Did you witness them stabbing her with knives?
Yes, of course, I barely had time to turn around when they were already stabbing her. So I left and took the children with me, to find safety.

What did you feel when you saw them killing her?
How do you think I felt? It was excruciating. I spent eight days crying. I did not raise my head, I did not eat, I did not drink. Not one drop of water. How do you think I felt, with all these small children with me, all of them crying? I suffered a lot ... a lot.

When her mother saw them killing her...
When she saw her, she dropped dead. When they took away the young men, it was different, because they came to take them, so we knew in advance. But with her, they had not touched her before. The mother died of sorrow at the sight of her slaughtered daughter.

So the mother died seeing her daughter...
She died, when she saw them stabbing her, she died for her daughter.

What was her mother's name?
Her name was Rima.

Rima Salama?
Yes.

When you saw them stabbing her with knives, where did you go?
I kept running and running. Israel showed up and I saw them. So I took the children, who didn't want to leave their grandmother and their aunt. I took the kids and walked up to the middle of town and stayed in a house where I found other women and men. My sister-in-law's son was with me; he was a young man. They came and took him from among us. And they took the other young man from among us too.

Were they gathering the young men?
They were and they lined them up, but I did not see them when they shot them.

Were they far from you?
Not really far, they were in the middle of town. They lined them up and killed them.

When they came to take the young men, did you have a feeling that they were going to kill them?
Of course we had a feeling. There were three brothers from the Yunis house, three beautiful young men. Three young men died. One woman was so sad for her one and only brother who was from Safsaf. So she took off her dress and put it on him, and she removed her scarf and put it on him. They came and took him. They found him out and they took him.

What was her name?
Bakriya Yunis.

What was her brother's name?
I don't know.

So they took him.
They took him.

Would they come and search among the women?
Yes, they searched among the women; they came and took him from among the women.

Did they separate the women on one side and the men on the other?
No, they didn't separate the women. They gathered us all together in one house, and started picking out each young man one by one and taking him away. They didn't gather the men in one house. People stuck together out of fear.

Did you hear them shoot the young men?
Of course. The firing sounded like a rainstorm.

Did you hear of anybody being killed in circumstances other than firing, or knives in the way your sister-in-law was killed?
No, I didn't hear of anything else, it was all by gunfire. I only heard of my sister-in-law being stabbed.

After they shot these young men, what happened in the village?
After they shot them, the women stayed together. Some of them fled during the night, and some of them stayed until the end, as they say. They had placed a guard to watch us in the village. He would take the elderly and let them slaughter [meat] and he would bring them food.

How long did you stay after they killed the young men?
I stayed in Safsaf for seven days after the massacre.

Amina Hasan Banat
born 1931 in Shaykh Dannun, Palestine
Interview with Bushra Mughrabi and Mahmoud Zeidan
Burj al-Barajneh, Beirut, 2003

2'00"–3'29"

Amina Hasan Banat: We never needed to buy any fruit or any vegetables. All our vegetables would grow in nature, and we were living the natural way. We didn't know any sickness; we didn't use any chemicals or anything. We were living a slow life. We would never hear about dangerous illnesses. We were just being, we were happy. One day, we did not know why, they said: 'War is about to break out, there will be skirmishes. Each individual must buy a rifle and keep it at home, in order to defend himself, in case something happens to us.' That is what the elders said.

***Bushra Mughrabi and Mahmoud Zeidan**: How big was your family? How many brothers and sisters were you?*
Are you asking how many brothers I have?

Yes.
Three of them. One of them is blind, they got him in the eye when he was young and he lost his vision in both his eyes. He is still with us. I have one brother who is still alive. My older brother died, I did not see him. My mother died, I did not see her. My father died, I did not see him. I have two sisters, they died, I did not see them. I am here in Lebanon, all by myself. I do not have a brother, nor a mother, nor a father, nor anybody at all. I only have a son, here in Lebanon, and two daughters. Nobody else. My four sons went missing in 1982. My husband received a projectile on his head while he was at home. His brains spilled on the ground and we buried him. And there I was, looking for my missing children.

9'05"–15'40"

Did the women work outside of the house, in your village?
Yes, on their own lands. *Fellahin* would work on their properties. But people in cities were not *fellahin*. They would buy from us *fellahin*. My father used to pick figs for me, which I would bring down to ʿAkka. He would harvest cactus fruit, enough to fill two crates. He would load them on a donkey for

me, and I would ride it and bring everything over to the city. There was never any fear or any danger upon us.

Would you go on your own?
Yes, I would. No, there were other people going there as well. But even if I was late and lagging behind them, I would not be worried. There would always be other people behind me. As soon as the shaykh would sound the *adhan*, for Fajr prayer, we would go down to ʿAkka. We would be selling by ten in the morning and then we'd come back. We did not get around by car or anything.

How?
We rode our donkeys, excuse my language.[5] We would load our crates on the donkeys and bring them down. And wherever there were streets, for example, near Nahr, al-Kabri, al-Mazrʿa or al-Manshiyya … the car would come. There was a member of my family named Muhammad Banat Abu Rashid. He was living in al-Rashidiyya, but he passed away, his children are still there. He used to have a pick-up truck. He would charge by the trip, and would load up in the village and bring everything over to ʿAkka and display it at the *hisbeh*. And those in the villages, including myself, would pull out our boxes, and people would come and we would tell them, 'My okras are better … Your okras are better … Your tomatoes … Your cactus fruits … Your figs.' This is how we were living, in Palestine.

What would you grow in your town?
We would grow everything. As I told you, cactus fruit was part of our produce, figs were part of our produce, and olives as well. If I had to tell you how many olive groves my father had, you wouldn't believe me. How many plots of land … When my father would find a watermelon that had grown this big from the sun, he would dig a deep hole in the ground and bury it, leaving only the top side uncovered. We would put grass on it to protect it from the rays, so that it wouldn't ripen too fast. Later on, we would bring it out of the ground and it would be that big. We would try to fit the watermelon in a *khurj*, and it would not even go through the hole. You don't know what a *khurj* is, do you?

Yes, I do.
We would put the watermelon inside it and it would not even get to the bottom of it. There were corn ears too. Imagine you were growing corn, and I wasn't. Or you were growing watermelon and I wasn't, or figs. I would

come to you and pick out some of your produce, you would come and you wouldn't say anything other than 'Enjoy your meal'. Say you had watermelons and I didn't, and I came over to choose, you would not make me pay for it. Wild cucumbers, tomatoes ... I would take a basket and pick out tomatoes from a brother's crops. And if you were the landowners and you saw me picking, you would not say anything to me. If you knew I did not have much, you wouldn't say anything. We were living in abundance. We would all sit and share the same meal. All the neighbours and all the village women would sit together, and whatever each woman brought, they would offer it to you. There would be seven or eight women sitting in a circle over here, and another circle over there in another neighbourhood, and there in yet another neighbourhood. This is how they sat ... at a common table. You would not think of your neighbour as a stranger. Same town, same brothers and sisters. Are we living that way now? No. Here, even brothers wouldn't mind killing each other. We are living in oppression, here. What if I told you that we've been here for 23 years, and we barely have a drop of drinking water for the whole camp. And that throughout this whole camp, there is not one house that directly receives drinking water. We have to buy the water. It's been 23 years.

Hajjeh, who were the biggest landowning families in your town?
The Rustum family. Their name was Rustum 'Abd al-'Al; they used to own land. We did not associate being a farmer with being poor. If I counted my father's plots of land, the ones I still remember, you would not believe me. That was my so-called poor father. Not really poor, only financially poor. Since my father did not have young men helping him, and he was alone – because we were four daughters first, until the boys were born ... He did not have anybody to help him. He was not able to cultivate all of the land. He would farm according to his needs.

Would the villagers help each other out with farming?
Of course, they would. Whoever was harvesting ... Say you were harvesting your wheat and I was done before you, I would come over and help you. Say I was still picking olives and you were finished before me, you would come over and help me. Our family built a house, we did not have any wheelbarrows, whoever was a construction worker would come and help me. This is how they were in 1948. I went back, I've been back three times. Whoever needed to build a house, but did not have any money ... Whenever there was an evening gathering in town, people would create a *diwan*. A *diwan* is like a huge living room, where people set up sofas.

Strangers who didn't know anybody came, as well as guest who might be lost or late to show up at their hosts. They would call this *madafeh* in that living room. An example of *madafeh* would be when someone would say, 'People! Umm ʿAziz wants to build a house and she does not have enough.' And three or four construction workers would step up and say, 'We will be there tomorrow.' They would bring rocks. 'We will go help him tomorrow.' 'So-and-so wants to pour cement tomorrow.' We would go help them out. They would mix the cement and place five or six ladders. Then, men would carry tanks on one shoulder, and women [would carry them] on their heads. And that is how they would help whoever needed to pour cement for his house. Whether there were two or five rooms, they would help. This is how we would help each other in everything. We were together, even the British in our town. In Palestine, there were British people, I remember them. And there were Jews who would go from Nahariyya to [Khirbat] Jiddin. They would pass through our town. They would see a child and say: 'Come, come'. The child would go to them, and they would carry him, kiss him, and give him a biscuit, or candied almonds or money. So, every time we saw a Jew going to his town of Jiddin, in the mountains, we would run to him so that he could give us a biscuit or a candied almond or a coin, and we would be happy. He would carry us and kiss us. It didn't matter if it was a little boy or a little girl.

There wasn't any enmity at the time.
There wasn't any enmity. To the point where, when the Jew came, as I said, kids would run towards him, and young and old would welcome him and salute him as if he were an Arab. We were living together with them. There was Tel Aviv, there was Nahariyya. I was born in Nahariyya. There were Jews living there. There was no enmity between the Arabs and the Jews. There were still Jews in Palestine in 1948, right? Well, there are many Palestinian men who married Jewish women. But a Palestinian woman never married a Jewish man.

29'45"–32'44"

So they would marry one of your villagers out to a stranger, then. It wasn't a problem, right?
Yes, I am from Shaykh Dannun and I got married in ʿAmqa. Who did I marry? My cousin on my mother's side. I am my husband's cousin, his aunt's daughter on his father's side, and he is my uncle's son, my mother's

brother. My uncle came over. He came over and he said, 'I want the girl', and my mother gave me to him...

I swear to God, when my father gave me, I had no idea. All I saw was them coming to read the *Fatiha*, and a group of men entering. My mother said to me, 'Go get dressed.' I asked, 'Why?' I was playing, I was just a 14-year-old girl; I was playing with my friend, her name was Fatma al-Khalid and there was also Nihaya al-Hanil. [My mother] said, 'People are coming to read your *Fatiha*.' 'To read my Fatiha?' She said, 'People are coming, your cousin wants to get engaged to you, people are coming to read your *Fatiha*.' As soon as she said that, there they were coming through the door. There were mangers behind the door; they had placed them there for the *dawab* to eat hay out of them. I got up, I was in a shocked state, so I went to hide behind the door. I didn't want to see anybody, I hid behind the door. They started asking, 'Where is the bride? We want to see her already, we want to know what she looks like.' They would say that if someone wanted to take one from another town, surely she must be better than from the hometown. I was not pretty. My sisters were very beautiful. I was not pretty. But my uncle would come over and say, 'I do like Amina, she has vigour, she is agile, I want her for my son.' So my mother gave me away. And they kept asking, 'Where is the bride?' while the bride was hiding and listening in on everything. They ended up reading the *Fatiha* and leaving, and they did not see me and nor did I see them. When I came out, my mother said, 'Where were you?' 'Where were you?' I said, 'I was hiding where the mangers are.' She said, 'You are not getting away with this. Why did you hide?' I said, 'Because I don't want to see anybody.' I swear, it was my wedding day, and my girlfriends were there and there was cactus fruit. I went with these friends, the ones I was telling you about, Nihaya and Fatma. And I hope they can hear me saying this now. We went and made a house out of stones – pretend houses. I made myself a house like this, she made a house over there, and she made one like that, and we took rocks and I said, 'This is my son,' and she said, 'This is my daughter...' And we made three houses next to each other, by playing with stones, and my hands and feet had henna on them and it was my wedding day. They were coming to get me at noon. People came to prepare me to be a bride, and my mother could not find me. She said to my sister, 'Go call her, see where she is.' My sister went up to the roof and kept calling me while I was on the other side, playing house with my friends on the grass, because I was young. And today's generations of ten year olds and nine year olds are more aware than we were. As for us, we were under God's will. We did not know how, nor did we want to know.

33'57"–35'00"

Hajjeh, how long did you stay in 'Amqa before the skirmishes started with the Jews?
I was there for three years ... three or four years. I know that when I left Palestine, I was 18 years old. I got married at the age of 14.

What happened before you left? What was the thing that made you leave your house?
The war that was brought upon us, dear. The tanks came for us and because we fought against them, we had nothing left when they invaded the town. They started bombing the town, they burnt down the houses, they bombed, and after they bombed the whole village that had resisted against them, they brought bulldozers and bulldozed the entire town.

Where were you when they brought the bulldozers?
We were in the Druze regions – in Jat and Yanuh and Yarka – these were Druze towns. The Druze were peaceful, they did not fight. We sought refuge in their towns. When we heard that the borders would close down, we left the Druze regions and went to the borders...

35'54"–40'56"

Did the men come with you?
No, the men had crossed and fled before the borders had closed. They had run away; they had no more ammunition left. I had two daughters – my husband could not even take one of them. He left me and he went. When we got to the borders, they told us, 'These are the borders with Lebanon, you can go through. These are the borders with Palestine, and we will be going back.' We went from the Lebanese borders. First, they dropped us off on the street, at the border. When my daughter saw the armed Jew, she got scared and started crying. If you could see how beautiful she was, how beautiful my daughters are. Even though I'm not pretty, their father is handsome. The girl started crying, so the Jew told me: 'Madam.' That street was at the Palestine–Lebanon border. I said, 'Yes?' and stayed like this (pulls headscarf over face). He said, 'Silence bubu, why is he crying, this bubu, why does he cry?' I told him, 'Khawaja, he wants water to drink.' He went like this on his water bottle (taps on right hip) and said, 'No water. You be waiting here, me go get water?' I looked this way over to the Lebanese borders and saw people on camels and donkeys stocking up on water. So I told him, 'Khawaja, if you

do favour to God, not to me, to God and to bubu, you allow me to go. I go down there, there is water, and I make bubu drink.' What did he answer? He said this and that, ' '*Ukhtu* Arab. '*Ukhtu* Arab, '*Ukhtu* Arab. All Arab not good.' The Druze that had brought us there had also loaded a few things on a camel. A bit of semolina and a bit of wheat, and two blankets and a mattress, on one camel, and they brought us over, the two Druze. They had surrounded the camel and they were searching it. I had 70 Palestinian liras and a couple of spiral bracelets. I had slid them inside my girl's pillow, it was this size, and then under the laundry basin, and had her sitting on it. They came and said, 'Take girl off.' I removed her, and they tore out the seams of the pillow. They wanted to see what was in it, but they still hadn't broken the inside. When the Jew – who I'd asked to let me get water as a favour to God – came back, he told me, 'All gold you carry, you leave here so bubu can go. *Yalla*, leave it and you go for bubu. Leave all of gold, and you can go.' I told him, 'God bless you, *khawaja*. May God protect you, *khawaja*.' They put the things on the camel and we left. They did not take one piastre from us. They did not humiliate us, nor did they beat us, nothing at all. That was at the border. We went down to 'Ayta al-Sha'b. In 'Ayta, we were boiling to death, out of fear and out of thirst. We went to sit down, they had made a cabin and were guarding the fig tree so that nobody would pick it. We went into the cabin and found it full of fleas. We left it and sat outside, with the girls under the sun. One of them was crying of thirst and I was thirsty as well. We looked over and found a well, there was a dead goat beside it. I swear, the worms inside it were moving like boiling rice. We opened the well and found a puddle of water at the bottom. We wanted to drink, but we could not reach the depths of the well. My cousin and I took off our scarves and tied them together with my girl's blanket, and we dipped them into the puddle at the bottom, and then we wrung them in a plate, like this. The water came out. You know how the water gets when it rains, the dirt, the redness ... I swear to God, we drank it. But what about the girls? I went into a nearby house and I told him ... I went in ... I knocked on the door, he said, 'What's wrong with you, who are you, lady?' I told him, 'I am Palestinian. God bless you, brother, may God extend your life, what is your name?' He said, 'My name is Abu Kamil.' I said, 'May God protect your children, Abu Kamil, would you please give me just a bit of water in a jug so these poor girls can drink? They are thirsty and little and they are dying in front of me.' He told me: 'Shoo shoo, go out, leave, leave, leave,' I told him, 'Why, my brother, what did I do to you?' He said, 'You Palestinians, we don't welcome you. We don't welcome you, you are unclean.' I said, 'No, my brother, I swear we didn't do anything. Maybe you could give me a bit of water as a favour towards God.' He told me, 'I won't give you.' I said, 'If I gave you a jug of oil, would you give me a jug of water?' He said, 'Do you swear that nobody else touched the olives?' I told him, 'I swear, I was the one who picked it and pressed it into the gallon and who brought it with me.' So I gave him a jug of olive oil and, I swear, he gave me a jug of water. And we stayed 13 days in 'Ayta al-Sha'b, and then we went to Juwaya and then from there to Hay al-Maslakh. I swear, we kept in touch and asked about him and he came to visit us from 'Ayta al-Sha'b to Hay al-Maslakh, and we went to visit him as well. We became friends. He gave me a jug of water, I gave him a jug of olive oil. We suffered a lot, my dear.

48'51"–50'06"

Do you express your longing towards Palestine, or to the town of Shaykh Dannun where your children live ... or where your siblings live? I mean, despite the catastrophe of your children whose fate you do not know about...
In the same way that the memory of my children remained ... Although the memory of my country does not equal the memory I carry of my children, I will never forget my country. I will never forget my nation. I will never forget my hometown. And I don't wish to be buried anywhere other than in my country, over there, because that is where my brother, my mother, my father and my sister are, and I would be with them. If I told you that my country could compare to my children, I would be lying. A child is more precious than one's own soul. A mother is not more important than her child. As they say, 'I'd rather wish for death to have me and to spare my child.' As for my country, I could never forget it, and it remains in my thoughts, but not as much as my children. Even my husband who was martyred, not as much as my children. Not even my sister, not as much as my children. Nor my brother, not as much as my children. My older brother who died, not as much as my children. And my sister died, and they all died, but none of them compare to my children. My children were born from my heart.

1h 26'43"–1h 27'38"

When we arrived in Juwaya, the weather change bothered them. My older daughter's head started swelling – she was three years old. Her head, her hands and her feet became swollen, and she died and I had no money to treat her. And the other girl got a disease in her mouth and she died. We arrived in Hay al-Maslakh and I gave birth to my kids here in Hay al-Maslakh. My oldest son was born in 1950. I left in 1948. I raised them into young men and they are now married. The ones I lost, I did not find again. They left in an instant while I was with them. And here I am, 23 years later and still searching. Still crying and still searching. After everything that happened to me, it's good that I can still stand up, it's good that I can still see, it's good that I still have my brain and I can still come and go.

1h 28'46"–1h 29'07"

Why did you not stay with [your parents in Palestine]? When you told me...
I am married, dear.

Didn't you say your husband departed and left you?
I am married, I am from the village of Dannun and I married in ʿAmqa. When the war started, and the tank was bombing us with missiles, he ran, I never saw him leave. His mother was running in front of him, he took her and his siblings, and he came to Lebanon, and I was still inside Palestine.

13

The Politics of Listening

Cynthia Kreichati

At her home in Burj al-Barajneh camp, in a southern suburb of Beirut, Fatima Sha'ban sits on the edge of a colourfully patterned couch. She wears a long black *abaya* dotted with tiny white motifs. The ivory curtain behind her is adorned with grey flowers. Her left arm rests on a white cushion. Fatima, who was born in the coastal village of al-Zib, in the *kaza* of 'Akka, is narrating her life and her experience of Palestine. The entire tableau seems familiar, drawn from the everyday – a *hajjeh* sitting on her couch – but the vivid stories she tells are apertures in space and time. Fatima is a formidable storyteller. She knows how to make you laugh through tears and how to share her pain. She recounts how she posed at her wedding and how her husband's uncle once beat her with the reins of his donkey on her way back from the village spring. Fatima's stories speak of love, desire and violence, music and dancing, poetry and death.

Fatima pays tribute to her husband Ali Ahmad al-Hajj, with whom she had 15 children. Although she was forced to marry when she was not yet 13 (after her family bribed the *qadi* with gifts and stuffed her chest with towels to make her look older), she seems proud of their life together, through thick and thin, as husband and wife for 60 years. She describes her husband's arduous labour – the farmers he would hire to care for the cattle, the orchards and the land they leased. There is no land more abundant than the land of al-Zib and no sea richer than the Mediterranean, which features prominently in Fatima's account. She retells stories of men at sea, those who went fishing and returned, and those who drowned in 1948. 'One of my brothers left by sea, in the boats. Those who left by boat were shot. They died in the sea,' she says. She also conjures al-Zib's coastal landscapes: the stone houses by the water, the village mosque, an ancient olive oil press on the beach, owned by the Yusif family. Fatima expresses some ambivalence towards family life. She recites poetry, the kind usually sung at weddings, and invokes the dead. 'May God rest their souls,' she says repeatedly. She recreates the intimate worlds of women and condemns the patriarchal

violence inflicted on her and other women and girls she knew. Her celebration of the anti-colonial resistance of men and women during the British
Mandate is equally personal. She commemorates the armed struggles of
people she knew from her village against Zionist militias on the coastal
railway roads, and evokes in her listeners the throbbing pain of her departure from Palestine on 14 May 1948, with her newborn daughter, who was
just nine days old.

To listen to Fatima's narrative is to become embedded in all the things,
people and places that make al-Zib and mark the Nakba as a process that
is ongoing. 'I used to go to the olive press on the beach. You know, it's right
after the *tal*, you go down towards the sea, past where the old houses are, this
is where we had the olive press,' she says.[1] The stories she imparts are both
independent from and intricately determined by the temporal, socio-political and environmental contexts in which they originally took place. This
layering makes possible the recovery of personal experiences (the death
of a relative, a young girl's encounter with her future husband, the *qadi*'s
questions about menstruation) together with the vitalities of many life-
times (drawn not only from Fatima's experiences but also from those of
others, in Palestine and in Lebanon). Because they can be both appreciated
on their own terms and comprehended only in relation to the context of
al-Zib, these stories impress themselves on and transform those listening.
We come to fully grasp and interpret Fatima's narratives only after building
our own visceral, cognitive and emotional relationships with al-Zib.

As Rosemary Sayigh observes, it is difficult to '*feel*' the history one reads
in books.[2] Speaking from her own lived experience, Fatima's recollections
are acute and vivid; they make events 'real' and felt for her listeners.[3] This
mode of storytelling, which embeds listeners in another space and temporality, does more than '[bring] to light hidden, suppressed or marginalized
narratives'.[4] By re-inscribing women's voices in official narratives as 'tellers
of history', Fatima's story challenges certain established notions of what constitutes history, who is authorised to recount it, and how it should be told.[5]
And yet, rather than merely reclaiming the experiences of women that have
been silenced and ignored, Fatima's account also sets the stage for another
kind of listening that is deeply transformative and inescapably contingent.
This is a listening that pays attention to the particularities of voice and the
act of communication, and that is understood not simply in physical terms
but also as receptiveness to the ways selves become blurred and entangled
through storytelling and shared experience.

Apprehending the multivalent and potent meanings of these stories
requires, then, a particular mode of attunement to the storyteller. As I listen

to Fatima, I wonder how we might engage the oral archive in a manner that incites us, as listeners, to consent to the reconfiguration of our relations to people, places and things? I search for a mode of engagement that is intimate, personal, visceral and irreducible – one that might also critically recognise how wounds of history and politics, as well as practices of collective remembrance, shape subjectivity and become part of the warp and weft of stories like Fatima's. To better grasp this politics of listening, I turn to Edward Said's theory of the 'concert occasion' – a unique performative event at once intimately personal, embodied and collective, and informed by complex socio-historical and political processes.[6] Listening to music performed in concert settings structures thought and emotion.[7] For example, a particularly powerful encore (or a *bis*) can radically alter what we, the audience, retain from a concert experience. We leave deeply affected by the last piece we heard, how it was performed for us and how we received it. Listening to an oral history interview drawn from the archive works on us in much the same manner – its effects are concentrated, embedded, rare, dislocated, collective, institutionalised and individual. In this way, listening as a mode of attunement also precedes, exceeds and structures language, speech and meaning.

In Arabic, the verb to listen means three things: to perceive sound, to acknowledge meaning, and to respond. I want to suggest here that the act of listening to Fatima is literal, figurative and methodological. Unlike looking, listening is a mode of paying attention to the fragmentary, the composite and the accretive. It is as a mode of attunement that attends to silences: hiatuses and breaks in time and space serve to separate or bring together seemingly distinct elements, both auditive and visual (picture a visual silence). Fatima's interview is marked by such ruptures. When she recounts how her family, future husband and in-laws took her to ʿAkka for her Katb al-kitab, she re-enacts her conversation with the *qadi*, whom her family had bribed.[8] She recalls how the *qadi*, seeing she looked too young for marriage, had asked her how old she was and whether she had washed. 'We washed the sheets and made the beds just yesterday!' she recalls telling him. Incrementally, these seemingly incoherent narrative fragments lend context and meaning to the experiences she shares. It is only retrospectively that we come to understand the significance of the *qadi*'s questions, which are rooted in both shariʿa and customary law. In asking whether she had washed, he was inquiring about *ghusl* or ablution, the cleansing ritual that women perform after menstruation.[9] Fatima admits her younger self 'knew nothing at the time'.

If listening also means responding, then how do we respond to oral histories? I am reminded of the stories of Umm Faris (Halima Hasuna) recorded and published by Rosemary Sayigh in *Voices: Palestinian Women Narrate Displacement* (2007). When an oral history encounter such as Sayigh's with Umm Faris is recorded aurally, visual perception, in its literal sense, is denied. This denial is powerful because it makes way for revelations that the gaze of a camera would render impossible. Sayigh describes Umm Faris, as 'a pleasant-faced woman of brisk appearance.'[10] Beyond this brief introduction, we know only what Umm Faris tells Sayigh during the conversation recorded on 12 April 1998 in Gaza City. Umm Faris begins by hesitantly mentioning that she does not seek to address 'political sufferings'. Instead, she wants to share her 'own personal sufferings'.[11] At the time of the interview, Umm Faris, who had been working with UNRWA, had just been evicted from al-Shati' refugee camp and spent significant effort, time and money rebuilding a home for herself and her two children, with her own two hands.

The vast majority of Umm Faris' painful recollections concern her peripatetic travels between 1978 and 1998, to places and cities as different as Gaza, Baghdad, Geneva, Damascus, Sayda and Badawi. During this period she accompanied her husband, a freedom fighter and a high-ranking member of Fatah she had married and moved to Iraq with in 1978. From this marriage she had two children: Youssef, born at Baghdad Medical City in 1979 and Mohammad, born at al-Shifa' hospital in Gaza in 1981. Both sons were delivered by caesarean section. In 1991, Umm Faris, by then a widow following her husband's assassination at the hands of the Abu Nidal Organization, was forcefully evicted from the southern Lebanese city of Sayda with her two children. From there, she moved to Badawi camp in north Lebanon, where she managed to forge identity papers with which she returned to her native Gaza with her two children in 1998.

Most of Umm Faris' travels were prompted by life-threatening complications she developed after giving birth to Mohammad. When she underwent surgery in Baghdad following her return from Gaza, doctors discovered 'cotton and gauze left inside her belly' after her second C-section.[12] The staff at Baghdad Medical City, already working under hardship and duress because of the Iran–Iraq War, were unable to provide proper care. Umm Faris' husband, through his connections, arranged for her transfer to Switzerland, where her condition began to improve following treatment. By then she weighed 35 kg and had undergone several surgeries, including a colostomy. The medical error had put so much pressure on Umm Faris' vital organs that her 'guts and her intestines were now ruined and rotten' because of this 'foreign substance that remained and reacted with blood and organs and coagulated to ruin everything'.[13] From Gaza to Baghdad and beyond, Umm Faris' body bore witness to her physical ailments as well as her experience of displacement, exile and migration.

At one point in the recording, in the midst of recounting her succession of difficult surgeries, Umm Faris suddenly breaks off the conversation. A prolonged silence ensues. 'Would you come see my abdomen?' she asks Sayigh. A long moment of silence follows. In this lull, I imagine her reaching for Sayigh's hand. I cannot see, but in listening to the silence, I intuit that Umm Faris lifts her garments to reveal her scars. In this very moment, Sayigh's response (which is also mine) bursts forth: 'Oh … is that … is all that from these surgeries? It goes straight into your heart.'[14] Sayigh's response appears contrapuntal: it is both empirical, reading the scars as medical signs or symptoms; and alive to the experiential, or what the scars reveal about Umm Faris' life, her passion, her pathos. It highlights what the medical language of clinical diagnosis (as one that seeks to establish meaning from relationships drawn between signs and disease) excludes, namely, the continuity between the physical and the psychosocial.[15] Umm Faris' scars, which extend from her navel to her heart in a suturing of literal, organic and anatomical connections, are a physical reminder of invasive and distressing abdominal surgeries. And yet the long, deep midline incision bisecting Umm Faris' abdomen also points to her own heart's content, and perhaps this was also what Sayigh meant.

To privilege listening as a mode of attunement is to retain the serendipitous potential of our encounter with the archive. Certain tropes of Palestinian oral histories provide invaluable frames through which we might think about peasant moral economies in pre-1948 Palestine, explore the relationships between memory and trauma, or question the centrality of women's bodies to nationalist narratives. Conversely, storytellers like Umm Faris and Fatima also instruct us in the practice of careful listening, enabling us to apprehend more keenly the reality of lived experiences that are firmly rooted in history. Their stories unfold within at least three transecting socio-political temporalities: the ongoing Nakba, the moment of the oral history interview, and the moment when the listener encounters the archive. Clearly, the presence of an interviewer materially affects the way stories are told. The particular context within which these narratives take shape is equally important; it inflects the storytelling and modulates its reverberations.

Umm Faris' opening statement, in which she conveys her desire to talk about her personal sufferings and not politics, gestures to the separation of the personal from the political. Umm Faris implicitly resists this distinction – one that oral histories, and women's accounts in particular, tend to blur. If she suggests that personal stories like her own are not typically recorded because they seem to lie outside established historiographical concerns (nationalist frames, recollections of the homeland, the experience of being a refugee in a camp), she also assumes that oral historians like Sayigh are not looking for them. In spite of (or perhaps because of) this, she remains keen on narrating how she suffered for years on end after her complicated childbirth in Gaza. Similarly, in Fatima's account, the personal and the political are thoroughly intermeshed. In response to interviewer Jihad al-'Ali's prompts about cultural practices of pre-1948 Palestine that are 'threatened with extinction', Fatima sings the folk songs she remembers; speaks of traditional medicine in 1930s Galilee (olive oil cures everything!); describes the gifts a bride would receive on her wedding day; lists every crop and tree farmers around al-Zib planted; and enumerates the various trades and professions of the men in her village. In between and through all of these details, spurred on by her desire to transmit her memories of her marriage and the world she built for herself, Fatima narrates a life inseparable from the sea, al-Zib's olive groves, the coastal railway tracks, the Haganah's defeat at the al-Zib bridge near Tarshiha in Galilee, family feuds in the village, and Lebanon's changing social and political landscape as she experienced it in al-Bus in Tyre, in 'Ayn al-Hilweh, in Sayda and in Burj al-Barajneh.

The questions that haunt this essay concern not only the responsibility of listeners but also what a 'politics of listening' might reveal about Palestine and the Palestinian people. Oral history, as a mode of knowledge production, is resolutely engrained in socio-historical contexts.[16] Its risks are well known – misrepresentation (the archetype of the refugee, the othering of the suffering subject), salvage ethnography (the recording of histories and cultural practices perceived as vanishing), and the reification of personal and intimate experience (where, for example, attempts at constructing collective narratives, linked to broader, more majoritarian concerns, are considered dogmatic or oppressive). However, as I have suggested, listening as a mode of attunement might allow us to both reflect on and transcend the limitations of dominant narratives. I can think of three ways that attuned listening might deepen our understanding of history, and the enmeshment of the personal and the political. *Storytelling works against isolation*, as self and other become entangled: we are present with Fatima as she counts the chickens, apricots and fish that her family gifted to the *qadi* who consented to marry her. *Stories live through and mobilise multiple temporalities*, unravelling the pasts that make up the present, while also recreating many such presents in the past. When Fatima poses for the interviewer as she did at her wedding, she is not only conjuring the past; in remembering, she also relives her wedding as a young bride, her present in her past. Finally, *stories elicit responses.* We are left to wonder how a story might have ended (what happened to the uncle of Fatima's husband who beat her?), or what might have been left out. When the interviewer asks, 'Where do you live now?' Fatima spontaneously replies 'al-Zib'. The interviewer interjects and insists, 'No, no *hajjeh. Now.* Where do you live *now?*' to which Fatima, pressing her palm against the couch, responds, 'Ah now? In Burj al-Barajneh. Al-Zib was inside the sea but Burj al-Barajneh was a desert filled with cacti!' Oral histories such as Fatima's and Umm Faris' are meaningful, educational, provocative, poignant, enriching and moving – not only for academics or professional scholars interested in Palestine but, first and foremost, for members of the extended Sha'ban and Hasuna families (where are they?), other friends and families from Gaza and al-Zib, Palestinians who live in the camps in Lebanon and neighbouring countries, those who remained in Palestine, members of the diaspora and broader audiences around the world. Listening – as perceiving sound, acknowledging meaning and above all responding (how?) – is yet another way of enmeshing the personal with the political and tending to one's own lived experience.

Fatima Shaʿban
born circa 1928 in al-Zib, Palestine
Interview with Jihad al-ʿAli
al-Bus camp, Lebanon, 2003

2'07"–5'10"

Jihad al-ʿAli: *Hajjeh, I want you to tell me about al-Zib. How many brothers and sisters were you, what did your father do for a living?*
Fatima Shaʿban: We were four sisters and two brothers. When we evacuated, one of my brothers left by sea, in the boats. Those who left by boat were shot. They died in the sea. As for the rest ... My husband went to work with the workers. We were leasing land; we had orchards and farmers. He went to work, he took two of the farmers who were renting from him and they went along the road of Nahariyya. Do you know Nahariyya? It was further ahead. There was an orchard they used to call al-Mukhtar. He went there, but the Jews didn't capture him. He saw that the people before him had been killed, so he went back. He took his farmers and his cows and went back. He tied them up in the orchard we were leasing, and I was alone. I had given birth nine days earlier. What was I to do? I took my children and left, and I saw a guy who was beating a woman and yelling at her 'Kadima'. 'Kadima! Kadima!' She was dressed like a peasant. 'Kadima! Kadima!' When they reached the well, he shot her. When he shot her, I got scared. I told him, 'I have children.' My son Ahmad was four years old, my daughter was two years old, and I had given birth to a girl nine days before.

Hajjeh, before you got married ... When you were young and still at home, what did your father do?
My father was not alive; he died when we were young. When he died, we were about three years old.

What did he do for a living, before he died?
He was a *fellah*. We were *fellahin*, we worked the land for a living – orchards, agriculture – this is how we farmed. There were no *khawaja* or people of the sort in al-Zib; we were simple *fellahin* – the *hata* and *'igal* type – and the young women wore nothing on their heads. But the rest of us wore *hata* and *'igal*.

How did your father pass away?
I don't remember my father well, I was about three years old, I can't recall. I remember things like when my family married me off, when my brothers married me off – and so I was married.

How did you play when you were young?
When we were young, we played *la'awit*. We used to play it by throwing the *zi'wayta* up in the air, and we would spend the whole day catching it, since there was no girls' school.

What is a zi'wayta?
Rocks. Rocks we used to break apart and play with. We played with a skipping rope. We used to go to the seashore – there was an elevated plain you could jump from; we went there every day in the mornings and afternoons. We played games on the beach, we played *tawabin*. And then we would go back home. This is how we played – I mean, us girls. As for the boys, they had their school. It was governmental and they taught boys only; they did not teach girls. Only by the end – two years before our departure – did they start teaching girls. We weren't there in time for it. By that time, we had already grown up. And we fled Palestine.

11'14"–13'55"

Tell us how your husband asked for your hand in marriage, and how he met you.
I did not know him at all. He was older than me, he spoke to my family, my brothers, my mother, my sisters. He spoke about it and it happened. I was not an adult yet.

Are you related?
No, we're not related, but he's from my village. I was young when they took me. The man who was supposed to officiate my Katb al-kitab said to my husband, 'I'm not writing her Katb al-kitab'. My husband asked him why. He replied, 'she's a little girl, how could I officiate her marriage?' He was Abu Salih al-Jamil, his cousin. He said, 'So what if you're my cousin! She's a little girl.' I was 13 years old, minus three months. 'How can I do her Katb al-kitab? Take her to 'Akka.' So they took me to 'Akka. They placed a towel on my chest, and a belt around my waist, they made me wear high heel shoes, and they stuffed my chest with things to give me bigger breasts, and I became huge, like a barrel! Then they took me to 'Akka, with my sister,

my mother and my brother. They brought me to the shaykh's house, but they had bribed him! Goddamn that shaykh, how easily he was bribed, that *mufti*. They brought him a basket of fish, and two chickens, and a crate of apricots, and they took off. They bribed him – I wasn't aware at the time. We waited in 'Akka for the *qadi* to come, in a plain facing east. They sat us on a couch. They said, 'Hey, girl!' The *mukhtar*, notables, the witnesses and those who were officiating came along. They said, 'My cousin, didn't I tell you not to officiate Katb al-kitab for such girls?' My husband replied, '*Ya sidi*, just ask her your questions.' He said to me, 'Get up, girl, and walk.' I got up and I walked. He said, 'How old are you?' I told him, 'I am twenty *jawz wa fard*.' Twenty *jawz wa fard*! The *qadi* was stupefied. He said, 'Have you washed?' We had just washed and placed fresh sheets. I said, 'We washed the sheets and made the beds just yesterday!' He told my husband: 'Abu Sami, you're bringing me a girl who plays with a skipping rope and who says that she washes bed linen and makes beds? Didn't I tell you to bring me an 18-year-old girl?' He said, '*Ya sidi*, you know, it happens.' This man had already been engaged twice and both had left him, so he was hoping this little girl would stay with him. The *qadi* said, 'Ok *ya sidi*' – someone came and whispered in his ear. He said, 'Ok. Put your hand here. But you can only get married to her in two years.' He said, 'At your orders, *ya sidi*.' Two months later, they married me off to him! I had just turned 14 when I had Abu Ihab – my son, Ahmad.

Do you remember who the shaykh was?
It was Shaykh Yusif. And our *mukhtar* was Abu Sami, from al-Sa'adiyya. We had a *mukhtar* for the *fellahin* and a *mukhtar* for the Sa'adiyya. We were with the *mukhtar* for al-Sa'adiyya, because my husband was from al-Sa'adiyya, his mother was from al-Sa'adiyya. Our Katb al-kitab was made official and so was our destiny.

16'27"–19'27"

Tell us about your wedding.
My wedding? God help you! They married me off, they threw a wedding for me. They brought chairs, and they forced me to sit still on a sofa, and surrounded me with decorations – here, there and behind me – and they sat me on a sofa. They told me, 'Sit still' – I was young. 'Sit and place your hands like this. Don't move, sit up like this!' I sat and I placed my hands like this. 'Put this handkerchief!' (she places her hands on her knees). I put the handkerchief. I wasn't able to sit still. Little girls came up to me, and said,

'Come and play with us!" I left the seat to go play! I played *kalat*.[17] I jumped and went off to play *kalat*. 'Goddamn you, it's your Katb al-kitab! You're a bride, you should stand still! You're playing *kalat* instead?' What was I to do? I kept leaving and they kept bringing me back. There was an older woman, she said: 'Goddamn your Katb al-kitab, how are you ever going to get married?' They sat me down on that chair. I sat still. A little later, they started making me pose – they used to make the bride pose. How was I to pose? They said, 'To pose, you have to get up like this.' I stood up straight like this, wearing my dress and my jewellery. I started fiddling with the jewellery. 'Sit still Goddamn it!' I kept looking at the jewellery, looking this way, looking that way, looking at my hands, looking here and there, and at my nails. I was just a child, but wearing so much. 'Sit down!' I sat. 'Pose!' I posed. They said, 'Put your hand here' (she places her hand on her chest), but I put my hands up instead. 'Turn this way', but I turned the other way. My mother, may she rest in peace, said, 'What am I going to do with you? Just sit and rest your head on your hand.' So I sat and I did. What was I to do? I sat! My sister came (breaks into song): '*Eh wiha* raise your head, you whose head is raised above all![18] *Eh wiha* the eye protects you – ' My voice is raspy today: '*Eh wiha* raise your head, you whose head is raised above all! *Eh wiha* you are perfect no matter what they say! *Eh wiha* raise your head and tell your brother, *eh wiha* hand me the silk, look how well-dressed the people are!' And they trilled for me. A woman came and said to me – what did she say, dear? I'm forgetting! '*Eh wiha* God bless you, one! *Eh wiha* and the second one is two! *Eh wiha* and the third one is a blue pearl … *Eh wiha* that fends off the evil eye from you!'[19] They trilled while I sat there. Another woman came and said to me: '*Eh wiha* the apricot branch has dangled! *Eh wiha* it's tart and hasn't ripened yet! *Eh wiha* come and see, O people! *Eh wiha* see all the newlyweds together!' And they trilled for me! What else can I tell you? Then they brought out the *zafeh*: 'We took your girl, we took your dearest girl! We took your girl, we took your dearest girl! We took her and we didn't even sell our cows!' – my husband's brothers were singing this. 'We took her and we didn't even sell our cows! And we were not among the indebted!' They clapped for me and carried me with the *zafeh*.

46'31"–52'43"

We used to have abundance. If you wanted to marry your son off, do you know what that meant? You'd slaughter four, five, six sheep. You'd invite people for seven days of wedding and dancing. You'd spend an entire day kneading *marquq* bread. Four, five, six *saj* at once, working away and puffing the bread. You'd cook for entire villages and invite them – al-Bassa, al-Kabri, Tarshiha, the biggest villages would be invited to her house. You would spend a week – eight days! – cooking for people. This doesn't happen anymore. Weddings just happen in a rush. A bit of cake and the wedding is over. A guy with a *mizmar* plays two notes and it's done. The *daff* breaks and the lovers part ways.[20] At the time, things weren't like this.

Where did the bride live, after her wedding?
She lived with her parents, with her husband. They had homes.

You mean with her in-laws?
With her in-laws. Some people's homes were built on top of arches. My house was this big and it extended to the next house, it was built above arches. They would set up a corner for her and she would stay at her in-law's house. They would put a closet for her and a mattress with covers, and that's where she would sleep. She'd sleep alone and he'd sleep alone. I slept next to my sisters-in-law, one on this side and one on that side. She put her cover here and the other put her cover there, they put covers between them. This is how it was back in the day, in the old houses. Later on, when younger people got married, they built their homes in the *bayadir*, on the sand – one room, two rooms – and people would live there. It was fancier. And in the old houses, they lived together. I was living with my sister-in-law: me, my sister-in-law and my mother-in-law – and her mother, even. We were four women in one house. Me in this corner, her in that corner and the other in another corner. And when one goofed, two of them would be beaten. Sometimes the three of us, or all four of us would be beaten. I swear. Let me tell you this anecdote. One early morning, I went to fill up at our house. When I had my son Ahmad, I stayed at my parents' house. I left early, at around six, I took the jug and went to the well. While I was walking, I stumbled with my slippers. I tripped on a rock and the jug fell on my head. I was still on the ground, I turned my head left and right like this. Who did I see behind me? My husband's paternal uncle. He was riding a donkey. I turned towards my uncle. I had fallen, the jug broke and I went back home with no water. My husband's uncle kept following me on his donkey, until I entered my house. I went into the house – we had trees like the *zanzalakht*. 'Hish!' He stopped the donkey, took the reins off – I was pregnant with my daughter Amina – and started beating me to the point of no return, until I fell to the ground. Then he rode the donkey and left. What was I guilty of? I never found out. What did I do? No one else was there, except him, I turned to him and I laughed. Two months passed. Pomegranate season arrived

and all of a sudden, this donkey ... I was walking to go fill the jug – I used
to wear shoes but I stopped – I was walking to the well barefoot, so the jug
wouldn't fall off my head. Once again, his uncle was following me on his
donkey. I started shaking uncontrollably. At the time, a woman was afraid
of her in-laws; today nobody's afraid. I went and sat inside the house. He
yelled at me, 'Come here *wleh!*' He said, 'Take this basket!' I took the basket.
'Bring this chair, bring this chair!' I brought it. 'Come sit next to me.' I sat.
I was scared of another beating, I would probably die from it. He said sit
here and I did. He said, 'Bring this knife' – no, the sharpest knife. I brought
the sharpest knife. 'Bring this plate!' I brought the plate. 'Sit here!' and I
sat. He cracked open a pomegranate, of the *shalabi* kind. He said, 'Listen,
if even one grain escapes, I'll cut your head off with this knife.' I ate the
pomegranate without thinking. See the oppression we endured? I ate it. He
said, 'Do you know why I beat you last time?' I said, 'How would I know?
Because I broke the jug, my uncle! That's why you beat me. What now? I
didn't do anything, here's the jug.' He said, 'No!' He pulled me from my ear.
I was wearing golden earrings shaped like birds. He pulled me from my ear
like this, and he yelled, 'Where are you?' I said, 'I am right in front of you,
uncle.' He said, 'Remember, you broke the jug, and you looked behind you
and laughed. Next time, I'll rip your ear off.' I said, 'As you wish my uncle,
I will no longer break the jug.' He said, 'No! This is not about the jug. We'll
replace it with ten other jugs. But next time, don't you look behind you and
laugh! Do you understand me?' I said, 'No, I laughed because you were the
one behind me.' He said, 'No. It could have been someone other than me. A
woman – a girl – if she laughs, turns around, and shows her teeth, no man
will ever respect her.' God help me ... I said, 'No, my uncle, I won't laugh,
nor will my teeth show.' That beating was so deadly – what do you say of
this? Who would ever do this today? See how they were, back in the day?

What did your husband do, when [his uncle] beat you?
Nothing at all! He came and found me exhausted, and sleeping under the
covers. He said, 'What's wrong with you?' I said, 'My uncle beat me up.
Your uncle beat me up.' He said, 'I wonder what you did.' I said, 'I broke the
jug.' And because of that, he insulted me and beat me with the reins of the
donkey – while I was pregnant with my daughter. We didn't know if she was
dead or alive.

What do you think of this, are you for it or against it?
No, I'm not for it. This is oppression! He could have explained this to me
with kind and calm words. 'Come my niece, you laughed and you broke

the jug. Next time, don't turn around and laugh.' But to beat me to death instead? He beat me until I was half-dead! With the donkey reins! He took the reins off and started beating me. He hit me until I fainted, until I was no longer even aware that my son was in my arms. Do you consider this talking? This is not talking. This is a crime. Nowadays, instead of beating a girl, you explain to her. At the time, they didn't explain. They had their bad sides and their good sides. That's how it was for us.

Figure 7 Fouad Sayegh and friends, Palestine, circa 1945.
Courtesy of Hala and Clemence Sayegh and the Nakba Archive.

Afterword
Oral History in Palestinian Studies

Rosemary Sayigh

[A]s is the case with other marginalized groups, Palestinian oral testimony projects are a vital tool for recovering and preserving the voices of Palestinian peasants (fellaheen) *who for centuries (and until 1948) constituted the overwhelming majority of the inhabitants of Palestine.*

– Nur Masalha[1]

During my first year of marriage into a Palestinian Arab family, I made a conscientious effort to come to terms with *fus-ha*, the classical form of the Arabic language that enables communication between different regions of the Arabic-speaking world. However, its complex grammar and professorial resonance rapidly defeated me. I'd learnt French, German and Italian without difficulty, but it seemed that Arabic was too much for me. This was a serious set-back for someone whose life was set to be spent in the Arab region, through marriage and as a practitioner of journalism and would-be anthropologist. I began my approach to Palestinian refugees in camps in Lebanon by hanging around an UNRWA clinic where people were likely to speak English, in a craven postponement of the necessity of understanding Palestinians, as well as being understood by them.

From the offices of the United Nations Relief and Works Agency for Palestine Refugees in the Near East (UNRWA), I took home the documents prepared by the Agency to publicise its programmes in education, health and development. For someone who was interested in history but whose schoolbooks had excluded the non-European world, Palestinian refugees were an enigma. Where had they come from? Why had they left? None of this was explained in UNRWA's pamphlets. In these texts, the refugee advent resembled a natural disaster, unexplained and inexplicable, thus making more permanent their resettlement in the host countries. From the days of its establishment, UNRWA benefitted from the services of an exceptional photographer, Myrtle Winter. It was Winter's picture of an elderly woman's face, hands clutching her headscarf to her mouth, that has been most used to represent Palestinian refugees. If a good picture is worth a thousand words, it also stifles speech by making it seem unnecessary. And this is particularly the case when the subject/object of the picture is a member of a marginalized group, who do not speak but are spoken for. The historic causes of marginality are erased, to be replaced by the call for sympathy for present suffering.

Others have written about the excision of all references to Palestine in UNRWA fund-raising brochures and films.[2] UNRWA schools do not teach Palestinian history even though a UN resolution on cultural rights endorses the right of children to knowledge of the history of the community they belong to.[3] First- and second-generation refugees told their children something about Palestine, but their knowledge was likely to be locally specific; according to many refugees, even this knowledge is no longer passed on. The absence of Palestinian history books for children is compounded by general neglect, among professional historians, of oral histories of the decades following expulsion, with the exception of a single study by Nafez Nazzal, limited to refugees from Galilee.[4]

Nazzal carried out his study in the early 1970s, when the PLO controlled the camps in Lebanon; access was much easier than it had been under the rule of the Lebanese Army's Deuxième Bureau. I enjoyed the same luck of timing, beginning research on Palestinian experience in Lebanon for an MA thesis in 1971. Visits to my mother-in-law's cousin, Umm Joseph, who lived in Dbaya camp, helped to fill me in on village life in pre-1948 Palestine. Her village, al-Bassa, had been relatively well-off through the cultivation of tobacco, and benefitted from the early development of transport linking coastal villages to ʿAkka. Umm Joseph's father-in-law was the village *mukhtar*, and she had lived in a single room in his large stone house along with her husband, his six brothers and their wives. Though al-Bassa had a Muslim minority, the Lebanese authorities ordained that only Christian Palestinians could settle in Dbaya camp, leaving the village's Muslims to join ʿAyn al-Hilweh or Rashidiyya. During one of my stays with Umm Joseph, she received a visit from a pre-1948 Muslim neighbour, commemorating their relationship as well as a feast. In such small important ways, first-generation refugees subverted Lebanese sectarianism.

Venturing into the camps and making friends there resolved my problem with Arabic. *Daraj*, dialectical Arabic, is distinct from *fus-ha* in encouraging varied pronunciations and ethnically specific set phrases. More than this, Arabic dialects are accompanied by a rich repertoire of facial expressions, hand gestures and body movements that make colloquial Arabic easier to learn than body-straight *fus-ha*. Spoken Arabic invites expression of emotion (welcome, pleasure, disgust, anger) as bodily accompaniment, while *fus-ha*, like all classical languages, works to suppress it.

Palestinian refugees speaking to an outsider tend to emphasise emotions related to the Nakba, and to not belonging in Lebanon (or Jordan or Syria). I was frequently told, 'It would have been better to have died in our country.' Many older refugees began with this declaration when I asked them for the story of their life – a recording project that lasted from 1989 to 1994. A collectively crafted narrative would follow, one that included the politics of the loss of Palestine as the result of conspiracy and Arab dependence, the failures of Palestinian leadership and bad treatment in the host country.

I began visits to Shatila just after the 1982 massacre. It was an unpropitious time. No one wanted to talk to me. No one could understand why I was there. My simplest question was answered with, 'Why do you want to know?' I would have made no progress at all if it hadn't been for Umm Mahmud, who adopted me simply because I was a friend of another researcher she had helped. As I gradually became known in the camp as 'a friend of Umm Mahmud', mistrust softened and I was invited into homes. The brutality of the massacre had created contradictory reactions: fear and reticence, but also the need to speak out against the aggressors. Deprived of political representation, voice seemed to be the only weapon Palestinians had at that time against violence and exclusion in Lebanon, while witnessing against genocide seemed to me to be a valid extension of anthropology.

So I began to observe Umm Mahmud as a *mara nashita* (an active and politicised housewife). Her day began around 4am, when she would mix the dough for bread, then roll it into rounds which her oldest daughter would carry on a plank on her head to be baked in the *furn*, the community oven. Next, she did the family wash (no light task with 9 children under 16 – one newly born), using water that had to be carried up from a tank on the street and heated on a primus. The washing finished, she made snacks for the children and hurried them off to school. Then a trip to Sabra market to buy food for the day. When the kids had eaten lunch, she would take me to visit neighbours and friends, trips that often extended beyond the camp and included Lebanese as well as Dom families, whose daughters Umm Mahmud taught to read. She took a keen interest in politics, and some of her visits were to the families of the political organisation her husband was a cadre in. Photos I took of Umm Mahmud show her making bread, shopping in the souk and – most characteristically of all – reading the radical newspaper *As-Safir* while suckling her youngest child.

NAKBA SILENCING

I cannot say that my book, *Palestinians: From Peasants to Revolutionaries* (1979), unlocked a spate of oral history studies.[5] Though oral histories with Palestinians now far outnumber those with other Arab peoples, they were slow to take off.[6] Oral history was and still is not taught at most Arab universities. The Nakba's traumatic effect played a part in this silence. Palestinian scholar Salim Tamari has advanced a psychosocial explanation of this phenomenon:

> My only explanation is that people were so traumatized that they did not actually want to talk about it ... I know that families on the most intimate terms would hesitate in speaking about what had happened to them in '48 ... until today I am having difficulty with people who have critical information.[7]

In a study of attitudes towards recording Nakba memories in Shatila camp, Allan notes hostility to the project.[8]

It goes without saying that the Nakba has not been commemorated in the way the Holocaust has. Indeed, a primary factor suppressing the Nakba from global awareness is the power of Holocaust commemoration. The influence of the global North over education systems worldwide renders full coverage of the Nakba unlikely even in textbooks on the Middle East. The spread of human-rights curricula centred on the Holocaust as the major violation is another factor in the suppression of the Nakba. This linking has universalised Holocaust teaching to an exceptional degree, which can be problematic in a Palestinian context. 'No human-rights curriculum is complete without inclusion of the facts of the Holocaust, and its lessons', said UNRWA's field director, John Ging, when the subject was incorporated into the curriculum in Gaza in 2009.[9] Ging linked Holocaust denial to denial of other 'blights and stains in human history', from Hiroshima to Cambodia to Rwanda and including 'for that matter, the Nakba' – remarks at once high-minded and disingenuous, given that it is the Nakba, not the Holocaust, that UNRWA has no mandate to teach.

Silencing the Nakba has helped frame the Zionist takeover of Palestine as a legitimate reward for victimhood rather than an act of colonialism consciously projected along European lines, and intended to support Western hegemony over the Arab east.[10] The power of Holocaust commemoration suppresses not only the Nakba but also the causal connection between the Holocaust and the Nakba, just as a building constructed over another

buries the history embodied in the first.[11] Indeed, the siting of Israel's extensive Holocaust museum, the Yad Vashem, on the lands of the Palestinian
village of Dayr Yasin, renders its history of massacre and ruin invisible to all
but those who already know it.[12] Yad Vashem is 'a vast, sprawling complex
of tree-studded walkways leading to museums, exhibits, archives, monu-
ments, sculptures and memorials ... [with] 62 million pages of documents,
267,5000 photos, thousands of films and videotaped testimonies ... [and]
3.2 million names of Holocaust victims.'[13] The Kfar Shaul mental hospital
established in 1951 covers homes ruined during the massacre. The graves of
those who died in Dayr Yasin are unknown and unmarked.

Among Israeli measures to silence the Nakba are decrees banning use of
the term in schoolbooks on pain of withdrawal of state funding.[14] The police
force has been used to remove Nakba day demonstrators, and to besiege
Zochrot, an Israeli NGO that records Nakba memories.[15] Yet more powerful
than official Israeli interdiction has been informal American silencing. As
Lila Abu-Lughod and Ahmed Sa'di point out, 'The debilitating factor in
the ability to tell their stories and make public their memories is that the
powerful nations have not wanted to listen.'[16] It was not until the 1990s that
American university presses began to publish research-based Palestinian
studies. The publication in 2007 of Abu-Lughod and Sa'di's *Nakba: Palestine, 1948, and the Claims of Memory*, with its use of the hitherto censored
term Nakba as its main title, was a breakthrough that marked full 'permission to narrate'.

In 1995, Saleh Abdel Jawad, a scholar at Birzeit University, and one of the
contributors to this volume, appealed to a Palestinian cultural institution
to support a research project he called 'Race Against Time', which would
have used oral history to record memories of pre-1948 Palestine as well as
the Nakba. Nakba narratives recorded in the early years would have had
a greater immediacy and substantiating detail than later ones. Moreover,
they would have offered a basis for refuting Zionist versions of the 1948
'war', for example, that the Palestinians had left under orders from their
own leaders.[17] Children would have had an answer to the accusing question
they put to their parents, 'Why did you leave?' Unfortunately, Abdel Jawad's
proposal did not find funding.

EXPANSION

A host of mainly oral history initiatives have partially filled a gap left
by the national institutions, notably: Birzeit's 'Destroyed Village' series,
undertaken by the university's Centre for Research and Documentation

of Palestinian Society (CRDPS); Al-Jana's collection commemorating the Nakba's 50th anniversary (1998); the website PalestineRemembered initiated by Salah Mansour in 2000;[18] as well as the Nakba Archive recorded by Diana Allan and Mahmoud Zeidan in 2002–2008 in Lebanon, with over 500 survivors from 144 villages and towns. The Nakba Archive employed local Palestinians as interviewers, with an equal number of women interviewees as men, and with descriptions focused on lives in Palestine before 1948, the Nakba itself and reception of refugees in the host country. In its breadth and depth, the Nakba Archive offers the most substantial view of modern Palestinian history to date. It was the first Palestinian oral-history archive to be filmed, and the material is engrossing at a human level, in no small part because of its visual dimension: not just official history but embodied experience is its subject. (Allan has a separate career as a documentary filmmaker, in the 'sensory ethnography' tradition developed at Harvard University in the early 2000s). Zeidan and Allan's project returns, as it were, to the silent scream of Myrtle Winter's image and lingers there, long enough for the subject to speak.

The ranks of scholars using Palestinian oral history swelled during the 1990s, 2000s and 2010s, notably including Sam Bahour,[19] Yezid Sayigh,[20] Randa Farah,[21] Rosemarie Esber,[22] Saleh Abdel Jawad,[23] Mustafa Abbasi,[24] Zena Ghandour,[25] Faiha Abdulhadi,[26] and Karma Nabulsi and Abdel Razzak Takriti.[27] A scholar whose interest in Palestinians has increased their 'visibility' in Western academia is Sherna Berger Gluck, whose archives at California State University focusing on women, labour and ethnic histories formed a model in oral history archiving.[28] A study that greatly expanded interest in Palestinian oral history was Rochelle Davis' book, *Palestinian Village Histories: Geographies of the Displaced*, another scholar represented in this collection.[29] Davis based her research on voice recordings with village members who had become exiles or refugees. Research during this period tended to focus on the refugees in camps, the UNRWA, host country conditions and the birth of the resistance movement. Most recently, the publication of *An Oral History of the Palestinian Nakba* (2018), edited by Nahla Abdo and Nur Masalha, has validated and enhanced the use of oral history as methodology to make public the experiences of dispossessed and subalternised peoples.[30]

THEORISATION

Oral historians like myself, possessed by enthusiasm for a topic or a particular human group, tend to enter the 'field' with little theoretical preparation.

In my own case, I realised there were cultural and class differences between me and my Palestinian speakers, but I did not speculate on how this might affect their responses to my questions, or on how my cultural background might affect my understanding of people's narratives. I did sense that people hoped I would be a channel of communication to the world outside, particularly the British government. Indeed, Abu Muhammad, a barrow-seller whom I sometimes stopped to chat with, when he knew I was about to travel to England, positively commanded me to alert the British public about Shatila's health problems. It was a justified appeal that I, as social researcher, typically noted down in my logbook, without considering whether I was morally obliged to make a return for free and generous access to Shatila people and their lives. It was not until I began to teach oral history in 2014, using Lynn Abram's excellent *Oral History Theory*, that I began to understand the moral and political complexities of the discipline I had catapulted myself into so unthinkingly.[31]

In *An Oral History of the Palestinian Nakba* (2018), Abdo contests the 'intersectionality' concept current among radical Western feminists on the grounds that it omits indigenous women. By placing land and genocide at the centre of her analysis, Abdo emphasises the need for an anti-colonial feminism that defines settler colonialism as primarily genocidal in regard to indigenous women because of their essential relationship to land.[32] Masalha reminds us that most histories are written by 'the powerful, the conqueror, the coloniser', and that there is thus a 'need for articulating new counter-hegemonic narratives and devising new liberationist and decolonisation strategies in Palestine'.[33] Oral history work with Nakba survivors is 'not merely to practice professional historiography, it is also a profoundly moral act of liberation and a struggle for truth, justice, equality, return ... and a better future.'[34] These and other contemporary scholars approaching the history of the country and people of Palestine tend to adopt a more reflexive, critical and 'Third Worldist' approach than earlier writers. For example, a recent study of Palestine/Israel, *Trans Intifada* (2018), treats Israel as a key station in the United States' search for world hegemony rather than as a rival national movement to that of the Palestinians.[35]

CONCLUSION

The intrinsic interest of Palestinian oral histories, as well as their contribution to the present and future history of the Middle East, fully warrants their publication. As chronicles of human suffering, they point a finger of accusation at the colonialist Zionist project, and go far to explain post-1948

Palestinian political, economic and cultural activism. From an anthropological perspective, they form a palimpsest of different meanings of 'home', as these become politicised through prolonged separation, developing from lived memories of family and local habitation to abstract visions of an expropriated 'homeland', in the process shifting from a personal to a national framework. Excised from most Western studies of the Middle East, including university curricula and textbooks, Nakba stories not only restore a vital human perspective to our understanding of the region, but also subvert imperialist hegemony over knowledge and teaching of Middle Eastern history. To quote Masalha again:

> The trauma of the Nakba affected Palestinian national identity and memories in two contradictory ways. On the one hand the Nakba led to the destruction of much of Palestinian society and the dispersal and fragmentation of the Palestinian people. But, from the encounter with and rejection of neighbouring Arab states, the Nakba also led to the crystallization, remembering and collectivization of a distinct and resistant Palestinian identity... While the formation of a Palestinian national identity had taken root long before 1948, there is no doubt that the Nakba was a key event in the consolidation and reconstruction of a strong, clearly defined and vital contemporary Palestinian identity...[36]

Contributors and Translators

CONTRIBUTORS

Saleh Abdel Jawad is Professor of History and Political Science at Birzeit University, Palestine, where he has worked since 1981. He has published extensively on Zionism, the Nakba, the Palestinian national movement and Palestinian collective memory. Most recently, his research has documented the prevalence of Zionist massacres during the ethnic cleansing of Palestine.

Salman Abu Sitta is the founder and president of the Palestine Land Society, London, dedicated to the documentation of Palestine's land and People. He is the author of six books on Palestine including the compendium *Atlas of Palestine 1917–1966* (London: Palestine Land Society, 2010) and *Mapping My Return: A Palestinian Memoir* (New York: American University of Cairo Press, 2016).

Diana Allan is Associate Professor in the Department of Anthropology and the Institute of International Development Studies at McGill University, Montreal. She is a filmmaker and the co-founder of the Nakba Archive. Her ethnography, *Refugees of the Revolution: Experiences of Palestinian Exile* (Stanford, CA: Stanford University Press, 2014) won the MEMO Palestine academic book award (2014) and the American Anthropological Association, Middle East Section Award (2015).

Rochelle Davis is Associate Professor of Anthropology in the Center for Contemporary Arab Studies at Georgetown University. Her main research is on forced migration, war and conflict. Her first book, *Palestinian Village Histories: Geographies of the Displaced* (Stanford, CA: Stanford University Press, 2011), addresses how Palestinian refugees today write histories of their villages that were destroyed in the 1948 war.

Dyala Hamzah is Associate Professor of Arab History at Université de Montréal. She has edited *The Making of the Arab Intellectual: Empire, Public Sphere and the Colonial Coordinates of Selfhood* (Abingdon: Routledge, 2013), authored *Muhammad Rashid Rida ou le Tournant Salafiste* (Paris:

CNRS Éditions, 2020), and published with *CSAAME, REMMM, Égypte-Monde arabe*, and Princeton University Press and Oxford University Press. Her current project explores Mandate Pan-Arabism and Palestine.

Lena Jayyusi is Emeritus Professor at Zayed University, Dubai, and serves on the Editorial Board of *Global Media and Communication*. She edited *Jerusalem Interrupted: Modernity and Colonial Transformation 1917-the Present* (Interlink publications, 2015), which won a MEMO Palestine Book Award. She publishes on media, cultural studies, film, memory narratives, and the pragmatics of communication and reasoning.

Cynthia Kreichati is a PhD student in anthropology at McGill University, Montreal. Trained as a pharmacist, she holds an MA in sociology from the American University of Beirut and has worked in the field of public health. Her current research is an ethnography of the Litani River in Lebanon and its people.

Jacob Norris is Senior Lecturer in Middle Eastern History at the University of Sussex, UK. His first book is *Land of Progress: Palestine in the Age of Colonial Development, 1905-1948* (Oxford: Oxford University Press, 2013). His current work looks at the history of Bethlehem in the nineteenth and twentieth centuries.

Laila Parsons is Professor at McGill University in Montreal, where she teaches the history of the modern Middle East, including the history of Palestine. She has published extensively on the 1948 war, on rebel soldiers in the interwar period, and on the place of narrative and biography in the historiography of the modern Middle East.

Ruba Salih is Reader at the Department of Anthropology and Sociology, School of Oriental and African Studies (SOAS), University of London. Her research interests and writing cover transnational migration and gender across Europe, the Middle East and North Africa, as well as the Palestine question, refugees and diaspora.

Rosemary Sayigh is an oral historian, anthropologist and the author of *Palestinians: From Peasants to Revolutionaries* (London: Zed, 1979); *Too Many Enemies: The Palestinian Experience in Lebanon* (London: Zed, 1994; al-Mashriq 2015); and the eBook *Voices: Palestinian Women Narrate Dis-*

placement (al-Mashriq, 2007). She was Visiting Lecturer, at the Center for Arab and Middle Eastern Studies (CAMES), American University of Beirut.

Sherene Seikaly is Associate Professor of History at the University of California, Santa Barbara, and the author of *Men of Capital: Scarcity and Economy in Mandate Palestine* (Stanford, CA: Stanford University Press, 2016). Her book project, *From Baltimore to Beirut: On the Question of Palestine* is a global history of medicine and race.

Amirah Silmi is Assistant Professor at Birzeit University's Institute of Women's Studies. She has a PhD in Rhetoric from the University of California–Berkeley, and an MA in Gender and Development from Birzeit. Her research is in the fields of colonial discourse, anti-colonial and revolutionary writing, aesthetics and feminist theory.

Ted Swedenburg is Professor of Anthropology at the University of Arkansas. He is the author of *Memories of Revolt: The 1936–39 Rebellion and the Palestinian National Past* (Minneapolis, MN: University of Minnesota Press, 1995); and co-editor of *Palestine, Israel and the Politics of Popular Culture* (Durham, NC: Duke University Press, 2005) with Rebecca L. Stein and *Displacement, Diaspora, and Geographies of Identity* (Durham, NC: Duke University Press, 1995) with Smadar Lavie.

Alex Winder is a historian of Mandate Palestine based at Brown University's Center for Middle East Studies, and executive editor of the *Jerusalem Quarterly*. He edited and introduced *Between Jaffa and Mount Hebron: The Diaries of Muhammad 'Abd al-Hadi al-Shrouf (1943–1962)*, published in Arabic in 2016.

Mahmoud Zeidan is a Palestinian refugee born in 'Ayn al-Hilweh camp in Lebanon. An education and human rights specialist, he has gained extensive experience in oral history with Palestinian, Iraqi and Syrian refugees. Mahmoud co-founded the Nakba Archive and Lens on Lebanon, a grassroots documentary initiative formed during the Israeli bombardment of 2006.

TRANSLATORS

Hoda Adra is a spoken word poet and filmmaker. She was born in Lebanon, raised in Saudi Arabia and adopted by Montreal. Her practice is rooted in writing as resistance and self-inscription, employing vocal and somatic inquiry to explore aborted oral histories and the suppression of movement from female bodies.

Rayya Badran is a Beirut-based writer and translator whose work features in various local and international publications. She has taught contemporary art and sound studies courses in the Fine Arts & Art History department at the American University of Beirut, and at the Académie Libanaise de Beaux-Arts, since 2014.

Lindsay Munford is a freelance language and research professional, and a Russian and Arabic specialist. She has worked for the UK government and an international law firm in Oman, and now supports clients in academia, research, corporate investigations, and human rights advocacy from her home in the UK.

Glossary

abaya: a loose, robe-like dress

adhan: Islamic call to prayer

ahliyya: national secular school

'*ajamiyya*: robe-like dress

Alhamdulillah: literally, 'praise be to God', a common expression of gratitude, reverence or relief; sometimes analogous to 'thank God' or 'thank goodness'

akhwalna: our maternal uncles; our relatives

'Akka: Acre

'*ambar*: sweets

'*amm*: paternal uncle; honorific for a male elder

'*ammo*: colloquial form of '*amm* or uncle

'*arif*: student selected to maintain order while the teacher is away from class

Ariha: Jericho

Astaghfirullah: phrase asking Allah for forgiveness, used in moments of difficulty or distress; pronouncing *Astaghfirullah* constitutes Istighfar, a core component of Islamic worship

'*atawiya*: informal reconciliation and mediation committee, convened to solve communal conflicts

athwab (plural of *thawb*): traditional embroidered dresses fashioned with fabrics, dying techniques and intricate cross-stitch motifs distinctive to villages and regions across Palestine

'*ayfa hali*: tired, exhausted (feminine adjectival form)

'*awwameh*: sweet dumplings

babor: kerosene stove

bakhsheesh: monetary donation that can serve as a tip, alms or bribe

baklaweh: filo pastry dessert with chopped nuts

ba'l: crops that do not need to be irrigated, named after Ba'al, the god of fertility, seasons and rain

bayadir: threshing ground

bayyarat (plural of *bayyara*): orchard or house garden

Bismillah il-Rahman il-Rahim: in the name of God, the merciful and compassionate

boqja: embroidered fabric wrap for transporting clothes and belongings

dabkeh: Palestine's national folk dance, involving diverse line and circle formations, a variety of footwork and intermittent solos; *dabkeh* also manifests solidarity, steadfastness, and resistance to settler colonialism and oppression

dawab (plural of *dabba*): four-legged animal that can pull a cart; it can refer to a donkey, horse, mule, ass or even a bull

dhimmi: a non-Muslim under the protection of Muslim law

dhira': cubits; a measure of length typically close to half a metre or the length of a forearm

al-Difa al-Gharbiyya: the West Bank

dirbakkeh: goblet-shaped drum; a core percussion instrument in Palestinian and Arab music (also known as a *tabla*)

dist: very large cooking pot

diwan: community reception or sitting room; also used to signify the social, civic and political gatherings that took place therein

Eid: holiday, feast or festival

fas: axe

Fatiha: engagement ceremony at which the first sura of the Qur'an (al-Fatiha) is read as a blessing in the presence of the couple's families

faza'a: long-standing practice of Palestinian village resistance dating back to the Ottoman period; analogous to 'sounding the alarm', 'mobilising'

fellahin (plural of *fellah*): peasant farmer

fida'iyin (plural of *fida'i*): freedom fighters central to Palestine's anti-colonial tradition of popular mobilisation towards national liberation

ghabaneh: wrapped head scarf

gineh: pound; currency instituted in 1927 during the British Mandate and replaced by the Israeli lira in 1952

habibi: literally, 'my love'; also used to mean 'dear', 'darling' or 'buddy'

hadayeh (plural of *hada*): poets who engage in a duel of sung poetry, often accompanied by supporters who also sing refrains and clap along; *hadayeh* also refers to the competition itself, often held during wedding celebrations

Halab: the Syrian city of Aleppo

halaweh: sesame- or tahini-based sweet

Hajjeh: honorific for addressing a respected female elder, traditionally attributed to Muslims who have completed the *hajj* to Mecca

hammam: place of public bathing or steam bath; a prominent feature of the Islamic culture of the Middle East and North Africa

harisseh: semolina cake

hata: traditional headdress (also known as *kaffiyeh*)

hayat: literally, 'life' in Arabic, is sometimes used to refer to a friend or relative who has died *hisbeh*: produce market

'igal: rope headband worn across the forehead to secure a headdress

jawz w fard: 'believe it or not'

Jaysh al-Inqadh: the Arab Liberation Army

al-jihaz: a bridal trousseau that forms part of the bride's dowry and includes different fabric items (nightgowns, sheets, towels, tablecloths, linens, beddings, etc.)

al-Jalil: the Galilee

ka'b-l-ghazal: traditional dessert

kadima (Hebrew): forward, hurry up, quickly

kaffiyeh: Arab headdress consisting of a square cloth folded to form a triangle and held on by an *'igal* cord

ka'k ban: a traditional sweet

Katb al-kitab: Islamic marriage ceremony during which the couple signs a contract before witnesses

kaymakam: subgovernor of a provincial district; a title originally used under the Ottoman Empire

kaza: a term that derives from Ottoman Turkish and refers to an administrative division (usually a district or subdistrict)

khalas: enough, finished, done

al-Khalil: Hebron

khamorim (Hebrew): donkeys

khawabi (plural of *khabiya*): jar

khirbeh: literally 'ruin'; usually refers to a site with visible architectural features

khurj: travelling bag or basket

krayk: shovel

kubbaniyat (plural of *kubbaniyya*): Jewish settlement

kubbeh: traditional meat dish made with ground meat, crushed bulgur wheat, pine nuts and spices

la'awit: children's game, similar to jacks

labneh: a strained yoghurt with the consistency of soft cheese

La ilaha illallah, Muhammad rasulullah: 'There is no god but God, Muhammad is the messenger of God'; these two *shahadas* or assertions of faith comprise the first pillar of Islam

lirat or *jahadiyat*: golden coins woven into women's hair, to adorn braids

madafeh: the meeting of elders, notables and men of the village in the *diwan*; the word also refers to the practice of receiving guests in the *diwan* itself

majawiz (plural of *mijwaz*): a double-piped, single-reed woodwind instrument

mansaf: traditional Bedouin rice dish

mara: woman

marja: authority, expert, reference source

marquq: thin, unleavened flatbread

mastabeh: raised platform with balustrade forming the upper level of *fellahin* houses where families lived; the lower level (known as the *rawieh* or *qa' al-bayt*) was used for livestock and agricultural equipment

Matawliyyat (feminine plural form of *Matawleh*): derogatory term used to refer to Shi'a communities originating from Jabal 'Amil, South Lebanon

mawasim (plural of *mawsim*): seasonal festivals typically involving pilgrimages to *maqamat* (shrines), where religious and popular celebrations were held

mizmar: a double-reed woodwind instrument with a conical bell

mohawraba: a genre of song sung before or during battles to raise the spirits of fighters

mouneh: food stores

mujadara: popular dish composed of brown lentils, rice or bulgur wheat, and caramelised onions

mukhtar: head of the village, chosen to represent the community to outsiders

mulukhiyya: mallow leaves (of the *Corchurus olitorius* plant); a popular vegetable in Palestine and the Arab world

al-Muqattam: the hill on which Cairo's citadel stands

al-Nasira: Nazareth

nawraj: a wooden bench on rails originally towed behind donkeys to thresh grains; when threshing machines replaced this traditional method, *nawraj* seats (which were carved and decorated) were often used as furniture

nidr: contractual prayer; oath

qandil: gorse (*Calicotome Spinosa*), a large, thorny shrub with luminous yellow flowers

qawaleen: refers to singers of 'ataba laments and *dal'una*, a structured, participatory dance form

qayazeen (plural of *qizan*): a term used to refer to barrel bombs thrown from aeroplanes

qazma: pickaxe

qibla: the direction of the Ka'ba in Mecca, which Muslims face when praying

qirsh: currency denomination issued during the Ottoman Empire, equivalent to one-hundredth of a lira or *gineh* (pound) and known in European languages as a piastre

al-Quds: Jerusalem

qumbaz: traditional men's robe

quwayir (plural of *quwwara*): large grain storage receptacles made of mud and straw *rawzana*: cramped basement lit by a small opening in the roof

al-Sa'adiyya: Bedouin tribe of the Upper Galilee.

al-Sahja: party in honour of the groom, one day before the wedding, held in the main square of the village or gathering place, often lit by bonfires; during the festivities, men dance *dabkeh* to the rhythms of sung poetry

saj: convex metal griddle for baking bread

salam: Arabic greeting meaning 'Peace be upon you'

sarab: the verb *sarab* (to leak) is commonly used to describe the actions of collaborators who sold Palestinian lands to 'Jewish settlers'

Sayda: the Lebanese city of Sidon

al-Sham: Greater Syria

shawahat: harvester paddles

sidi: masculine title of respect, similar to 'Mister' or 'Sir'

suwayd: Palestinian Buckthorn (*Rhamnus palaestina*), a medium-sized evergreen shrub

taboun: outdoor stone oven

tarbush: red felt, tasselled hat (also known as *fez*)

tarsh: herd of cattle, usually sheep or goats

tawabin: children's game

tawteen: 'settlement', 'resettlement' or 'naturalization', is used to refer to the 'settlement of non-Lebanese', primarily Palestinian refugees

teta: informal term for grandmother in Lebanese colloquial Arabic

tiz al-habuba: literally, 'lover's arse'

touriya: hoe

turmus: lupini beans

Walla: literally, 'by God', an exclamation with a range of meanings, from 'I swear' to 'Well...'

wleh: vulgar or disrespectful term of address

ya: vocative particle implying 'You', 'O' or 'Hey' in direct address

Yafa: Jaffa

ya hala: colloquial welcome

yalla: colloquial expression variously comparable to 'Hurry up!', 'Come on!' or 'Let's go!'

yam: colloquial expression that means 'just as I am', or 'just like that'

ya wayli: expression of grief roughly equivalent to 'Woe is me!'

zafeh: Arabic wedding procession

zalameh: man

zanzalakht: Persian Lilac (*Melia azedarach*), a deciduous tree in the mahogany family

zeft: rotten, awful

zinco: corrugated metal roofing

Notes

INTRODUCTION

1. Constantin Zurayk's book *Ma 'na al-Nakba* (Beirut: Dar al-'llm-lil-Malayyin, 1948) was translated into English eight years later, *The Meaning of the Disaster* (Beirut: Khayat's College Book Cooperative, 1956).
2. Frances Hasso's critique of progressivist modern Palestinian/Arab accounts of 1948 by leading Arab intellectuals like Zurayk examines how the very form of these texts could not account for the idea of protecting women's honour as a reason for Palestinian flight. 'Modernity and Gender in Accounts of the 1948 and 1967 Defeats', *International Journal of Middle East Studies*, 32 (2002): 491–510.
3. The term 'Nakba' was also used to describe Arab dispossession at the hands of British and Allied forces in 1920. In George Antonius' classic text, *The Arab Awakening* (1938), he writes: 'The year 1920 has an evil name in Arab annals: it is referred to as the Year of Catastrophe ('Am al-Nakba).' This is in direct response to 'the decisions of the San Remo conference, the occupation of the whole of Syria by the French, the consolidation of British control in Iraq on a basis which denied even the outward forms of self-government, and the emergence of a policy of intensive Zionist development in Palestine.' George Antonius, *The Arab Awakening* (Phoenix, AZ: Simon Publications, 2001 [1938]), 312.
4. Elias Sanbar, 'Out of Place, Out of Time', *Mediterranean Historical Review* 16(1) (2001), 1.
5. Following the collapse of the Ottoman Empire in 1918, the partitioning of Levantine territory into French and British mandates – in accordance with the covertly devised Sykes–Picot Agreement – foiled Arab nationalist aspirations, and placed Palestine and Transjordan under British control. See Rashid Khalidi's *The Hundred Years' War on Palestine: A History of Settler Colonialism and Resistance, 1917–2017* (London: Metropolitan Books, 2020); James Barr's *A Line in the Sand* (London: Simon & Schuster, 2011); Bernard Regan's *The Balfour Declaration* (London: Verso, 2018); and Antonius, *The Arab Awakening*.
6. Ilan Pappe, *The Ethnic Cleansing of Palestine* (Oxford: Oneworld Publications, 2006).
7. Joseph Massad, 'Resisting the Nakba', *The Electronic Intifada*, 16 May 2008, https://electronicintifada.net/content/resisting-nakba/7518.
8. Noura Erakat, *Justice for Some: Law and the Question of Palestine* (Stanford, CA: Stanford University Press, 2019).
9. Khalidi, *The Hundred Years' War on Palestine*.
10. Edward Said, *The Question of Palestine* (New York: Times Books, 1979), 9.

11. For more on the racial genealogies that shaped the 1948 Palestinian displacement and humanitarian governance since, see Shaira Vadasaria, '1948 to 1951: The Racial Politics of Humanitarianism and Return in Palestine', Õnati Socio-Legal Series, *Governing the Political: Law and the Politics of Resistance* (Gipuzkoa: Õnati International Institute for the Sociology of Law, forthcoming, 2020).

12. This set of agreements between the PLO and the Israeli government instituted the Palestinian Legislative Council and interim Palestinian Authority, which was supposed to form a self-governing Palestinian state within five years. Presented as a pragmatic solution, the Oslo process ultimately postponed vital issues – notably the question of Palestinian refugees – and sought to erode international legal mechanisms that uphold core Palestinian rights. A moment of profound rupture and alienation, the Accords terminated three decades of collective mobilisation under the banner of the Palestinian revolution, and disenfranchised the vast majority of Palestinian refugees.

13. Palestinian Oral History Archive, https://libraries.aub.edu.lb/poha/ (accessed 3 October 2019).

14. For further details, see Doug Boyd, 'OHMS: Enhancing Access to Oral History for Free', *Oral History Review* 40(1) (2013): 95–106.

15. The interviews included in this collection will soon be available with English subtitles through the Nakba Archive website, at: www.nakba-archive.org.

16. James Agee and Walker Evans, *Let Us Now Praise Famous Men* (London: Penguin, 2006), 10.

17. Edward Said, *After the Last Sky: Palestinian Lives* (New York: Columbia University Press, 1999), 4.

18. For instance, Rosemary Sayigh, *From Peasants to Revolutionaries: A People's History* (London: Zed Books, 1979); Nafez Nazzal, *Palestinian Exodus From the Galilee* (Beirut: Institute for Palestine Studies, 1978); 'Arif al-'Arif, *al-Nakba: Nakbat Bayt al-Maqdis wal-firdaws al-mafqud* [*The Catastrophe: The Catastrophe of Jerusalem and the Lost Paradise*] (Beirut: Institute for Palestine Studies, 2013); and Ilan Pappe, *The Ethnic Cleansing of Palestine* (Oxford: Oneworld Publications, 2006).

19. For instance, Nur Masalha, *The Palestine Nakba: Decolonizing History, Narrating the Subaltern, Reclaiming Memory* (London: Zed Books, 2012); Lila Abu-Lughod and Ahmed Sa'di (eds), *Nakba: Palestine, 1948, and the Claims of Memory* (New York: Columbia University Press, 2007); and Nur Masalha and Nahla Abdo (eds), *An Oral History of the Palestinian Nakba* (London: Zed Books, 2018).

20. Mladen Dolar, *A Voice and Nothing More* (Cambridge, MA: MIT Press, 2006), 13.

21. Hana Sleiman and Kaoukab Chebaro note that in 1944, 66 per cent of Palestinian society was agrarian, with literacy levels estimated at around 15 per cent. 'Narrating Palestine: The Palestinian Oral History Archive Project', *Journal of Palestine Studies* 47(2) (Winter 2018), 66.

22. See Mayssoun Soukarieh, 'Speaking Palestinian: An Interview with Rosemary Sayigh', *Journal of Palestine Studies* 38(4) (Summer 2009): 12–28.

23. Soukarieh, 'Speaking Palestinian'.

24. See Diana Allan, *Refugees of the Revolution: Experiences of Palestinian Exile* (Stanford, CA: Stanford University Press, 2014), 202.
25. For more information on these initiatives, see www.palestineremembered. com; http://al-jana.org/programs-activities/active-memory/; and http://learn-palestine.politics.ox.ac.uk.
26. According to UNRWA's registration files, 144 towns and villages are represented in the Palestinian diaspora in Lebanon.
27. While the majority of interviews were conducted in the camps, middle-class and elite Palestinians were also interviewed during the latter phase of the project.
28. In an effort to contribute to the preservation of these histories within families and camp communities, we also duplicated interviews and scanned precious family documents for participants.
29. While scholars like Rosemary Sayigh, Jaber Suleiman and Moatez Dajani's organisation, Al-Jana, had recorded interviews in audio format with Palestinians in the camps in Lebanon, video had not been used.
30. Lena Jayyusi, 'Iterability, Cumulativity, and Presence: The Relational Figures of Palestinian Memory', in Lila Abu-Lughod and Ahmed Sa'di (eds), *Nakba: Palestine, 1948, and the Claims of Memory* (New York: Columbia University Press, 2007), 110.
31. Amina Banat, interviewed by Mahmoud Zeidan on 23 August 2005, 49:49–50:06.
32. Abu Ammar: Yasser Arafat's *kunya*, or nom de guerre.
33. Edward Said, *After the Last Sky: Palestinian Lives* (New York: Columbia University Press, 1999), 32.
34. Vadasaria, '1948 to 1951', 23.
35. Hoda Adra, personal communication, 13 May 2020.
36. Adra, personal communication, 13 May 2020.
37. Roland Barthes, *The Responsibility of Forms* (Berkeley, CA: University of California Press, 2003), 256.
38. Mladen Dolar cited in Pooja Rangan, 'Audibilities: An Introduction', *Discourse* 39(3) (Fall 2017), 281.
39. Lisa Stevenson, 'Sounding Death, Saying Something', *Social Text* 130, 35(1) (March 2017), 73.
40. Verne Harris, 'The Archival Sliver: Power, Memory, and Archives in South Africa', *Archival Science* 2(1–2) (2002), 84.
41. Walter Benjamin, *Illuminations* (New York: Schocken Books, 2007 [1968]), 91.
42. Benjamin, *Illuminations*, 87.
43. Benjamin, *Illuminations*, 94.
44. Ann Laura Stoler, *Duress: Imperial Durabilities in Our Times* (Durham, NC: Duke University Press, 2016), 26.
45. Allan, *Refugees of the Revolution Experiences*, 51.

CHAPTER 1

1. The British established administrative departments – Education, Public Health, Antiquities, Surveys, etc. – to replace the Ottoman administration in Palestine.

Villagers were most impacted by the policing and military, taxation, education and public health administrative arms of the Mandate government. For details on the Mandate's administration of Education and Religion, see A.L. Tibawi, 'Religion and Educational Administration in Palestine of the British Mandate', *Die Welt des Islams*, 3(1) (1953): 1–14.

2. J.V. Shaw (ed.), *A Survey of Palestine Prepared in December 1945 and January 1946 for the Information of the Anglo-American Committee of Inquiry*, 2 vols and supplement (Washington, DC: Institute for Palestine Studies, 1991), Vol. 1, 147–58. The last census of Palestine was conducted in 1931. In 1944, the rural population was estimated at 872,090 (693,820 Muslims, 138,220 Jews and 27,760 Christians) and the urban population at 825,880. According to these figures, the urban population of Palestine grew by 97 per cent between 1931 and 1944, while the rural population increased by 52 per cent.

3. Beshara Doumani illustrates this interconnection with the case of Jabal Nablus in the eighteenth century: the olive oil soap industry's dominance throughout the Mediterranean and beyond was made possible by vast olive production in the city's surrounding. Beshara Doumani, *Rediscovering Palestine: Merchants and Peasants in Jabal Nablus, 1700–1900* (Berkeley, CA: University of California Press, 1995).

4. Relentless British repression of organised political activity during this period decimated Palestinian capacity for resistance during the Nakba.

5. This material is reproduced in the village books written by Palestinians about their villages that were destroyed in 1948. See Rochelle Davis, *Palestinian Village Histories: Geographies of the Displaced* (Stanford, CA: Stanford University Press, 2010).

6. Blaybil is referring to the 1929 *Thawrat al-Buraq* or Buraq Uprising, an intensification of ongoing popular mobilisation against foreign domination and increasing Jewish settler immigration. Organised Palestinian resistance was sustained from the outset of British military rule in 1917, through European leaders' allocation of the Mandate to Britain at the 1920 San Remo conference, and for the duration of the Mandate period.

7. 'Izz al-Din al-Qassam – an influential anticolonial scholar, educator and revolutionary born in Syria – organised collective resistance to Italian, French, British and Zionist occupation, oppression and colonisation in the Arab world from the 1910s until he was killed in battle by British forces in 1935. The popular movement he built in Palestine was the central mobilising force of the 1936–39 Revolt.

8. *Matawleh*: relating to Shi'a communities originating from Jabal 'Amil, South Lebanon, where Mana' was living when this interview was recorded.

CHAPTER 2

1. 'Abdallah al-awal ibn al-Husayn (Abdullah I) ruled as Amir of Transjordan from 1921–46, when Jordan gained independence from Britain; then as King of Jordan until his assassination in 1951.

2. Hajj Amin al-Husayni (c.1897–1974): Palestinian nationalist leader from an upper-class Jerusalem family. Appointed Grand Mufti of Jerusalem by Mandate authorities in 1921, he remained a prominent political figure in subsequent decades.

3. al-Ma'mun: an eminent scholar who ruled the 'Abbasid caliphate from 813–33.

CHAPTER 3

1. For a detailed account about how colonisers treated the colonised as children, see Frantz Fanon, *Black Skin, White Masks* (New York: Grove Press, 1967).

2. For a fuller discussion of the relationship between peasant women and paid labour, see, for example, Maria Mies, *Patriarchy and Accumulation on a World Scale* (London: Zed Books, 1986); and Maria Mies and Veronika Bennholdt-Thomsen, *The Subsistence Perspective: Beyond Globalized Economy* (London: Zed Books, 2000).

3. Blida is a village in Southern Lebanon; its lands extend to Qadas in Palestine, and these were occupied in 1948. The people of Blida shared neighbourly, trade and work relations with the Palestinian villages in the Northern Galilee. In Hamda's story, women from the Southern Lebanese villages came to participate in the Nabi Yusha' festival. But she only mentions Blida women as those who came to work in the construction of the British airport. Her story, however, does not refer to differences in payment or treatment of the Lebanese women by the British employers, which was the case when other Arab workers were brought to work among Jewish and Palestinian workers. Hamda focuses more on the differences in dress and costumes between the two groups of women.

4. The people of al-Nabi Yusha' held a festival on the fifteenth of Sha'ban (the eighth month of the Muslim calendar). The festival was similar to that of al-Nabi Rubin's festival in al-Ramla District; see Walid al-Khalidi (ed.), *All That Remains: The Palestinian Villages Occupied and Depopulated by Israel in 1948* (Washington, DC: Institute for Palestinian Studies, 1992). On al-Nabi Rubin and al-Nabi Yusha' festivals, see also Andrew Peterson, 'A Preliminary Report on Three Muslim Shrines in Palestine', *Levant* 28(1) (1996).

5. Although the Kirad al-Baqqara were expelled multiple times, between 1948 and 1956, with the village eventually destroyed in 1956, a massacre in the village has not been documented, its story as 'Arab al-Zubayd's is that people were told to leave by the Jaysh al-Inqadh, fearing a massacre by the Zionist gangs. For more information on the expulsion of Kirad al-Baqqara, see Dan Rabinowitz and Sliman Khawalde, 'Demilitarized, Then Dispossessed: The Kirad Bedouins of the Hula Valley in the Context of Syrian–Israeli Relations', *International Journal of Middle East Studies* 32(4) (2000): 511–30.

6. Frantz Fanon, *The Wretched of the Earth*, trans. Charles Lam Markmann (New York: Grove Press, 2004).

7. The peasants were the main force leading the 1936 revolution, while the urban middle classes as well as the bourgeoisie were reluctant to join, and many were

relieved, for economic reasons, when the revolt ended. See Ghassan Kanafani, *1936–39 Revolt in Palestine* (London: Tricontinental Society, 1980).

8. In his *Black Skin, White Masks*, Fanon describes the urge and obsession among colonised black men to court white colonialist women.

9. With respect to work conditions and relations between Arab and Jewish workers in Haifa, see, for example, Zachary Lockman, *Comrades and Enemies: Arab and Jewish Workers in Palestine, 1906–1948* (Berkeley, CA: University of California Press, 1996).

10. The Arabic verb *sarab* (to leak) is commonly used to describe the actions of collaborators who sell off Palestinian land to the Israelis.

11. Ghassan Kanafani argues that in the latter stages of the revolt the Palestinian revolutionaries were targeting British colonialists as the main enemy. Nevertheless, he also shows that the British responded by relegating the task of crushing the revolution to Zionist forces, a process that began with the organisation of a Zionist voluntary defense force, and which continued in the 1940s, paving the way for the Zionist take over in 1947–48. See Kanafani, *1936–39 Revolt in Palestine*. Except for the Zionist branch of the communist party (see note 12), the Palestinian Communist Party's position was that Britain used Zionism as a key tool in its imperialist project.

12. Muhammad's position here is curious, for it is closer to the Zionist branch of the Palestinian Communist Party than it is to the Arab branch. It also reflects the ideological and political contradictions and ambiguities from which the Palestinian Communist Party suffered. As Maher al-Sharif demonstrates:

> The Communists in Palestine saw the Zionist movement as representing the bourgeois Jewish interests and as a tool in the hands of British imperialism used to crush the Arab movements struggle against imperialism. But they failed to see the danger this movement had on the interests and even existence on the Arab Palestinian people.

See Maher al-Sharif, 'al-Hizb al-Shuy'i al-Falastini wa al-Mas'ala al-Qawmiyya al-Arabiyya fi Filastin 1930–1933', *Shu'un Falastiniyya* 113 (1981), 22. Ghassan Kanafani, al-Sharif, as well as Muhammad Dakrub agree that the Palestinian communists lacked the ability to analyse and understand the material reality in Palestine – most importantly, the fact that the struggle was over the land and that it was mainly a peasant as opposed to a workers' struggle. Even when they decided to support the 1936 revolution, they maintained that workers should lead the revolution and its driving force, the peasants. Nevertheless, as both al-Sharif and Dakrub show, the communists in Palestine had to struggle between, on the one hand, the Zionists inside the party, who wanted to focus on imperialism, in an abstract form, as well as on organising Jewish and Palestinian workers, ignoring the contradictions and conflicts between the two groups of workers, they refused to fight against Zionist immigration to Palestine, or dissolve the group that was in the Haganah, while at the same time refusing the alliance between the party and the Independence Party; see Muhammad Dakrub, 'Qira'a Rahina fi al-Masirat al-Muta'rijah

lil-Hizb al-Shuyu'i al-Falastini: Rihlah fi Dahaliz al-Arshif al-Siri lil-Koment-
ern', *Majalat al-Dirassat al-Falastiniyya* 67 (2006): 149–170. On the other hand,
there were those who believed that the communists could join the Arab liberation movement, allying themselves with the Independence Party, which was
the more progressive party in the Palestinian national movement. However,
the main change in the orientation and focus of struggle in the party was in the
1940s, when the Palestinians in the party formed the Arab National League.
According to al-Sharif, the League was not formed as an Arab communist
party but as a leftist national liberation organisation, which was led by the Arab
communists. The League supported a democratic national liberation project;
its main aim was 'to rid the country of colonialism and Zionism'. See 'Usbat
al-Taharur al-Watani wa al-Mas'ala al Qawmiyya al-Arabiyya fi Filastin 1943–
1948', *Shu'un Falastiniyya* 108 (1980), 78. While declaring Zionism as the main
enemy, it took a different position from the Jewish community, separating their
interests from those of Zionism, a separation that both Dakrub and al-Sharif
thought was idealistic.

13. My criticism of the individual follows Marx's critique of the separation between
the individual and political, the private (religion, economic activity and civil
rights) from the social. For Marx, this separation turns the political into an
abstract category, where material life comes to be understood in private terms,
rather than as a collective political problem and the manifestation of oppressive, exploitative relations. See 'On the Jewish Question', in Robert Tucker
(ed.), *The Marx–Engels Reader* (New York: W.W. Norton and Company, 1978),
26–52.

14. The Qasmiya Bridge was the main crossing point over the Litani River, approximately 50 kilometres south of Beirut on the coastal road north of Sur (Tyre).
It was destroyed by Israeli air strike on 12 July 2006.

15. al-Nabi Yusha': a *maqam* (shrine) on the burial grounds of the Prophet Yusha'
(Joshua), developed into a village with a mosque and visitors' building for
pilgrims in the late eighteenth century. Qadas and al-Nabi Yusha' were among
seven Palestinian villages occupied by French colonial forces after the First
World War (in line with the secret 1916 Sykes–Picot Agreement) and transferred to British Mandate control in 1923.

16. Ziyarat al-Nusf [min shahr Sha'ban]: pilgrimage halfway through the month
of Sha'ban, the eighth month of the Islamic calendar.

17. *jukh*: felt; *balashin, faramil*: Hamda is likely referring to the *thawb* and small
matching headdress, traditionally worn for weddings and ceremonies.

18. Hamda is referring to the Hula Arab Bus Company owned by Ahmad Kuri
of Safad, which still exists to this day. A similar attack is described in Benny
Morris, *1948: A History of the First Arab–Israeli War* (New Haven, CT: Yale
University Press, 2009), 105.

19. The two towns of Kirad al-Baqqara and al-Ghannama are Kurdish Bedouin
settlements, where shepherds took care of cows and sheep, respectively.

20. 'A *taltamees* who can't distinguish a Friday from a Thursday' is a common
Arabic expression indicating disorientation or confusion.

21. 'Abdallah al-Asbah (Abu al-Abid): anti-colonial commander renowned for his actions in the Safad district during the 1936–39 revolution. He was besieged and killed by British forces in 1937.
22. On pre-1948 maps of Palestine, Abu Zuwaytina is found just below 'Arab al-Zubayd, outside the village of Mallaha.
23. 'Athroun is the former name of the village of Aitaroun, near Marun al-Ras.
24. 'athra: misstep, stumble, blunder. A pun on the village name 'Athroun.
25. Aravi and Yehudi: Hebrew for 'Arab and Jew'.
26. kham: 'Arabi is likely referencing the Hebrew word hakam, which designates a sage or (in Sephardic Judaism) a rabbi.

CHAPTER 4

1. Ziadeh contributed to Idha'at al-Quds (Jerusalem Calling, Palestine Broadcasting Service, 1936–1948), Idha'at al-Sharq al-Adna (Voice of Britain, Near East Broadcasting Company, 1942–1956), the BBC Arabic service, and countless programmes and talks aired by Arab broadcasting companies in locations including Beirut, Bahrain, Kuwait and the Maghrib. Sayigh played a central role in institutionalising Israeli broadcast monitoring. He oversaw the Palestine Research Centre's daily Monitor of Israeli Broadcasts, a bulletin published daily from 1977 to 1982.
2. Ziadeh contributed articles to early Nahdawi papers such as al-Muqtataf and al-Hilal, as well as to highly significant interwar Egyptian papers including Hasan Zayat's al-Risala and Ahmad Amin's al-Thaqafa. He also published countless papers in national papers. In the 1950s, Sayigh contributed to al-Nahar and al-Usbu' al-'Arabi as well as to al-Hayat and al-Thaqafa al-'Arabiyya. In the 1960s and 1970s, at the head of the PLO Research Centre, he oversaw the monthly Shu'un Filastiniyya. In the late 1970s, he edited the Center for Arab Unity Studies' al-Mustaqbal al-'Arabi, the Arab Institute for Research and Publications' Qadaya 'Arabiyya, and in the early eighties, the Arab League's Shu'un 'Arabiyya. One of the last papers he contributed to was as-Safir.
3. Among such narratives and key political texts that shaped the political discourse about the Nakba is Constantin Zurayk's Ma'na al-Nakba (Beirut: Dar al-'Ilm-lil-Malayyin, 1948). It was translated into English eight years later, The Meaning of the Disaster (Beirut: Khayat's College Book Cooperative, 1956).
4. al-Bassa, a Palestinian town north of Acre, was twice martyred. It fell to the Zionists on 14 May 1948, after an attack by the Palmach forces. Inhabitants were rounded up in the church and forcibly expelled or shot, before the village was razed to the ground. A house, a maqam and a church are all that remains today. A decade earlier, in 1938–39, al-Bassa and its sister town Halhul sustained the worst atrocities of British counterinsurgency. See Matthew Hughes, 'The Practice and Theory of British Counterinsurgency: The Histories of the Atrocities at the Palestinian Villages of al-Bassa and Halhul, 1938–39', Small Wars & Insurgencies 20(3–4) (2009): 528–50. On communal life in al-Bassa, see Sayigh's brother's endearing recollections in Rosemary Sayigh (ed.), Yusif

Sayigh: Arab Economist and Palestinian Patriot (Cairo: American University in Cairo Press, 2015).

5. Elizabeth Brownson 'Colonialism, Nationalism and the Politics of Teaching History in Mandate Palestine', *Journal of Palestine Studies* 43(3) (2014): 9–25; and Rochelle Davis, 'Commemorating Education: Recollections of the Arab College in Jerusalem, 1918–1948'. *Comparative Studies of South Asia, Africa and the Middle East* 23(1) (2003): 190–204. One of just two public high schools in Palestine at the time, the Arab College was the only secondary institution established by Mandate authorities. From 1944 onwards, Rashidiyya College (founded as a primary school under Ottoman rule in 1905) also offered a two-year post-matriculation curriculum leading to the Palestine intermediate examination.

6. Classical history formed the backbone of British imperial education, and Ziadeh describes Mandate Director of Education, Jerome Farrell, as a Roman history specialist. Farrell, who worked under Humphrey Bowman before succeeding him as director in 1936, oversaw the Department of Education's grant programme and developed a patronising friendship with Ziadeh.

7. In the interview, Ziadeh states that he never engaged in (political) discussions of Palestine's position within the Arab world, though he did broach the topic from an academic and historic point of view. In his memoirs, he details the crisis he underwent after the failure of the United Arab Republic (1958–61), and his subsequent silence with regard to Arabism and the question of Palestine. See Nicola Ziadeh, *Ayami: Sira Dhatiya* (London: Hazar, 1992), Vol. 2, 255.

8. The Palestine National Council has been the sovereign legislative body of the Palestinian people since it was founded in 1964.

9. Anis was brother to Yusif, Munir, Tawfiq, Fayez and Mary Sayigh; and brother-in-law to Rosemary Sayigh.

10. Founded by the PLO in 1965, the Palestine Research Centre (PRC) was systematically looted by the Israelis following their 1982 invasion of Lebanon, its vast library and archive 'emptied' in an attempt to hollow out the Palestinian revolution. In 1983, a car bomb destroyed the centre, killing 14 and injuring 107. The PRC closed, then relocated to Cyprus. On the PLO Archive, see Hana Sleiman, 'The Paper Trail of a Liberation Movement', *Arab Studies Journal* 24(1) (2016): 42–67.

11. Sayigh, who stressed the PRC's commitment to training and supporting researchers of all educational, social and economic backgrounds, championed objective analysis, neutrality and freedom of expression. See Anis Sayigh, *Anis Sayigh 'an Anis Sayigh* (Beirut: Riyad al-Rayyis, 2006), Chapter 5.

12. On the eleven-volume *Palestine Encyclopaedia*, see Anis Sayigh, *Anis Sayigh 'an Anis Sayigh*, Chapter 5.

13. After an exacting search of the Damascus mosques, *takaya*, and churches where Ottoman recruits were garrisoned before being sent to their death without prior training, Ziadeh and his mother finally located his father in a mosque that only the boy was permitted to visit. When the father subsequently disappeared, they desperately searched the city's hospitals – which Ziadeh recounts

in horrifically vivid detail, likening corpses awaiting burial, immersed in cold water to delay decomposition, to floating pickles – only to be informed that he had died and been buried in the St George's Christian cemetery.

14. In 1972, Israel inaugurated a brutal campaign to systematically eliminate Palestinian intellectuals and activists all over the world. In 1972, Sayigh was a victim of a letter bomb that impaired his hearing and vision, and blew three fingers off his left hand.

15. See Sayigh's interview at 43'07". Sayigh reports that after the Arab Revolt broke out in the mid-1930s, interaction and intermingling between Jews and Arabs in 'mixed towns' ceased. However,

> the relationships between Arabs were very strong and I swear and attest (uqsim wa u'akid) that there was no sectarian sentiment between Arabs, and if at all then it was between Christians of different denominations, but not between Muslim and Christian as there might be to a certain point today between Palestinians.

Sayigh authored a book on Lebanese sectarianism: *Lubnan al-Ta'ifi* (Beirut: Dar al-Sira' al-Fikri, 1955).

16. See Ziadeh's interview at 4h 58'13". Mandate authorities appointed Shaykh Husam al-Din Jarallah (1884–1954) as chief inspector of Islamic courts and Arabic public education after his unsuccessful bid against Hajj Amin to become the president of the Supreme Muslim Council.

17. A member of the Greek Orthodox Patriarchate of Antioch and All the East, a Christian community of which the Apostles Paul and Peter are considered co-founders.

18. What Sayigh does and does not say about Levantine Protestantism and his family's connection to the Scottish Mission in Palestine is among the most fascinating aspects of his interview. He tells of missionaries' expansive plans for Tiberias, where his father was a pastor and where Scots established the Sea of Galilee Medical Mission in 1885, as well as the huge rectory in which Sayigh grew up (the grounds, he says, were bigger than the American University in Beirut campus). These developments were made possible by the ominous Ottoman Land Code of 1858, which paved the way for the transformation of public land (previously administered according to local Palestinian customs and traditions) into purchasable private property. Ottoman land reform likewise facilitated the construction of the Bishop Gobat School, one of the first buildings erected outside Jerusalem's city walls. British colonial authorities comprehensively implemented the 1858 code upon occupying Palestine in 1917. See Frantzman et al, 'The Anglican Church in Palestine and Israel: Colonialism, Arabization and Land ownership,' *Middle Eastern Studies* 47: 101–126.

19. Ziadeh's utter disregard for Tibawi, an esteemed educator and historian, who was also studying in London when the Nakba occurred, is truly remarkable. Unlike Ziadeh (who discounts the need to discuss Palestine's Islamic schools in the interview), Tibawi was concerned with the fate of the *katatib*, elementary village schools that taught the Quran, reading and writing, and which he himself had attended. See Tibawi, 'Religion and Educational Administration

in Palestine of the British Mandate', *Die Welt des Islams* 3(1) (1953): 4–6; and *Arabic and Islamic Garland: Historical, Educational and Literary Papers Presented to Abdul-Latif Tibawi* (London: Islamic Cultural Centre, 1977), 11–13.

20. The first expression is Anis Sayigh's (interview at 38'40"); the second is Rosemary Sayigh's (*Yusif Sayigh*, 4).

21. Consider Anis Sayigh's absence from the 'prominent figures' page of the National Evangelical School for Boys and Girls in Sayda (NGEIB) website. The NGEIB grew out of the Gerard Institute, to which Sayigh transferred after the Bishop Gobat School closed on 30 November 1947, and from which he graduated in 1949. See NGEIB, 'History', www.neigb.edu.lb/history/ (accessed 1 May 2020). Consider, too, the absence of Ziadeh's biography on the otherwise remarkable Palestinian Journeys website, an 'online portal into the multiple facets of the Palestinian experience, filled with fact-based historical accounts, biographies, events, and undiscovered stories (...)'. An ongoing project, it tellingly did not prioritize documenting Ziadeh's life, due in all likelihood to Ziadeh's non-activist stance on Palestine. See: https://www.paljourneys.org/en/timeline/biographies (accessed 1 May 2020).

22. Accounts of the Arab College in the early 1920s associate resistance and organising with such prominent educators as Darwish al-Miqdadi (1897–1961), a history lecturer who delivered fiery anti-colonial speeches, coordinated Arab scouting brigades and organised strikes. Though colonial administrators controlled syllabi, nationalist education continued under the guise of extra-curricular activities. Teachers were subject to strict surveillance, and those deemed too subversive were expelled, demoted or driven to resign (Tal'at Sayfi, the school director described in Sayigh's interview, is a case in point). See Brownson, 'Colonialism, Nationalism and the Politics of Teaching History in Mandate Palestine', 15.

23. I borrow this fitting descriptor from the title of Diana Allan's introductory chapter.

24. Ilan Pappe, *The Rise and Fall of a Palestinian Dynasty: The Husaynis, 1700–1948* (Berkeley, CA: University of California Press, 2010), 137. The Bishop Gobat School was initially a mission of the London Society for Promoting Christianity Amongst the Jews, and an early project of the joint Anglo-Prussian Protestant bishopric of Jerusalem established in 1841. On the school's history, missionary work among local (mainly Orthodox) Christians, and reliance on Church Mission Society (CMS) support, see Abdul Latif Tibawi, *Arab Education in Mandatory Palestine* (London: Luzac, 1956).

25. Walid Raghib Khalidi, 'al-Kulliyya al-'Arabiyya fi al-Quds: Khalfiya Tarikhiyya wa Nadhra Mustaqbaliyya', *Majalat al-Dirasat al-Filastiniyya* 11(44) (2000): 136–148.

26. Edward Said (1935–2003) was a pre-eminent Palestinian public intellectual, academic and educator, whose pivotal publications include *Orientalism* (1978) and *Culture and Imperialism* (1993). From 1977 to 1991, he served as a member of the Palestinian National Council (the parliament-in-exile representing all Palestinians, both inside and outside of Palestine).

27. Khalil al-Sakakini (1878–1953), first director of the Arab College (1919–1920), resigned after the appointment of Herbert Samuel, a Zionist Jew, as the high commissioner for Palestine:

> Active in many of the intellectual pursuits of the time, he was a visionary educator, debated politics with other Palestinians in a number of forums, founded literary clubs, and took part in the leadership of the Arabization movement within the Greek Orthodox church.

Davis, 'Commemorating Education: Recollections of the Arab College in Jerusalem, 1918–1948', 192.

28. Khalil Abdallah Totah (1886–1955), second director of the Arab college (1920–1925), resigned in 1925 after Lord Balfour visited Palestine for the inauguration of the Hebrew University. He was a Palestinian educator, advocate and author, whose work stressed the role of education in liberation and progress.

29. Ziadeh is referring to Montessori, although Pestalozzi (1746–1827) was also revered by Arab educators at the time.

30. Iskandar al-Khuri al-Baytjali (1888–1973) was a Palestinian polyglot translator, journalist, poet, writer and lawyer, educated at the Russian school, where he would teach Arabic and theology.

31. *al-Muqattam* is the name of the hill on which Cairo's citadel stands.

32. Taha Husayn's *On Pre-Islamic Poetry*, published 1926, was critical of the authenticity of the pre-Islamic and Islamic canon (of ancient Arab poetry and of portions of the Qur'an). The book caused an uproar and cost Husayn his position at Cairo University. He was to be eventually reinstated therein but his book was censored in Egypt.

33. 'Abd al-Rahman Bushnaq (1913–1999) was a Palestinian writer, translator, BBC broadcaster, and later, manager in the Arab Bank. He was educated at the Arab College, the American University of Beirut and Cambridge University, before returning to teach at his alma mater in Jerusalem until the Nakba. Ishaq Musa al-Husayni (1904-1990) was a Palestinian writer, critic, philologist, translator and academic. He studied in many Jerusalemite and Middle Eastern establishments and then taught in a certain number of them. Jamil 'Ali was a professor of mathematics at the Arab College.

34. *sarf wa nahw*: rules of grammar in Arabic, including the conjugation of verbs (*sarf* or *tasrif*) and the modulation of words and declensions (*nahw* or *i'rab*).

35. *Kana wa akhawatuha*: *kana* and its 'sisters', in Arabic grammar. When inserted in a sentence, these incomplete verbs shift the subject or predicate into the accusative case.

CHAPTER 5

1. Figures throughout are from British reports to the League of Nations and Palestine Police administrative reports, collected in a 16-volume set: Robert L. Jarman (ed.), *Palestine and Transjordan Administration Reports, 1918–1948* (Slough: Archive Editions, 1995).

2. The Palestine Police drew British 'experts' and personnel experienced in repressing colonised populations from elsewhere in the British Empire, including Ireland, South Asia and Africa. The most notorious collaboration between the Palestine Police and Zionist paramilitaries was the formation of the Special Night Squads during the 1936–39 revolt. Laleh Khalili, 'The Location of Palestine in Global Counterinsurgencies', *International Journal of Middle East Studies* 42 (2010): 413–433.

3. John L. Knight, 'Securing Zion? Policing in British Palestine, 1917–39', *European Review of History* 18(4) (2011): 523–43; and Charles Smith, 'Communal Conflict and Insurrection in Palestine', in David M. Anderson and David Killingray (eds), *Policing and Decolonisation: Nationalism, Politics, and the Police* (Manchester: Manchester University Press, 1995), 62–83.

4. David Ben-Gurion, 'Britain's Contribution to Arming the Haganah', in Walid Khalidi (ed.), *From Haven to Conquest: Readings in Zionism and the Palestine Problem until 1948* (Washington, DC: Institute for Palestine Studies, 2005), 372–74; Martin Kolinsky, 'The Collapse and Restoration of Public Security', in Michael J. Cohen and Martin Kolinsky (eds), *Britain and the Middle East in the 1930s: Security Problems, 1935–39* (London: Palgrave Macmillan, 1992), 157.

5. David Cesarani, 'The War on Terror that Failed: British Counter-Insurgency in Palestine 1945–1947 and the "Farran Affair"', in Matthew Hughes (ed.), *British Ways of Counter-Insurgency: A Historical Perspective* (New York: Routledge, 2013), 73–96.

6. Khalili, 'Location of Palestine in Global Counterinsurgencies'; and Georgina Sinclair, *At the End of the Line: Colonial Policing and the Imperial Endgame, 1945–80* (Manchester: Manchester University Press, 2010).

7. See, for example, Itamar Radai, *Palestinians in Jerusalem and Jaffa in 1948: A Tale of Two Cities* (New York: Routledge, 2016), 43–44.

8. On the historiography of the Palestine Police, see Yoav Alon, 'Bridging Imperial, National, and Local Historiographies: Britons, Arabs, and Jews in the Mandate Palestine Police', *Jerusalem Quarterly* 75 (2018): 62–77.

9. British authorities used employment and appointments both to cultivate members of Palestinian notable families as reliable intermediaries and to stoke rivalries among these families to undercut unified nationalist organising. See Rashid Khalidi, *The Iron Cage: The Story of the Palestinian Struggle for Statehood* (Boston, MA: Beacon Press, 2006), Chapters 2 and 3.

10. These trends are based on an analysis of some 750 service record cards of Arab policemen serving at the Mandate's end, held in the Middle East Centre Archive at St. Antony's College, Oxford, Boxes 1–12, MECA GB165-0365.

11. British authorities maintained the Ottoman Penal Code as the criminal law of Palestine, adding new ordinances to it piecemeal, until instating a new Criminal Code Ordinance in 1936. Palestinians participated in the Mandate's criminal legal system as judges, lawyers and policemen (not to mention as complainants, defendants and witnesses), but the Mandate structure offered them no input on legislation.

12. On the targeting of Arab policemen, especially during the 1936–39 revolt, see Hillel Cohen, *Army of Shadows: Palestinian Collaboration with Zionism, 1917–1948* (Berkeley, CA: University of California Press, 2008).

13. See, for example, Alex Winder, 'With the Dregs at the Sambo Café: The Shrouf Diaries, 1943–1962', *Jerusalem Quarterly* 54 (2013): 37–41.

14. Sarona colony was established by German Protestant Templers under Ottoman rule. British colonial forces established a compound comprising a Palestine Mobile Police station on the site, which they initially raided and occupied in 1917.

15. Menachem Begin was commander of Irgun, a Zionist paramilitary splinter faction of the Haganah, from 1943 to 1948. The Irgun – together with other Zionist groups – perpetrated wanton, ruthless violence against Palestinians (including the Dayr Yasin massacre of 9 August 1948); and attacks against British military and civilian targets in Palestine (such as the attack Agha describes). Begin was elected Israeli prime minister in 1977.

16. Agha here refers to the Palestine Post and Telegraphs company. In the incident, he is describing, the Irgun hijacked a van belonging to this company then blew it up at the Sarona Police Camp.

17. This attack, which took place on 25 April 1947, killed four policemen at the scene, with another dying later from injuries sustained in the bombing.

CHAPTER 6

1. For examples, see Michael Provence, 'Ottoman Modernity, Colonialism, and Insurgency in the Interwar Arab East', *International Journal of Middle East Studies* 43 (2011): 205–225; and Leila Parsons, *The Commander: Fawzi al-Qawuqji and the Fight for Arab Independence, 1914–1948* (New York: Farrar, Strauss and Giroux, 2016).

2. For examples, see John Harte, 'Scouting in Mandate Palestine', *Bulletin of the Council for British Research in the Levant* 3(1) (November 2008): 47–51; and Issam Khalidi, 'Body and Ideology: Early Athletics in Palestine (1900–1948)', *Jerusalem Quarterly* 27 (Summer 2006): 44–58.

3. Ted Swedenburg, *Memories of Revolt: The 1936–1939 Rebellion and the Palestinian National Past* (Minneapolis, MN: University of Minnesota Press, 1995).

4. For studies of the narrative tropes employed in various forms of Palestinian storytelling, see Nadia R. Sirhan, *Folk Stories and Personal Narratives in Palestinian Spoken Arabic: A Cultural and Linguistic Study* (London: Palgrave Macmillan, 2014); and Ibrahim Muhawi and Sharif Kanaana, *Speak, Bird, Speak Again: Palestinian Arab Folktales* (Berkeley, CA: University of California Press, 1989).

5. Maryam mentions her husband, Yusif Taha, earlier in the interview.

6. B'nai B'rith, a US-based Jewish fraternal society, opened lodges in Arab cities including Cairo, Alexandria, Jerusalem and Safad under Ottoman rule. During the Mandate period, B'nai B'rith expanded in Palestine, installing two colonies in the Lower Galilee, among other activities.

7. The *salam*, an Arabic greeting meaning 'Peace be upon you', and the customary response.
8. Ma'souba: the Arabic name for kibbutz Matzuva.
9. Colonial records and Arab periodicals testify to brutal reprisals against al-Bassa after a British armoured vehicle hit a mine near the village on 6 September 1938, killing four soldiers. The Royal Ulster Regiment, which was stationed in the area, proceeded to terrorise villagers, burn al-Bassa to the ground, and contrive an explosion to massacre around 50 men under a bus. See Matthew Hughes, *Britain's Pacification of Palestine* (Cambridge: Cambridge University Press, 2019), 330–334.
10. *kouseh*: likely refers to British cannon artillery and high-calibre shells, which weighed well over 1,000 pounds. Prison camps – which Mandate forces established throughout Palestine, in addition to permanent prisons and torture centres – were situated on military bases and run by British Army personnel. 'Abd al-Rahman Sa'ad al-Din was likely detained in the notorious crowded Mazra'a camp, just north of 'Akka. For more on the Mandate detention system, see Hughes, *Britain's Pacification of Palestine*, 235–252.
11. Daboya: Described in Mandate documents and administrative reports as a 'triangular piece of land' north of 'Akka on the Ras al-Naqura road, where the colonial government's Stud Farm adjoined its Stock Farm and Agricultural Station. These facilities comprised acres of stables and storehouses; and relied heavily on the forced labour of Palestinian political prisoners.

CHAPTER 7

1. Husayn Ali Lubani, *Mua'jam al-Aghani al-Sha'biyat al-Filastiniyya* (Beirut: Maktaba Lubnan Nashirun, 2007).
2. David McDonald, *My Voice is My Weapon: Music, Nationalism, and the Poetics of Palestinian Resistance* (Durham, NC: Duke University Press, 2013), 54–55; and Ted Swedenburg, *Memories of Revolt: The 1936–39 Rebellion and the Struggle for the Palestinian National Past* (Fayetteville, AR: University of Arkansas Press, 2003), 72–73.
3. McDonald, *My Voice is My Weapon*, 43-46.
4. Samih Shabeeb, 'Poetry of Rebellion: The Life, Verse and Death of Nuh Ibrahim during the 1936–39 Revolt', *Jerusalem Quarterly* 25 (2006): 65–78.
5. Nimr Hasan Hijab, *Al-Sha'ir al-Sha'bi al-Shahid Nuh Ibrahim* (Amman: Dar al-Yazuri, 2006).
6. Swedenburg, *Memories of Revolt*.
7. Laila Parsons, *The Commander: Fawzi al-Qawuqji and the Fight for Arab Independence 1914–1948* (New York: Hill & Wang, 2016).
8. Ibid. See also Charles Anderson, 'From Petition to Confrontation: The Palestinian National Movement and the Rise of Mass Politics, 1929–1939', PhD diss. New York University, 2013.
9. Parsons, *The Commander*. See also Matthew Hughes, *Britain's Pacification of Palestine: The British Army, the Colonial State, and the Arab Revolt, 1936–1939* (Cambridge: Cambridge University Press, 2019).

10. Al-Layyeh: the bend in the road at Bal'a. A non-standard transliteration is used here, to preserve the rhyme.
11. See Parsons, *The Commander*; Anderson, 'From Petition to Confrontation'; and Subhi Mohammad Yasin, *Al-Thawra al-'Arabiya al-Kubra fi Filastin, 1936–1939* (Cairo: Dar al-Katib al-'Arabi, 1959).
12. Nabil 'Awda, 'Al-Sha'ir al-Tha'ir Farhan Salam', *Majalat Anhar al-Adabiya*, www.anhaar.com/ar/?p=3829 (accessed 1 May 2020). See also Nimr Sirhan, Mawsu'at al-*Fulklur al-Filastini*, Vol. 2 (Amman: E.P.F. Bayader-Jordan, 1977).
13. Swedenburg, *Memories of Revolt*; and Hughes, *Britain's Pacification of Palestine*.
14. Sonia Nimr, 'A Nation in a Hero: Abdul Rahim al-Hajj Mohammad and the Arab Revolt', in Mark LeVine (ed.), *Struggle and Survival in Palestine/Israel* (Berkeley, CA: University of California Press, 2012).
15. British Liberal politician Herbert Samuel was appointed first High Commissioner for Palestine in 1920, when the League of Nations had yet to approve the colonial Mandate. He was an avid supporter of Zionism.
16. The actual date was 17 June 1930.
17. The Martini-Henry rifle was standard issue for British imperial forces from 1871, and was used until 1918 to subjugate indigenous populations in South Africa, Afghanistan, the Arab world and beyond.
18. *The Isra' of the Prophet Adnan*: the Prophet Muhammad's night journey from Mecca to Jerusalem on the back of Buraq, a winged equine creature; introduced in Chapter 17 of the Qu'ran.
19. Al-Qahtan: ancient ancestor of Arab tribes in the Mashriq, dated to some 3,000 years before Islam.
20. On 2 November 1917, in a letter destined for the Zionist Federation, British foreign secretary Arthur James Balfour affirmed his government's support for 'the establishment in Palestine of a national home for the Jewish people'. A statement of imperial intent, the Balfour Declaration presaged Britain's 30-year occupation of Palestine.
21. *Zaqqum*: a tree that grows in Jahannam (Hell), referred to in Chapter 37 of the Qur'an.
22. It is not clear what *Zlut* refers to.
23. The second half of the Surat al-Fil ('The Elephant'), Qur'an 105:1–5 (Saheeh International translation).
24. The Supreme Throne, or Throne of God ('arsh), is considered to be one of the greatest things ever created by God in Islamic theology, located above the highest level of Paradise.

CHAPTER 8

1. As detailed in annual reports by the British Government to the Council of the League of Nations on the Palestinian Administration, 1923–1926 (accessible via the UN Information System on the Question of Palestine). See also Sahar Huneidi, *A Broken Trust: Herbert Samuel, Zionism and the Palestinians, 1920–1925* (New York: I.B. Tauris, 2001).

2. See Justin McCarthy, *The Population of Palestine: Population History and Statistics of the Late Ottoman Period and the Mandate* (New York: Columbia University Press, 1990).

3. See details of recently revealed files in Matthew Hughes, *Britain's Pacification of Palestine: The British Army, the Colonial State and the Arab Revolt, 1936–1939* (Cambridge: Cambridge University Press, 2019).

4. Hughes, *Britain's Pacification of Palestine*, 281–288.

5. Hughes, *Britain's Pacification of Palestine*: on cooperation in intelligence, see 295–306; dressed in British uniforms, 301; cooperation with Haganah, 91–92; and translation, 297–304.

6. See, for example, Hansard, Parliamentary Debates (Commons) on Jewish Terrorism (28 January 1947, Vol. 432 col. 772–6; 31 January 1947, Vol. 432 col. 1300–58; etc.)

7. This handwritten document was gratefully received from the family of a British soldier.

8. UN DAG-13/3.3.1:10.

9. C.N. Ezard, HM Consul General, Haifa to Foreign Office, 12 July 1950, covering letter 17 July 1950, in Robert L. Jarman (ed.), *Israel, Political and Economic Reports 1948–1953: Israel under the Premiership of David Ben Gurion, 1948–1953*, Vol. 3: 1950 (Cambridge: Cambridge Archive Editions, 1950), 447–508.

10. Schmeisser: a German MP 40 sub-machine gun.

11. *hannaneh* is a neighborhood of Sha'b in the district of 'Akka that included a water spring ('Ein al-Hannaneh), which flowed out of an old fountain carved in a rocky wall. According to Palestine Survey maps from the 1940s, a mosque was also located in the vicinity of 'Ein al-Hannaneh.

12. Hadera: a Jewish settlement in the district of 'Akka, founded in 1890 by members of Hovevei Zion, a group of Zionist immigrants from Russia and Eastern Europe.

13. *khawaja*: title of respect analogous to 'Sir'. The Jewish soldier assumes he is addressing her husband.

14. *khirbeh*: literally 'ruin'; usually refers to a site with visible architectural features (remnants of walls, wells, etc.). Some Palestinian villages are situated on or near such ruins, and named after them. See Walid al-Khalidi (ed.), *All That Remains: The Palestinian Villages Occupied and Depopulated by Israel in 1948* (Washington, DC: Institute for Palestinian Studies, 1992).

CHAPTER 9

1. Hannah Arendt, *The Origins of Totalitarianism* (New York: Harcourt Brace, 1966), 439.

2. Of the eleven cities and towns that were occupied by the Israeli forces in 1948, al-Nasira (Nazareth), because of its religious status for Christians worldwide and for the Vatican, was the only town not to suffer destruction, displacement or looting. Ben Gurion gave his army strict orders that the town should not meet the same fate as the others, as it would anger the Christian world. For more details about the case of al-Nasira and its significance, see my compre-

hensive study about the 1948 massacres: Saleh Abdel Jawad, 'Zionist Massacres: the Creation of the Palestinian Refugee Problem in the 1948 War', in Eyal Benvenisti, Chaim Gans and Sari Hanafi (eds), *Israel and the Palestinian Refugees* (Berlin: Springer, 2007), 59–127.

3. Israeli Radio was introduced in the 1950s as part of a propaganda campaign aimed at casting Israel in a favourable light. The programmes were in Arabic and featured family members who had stayed behind in Israel sending recorded greetings in their own voices to their children, who had fled their home country. A message would usually include the latest family news such as births and marriages in the family … The programmes were also used to send coded messages to Israeli agents in the Arab world.

4. This preferred method of the Israeli Army persisted after the emergence of the state; it happened in the small town of Qalqilya (1956), the village of Qabiya (1953) and other locations in the West Bank in the mid-1950s.

5. The Israeli forces' code of ethics continues to propound the precept/myth that the Jewish weapons are employed only in cases of self-defence, strictly out of military necessity, against armed forces and never civilians or prisoners of war, and proportionate to level of violence used by the other side. On the mythical nature of this principle, see Avi Shlaim, 'The Debate About 1948', *International Journal of Middle East Studies* 27(3) (1995): 287–304; and Benny Morris, *1948: A History of the First Arab–Israeli War* (New Haven, CT: Yale University Press, 2008).

6. My research was published by the long-established Max Planck Institute in Heidelberg, Germany. This despite the fact that, due to the Holocaust atrocities, the Institute was sensitive to any criticism of Israel. Not a single Israeli historian refuted or questioned the validity of the number or details of massacres given in my study, although certain aspects of the analysis did come in for some criticism. In fact, the language had already been toned down substantially in those parts at the insistence of the Institute and an editor of the paper, who is an Israeli historian.

7. The village suffered two attacks in mid-March 1948, just days apart. The massacre that was committed during the second attack claimed the lives of dozens of inhabitants of the village, which, although small, was a vital transportation hub.

8. Circassians: It is likely that al-'Abd Tahir is referring to the Circassian community of Rihaniyya (a village near Saliha) that surrendered to the Israeli army in October 1948 and was allowed to remain in the village.

9. *ruh*: The Jewish man incorrectly addresses Kamila using the male singular, demonstrating poor knowledge of Arabic.

10. Marun al-Ras, village in South Lebanon.

11. Maryam is likely referring to a Jewish settlement in the vicinity of 'Arab al-Zubayd, a village near al-Husayniyya.

12. Hulata, a kibbutz near al-Husayniyya, mentioned earlier in the interview.

13. *qibla*: the direction of the Ka'ba in Mecca, towards which Muslims should face when praying. In al-Husayniyya, the *qibla* is towards the south.

14. Maryam may be referring to al-Shuna, another village in the Safad Subdistrict.

CHAPTER 10

1. Safsaf was occupied during Operation Hiram (29–31 October 1948), the Israel Defense Force's final push to clear Arab forces from the Upper Galilee. Bal'awi left the area months before Israeli forces committed a horrific massacre in the village, on 29 October 1948.
2. In this case, the *qibla* is towards the west.
3. Adib al-Shishakli (1909–64): a prominent Syrian commander during the 1948 war.
4. Shafa 'Amr: a large Christian, Druze and Muslim town which fell to Zionist forces between 8 and 12 July 1948, partly as a result of Druze collaboration.
5. The Arab Higher Committee, or Higher National Committee, was represented by Local National Committees at the district, subdistrict and village levels. Abu Raqaba is likely referring to the Acre National Committee.
6. The Arab Liberation Army's main training base was in the Qatana military camps, near Damascus. Many Palestinian officers were trained there.
7. Ahmad Shuqayri (1908–80): Palestinian representative who played a crucial role in founding the Palestinian National Council (PNC), the sovereign legislative body of the Palestinian people, in 1964. The Palestine Liberation Army was officially declared at the third PNC session in 1966.
8. Ahmad Jibril was a military leader in al-Jabha al-Sha'biyya li-Tahrir Filastin (the Popular Front for the Liberation of Palestine) in Jordan before 1968.
9. Wasfi al-Tal (1919–71) and Shawkat Shuqayri (1912–82) were both leading commanders during the war, from Jordan and Lebanon respectively. They were reputed to be highly capable, as was al-Shishakli.
10. Haifa fell on 22 April 1948, following a sweeping Haganah attack on the city's Arab quarters, in close coordination with British forces.
11. Abu Is'af was a leading local Palestinian commander and hero of 1948. His headquarters were in Sha'b. After the fighting was over, in December 1948, Zionist forces went back to Sha'b and expelled villagers who had returned after they were forced to flee in July, when their village was first seized.
12. Qal'at Jiddin: a destroyed crusader fortress around which Khirbat Jiddin village was built. It was the site of fierce fighting and a Palestinian victory when a convoy headed to Yehi'am, a nearby Jewish settlement, was attacked and defeated in March 1948.
13. 15 May 1948: the day Arab armies would enter Palestine, following the withdrawal of British forces (the British Mandate for Palestine expired at midnight on 15 May).
14. The harvest of 1948.

CHAPTER 11

1. Ilan Pappe, *The Ethnic Cleansing of Palestine* (Oxford: Oneworld Publications, 2006), 156. See also Donald Neff, 'Expulsion of the Palestinians – Lydda and Ramleh in 1948', *Washington Report on Middle East Affairs* (July–August 1994),

www.wrmea.org/1994-july-august/middle-east-history-expulsion-of-the-palestinians-Lydda-and-ramleh-in-1948.html.

2. Born in 1930, Shammout is considered one of Palestine's leading painters. His first exhibition – in 1953, in Gaza – was inspired by the forced march out of Lydda, a theme that reappeared in various ways throughout his work. In 1965, he became the Director of Arts and National Culture within the PLO. Elected in 1969 as the first Secretary General of the Union of Palestinian Artists, he was also elected Secretary General of the Union of Arab Artists in 1971.

3. Born in Lydda in 1925 to a Christian family, Habash was a medical student at the American University of Beirut during the 1948 war. He was present in Lydda at the time of the Jewish assault, worked in field hospitals to treat the wounded, and was forced out with everyone else. In 1951, he was one of a group of young Arabs (including Hani al-Hindi, Wadiʿ Haddad, Ahmad al-Khatib and others) in Beirut who founded the Movement of Arab Nationalists (MAN), which was announced at its first conference in 1956. After the Arab defeat in the 1967 war, Habash founded and led the left-wing secular Popular Front for the Liberation of Palestine, dedicated to armed struggle. For an account of the fall of Lydda and his experiences there, see his memoir *al-Thawriyun La Yamutun Abadan* (Beirut: Dar al-Saqi, 2009), 27–30.

4. The first truce of the 1948 war fell between 11 June and 8 July. By that time, there were already about 300,000 Palestinian refugees – a result of the Jewish military operations of Plan Dalet, intended to clear the Galilee of Arabs. As the Arabs were demanding the refugees' return, the Jewish command took advantage of the truce to demolish many then emptied villages to prevent this. The truce marked the end of the first wave of ethnic cleansing, and the beginning of the second wave, which saw the launch of Operation Dani against Lydda and Ramla. See Benny Morris, *The Birth of the Palestinian Refugee Problem Revisited* (Cambridge: Cambridge University Press, 2004). On Plan Dalet, see Walid Khalidi, 'Plan Dalet: Master Plan for the Conquest of Palestine', *Journal of Palestine Studies* 18(1) (Autumn 1988): 4–33.

5. Consequent on the announcement by the British government that it wished to withdraw from Palestine, and a report by the UN Special Committee on Palestine (UNSCOP), the UN adopted Resolution 181, on 29 November 1947, which called for partition of Palestine into an Arab and Jewish state. The Palestinian Arabs, who composed two-thirds of the population at the time, were allotted 43 per cent of Mandatory Palestine. The Jews, who constituted one-third of the population (most of whom had immigrated within the previous three decades) and who owned only 7 per cent of the land, were allotted 56 per cent of the country. Almost half (45 per cent) of the population of the proposed Jewish state would be Arab. The city of Jerusalem would be internationalised. The Jewish Agency accepted the plan, but the Palestinian Arabs rejected it as a denial of their right to self-determination, which they had been demanding for the previous three decades, since the British occupied Palestine in 1917.

6. See also Morris, *The Birth of the Palestinian Refugee Problem Revisited*, 425.

7. Pappe, *The Ethnic Cleansing of Palestine*, 167.

8. 'Yerachmiel Kahanovich, Palmach Soldier', *Zochrot*, https://zochrot.org/en/testimony/54345 (accessed 1 May 2020).
9. Pappe, *The Ethnic Cleansing of Palestine*, 167. See also Morris, *The Birth of the Palestinian Refugee Problem Revisited*, 426.
10. Spiro Munayyar, 'The Fall of Lydda', *Journal of Palestine Studies* 27(4) (Summer, 1998): 80–98.
11. The village of Dayr Yasin was the site of a brutal massacre by Irgun forces on 9 April 1948, which was pivotal in producing panic among the civilian population of Palestine. See Daniel McGowan and Marc H. Ellis (eds), *Remembering Deir Yassin: The Future of Israel and Palestine* (New York: Olive Branch Press, 1998).
12. Operation Nachson was the first operation of Plan Dalet. See Pappe, *The Ethnic Cleansing of Palestine*, 87–91.
13. Avi Shlaim, 'Israel and the Arab Coalition in 1948', in Eugene Rogan and Avi Shlaim (eds), *The War for Palestine: Rewriting the United States and the Israeli–Palestinian Conflict History of 1948* (Cambridge: Cambridge University Press, 2001), 79–103. See also Munayyar, 'The Fall of Lydda'.
14. Arnon Golan, 'Lydda and Ramle: From Palestinian-Arab to Israeli Towns, 1948–67', *Middle Eastern Studies* 39(4) (October 2003): 121–139. See also Pappe, *The Ethnic Cleansing of Palestine*.
15. Pappe, *The Ethnic Cleansing of Palestine*, 169.
16. Golan, 'Lydda and Ramle', 124. See also Morris, *The Birth of the Palestinian Refugee Problem Revisited*, 423–24.
17. Pappe, *The Ethnic Cleansing of Palestine*, 166.
18. Munayyar, 'The Fall of Lydda', 188; and Morris, *The Birth of the Palestinian Refugee Problem Revisited*, 425.
19. Morris, *The Birth of the Palestinian Refugee Problem Revisited*, 426; and Munayyar, 'The Fall of Lydda', 82.
20. Morris, *The Birth of the Palestinian Refugee Problem Revisited*, 251 and 523.
21. *mawasim* (plural of *mawsim*): seasonal festivals, typically involving pilgrimages to *maqamat* (shrines) where religious and popular celebrations were held. The *maqam* to *al-Nabi* (the Prophet) Salih is located in al-Jami' al-Abyad (the White Mosque) in Ramla.
22. Istiqlal (Independence) Party: a progressive party founded in the early 1930s, when various parties emerged to offset notable families' dominance of Palestinian politics. Istiqlal called for parliamentary Arab rule in Palestine, and active resistance to both Zionism and the British Mandate. The Arab Higher Committee, a coalition of six parties formed in response to the 1936 Palestinian General Strike, was heavily influenced by Hajj Amin al-Husayni.
23. The name 'Adla (from the root 'adala) means just, balanced, upright.

CHAPTER 12

1. Nafez Nazzal, in his oral history book reporting the massacre of Safsaf, notes that Israeli soldiers had entered Safsaf around sunrise and ordered the villagers to line up in a spot in the northern part of the village. One villager says:

As we lined up, a few Jewish soldiers ordered four girls to accompany them to carry water for the soldiers. Instead, they took them to our empty houses and raped them. About 60 of our men were blindfolded and shot to death, one after the other, in front of us. The soldiers took their bodies and threw them on the cement covering of the village's spring and dumped sand on them.

In later days, Israeli troops visited the village, telling the inhabitants that they should forget what had occurred and could stay in their homes. But they began to leave under cover of the night towards Lebanon, about four at a time, until Safsaf was empty. Nafez Nazzal, *The Palestinian Exodus from Galilee, 1948* (Beirut: Institute for Palestine Studies, 1978), 95.

2. Primo Levi, *The Drowned and the Saved* (London: Abacus, 1989), 26.
3. Cathy Caruth, *Trauma: Explorations in Memory* (Baltimore, MD: Johns Hopkins University Press), 151.
4. Alessandro Portelli, 'The Peculiarities of Oral History', *History Workshop Journal* 12(1) (Autumn 1981): 96–107.
5. The word *hmar* (donkey) is also an insult.

CHAPTER 13

1. *Tal* here signifies both a hill or small mountain and al-Zib's archaeological *tal*. In her description of al-Zib, Fatima uses the word *tal* to designate the oldest, most ancient part of town.
2. Emphasis in the original.
3. Mayssun Soukarieh, 'Speaking Palestinian: An Interview with Rosemary Sayigh', *Journal of Palestine Studies* 38(4) (2009), 18.
4. Nur Masalha, 'Decolonizing Methodology, Reclaiming Memory: Palestinian Oral Histories and Memories of the Nakba', in Nahla Abdo and Nur Masalha (eds), *An Oral History of the Palestinian Nakba* (London: Zed Books, 2018), 8.
5. Rosemary Sayigh, 'Palestinian Camp Women as Tellers of History', *Journal of Palestine Studies* 27(2) (1998): 42–58.
6. Edward Said, *Musical Elaborations: The Wellek Library Lectures at the University of California, Irvine* (New York: Columbia University Press, 1991).
7. Said suggests that the concert occasion creates relationships between listening and the making of a dynamic social space with the concert itself a result of a series of socio-political, cultural, technological and historical processes; and the concert's reception an outcome contingent upon specific arrangements of aesthetic and social experiences.
8. Fatima uses the words *shaykh*, *qadi*, and *mufti* interchangeably. It is likely that this man was in fact a *qadi* (Islamic court judge). On distinctions and similarities between the roles of *qadi* and *mufti*, see Brinkley Messick, 'The Judge and the Mufti', in Rudolph Peters and Peri Bearman (eds), *Ashgate Research Companion to Islamic Law* (London: Routledge, 2016), 73–92.
9. The Ottoman Law of Family Rights (1917), which formed the basic family law code for Muslim communities in Palestine under the British Mandate, stipulated a minimum marriage age of 18 for men and 17 for women. However, a

qadi could authorise marriage at a younger age, if both parties were confirmed to be sexually mature. See, for example, Judith E. Tucker, 'Revisiting Reform: Women and the Ottoman Law of Family Rights, 1917', *The Arab Studies Journal* 4(2) (1996): 4–17.

10. Rosemary Sayigh, '"Umm Faris"', Sheikh Radwan, Gaza City, April 12', in *Voices: Palestinian Women Narrate Displacement* (Al Mashriq, 2007), http://almashriq.hiof.no/palestine/300/301/voices/Gaza/halima_hassouna.html (accessed 1 May 2020).
11. Ibid.
12. Ibid.
13. Ibid.
14. Ibid.
15. Byron J. Good and Mary-Jo Delvecchio Good, 'Toward a Meaning-Centered Analysis of Popular Illness Categories: "Fright Illness" and "Heart Distress" in Iran', in Anthony J. Marsella and Geoffrey M. White (eds), *Cultural Conceptions of Mental Health and Therapy: Culture, Illness, and Healing*, Vol. 4. (Dordrecht: Springer, 1982), 141–66.
16. For a detailed discussion of Palestinian oral historiography, see, for instance, Nur Masalha, 'Decolonizing Methodology, Reclaiming Memory: Palestinian Oral Histories and Memories of the Nakba', in Nahla Abdo and Nur Masalha (eds), *An Oral History of the Palestinian Nakba* (London: Zed, 2018), 6–39.
17. A popular game among girls at the time, *kalat* (plural of *kal*) involved throwing small rocks in the air and catching them with a single hand. Many variations were played, hence the plural form.
18. *Eh wiha…*: largely improvised phrases sung by women at a wedding to wish the bride prosperity, followed by collective ululating, a practice known as *zalghouta*.
19. The first two verses of this rendition serve merely to complete the rhyme.
20. Literal translation of a proverb used when nothing works out anymore. A *daff* is a large frame drum played at celebrations.

AFTERWORD

1. Nur Masalha, 'Decolonizing Methodology, Reclaiming Memory: Palestinian Oral Histories and Memories of the Nakba', in Nahla Abdo and Nur Masalha (eds), *An Oral History of the Palestinian Nakba* (London: Zed Books, 2018), 9.
2. See Stéphanie Latte-Abdallah, 'La part des absents: Les images en creux des refugies palestiniens', in Stéphanie Latte-Abdallah (ed.), *Images aux frontières: representations et constructions sociales et politiques: Palestine, Jordanie 1948–2000* (Beirut: Institut français du Proche-Orient, 2005).
3. Resolution on Cultural Rights: A/RES/44/25.
4. Nafez Nazzal, *The Palestinian Exodus from Galilee, 1948* (Beirut: Institute of Palestine Studies, 1978).
5. Rosemary Sayigh, *Palestinians: From Peasants to Revolutionaries* (London: Zed Press, 1979).

6. Rosemary Sayigh,'Oral History, Colonialist Dispossession, and the State: The Palestinian Case', *Settler Colonial Studies* 5(3) (2015): 193–204.
7. Salim Tamari, 'Special Issue on Oral History, *Al-Jana: The Harvest* (Beirut: Arab Resource Center for Popular Arts [ARCPA], 2002), 57.
8. See Diana Allan, 'The Politics of Witness: Remembering and Forgetting 1948 in Shatila Camp', in Ahmad Sa'di and Lila Abu-Lughod (eds), *Nakba: Palestine, 1948, and the Claims of Memory* (New York: Columbia University Press, 2007), 274.
9. Donald MacIntyre, 'UN to Teach Children about Holocaust in Gaza Schools', *The Independent*, 23 October 2011.
10. See Edward Said, *The Question of Palestine* (New York: Times Books, 1979), 29.
11. Michel Rolph Trouillot, *Silencing the Past: Power and the Production of History* (Boston, MA: Beacon Press, 1995).
12. Daniel McGowan and Marc Ellis (eds), *Remembering Deir Yassin; the Future of Israel and Palestine* (New York: Olive Branch Press, 1998).
13. Nur Masalha (ed.), *Catastrophe Remembered: Palestine, Israel and the Internal Refugees* (London: Zed Books, 2005), 6–7.
14. 'Israel Bans "Catastrophe" Term from Arab Schools', *Reuters*, 22 July 2009; in 2011, Israeli law criminalised Nakba commemoration.
15. Hagai Matar, 'Police Besiege, Arrest Activists Planning to Commemorate Nakba', *+972*, 26 April 2012.
16. Ahmad Sa'di and Lila Abu-Lughod (eds), *Nakba: Palestine, 1948, and the Claims of Memory* (New York: Columbia University Press, 2007), 11.
17. Erskine B. Childers, 'The Other Exodus', *The Spectator*, 12 May 1961.
18. See 'Mission Statement', *Palestine Remembered*, 7 April 2007, www. www.palestineremembered.com/MissionStatement.htm; and see 'Nakba's Oral History Interviews Listing', *Palestine Remembered*, www.palestineremembered.com/OralHistory/Interviews-Listing/Story1151.html.
19. Staughton Lynd, Sam Bahour and Alice Lynd (eds), *Homeland: Oral Histories of Palestine and Palestinians* (New York: Olive Branch Press, 1997).
20. Yezid Sayigh, *Armed Struggle and the Search for State: The Palestinian National Movement* (Oxford: Oxford University Press, 1997).
21. Randa Farah, 'UNRWA in Popular Memory al-Baqa Refugee Camp', *CERMOC A History within History: Humanitarian Aid and Development* (CERMOC: Amman, October 1998).
22. Rosemarie Esber, 'The 1948 Palestinian Exodus from Haifa', *The Arab World Geographer* 6(2) (2003): 112–41, and Rosemarie Esber, *Under the Cover of War: The Zionist Expulsion of the Palestinians* (Alexandria, VA: Arabicus Books and Media, 2008).
23. Saleh Abdel Jawad, 'The Creation of the Arab Refugee Problem in the 1948 War', in Eyal Benvenisti et al. (eds), *Israel and the Palestinian Refugees* (Berlin: Springer, 2007).
24. Mustafa Ahmad Abbasi, 'The End of Arab Tiberias: The Arabs of Tiberias and the Battle for the City in 1948', *Journal of Palestine Studies* 37(3) (2007): 6–29.
25. Zena Ghandour, *A Discourse on Domination in Mandate Palestine* (New York: Routledge, 2010).

26. Faiha Abdulhadi, *Living Memories: Testimonies of Palestinians' Displacement in 1948* (Ramallah: Al Rowat, 2017).

27. Nabulsi and Takriti' project, 'The Palestinian Revolution', is an online teaching resource that explores Palestinian revolutionary thought and practice. See: learnpalestine.politics.ox.ac.uk

28. Sherna Berger Guck, 'Advocacy Oral History: Palestinian Women in Resistance', in Sherna B. Gluck and Daphne Patai (eds), *Women's Words: The Feminist Practice of Oral History* (New York: Routledge, 1991).

29. Rochelle Davis, *Palestinian Village Histories: Geographies of the Displaced* (Stanford, CA: Stanford University Press, 2010).

30. Nahla Abdo and Nur Masalha (eds), *An Oral History of the Palestinian Nakba* (London: Zed Books, 2018).

31. Lynn Abrams, *Oral History Theory* (London: Routledge, 2010).

32. Nahla Abdo, 'Feminism, Indigenous and Settler Colonialism: Oral History, Memory and the Nakba', in Nahla Abdo and Nur Masalha (eds), *An Oral History of the Palestinian Nakba* (London: Zed Books, 2018), 58.

33. Masalha, *An Oral History of the Palestinian Nakba*, 7.

34. Masalha, *An Oral History of the Palestinian Nakba*, 7.

35. Denjal Jegic, *Trans/Intifada: The Politics and Poetics if Intersectional Resistance* (Heidleberg: Universitätsverlag, Winter 2018).

36. Masalha, *An Oral History of the Palestinian Nakba*, 31–32.

Index

Note: *ill* refers to an illustration; *n* to a note; *port* to a portrait

335

Baydas, Khalil 92
Bayt Jibrin 114
Begin, Menachem 107, 322–3*n*15
Beirut 11, 82
Beit Shemen settlement 240–1, 244, 245
Ben Gurion, David 168, 237
Benjamin, Walter 17–18
Bernadotte, Count Folke 169
Beta Israel 80
Biltmore Conference (1942) 168
Birzeit University 'Destroyed Palestinian
    Villages' 188, 297–8
Bishop Gobat School 83, 85–6, 95,
    320*n*23
Blaybil, Ibrahim: interview with 30–5
B'nai B'rith 323*n*6
Bristol Café, al-Quds 91
Britain: colonial period in Palestine 1, 3,
    27–8, 34, 37, 52, 71–2, 87–8, 172,
    312–3*n*1
  collusion with Zionism 149, 168, 240,
    315*n*11
  see also Arab Revolt
B'rith camp 129
British Mandate for Palestine 3, 13, 25,
    28, 30, 43, 101, 102
Buraq Uprising 141, 149, 313*n*6
Burj al-Barajneh camp 18, 106, 215, 227,
    228, 267, 276, 281–2
al-Bus camp 211
Bushnaq, 'Abd al-Rahman 32, 321*n*32
Bushnaq, 'Ali 224

Cairo 91
California State University 298
Camp David Summit (2000) 4
camps 2, 8, 10, 12, 28–9, 45, 56
  Bedouin 189
  concentration camps 170, 171
  forced labour camps 171
  see also refugee camps; War of the
    Camps
Carmel, Moshe 3
Caruth, Cathy 256
Catholic Church 51
Christians 44, 45, 146, 243, 294
Church Mission Society 86
Church of the Nativity, Bethlehem 145–6
Circassians 195, 197, 327*n*8

colonialism *see* Britain; French colonial-
    ism; settler colonialism
communists 75, 76, 315*n*12
Contemporary Poets, The (*al-Nafa'is
    al-'Asriyya*) (magazine) 92

Dahmash mosque, Lydda 238
Dar al-Mu'allimin *see* Arab College
Davis, Rochelle 15
  Palestinian Village Histories 298
al-Dawayima 188, 192
Dayan, Moshe 241
Dayr Sharaf, battle of 132
Dayr Yasin massacre 169, 188, 189, 192,
    216, 239, 253–4, 297, 322–3*n*15,
    329*n*11
Defence (Emergency) Regulation (1945)
    172
Dolar, Mladen 5, 16
Druze 146, 272, 273

Eban, Abba 45
  My Country 58
education 26, 30–3, 47–50, 87–9
  see also schools
Egypt 82, 128
Eid 15, 26, 31, 37–9, 106, 243, 252, 306
Enemy Property Act (1953) 172
Etzel *see* Irgun
Ezard, C.N. 171

Faisal, King 140, 144
Falasha *see* Beta Israel
Fanon, Frantz 65
Umm Faris 279–80
fellahin 8, 32, 65, 267, 283
Firqat Aghani al-'Ashiqin (music group)
    141
French colonialism 128, 143
French schools 48–9
Fuda, Taliba Muhammad 170
  interview with 179–85

Galilee *see* al-Jalil
Gargour Shipping 53
Gaza 19, 114, 189, 279
Genocide Convention (1948) 193
Ging, John 296
girls: education of 39, 47, 50, 94, 284
  see also marriage

Glubb, Sir John Bagot (Glubb Pasha) 241
Gluck, Sherna Berger 298

Habash, George 237, 328–9*n*3
Hadad, 'Uthman Ja'far 224
Haggadah, 'Uthman Ja'far 224
Hadad, 'Uthman Ja'far 224
Haganah 86, 102, 168, 170, 214, 255, 281
Haifa 65, 81–2, 228, 239
Hasuna, Halima *see* Umm Faris
al-Hayja, Mahmud Abu 9–10, 12, 216–7
    interview with 228–32
Hebrew language xvii, 59, 77, 79, 117, 209
Hebron *see* al-Khalil
Herzl, Theodore 58–9
Hijazi, Fu'ad 149
Histadrut *see* Zionist Labour Federation
Hitler, Adolf 45, 60
Holocaust 45, 296–7
Holocaust Museum, Yad Vashem 296–7
Holy War Army 105
al-Hula 31, 186, 314*n*5, 316*n*18
Husayn, 'Abdullah 97*port*
Husayn, Taha *Fi al-Shi'r al-Jahili (On Pre-Islamic Poetry)* 91–2, 321*n*31
al-Husayni, 'Abd al-Qadir 105, 144, 147, 214
al-Husayni, Hajj Amin 45, 57, 59, 60, 144–5, 146, 147, 224–5, 314*n*2
al-Husayni, Hasan 16, 45–6
    interview with 57–60
al-Husayni, Ishaq Musa 92, 321*n*32
al-Husayni, Muhammad Amin 155
al-Husayniyya 186, 187, 190–2

Ibn Saud, King 143
Ibrahim, Nuh 141–2, 144, 145, 146, 147–8, 151–3
illiteracy *see* literacy
International Red Cross 86, 171
Intifada
    (1st) 121
    (2nd) 86
Iran-Iraq War 279
Irgun 102, 188, 240, 255, 322–3*n*5
Israel: narrative of founding of 5, 191
Israel Police 102, 297
Israel Radio 326*n*3
Israeli Philharmonic Orchestra 59
Istiqlal (Independence) Party 243, 330*n*22

Jabal al-Mukabbir 86
al-Jabi, Subhi 224
Jabra, Jabra Ibrahim *In Search of Walid Masoud* 17
Jaffa *see* Yafa
al-Jalil (Galilee) 45, 186, 147, 190, 214, 281, 294
al-Jamia al-'Arabiyya *see* Arab League
Jamjum, Muhammad 150
al-Jana (archive) 6, 298
Jarallah, Shaykh Husam al-Din 84, 319*n*15
Jawad, Saleh Abdel 297
Jaysh al-Inqadh *see* Arab Liberation Army
Jaysh al-Jihad al-Muqadas *see* Holy War Army
Jaysh al-Tahrir al-Filastini *see* Palestine Liberation Army
Jayyusi, Lena 10
Jerusalem *see* al-Quds
Jerusalem Girls College 49
Jerusalem University College 86
Jewish immigrants 44, 105, 109, 110, 167, 168
Jewish National Fund 45
Jewish Settlement Police 102
Jewish shops 51, 52
Jewish Symphony Orchestra 59
Jewish terrorism 106, 107, 169, 172
Jewish women 270
    as sexual decoys for Arab men 65, 107, 108–9
Jews: relations with Arabs *see* Arabs and Jews
Jisr al-Basha camp 79
Jordanian Army 241, 245
Umm Joseph 294
Jum'a, Hamda 7, 14, 61–4, 67–8
    interview with 69–74

al-Kabir, Abu Ibrahim 142
kaffiyyeh (Palestinian scarf) 29, 66, 121, 307
Kfar Shaub Mental Hospital 297
al-Khalidi, Ahmad Samih 90, 91
al-Khalidi, Hazim 224–5
al-Khalil 114, 118, 150, 224

Thanks to our Patreon Subscribers:

Lia Lilith de Oliveira
Andrew Perry

Who have shown generosity and comradeship in support of our publishing.

Check out the other perks you get by subscribing to our Patreon – visit patreon.com/plutopress.
Subscriptions start from £3 a month.